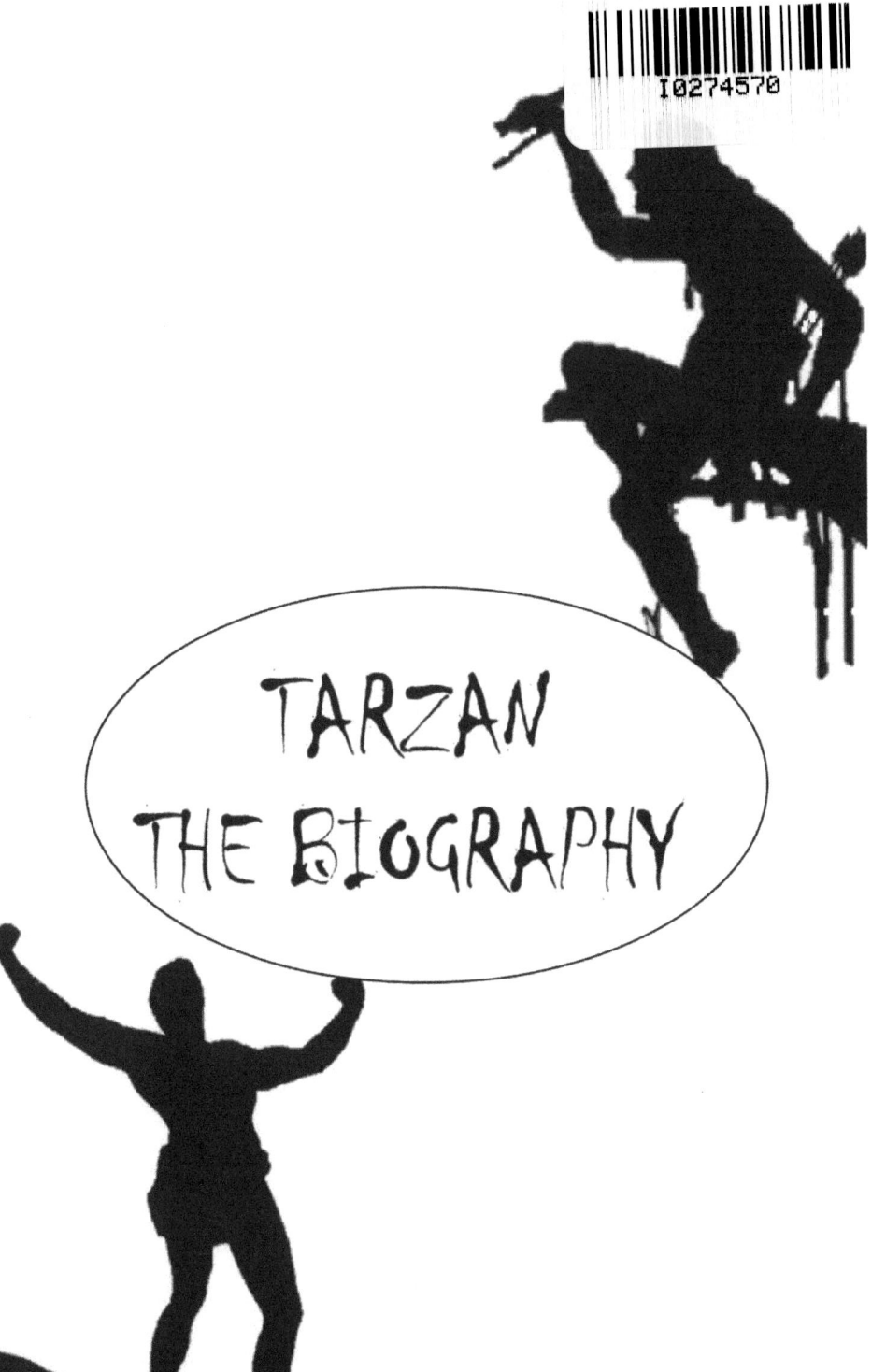

Tarzan: The Biography

First published in 2012 by Telos Publishing Ltd as *Ape-Man: The Unofficial and Unauthorised Guide to 100 Years of Tarzan.*

This new edition published in 2017 by Askill Publishing.

© 2012, 2017 Sean Egan

ISBN: 978-0-9545750-7-6

The moral right of the author has been asserted. No reproduction of this work, in whole or in part, is permitted without the written consent of the publisher.

This book is sold subject to the condition that it shall not by way of trade or otherwise, be lent, resold, hired out or otherwise circulated without the publisher's prior written consent in any form of binding or cover other than that in which it is published and without a similar condition including this condition being imposed on the subsequent purchaser.

CONTENTS

ACKNOWLEDGMENTS 7
INTRODUCTION 9
PART ONE: THE CREATOR 11
PART TWO: BIRTH OF THE APE-MAN 21
PART THREE: CONQUERING THE FUNNIES 77
PART FOUR: HERE'S JOHNNY 101
PART FIVE: EXIT WEISSMULLER 181
PART SIX: THE WEINTRAUB ERA 201
PART SEVEN: THE LEAN YEARS 245
PART EIGHT: THE KELLER ERA 311
PART NINE: ENTER DISNEY 337
PART TEN: POST-MILLENNIAL TARZAN 351
PART ELEVEN: SWINGING INTO AN UNCERTAIN FUTURE 397
APPENDIX: TARZAN IN THE MEDIA 405
SELECTED BIBLIOGRAPHY 415

ACKNOWLEDGMENTS

My grateful thanks to the following for granting interviews or providing quotes for this book: Robert R Barrett, Al Bohl, Andy Briggs, Danton Burroughs, Gerry Conway, Gary Goddard, Thomas Grindberg, Bill Hillman, Hugh Hudson, Len Janson, Micheline Keller, Robert Kline, Joe Kubert, Christopher Lambert, Joe Lansdale, Robin Maxwell, Denny Miller, Michael Moorcock, R A Salvatore, Dez Skinn, Roy Thomas and David Yates.

Joe Kubert and Denny Miller died between the publication of the first and second editions of this book. Attribution of their quotes has been kept in the present tense for purposes of stylistic consistency.

Thanks also to the following people for helping me with queries: Scott Tracy Griffin, Erin Herman, Robert W Lamb, Jim Sullos and Cathy Wilbanks.

Robert R Barrett kindly granted his expertise in matters ape-man by reading through the manuscript of the first edition of this book and correcting errors.

Last and emphatically not least, I extend my vast gratitude to lifelong Edgar Rice Burroughs fan Bill Hillman, who provided assistance over and above the endless queries he patiently answered simply via maintaining his multitude of ERB sites, the main one of which – erbzine.com – constitutes a staggering Burroughs resource.

All images herein are reproduced for illustrative purposes only. Except where noted, images are either public domain or their reproduction is covered by fair-use principles.

INTRODUCTION

Edgar Rice Burroughs' Tarzan is one of the great fantasy figures of modern times.

He made his first appearance in the issue of *The All-Story* magazine cover-dated October 1912. An English lord whose parents are shipwrecked, he is raised in the African jungle by a previously undiscovered type of great ape. He grows up both to claim his inheritance in civilisation and to adhere to the principles and skills he has learnt in the wild. It was a tale to which the public immediately took. The ape-man was such a cultural phenomenon that he was responsible for many firsts: after conquering the printed word, he proceeded to triumph in other media and markets almost as soon as they were invented, from movies to comic strips to radio to merchandising. Burroughs' tally of two-dozen Tarzan novels was impressive, but it was dwarfed by the array of film adaptations of his character. Although they weren't exactly faithful to the source, they were so pleasing to the public that they constitute, Sherlock Holmes excepted, the longest-running movie franchise of all time. The character's popularity crossed national boundaries, with boys from America to India to Russia miming swinging on a vine while emitting a deafening yodel. Not only was it global, the popularity was enduring: the boys in the early part of the 20th century who imitated their idol grew up and spawned a generation to whom the character was even more revered. Although inevitably the Tarzan craze lessened in intensity, it continues in significant form to this day, with an archive of Tarzan films and TV series in rotation on television screens across the planet, a comic strip still circulating and new Tarzan films, television shows and books continuing to be scheduled.

Yet ironically, almost from the moment he created him, Burroughs was bored by his character, seeing him as having little story potential. He continued to crank out his adventures only through financial necessity. Even more ironically, many of those resentfully-written stories were high-quality.

The course of the hundred years-plus of Tarzan's existence has seen many societal changes. They include the decolonisation of the African continent, the rise of ecological and animal-preservation concerns and the abolition of the heredity principle in the House of Lords: all of these things change the landscape for the Lord of the Jungle and may possibly undermine his very premise.

Tarzan: The Biography explores the Tarzan phenomenon across all cultural media. With the aid of writers, actors, directors and other creative talents who have been involved in purveying the ape-man to the world, it examines the history, appeal, impact and uncertain future of a truly remarkable icon.

PART ONE: THE CREATOR

Edgar Rice Burroughs was a restless soul.

Born in 1875 to a well-to-do Chicago family, by 1911 he had been, among other things, a cavalry officer, a cowboy, a goldminer, a store proprietor and the manager of a large Sears catalogue office. 'He tried just a huge number of jobs,' says Bill Hillman, lifelong Burroughs fan and supervisor of the official ERB website. 'I guess he was a daydreamer.'

'He wasn't a failure,' Burroughs' grandson Danton insisted to this author in his last-ever interview, conducted four months before his death in his sleep from heart failure in May 2008. (All Danton Burroughs quotes presented in this book are from that interview unless stated.) 'He just wasn't interested in those lines of work. When he took over the stenographic department at Sears and Roebuck, he shaped that place up. They'd never experienced anybody like my granddad. And then when he worked at Michigan Military Academy, he was manager of the football team. The horsemanship, he took care of that. He taught geology. He had so many varied jobs. He didn't fail at them, he just was moving on to what he really wanted to do.' Burroughs himself seemed to be of the inclination to beg to differ. In an outline for an unwritten autobiography, he noted of the years 1905-11, 'I am a flop.'

Hillman points out that the adult Burroughs was always artistic: 'In the Michigan Military Academy back in the early 1890s, he was editor of the school paper. He wrote quite a bit of stuff. He was an excellent cartoonist and artist. He wrote a lot of little-known stuff before he was published, mainly for family or for newspaper submissions with poetry and things like that. He turned to professional writing at a very late age.' Danton: 'He was starting to write around the turn of the century, when he wrote *Minidoka*.'

The latter fairytale-come-fantasy was something Burroughs never submitted for publication, but in 1911 he decided to do more than just write for fun. He was currently attempting to make a living as a pencil-sharpener agent. The business wasn't going well and he found he had empty hours to fill. He decided to try his hand at devising something for the 'pulp' fiction magazines that, in an era before radio and TV, when cinema was in its infancy, were massively popular. Hillman continues: 'He had dreams, nightmares and stuff and it all came together – all his past experiences. He thought, "I can write this drivel as well as the pulp authors." In his spare time he looked over some pulp magazines and checked out the advertising in them. *Under the Moons of Mars* or *A Princess of Mars* was the result.'

Under the Moons of Mars was written on the backs of pages carrying the mastheads of a previous failed Burroughs business. It was serialised across six issues of *All-Story* cover-dated from February to July 1912. Its protagonist John Carter is, on earth, merely a mustered-out Civil War soldier turned gold prospector. On Mars – Barsoom in native parlance – he becomes a fearsome warrior via the planet's lighter gravity, which enables him to make 20-yard leaps over the heads of the brutal six-limbed green men he soon finds himself in battle against on the side of the planet's more cultured red race. Carter finds his way to the titular planet by the pat manoeuvre of wishing himself there, and learns the language of Mars preposterously swiftly. Nonetheless, the author exploited superbly the then still widely-held belief that Mars was either inhabited or had been, painting an evocative and intricate picture of a world whose culture is of a decaying majesty.

Burroughs had finally alighted on a career that didn't make him restless. It was one that would ultimately see him hailed as a pioneer of science fiction and fantasy, become one of the most popular authors of all time and, if that wasn't enough, create an imperishable cultural icon. Said Danton, 'He was unique … My grandfather could describe action so vividly that the reader literally couldn't put the book down.' Danton was biased of course, but his comments reflect those of many with no bloodlink to ERB.

There would be ten Mars tales printed in Burroughs' lifetime.

The initial trilogy – the first story was printed in book form as *A Princess of Mars* in 1917 and was followed by *The Gods of Mars* and *Warlords of Mars* – are the strongest. However, unlike other Burroughs series demeaned by incrementally less interesting sequels, a consistent quality and invention was maintained in the Barsoom franchise, with only *Synthetic Men of Mars* (1939) considered to be truly bad.

When Burroughs' most enduring creation made his debut in *All-Story* in October 1912, he initially earned him $700. It was a goodly sum in those days, but would soon seem paltry in light of the multi-million dollar industry the character would become. *Tarzan of the Apes* saw Burroughs incorrectly place tigers in Africa, but otherwise it was an amazingly convincing tale of a child brought up in the jungle by a species – which the author would later name Mangani – halfway between ape and man.

The tiger references were corrected when *Tarzan of the Apes* became Burroughs' first published book in 1914. 'A book was just really beyond reach at that time, certainly with his imaginative stuff,' says Hillman. 'It took quite a number of years before actually they published some of his stuff in hardcover. The pulp magazines were the available market for him. Before that [book publication], he serialised things in American newspapers.'

Even when he started placing work with book publishers, Burroughs – ever a canny businessman – still ensured the extra remuneration that came with an initial appearance in the pulps. Hillman: 'He serialised things first, and he learned after his first effort to keep the publishing rights, which a lot of [other pulp writers] didn't do. And then he expanded and collated some of these serialised chapters into the finished product. He did that all his life.' This was a symptom of the fact that Burroughs unashamedly wrote not for art but money, playing hardball over fees and measuring out a story's worth by the time it took him to complete it.

Not all Burroughs stories made the transition from pulp to book in his lifetime, which is why all first appearance dates given in this section are for magazine publication, unless otherwise stated.

Burroughs' third franchise was Pellucidar, a physically inverted Inner World he posited deep beneath our very feet, one whose rising horizons are ruled over by repulsive winged reptiles called Mahars. *At The Earth's Core*, the first of seven Pellucidar books, appeared in 1914. It was filmed pulpily in 1976, with Doug McClure in the role of protagonist David Innes.

Burroughs' fourth series was Caspak, which debuted with *The Land That Time Forgot* (1918). Although the depiction of an undiscovered land in which dinosaurs still place their thunderous steps is clearly inspired by Arthur Conan Doyle's *The Lost World*, Burroughs' series also features real originality in the form of an ingenious truncated internal evolutionary system spanning not millennia but an individual's lifetime. A film appeared in 1975, with a sequel following in '77, both made by Amicus, the same company responsible for the *At The Earth's Core* film. A new movie adaptation of *The Land That Time Forgot* materialised in 2009.

These series and others have garnered Burroughs the title Grandfather of Science Fiction. Hillman offers, 'I've always qualified that by saying "American science fiction." Of course, H G Wells and Jules Verne and earlier people come before.' But Burroughs was not just the first major US SF novelist. Hillman notes: 'Science fantasy or science fantasy adventure – somewhere in a niche there, you could put him as a pioneer.'

Burroughs could also claim to have brought significant female characters into SF and fantasy for the first time. Danton observed: 'He combined the science fiction with romance, and you really took the part of his heroes and heroines.' Hillman adds: 'He's a much easier read. He's more captivating. He moves the plot along much faster than H G Wells or Jules Verne … He was the launch pad for so many authors to come. Pulp authors and authors right into the Golden Age of science fiction. They drew so heavily on his ideas. And he's always been criticised for not being scientific, but I've done a number of features where I've listed some of the inventions that he has come up with, and so many of these have eventually come true, like body transplants and x-rays and navigation devices. It goes on and on.'

Burroughs was never fêted by the critics. 'He was panned a lot,' admitted his grandson. 'I think the bottom line was, if he wasn't a great author he wouldn't have been so damn popular.' Danton also said, 'He would always downplay it. He was pretty humble about it.'

'I don't think you can take that at face value,' says Hillman of Burroughs' 'I'm-a-simple-storyteller' line. 'He put a lot of work into his writing and he was very successful and I think he was very proud of what he had accomplished ... He never really admitted that, but I think it bothered him when critics didn't realise the type of writer he was.' John Taliaferro's Burroughs biography *Tarzan Forever* certainly portrays a man frustrated by his inability to make the step up from the low-rent pulps to the respectable 'slicks'. Hillman reasons, 'He was writing for a certain market and he was top of his field. In his own way, he was a great writer.'

Burroughs' other major series was Amtor, which debuted with *Pirates of Venus* (1932). Opinion on these stories – four of which were published in Burroughs' lifetime – is sharply divided. Many find them dull and their blundering protagonist Carson Napier irritating. As Danton pointed out, 'He was on his way to Mars. He ended up on Venus.' Others feel Napier's pointedly unheroic nature was an indication of Burroughs' development as both writer and human being. In the Amtor series, his normal glorification of battle – and at times almost sexual celebration of muscle-bound heroes – gave way to a more mature outlook, a parallel of the way Burroughs' writing style had become leaner and less inclined to floridity down the years. 'Sure,' said Danton when asked if Burroughs was satirising hero novels, but also points out that the period saw Burroughs divorce his grandmother, marry a much younger woman, lose the El Caballero country club he had founded and wrestle with the multi-media success of Tarzan. 'It was just a time of turmoil,' he says.

Certainly, a mature outlook was evinced by *Beyond the Farthest Star* (1942). That the planet Poloda is in the midst of a hundred-year war is portrayed as a matter for depression rather than derring-do. Quasi-ironically, Burroughs – an eyewitness at the bombing of Pearl Harbor – became World War II's oldest war correspondent around this time.

Other Burroughs SF and fantasy novels are: *The Moon Maid* trilogy, an anti-communist alien invasion story collected in one volume in 1926; *Beyond Thirty* aka *The Lost Continent* (1915), a rare Burroughs future-set story; *The Eternal Lover* aka *The Eternal Savage*, a high-quality pair of stories from 1914 and 1915 concerning a primeval man who awakens in modern Africa; *The Monster Men* (1913), a cross between *Frankenstein* and *The Island of Doctor Moreau* with a romance thrown in; and *The Resurrection of Jimber-Jaw* (1936), a battle-of-the-sexes story featuring a reawakened caveman.

Danton said of his grandfather, 'He would inject quite a bit of himself in all of his work,' but he also admitted, 'He stayed away from the realistic.' Even several Tarzan books feature science fiction elements. However, Burroughs' *oeuvre* is not exclusively fantasy and SF. The prolific author tried his hand at virtually every writing genre imaginable. The least interesting of his non-fantasy fare are jungle-set Tarzan variants like *The Cave Girl*, *Jungle Girl* and *The Lad and The Lion*, and naturalistic works such as *The Oakdale Affair* (filmed in 1919), *The Efficiency Expert*, *The Girl from Hollywood*, *The Girl from Farris's* and *Marcia of the Doorstep*. The latter is a novel with an ingénue protagonist. Written in 1924, it is by far his longest piece of work. Nobody could bring themselves to publish it, including Burroughs himself when he set up his own imprint. It saw the light of day only in 1999. Danton offered, 'I like *The Girl from Hollywood* because you could see the family background there.' In the so-so category of non-SF Burroughs are *The Prisoner of Zenda*-homage *The Mad King*, the realistic play *You Lucky Girl!* (published in 1999) and *The Outlaw of Torn*, set in 13th century England.

The historical *I am a Barbarian* – the narrative of a slave of

Caligula – is high-grade and it's surprising that this 1941 novel didn't see print anywhere in Burroughs' lifetime. Also impressive is the uncategorizable (and possibly intentionally parodic) *The Mucker*, the story of a no-good bum who discovers an inner moral fortitude when he is swept up in high-seas adventure.

The Wild West was no mythological place to ex-cavalryman Burroughs, so it's unsurprising that his Westerns are the most interesting of his non-fantasy works. *The War Chief* (1927) and *Apache Devil* (1928) are not only fine reads but predate *Dances With Wolves* by a good half-century in their sympathetic portrayal of Native Americans. 'He did a lot of research on those,' noted Danton.

Burroughs was one of the most widely-read English-language authors of the first half of the 20th century. Reliable sales figures for the era are difficult to find, but it is generally accepted that, of his contemporaries, only Western writer Zane Grey outsold Burroughs in America. Moreover, almost nobody can name a Zane Grey character today, whereas there are still few people on the planet who don't have at least a vague idea who Tarzan is. Burroughs naturally made a fortune from his vast readership. However, his revenue streams came from many sources other than writing. Tarzan spawned industries left, right and centre. Not only were Tarzan movies phenomenally lucrative for him, but, points out Hillman, 'He was one of the first big merchandising people.'

Unfortunately, Burroughs lost large chunks of his fortune. He was hit heavily by over-spending, the '29 Wall Street crash and divorce. He continually had to sell off parts of the 540-acre San Fernando Valley estate that he bought in March 1919 and turned into a ranch named Tarzana. Nonetheless, in the shape of the town of Tarzana – founded in 1928 on parts of the property he sold off – he left an enduring monument over and above his 80-odd books. 'He had a dream and he told his brother Harry that he wanted to start a community and name it Tarzana,' recalled Danton. 'And by God he did it. He wrote diligently to the postal department and got a post office brought here and got telephone service. He got a bus service, stage line. He really put this whole community on the map. He got the chamber of commerce going. We're thriving today with about 60,000 residents.'

Towards the end of Burroughs' life, a certain fatigue began to set in to both his writing and his private life. 'Burroughs' peak writing seemed to be in the ['10s] and early '20s and then he had a lot of personal problems and financial problems,' says Hillman. Burroughs' estrangement from his wife seemed to coincide with the disappearance from the Tarzan series of the character's iconic spouse Jane. His Tarzan books particularly became increasingly formulaic, featuring an endless procession of lost cities (all, with one exception, white settlements), safaris in peril and implausible Tarzan look-alikes.

When he returned to civilian life after World War II, Burroughs' publishing company – which he had set up in 1931 because, by his own admission, his hardball-playing had cut his previous publishers' profit margins to counterproductive levels – issued three more books, one each in the Tarzan, Mars and Venus series, before he passed away. The cause of his death on 19 March 1950 was a Parkinson's disease-related heart attack. Said Danton, 'My granddad was diagnosed with Parkinson's in 1949 – I've got the letter from the doctor – and then my dad acquired it in 1959 and I got Parkinson's in 1999.' This sad fact does rather complicate Burroughs' beliefs in eugenics, distasteful manifestations of which litter his work, and nature-over-nurture, which notion forms the bedrock of the Tarzan character, a person who, despite being brought up by wild beasts, possesses an innate decency supposedly by dint of being the offspring of English nobility. Yet Burroughs was no idiot. He admitted in correspondence that if a child really had been raised like Tarzan, far from exhibiting graciousness, he 'would develop into a cunning, cowardly beast' and, in contrast to the preternatural beauty he gave the ape-man, would be 'under-developed' through lack of nourishment and rest.

By the time of his death, a new generation of SF writers who had idolised Burroughs as children were making a mark. His swashbuckling blend of fantasy and SF is clearly evident in the works of Robert E Howard, Ray Bradbury and Michael Moorcock. H P Lovecraft and Isaac Asimov were also manifestly devotees. Superman – one of the few fictional characters as iconic and enduring as Tarzan – would not have been possible without John Carter and, by extension, neither would any other costumed superhero. Observes comics writer Roy Thomas of Superman's creator, 'Jerry Siegel was a Burroughs fan. The main Martian city is Helium and Siegel made his Krypton, which is another inert gas, and of course the idea of leaping that distance and being stronger in a weak gravity – there's an awful lot of John Carter in there.'

Another fictional hero was also clearly indebted to John Carter. Burroughs had tried to syndicate a John Carter newspaper strip. Three days after his negotiations fell through with the King Features Syndicate agency, newspapers began running its *Flash Gordon* strip. Gordon – in his original newspaper-strip incarnation – was, like Carter, a fearsome swordsman who found himself able to make giant leaps on a planet with lighter gravity.

Meanwhile, Philip José Farmer, although a considerable SF talent himself, throughout his career wrote what was almost Burroughs fan fiction, with several of his novels featuring Tarzan-esque characters. Burroughs even influenced hack Western writer J T Edson, who wrote a series of jungle-set novels about one Bunduki, posited as Tarzan's adopted grandson.

Burroughs' legacy continues. In 2012, a big-budget John Carter film hit the cinema screens. New Tarzan movies appeared in 2013 and 2016. Fresh ape-man books and comics appear to this day. A Disney Tarzan musical continues to wend its way successfully around the world. Even Carson Napier is slowly making his way to a film adaptation.

Burroughs' brand of SF and fantasy may now seem old-fashioned, what with its Victorian morality, over-reliance on coincidence and flamboyancy of dialogue. However, his captivating, pacey narratives, futuristic visions leavened with romance, and universes imagined to the tiniest detail could still teach a thing or two to contemporary writers of speculative and fantasy fiction who may feel a sense of superiority about their more edgy styles. Moreover, a patina of age has not precluded much of Burroughs' work possessing an immortal status: who of his disciples has created the likes of Tarzan and John Carter, characters so iconic that they are still the subject of adaptations when the world in which they first made an appearance is barely recognisable as our own?

PART TWO: BIRTH OF THE APE-MAN

In the early years of the 20th Century, the market for the printed word was vast. Unlike now, the educated classes were not in a minority in their love of reading. In an era when there was no TV or radio and where cinema was in its silent, histrionic infancy, the working classes could only keep themselves entertained by going out to the theatre and vaudeville/music hall or staying in and consuming prose. On the latter front, those who favoured fiction and who were modest of pocket gravitated to cheap novels and magazines. In the American market, magazines were divided into the 'slicks' and the 'pulps'. The former were more highbrow, printed on good-quality paper and priced accordingly. The latter cost (originally) just a dime because they were printed on untrimmed, low-grade paper (pulp). The pulps' content – stories, often book-length, of adventure, crime, science fiction, cowboys and romance – was geared toward the reader with a less sophisticated palate. Modern sensibilities might scoff at its moral, structural and stylistic simplicity but, while much pulp writing can now really be taken seriously only by children and teens, it remains a quite sobering fact that a century ago often poorly educated people devoured words in volume unimaginable to their modern, nominally more sophisticated counterparts.

The All-Story Magazine began life in 1905 as a monthly publication. It dropped the 'magazine' part of its title in 1910 and became a weekly in 1914. It was published by Frank Munsey, who pioneered the pulp format with *Golden Argosy* aka *Argosy*. Burroughs was well-acquainted with the Munsey magazines from regularly handling them in a spell working as a newsagent. Although, like much of Burroughs' science fiction, *Under the Moons of Mars* was ingenious, one wonders whether this back-up *All-Story* feature would have ever made it to book form had it not been for the slipstream of success created by the second novel-length narrative the magazine accepted from him. Three other, much shorter, stories appeared in that edition of *All-Story* cover-dated October 1912 (on sale 27 August); but whereas 'The Spaniard' by Frank Comstock, 'The Goat of Dolores Valdez' by John D Swain and 'On the Zodiac Turnpike' by Ella B Argo have now disappeared into history, *Tarzan of the Apes* emphatically has not. Even Clinton Pettee's cover illustration is immortal: his beautiful painting of a headbanded Tarzan astride a rearing lion, preparing to plunge a knife into its flank as a cowed visitor from civilisation looks on, remains one of the definitive images of the ape-man (something assisted in recent years by it becoming public domain).

Burroughs himself stated in a letter to a scholar who inquired about his inspirations for the work, 'It may have originated in my interest in Mythology and the story of Romulus and Remus. I also recall having read many years ago the story of a sailor who was shipwrecked on the Coast of Africa and who was adopted by and consorted with great apes to such an extent that when he was rescued, a she-ape followed him into the surf and threw a baby after him. Then, of course, I read Kipling; so that it probably was a combination of all these that suggested the Tarzan idea to me.'

Rudyard Kipling was the author of *The Jungle Book* (1894) and *The Second Jungle Book* (1895), collections of short stories mainly set in India. Eight of the fifteen stories across the two volumes feature Mowgli, a boy who is raised by wolves after appearing, unexplained, as a baby in their lair. Mowgli learns to speak to animals, especially panther Bagheera, bear Baloo and snake Kaa. Ironically, just about the only members of the animal kingdom with whom Mowgli is not friendly are monkeys, who are portrayed as stupid, cruel and – because of their location in the jungle canopy far above the other wildlife – outsiders. Nonetheless, in the trees Mowgli becomes as agile as an ape.

There are many similarities between the Jungle Books and the Tarzan stories over and above the overarching theme of a feral child who can converse with wildlife. Among them are anthropomorphism and generic names for members of the animal kingdom alternate to those conferred by man but strangely constructed of human vowel sounds. They also include the protagonist's dominion over wildlife, preternatural strength forged by an outdoors existence and adoption of the trappings of man in the form of a loincloth and knife. Cold Lairs, an abandoned city of decaying majesty featured in the story 'Kaa's Hunting', would be echoed by Burroughs in his lost metropolis of Opar. Meanwhile, this line from the closing story of *The Second Jungle Book* is very reminiscent of the idolatry-inclined Burroughs: 'As he stood in the red light of the oil-lamp, strong, tall, and beautiful, his long black hair sweeping over his shoulders, the knife swinging at his neck, and his head crowned with a wreath of white jasmine, he might easily have been mistaken for some wild god of a jungle legend.'

Kipling himself felt certain of the link between Mowgli and Tarzan, but was relaxed about it. He wrote that the Jungle Books 'begat Zoos' of 'imitators,' and that 'the genius of all the genii was one who wrote a series called *Tarzan of the Apes*.' He added, 'I read it, but regret I never saw it on the films, where it rages most successfully. He had "jazzed" the motif of the *Jungle Books* and, I imagine, had thoroughly enjoyed himself.'

Although it might be said that Kipling was operating on a far higher literary plane than Burroughs – he wrote many acknowledged classics and continues to be widely read and taught today – his Mowgli stories don't have the narrative propulsion and intriguing character development of Burroughs' early Tarzan books.

Burroughs scholars like Richard A Lupoff spent chunks of their lives searching in vain for the shipwrecked-sailor story Burroughs also cited as an inspiration. Some have concluded that Burroughs did not in fact see it in print, but heard a piece of folklore.

Some have also cited the possible influence on Burroughs of *Captured by Apes* (1888) by Harry Prentice, although this tale of a sailor shipwrecked on an island who becomes king of the resident simians by wearing the hide of the former ape king only seems persuasive as an influence in combination with the similarity of the same author's later *Captured by Zulus* to the plot of the Burroughs Tarzan book for children *The Tarzan Twins*. A 1910 *All-Story* inclusion titled 'The Monkey Man' and the 1906 Jack London novel *Before Adam* also contain elements that are reminiscent of components of *Tarzan of the Apes*, as does Albert Robida's 'Monkey King', published in *Puck* in 1880.

Non-fiction works by which Burroughs may have been influenced include *In Darkest Africa* by Henry M Stanley (1890), *Heroes of the Dark Continent* by J W Buell (1890) and *Explorations and Adventures in Equatorial Africa* by Paul Du Chaillu. The latter was the man who proved the existence of the gorilla, even if he (like Burroughs) inaccurately portrayed them as aggressive. He also posited a form of talking ape. In another work, Du Chaillu described monkeys as 'nkemas', a word similar to 'Nkima', the name of Tarzan's monkey companion in later ape-man novels. Paul Du Chaillu's own name is conspicuously redolent of that of Tarzan's friend Paul D'Arnot.

As well as the mythical story of how Romulus and Remus were raised by a she-wolf before founding Rome, Burroughs must surely have been influenced, even if subliminally, by real-life stories of feral children, i.e. human young who by virtue of a combination of rural location and abandonment/tragedy live for a period cut off from man, in some cases in the company of wild animals, before re-entering human society. Stories about the likes of Wild Peter of Hanover, the Bear Girl of Hungary and the Wild Boy of Aveyron had been appearing in print for hundreds of years and, in more credulous times, tended to be accepted at face value. Subsequently (mostly after Burroughs' time), many of the stories were exposed as false. However, even a hundred years ago it was widely known that, in the confirmed cases, if a child was feral during its baby-to-toddler years, it was never able to re-assimilate fully into society: such experiences leave speech faculties irreparably impaired, as well as any perception on the part of the child of being human. In order to tell the story he had in mind of the triumph of nature over nurture, Burroughs had to ignore all of the evidence about its impossibility.

Tarzan of the Apes reads surprisingly like Jane Austen in places, what with its often courtly narrator's voice, belief in idealised love and talk of marriage based on financial imperatives. Sometimes it reads like a parody of Austen, what with its flowery prose ('But what of Alice and that other little life so soon to be launched amidst the hardships and grave dangers of a primeval world?') and laughably stilted dialogue ('Hundreds of thousands of years ago our ancestors of the dim and distant past faced the same problems which we must face, possibly in these same primeval forests. That we are here today evidences their victory'). In other places, though, the story reads like Conrad, with much exciting shipboard intrigue and ferocious jungle conflict.

Although he may have taken his cue from Kipling, Burroughs' vision is somewhat more blood-drenched, for the world traversed by Tarzan is a far more savage one than that negotiated by Mowgli. In one passage, Tarzan's scalp is left hanging over his eyes during a fight with a simian. In another, a squabble amongst pirates sees the point of a pick-axe brought fatally down upon a head. Jane, meanwhile, is narrowly saved from being raped by a bull ape.

The tale begins with Burroughs informing the reader, 'I had this story from one who had no business to tell it to me, or to any other.' The framing device is illogical. Burroughs cannot possibly have had the manifold and minutely detailed events that follow related to him in mere conversation, even if it is supposedly corroborated by 'the yellow, mildewed pages of the diary of a man long dead, and the records of the Colonial Office.' However, it is also clever, drawing in the reader with its tone of a shared secret and its intriguing implication of being a true story.

In the year 1888, someone whom Burroughs calls John Clayton, Lord Greystoke ('the fact that ... I have taken fictitious names for the principal characters quite sufficiently evidences the sincerity of my own belief that it *may* be true'), accompanied by his pregnant wife Alice, is sailing on the HMS *Fuwalda*. His destination is 'a British west coast African colony,' where he is to investigate on behalf of the British Colonial Office the maltreatment of natives. The brutality of the captain of the vessel provokes a mutiny, and it is only the concern Greystoke has previously displayed about the conditions on board that sees his and Lady Greystoke's lives spared. They are put ashore with their (considerable) belongings in a place identified only as 'West coast of Africa, about 10° degrees south latitude.' (Burroughs scholar H H Heins later asserted that this identified Tarzan's birthplace as the country of Angola, then a Portuguese colony.)

Disbelieving of the mutineers' promise that they will alert the authorities of their whereabouts, Greystoke throws himself into creating a safe haven for Alice and their imminent child. Alice shortly gives birth to a healthy baby boy in the sturdy log cabin Greystoke has constructed. They call him John. However, a frightening encounter with one of the human-like apes they have frequently spotted lurking in the vicinity sends Alice into a bed-ridden delirium from which she never quite recovers until her death a year after giving birth. The cause of death is never specified; the perception of the time of women's general fragility is apparently sufficient explanation. Greystoke follows Alice into the afterlife shortly thereafter when the cabin is invaded by examples of these apes. His baby, however, is spared due to the coincidence of there numbering amongst the apes Kala, a female who lost her own infant only hours before when Kerchak, the king of her tribe, embarked on a bad-tempered treetop rampage that culminated in it falling to the jungle floor. After snatching up the crying human babe, Kala – to the derision of her hairy friends – nurses the child and raises it as her own. The Mangani tribe give their new, strange, hairless member the name 'Tarzan', which in their language means 'White-Skin'.

Danton notes of his grandfather, 'He created the name "Tarzan" from nonsense syllables. You could see him in his original handwritten draft where he scratches out different names and things.' The manuscript shows Burroughs toying with 'Zantar' and 'Tublat-Zan'. Danton: 'And he finally hits on "Tarzan". It's just amazing how that man's mind worked.' In time, Burroughs would evidently realise that such a non-guttural word was not the sort of sound that naturally emanates from the mouth of even a man-like simian and would do a little backtracking when he came up with a Mangani name for the ape-man's son, explaining that the word "Korak" was 'as near as it may be interpreted into human speech.' Filmmakers down the decades, however, have consistently failed to acknowledge the incongruity of Tarzan's name, with a few exceptions. The 1998 movie *Tarzan and the Lost City* and the 2017 Netflix series *Tarzan and Jane* came up with a logical get-around by making the name one bequeathed by Africans. *Greystoke* (1984) dispensed with the problem by jettisoning the name entirely.

Burroughs depicts the primates who raise young Clayton not as a known species such as chimpanzees (which barely appear in any Burroughs Tarzan book) or gorillas. Instead, he renders them 'a species closely allied to the gorilla, yet more intelligent; which, with the strength of their cousin' makes them 'the most fearsome of those awe-inspiring progenitors of man.' They can grow to a height of seven feet, but they swing through the upper branches of the trees like chimps and (although the world did not understand this at the time) unlike gorillas. However, they engage in rituals similar to those of primitive man, such as the fevered, drum-beating Dum-Dum, designed to mark milestones like tribal killings or the ascension of a new king. They are also omnivores, and quite bloodthirsty ones: they ceremoniously place one foot upon the neck of killed prey and vanquished enemies as they emit a blood-curdling victory cry.

In later books Burroughs would flesh out the undiscovered species, including belatedly giving them a name. Slightly confusingly, Mangani means Great Apes, ordinarily an umbrella title for the larger primates: chimps, gorillas, orangutans and, indeed, humans. The Manganis' name for themselves distinguishes them in their language from different races of man ('Tarmangani' are 'white great apes', 'Gomangani' 'black great apes').

In *The Son of Tarzan*, Burroughs described the Mangani as 'almost extinct.' In one of the stories in *Jungle Tales of Tarzan*, the author explicitly differentiated Mangani from chimpanzees and gorillas by stating that unlike them they 'walk without the aid of their hands quite as readily as with.' In *Tarzan and the Leopard Men*, two decades after Tarzan's first appearance, a character observed of the species, 'It was evident that they were not gorillas, and that they were more man-like than any apes he had seen.'

We follow Tarzan's progress amongst these primates from helpless infant, to nervous child, to mischievous teen and finally to an adult who becomes king of his tribe after a battle to the death with Kerchak. Outside of his tribe, Tarzan's best friend is Tantor, Burroughs' generic Mangani name for elephant. Over time, Burroughs would establish that Tarzan held no respect for Gimla the crocodile, was naturally wary of Numa the lion, felt the closest thing he knew to fear when contemplating Histah the snake and despised Dango the hyena for his cowardly scavenging.

In the book version, Sabor the lioness took the place of the tiger Burroughs erroneously placed in Africa in the *All-Story* original. However, it would have been just as apt to object to the presence in the African bush of Numa and Tantor, which creatures overwhelmingly inhabit the continent's plains. Hillman notes, 'His Africa is not a real place: to swing from the upper terraces of the rainforest and [have] lions and elephants running through the rainforest. But his Africa was picked up by so many films and authors later on.'

Burroughs' jungle opera is, on one level, ludicrous. However, we in the main buy into it because the narrative is engagingly written by an author who displays no embarrassment about the unlikely tapestry he is weaving. By investing the apes with human-like personalities and motivations, Burroughs keeps the narrative compelling, even if the apes' vocabularies are absurdly wide ('Let us leave him quietly sleeping among the tall grasses, that you may bear other and stronger apes to guard us in our old age'). He manages to refrain from indulging in the more sentimental aspects of anthropomorphism. He even has us half-believing that Tarzan really could unlock the mysteries of the written word by spending hours poring over the children's primers and books owned by his parents, which have been preserved in the rudimentary house his father built. In fact, these sections of head-scratching absorption and dawning enlightenment are rather sweet. Their convincing spell is broken only when the grown Tarzan leaves a note signed in his ape name for foreigners who have taken over his treasured cabin, and we recall that Burroughs has already explicitly stated that his silent, solitary studies mean that Tarzan doesn't understand the connection between the written word and speech, so would not know how to write 'Tarzan'.

Less sweet are Tarzan's murderous games with a black tribe who set up camp in his part of the jungle. He has learned from his father's books that he is not an *ape* but a *man*, hence his compulsion to shave his face with his father's hunting knife. But when the first human on which he can ever recall having laid eyes kills his adoptive mother Kala, he wreaks terrible revenge. Fair enough in regard to the actual killer, perhaps, but Tarzan then torments the man's tribe, who are characterised by 'yellow teeth … filed to sharp points…', 'great protruding lips' and an overall appearance of 'low and bestial brutishness.' It would probably be unwise to be over-sensitive about depictions of cannibalism – such phenomena did exist – but the way that Tarzan kills these 'savage natives of the interior' whenever he desires arrows, jewellery or a loincloth (another deliberate adoption of the trappings of man) is somewhat disturbing. Burroughs does at least posit the savagery of the natives as partly the legacy of their bitterness at their treatment by 'that arch hypocrite, Leopold II of Belgium, because of whose atrocities they had fled the Congo Free State.'

His adoption of the family hunting knife puts Tarzan on equal footing with the ferocious animals by which he is surrounded, making him able to defend himself from gorillas and lionesses. Not that Tarzan can use only physical power to overcome his opponents. Burroughs' belief in the beneficial effects of a noble lineage are revealed in his comments on 'the hallmark of aristocratic birth, the natural outcropping of many generations of fine breeding and hereditary instinct of graciousness.' One product of Tarzan's supposedly hereditary intelligence is his working out that he can kill lions and apes with a full-nelson wrestling hold.

Although investing such stock in noble blood seems preposterous from a modern perspective, where lords are more likely to be perceived as upper-class twits than a superior breed, it should be noted that the word 'lord' was in 1912 and for a long time thereafter as synonymous with glamour as the word 'princess'. It might be the case that, even as Burroughs was writing *Tarzan of the Apes*, peers were losing a certain allure: the 1911 Parliament Act took away the House of Lords' ability to reject the legislation of the democratically elected Commons. However, only after the Second World War and the arrival into the mainstream of leftist politics did 'lord' begin to tip over into a pejorative. The word and concept never really regained its previous allure even as the political fashions swung back to the right.

Burroughs' description of Tarzan is idealised to the point of homoerotic. He is a giant of six foot (even today, after a century of increasing average height, western men tend to be around 5' 10") with a 'straight and perfect figure, muscled as the best of the Roman gladiators must have been muscled, and yet with the soft and sinuous curves of a Greek god.' By the time two paragraphs later Burroughs is enthusing over 'the noble poise of his handsome head upon those broad shoulders, and the fire of life and intelligence in those fine, clear eyes' we imagine he is all but slavering. (For the record, Burroughs fathered three children and there seems no obvious indication of a gay leaning.)

Act II of the book starts at around the 100-page mark when a party of outsiders is put ashore almost exactly where Tarzan's parents were marooned 21 years previously and in almost identical circumstances: they are the spared survivors of a ship mutiny. This event is just about plausible, but by a quite astonishing/ridiculous coincidence one of the party is Tarzan's cousin, William Cecil Clayton, who has inherited his title and estates on the assumption that the Greystokes who disappeared on the high seas are dead.

Another of the party is Miss Jane Porter of Baltimore, a young woman by whose beauty the observing Tarzan is immediately enraptured. When Tarzan recues Jane from mortal danger and takes her on an exhilarating swing through the treetops, she begins feeling the same way about him.

The story begins to unravel when Tarzan starts his transformation into a gentleman, which process is not only absurdly accelerated (maritime man Paul D'Arnot – the rescuer of the Porter/Clayton party – has him eloquent in French within weeks), but also makes him intrinsically less interesting and likeable: by killing a lion to win a bet, Tarzan turns from noble savage to glorified big-game hunter. Burroughs also misses a trick in not showing Tarzan's reaction to his first metropolis (Paris). Tarzan expertly driving a car not long after reaching America, meanwhile, leaves the reader more incredulous than had any aspect of the jungle opera.

Burroughs does at least introduce an impressive twist at the end when a miserable Jane is contemplating marriage to a man she hates but to whom her father is financially indebted. Tarzan rescues Jane from a forest fire and then from her marriage, both by brute physical force. However, Tarzan doesn't get the girl, or the title and estates that he knows his fingerprints prove are rightfully his. When Jane tells him she has promised to marry William Cecil Clayton, Tarzan keeps his counsel rather than take away status and riches from his beloved's intended. Asked by William Cecil about his background, Tarzan says, 'My mother was an ape ... I never knew who my father was.' It is a pleasingly unusual and poignant conclusion in an era in which a manufactured happy ending would have been expected by much of the readership. This is in keeping with the book as a whole, for despite its expedient gaps in logic and the idealised nature of the hero – and he is a hero, not a protagonist – it sidesteps simplistic patterns. One example is Tarzan being given the handicap of initially not being able to speak the words he has learnt to read. Even Jane's improbable instant love for Tarzan is undercut by her subsequent apprehension that he will eat like an animal at table and her realisation back in civilisation that context was the main reason for her feelings for her 'forest god'.

Burroughs employs a stately pace for his varied and sometimes complex tale. He is often ornate, but such is the quality of his writing that the reader can sink into this stylistic plushness quite happily: 'For a moment he scrutinised the ground below and the trees above, until the ape that was in him by virtue of training and environment, combined with the intelligence that was his by right of birth, told his wondrous woodcraft the whole story as plainly as though he had seen the thing happen with his own eyes.' The omniscient narrative voice that was so prevalent in literature of the time, and which can be insufferable to the modern reader, is here the only apt method to relay a story that must explain the motivations of not just sophisticated adults but savage beasts and a feral boy.

The book's comedy elements are its weakest parts. The 'Lawdy'/'No sah!' speech patterns of Jane's black maid Esmeralda might in isolation be simple colloquialism, but, combined with Esmeralda attempting to jam her bulk into cupboard shelves and fainting away at every sign of danger, become part of a bad-taste cartoon. In fairness, Burroughs also portrays Jane's intellectual father Professor Archimedes Q Porter and his secretary and assistant Samuel T Philander as effete and absurd, engaging in intellectual babble about a lion trailing them instead of running for their lives.

The presentation of the attraction between Tarzan and Jane as pure love is a sign of times in which lust was a reality that dared not speak its name. Another indication of olde worlde mentality is the fact that the only profanities throughout – uttered by the sailors – are rendered as black lines. On a related note, some of the expressions used in the text have long passed out of the language (Burroughs tells us that 'Tarzan sat in a brown study' to indicate that he is absorbed in thought).

Burroughs' story was not only engaging and exciting, it was also highly unusual – something that quite quickly became forgotten through the familiarity of the Tarzan character in the culture. Unsurprisingly, *Tarzan of the Apes* was an immediate sensation with *The All-Story*'s readers. Burroughs had very cannily sold Munsey only first magazine publication rights. It was a move so unusual that it could be said to have jeopardised publication – there was considerable correspondence between the magazine and the author about it before Munsey acquiesced – but by sticking to his guns Burroughs laid the foundation stone of his fortune.

Thomas Metcalf, managing editor of *The All-Story*, virtually begged Burroughs for a sequel to *Tarzan of the Apes*. However, when the author did agree to the resumption of the adventures of the hero who had enraptured his magazine's readership like no other, Metcalf dismissed the result as unprintable.

Burroughs was so distraught at the rejection of the tale which he first titled *Monsieur Tarzan* that he told Metcalf he was giving up writing. 'I put a lot of work on it,' he wrote. 'Mapped it out carefully so that I was quite sure that it would be smooth and consistent. You approved of the plans, and I did not deviate from them except in such minor details as seemed necessary ... I certainly cannot afford to put months of work into a story thinking it the best work that I had ever done only to find that it doesn't connect. I can make money easier some other way ... I think I'll chuck it.' Metcalf wrote back to implore him, 'For the love of Mike! Don't get discouraged!' Burroughs was actually a bit of a drama queen when it came both to rejection and to what he felt to be unjustly low remuneration, and it's doubtful that he contemplated longer than a few minutes abandoning his new writing career. After all, he wasn't a stranger to knock-backs: his historical novel *The Outlaw of Torn* had been rejected by *All-Story* following the acceptance of *Under the Moons of Mars*. Perhaps Burroughs was a little fed up with Metcalf: he had rejected *The Outlaw of Torn* after being the one to suggest an historical novel to him, and likewise it was at his suggestion that Burroughs transplanted Tarzan to an urban setting for his second adventure.

Burroughs sent what he now retitled *The Ape-Man* to *New Story Magazine*, published by Munsey rival Street & Smith. Although it was accepted, it's highly probable that it was simply the acclaim and profit the first Tarzan adventure had yielded for Munsey that engendered this happier result for the author. Nonetheless, Burroughs was probably less concerned by this than the fact that his payment was three hundred dollars more than he had secured for his first Tarzan story.

Approaching in terms other than those of naked commerce what was eventually serialised in *New Story* from June to December 1913 as *The Return of Tarzan*, it becomes understandable why Metcalf was not impressed. It's laughable. The juxtaposition of a wild man's savagery with the mores and customs of civilisation is a valid idea. However, as had already been demonstrated by the last section of *Tarzan of the Apes*, Burroughs did not know how to bring off this literary conceit. Here, the faults of the way he depicted his urbanised Tarzan in the first book are magnified several-fold. A year or so after his first glimpse of city people, Tarzan is cruising through society enjoying cigarettes and absinthe ('… it was because he took civilisation as he found it'), attending libraries and picture galleries, devouring books and doling out personalised cards declaring 'M. JEAN C. TARZAN.' Barely a year after first speaking, he is preternaturally eloquent ('I am convinced that their enmity is a sufficient guarantee of the integrity of its object') and steeped in American culture ('She is from an old southern family in America, and southerners pride themselves on their loyalty,' he observes of Jane's promise of marriage to his cousin). Meanwhile, the book is riven with unlikely coincidences, from

Jane's best friend Hazel Strong being at a critical juncture on the same liner as the ape-man, to Tarzan – thrown overboard said liner – finding himself washed ashore at, of all the places in the world, the log cabin where he was born. Elsewhere, there are lapses more grave than offences against probability: '…the black men … to my mind are in most ways lower in the scale than the beasts,' offers Tarzan easily.

The plot begins with Tarzan loafing around Paris through the aegis of Paul D'Arnot. His honourable behaviour in a duel – one engineered by his new nemesis, high society criminal Nikolas Rokoff – lands him a job as a secret agent for the French government in Algeria. It is Rokoff who arranges for Tarzan to be thrown over a ship's rail when he is headed for Cape Town on business. Back in the Africa in which he feels far more comfortable than the metropolis – even despite a lukewarm welcome from the Mangani and the lack of cigs and booze – he becomes head of the Waziri tribe, who will feature in many Tarzan adventures to come. It is the Waziri who take Tarzan to a lost city from which they obtain their ornaments: Opar. This is the first, and for many the best, of the numerous isolated and antediluvian civilisations that will feature in Tarzan stories, not least because of its high priestess, the beautiful La. Cut adrift from its imputed motherland Atlantis after the latter's watery fate, Opar is populated by repulsive savage men, who are the result of carnal relations with apes, and physically perfect women, who are the result of careful breeding. Little wonder that La – a recurring character in the series – would forever hold a torch for the buff Tarzan. It is rumoured that Burroughs always regretted not pairing the two. Although Jane did develop into a resourceful character in her own right rather than the prim near-cypher of the debut, La – with her haughty demeanour, steely determination, scantily clad sensuality and facility in the Mangani language – is in several ways a far better match for Tarzan.

Tarzan finds Jane on his patch again when she, her intended and Rokoff are, in another ludicrous coincidence, washed ashore on the stretch of the African coast where he grew up. Jane's southern loyalty evaporates when her fiancée fails to protect her from a lion (leaving a hidden Tarzan to save them with a spear). Tarzan subsequently rescues Jane from Opar's blood-drenched sacrificial altar. The treasures Tarzan has looted from Opar mean he will never be skint, but William Cecil Clayton ensures his further security by acknowledging on his fevered African deathbed that Tarzan is the real Lord Greystoke. At book's end, Tarzan and Jane are married by Jane's father. They sail to civilisation, Tarzan comfortable in the knowledge that his love for his new 'mate' will quell his misgivings about never seeing the jungle again.

There are occasional flashes of good writing in *The Return of Tarzan*, such as the depicted terror of the inhabitants of an upmarket house through which rings the victory cry of the bull ape after Tarzan has pitilessly dealt with an antagonist. Generally, though, the prose is utilitarian and stiff. It also suffers from a comic book-like tenor: in action scenes, we never feel anxiety over Tarzan's fate. In fact, sometimes we wish for harm to befall the ape-man, so pompous is he in his assumption of the mantle of do-gooder. Additionally, the omniscient narration that was so appropriate in *Tarzan of the Apes* is here somewhat suffocating: four points of view are represented in the first three pages alone.

Despite the hectic plot, throughout *The Return of Tarzan* Burroughs doesn't seem to know what to do with the character he had dreamed up in a fit of sublime creativity. That, the poor writing and the utter lack of believability would have confirmed to some that *Tarzan of the Apes* – with its now ruined perfect, tragic ending – never needed a sequel.

Tarzan's phenomenal success in the pulps created a commensurate demand for more. Yet that demand was in a way illogical. Tarzan was intrinsically a one-off. Once the concept had been depicted of a nobleman raised in the jungle and then being reclaimed by civilisation, there was, apparently, nowhere else to go with it. For this reason, it's probable that Burroughs had originally not considered *Tarzan of the Apes* to be anything other than self-contained. The Tarzan universe was far more obviously limited than those of the two other franchises he had begun. Two sequels to *Under the Moons of Mars* had seen magazine publication by 1914, and in neither had Burroughs been visibly straining for a way to perpetuate his original idea. Similarly, the ideas on which he had begun expounding in *At the Earth's Core* would be ingeniously, rather than contrivedly, elaborated on in half a dozen further volumes set in Pellucidar. We should also note that Tarzan at this juncture was probably not a huge priority for Burroughs. Between the first and the third Tarzan stories, Burroughs published in the pulps the novel- or novella-length stories *The Cave Girl*, *A Man Without a Soul* (later re-titled *The Monster Men*), *The Mucker*, *The Mad King* and *The Eternal Lover*. These tales – which don't even include some unpublished short stories – range from science fiction to a form of dirty realism. Burroughs was clearly enjoying his newly assumed status of author and Tarzan was just one of the characters whose stories he was veritably cranking out. He may well have been thinking that there was no reason to believe he could not create something just as popular as Tarzan.

Yet, as a cold-eyed realist and someone with a family to support, Burroughs was naturally happy to accede to public demand for more Tarzan. Sandwiching the third *bona fide* entry in the Tarzan series were two stories that shamelessly exploited the ape-man's success. Burroughs shoehorned Tarzan into the otherwise unrelated *The Eternal Lover* by making the protagonist a big-game hunter visiting the estate of Lord and Lady Greystoke at the start of a fantastic adventure wherein he is transported back to primitive times. In doing so, Burroughs created severe continuity problems, as his depiction of the Claytons' son Jack as a babe in arms doesn't chime with the fact that he subsequently placed him in the thick of the action in the First World War. The other sandwiching story, *The Lad and the Lion*, in fairness ties in just as much to *The Mad King*, but with it Burroughs effectively gave himself another bite of the Tarzan cherry by proffering what is essentially a re-tooled *Tarzan of the Apes*: the young heir to a European crown is washed up on an African shore and has to fend for himself in the company of only a lion he has befriended onboard; ultimately he returns to his royal birthright.

Despite its warmed-over nature, in 1917 *The Lad and the Lion* became the first-ever Burroughs story to be adapted to the young medium of the moving picture. The première of the five-reel movie occurred simultaneously with the story's magazine publication, an indication both of the prevailing short turnaround times for films and of Burroughs' business canniness in proactively pitching his properties. Sadly, there is no known surviving print of *The Lad and the Lion*, which was very loosely remade in 1936 as *The Lion Man*. Curiously, at first no movie studio seemed interested in *Tarzan of the Apes* itself.

The inherent limitations of Tarzan were made almost embarrassingly manifest by *The Beasts of Tarzan*, published in May-June 1914 by the magazine that, following a merger, was now called *All-Story Cavalier Weekly*. Even expanded for book publication in 1916, it would be one of the slimmest of Burroughs' Tarzan volumes. It is just as insubstantial aesthetically.

At the beginning of the story, a shadow is cast over the nuclear-family bliss of Tarzan, Jane and Jack by news that Nikolas Rokoff has escaped from prison. Naturally, the villain from *The Return of Tarzan* is out for revenge. He abducts both Jane and Jack and strands Tarzan on a remote island, giving him something on which to dwell by telling him he is going to allow Jack to be raised by cannibals in Africa, while Jane's fate he leaves 'to your imagination.'

The beasts of the title are the creatures on the island that Tarzan enlists to help him get back his family. One is Akut, a Mangani with whom Tarzan is understandably able to converse. Somewhat less comprehensible is how he is able to communicate with Sheeta the panther, who becomes his obedient (if admittedly edgy) ally after he rescues him from beneath a fallen tree. The final ally he picks up is the warrior Mugambi, and if his implicit bracketing with 'beasts' will set twitching the antennae of those who have already perceived racism in Burroughs, it has to be said that the character is at all times depicted as noble and brave, with it actually being stated that he is the ape-man's 'black counterpart.' Tarzan battles a crocodile for the first time in the series before reaching Africa, killing Rokoff and saving Jane and Jack from their respective intended doom.

If Tarzan has become far too civilised for plausibility over the previous two stories, Burroughs also at least tries to keep him connected to his savage upbringing: at one point Tarzan smears his face almost orgasmically with his quarry's hot blood; at another he dismisses Jane's pleading for an enemy's life as he methodically breaks his neck. Such realism is rather spoilt by a feeble ending in which Burroughs takes to the farthest, most ludicrous degree his penchant for omniscience by addressing the reader like some vaudeville turn. Referring to Tarzan's African estates, on which the ape-man is proposing to allow Mugambi and his lover to live, he writes, 'Possibly we shall see them all there amid the savage romance of the grim jungle and the great plains where Tarzan of the Apes loves best to be. Who knows?'

This hardly enthusiastic closing remark is in keeping with the tentative and aimless air surrounding *The Beasts of Tarzan*, a book that sums up a problem that Burroughs would really face for the rest of his days. Within its pages, he gropes for something to do with a character who stubbornly persists in being his most successful invention.

The tight constraints in which Burroughs found himself *vis a vis* Tarzan presumably explain why the ape-man did not return to the newsstands for another 18 months. Although the author's solution to his creative impasse was not quick in coming, it was clever. *The Son of Tarzan* was serialised in *All-Story Weekly* (the *Cavalier* component having now been dropped from the title) in six parts from December 1915 to January 1916. The longest Tarzan story so far, it was streets ahead of its predecessor and is one of the most enduringly popular of all Tarzan adventures.

One wonders how much of the renewed inspiration evident in Burroughs' Tarzan writing was due to the fact that, a month after *The Beasts of Tarzan* began its serialisation, he had received confirmation that *Tarzan of the Apes* was to become his first published novel. This was no small achievement. Burroughs might throughout his life have bristled at the fact that his magazine writing was almost entirely restricted to the pulps, but a proper bound book was on a higher plateau than occupied even by the slicks. It was A C McClurg who finally consented to publish *Tarzan of the Apes* after several other publishers – as well as, previously, McClurg – had rebuffed Burroughs' entreaties to rescue it from its literary ghetto.

Once again, Burroughs was displaying his grounding as a businessman. Most other writers would simply have been bowled over to see their name in print, yet although Burroughs was no doubt pleased to get published in *All-Story*, he was also cognisant of the fact that, despite the estimated 200,000 pairs of eyes that had seen the edition in which Tarzan made his debut, it was a transient success: the shelf-life of the magazine was precisely one month (and it was presumably not the kind of periodical favoured by libraries). A serialisation of *Tarzan of the Apes* that started in January 1913 in the *New York Evening World* newspaper, in a deal brokered by Munsey's company, had brought welcome extra exposure and income. (The vast number of city and state newspapers in America prepared to pay to run a story already published elsewhere would provide a nice little bonus for Burroughs in coming years.) Although the shelf-life of an edition of a newspaper was even shorter than that of a magazine, the serialisation was an elongated one: it ran for 46 daily episodes, Mondays to Saturdays. More to the point, it was newspapers that gave Burroughs his foot in the door of book publishing. Friend Albert Terhune, fiction editor at the *Evening World*, did Burroughs a favour by testifying to publishers how popular were Burroughs' stories with his periodical's readers.

McClurg, based in Burroughs' home town of Chicago,

published *Tarzan of the Apes* on 6 June 1914. The approximately 10,000 copies of the novel's first edition may not sound too impressive considering that the readership of the *All-Story* stood at around 20 times that figure, nor might Burroughs' $250 advance on a royalty of ten percent (with escalator) of the $1.30 cover price immediately scream 'big time'. However, a book, if it remained in print, would generate money for many years.

There was an additional benefit incalculable in monetary terms. The *Tarzan of the Apes* McClurg hardback had a red binding on which the title and author's name were embossed in gold lettering. Over this was positioned a dust jacket whose quietly dignified wraparound illustration by Fred J Arting went in the other direction to Clinton Pettee's dramatic, full-colour cover art accompanying the same tale when featured in *All-Story*, it showing simply a human silhouette sitting in a tree, with a lion wandering around in the distance. Inside the covers, the crisp, thick pages were a world removed from the second-rate paper from which the pulps had taken their name. The whole artefact was the type of thing that would sit very nicely alongside the handsome volumes on the shelves in the learned Burroughs' library. Burroughs was now a *bona fide* author. Book versions of *The Return of Tarzan*, *The Beasts of Tarzan* and *The Son of Tarzan* followed at annual intervals.

This did not mean, though, that Burroughs began to spurn the likes of *All-Story*, especially when by no means all of his stories made the jump from magazines: *The Lad and the Lion*, for instance, couldn't be placed with a book publisher even despite having become a movie. However, from hereon Burroughs' main series – Tarzan, Mars, Venus, Pellucidar and Caspak – all found book publishers pretty effortlessly, as did several other mini-series and one-offs. The previously small McClurg became rich as Burroughs' – and especially Tarzan's – fame spread exponentially.

That Burroughs decided to re-invigorate the Tarzan franchise by giving the ape-man's son an adventure of his own was on one level a dangerous move. A Tarzan with a teenage progeny is by definition getting on a bit, which can't help but diminish the hero's aura of physical perfection. On the other hand, the coming-of-age story – with its built-in vulnerability, youthful vigour and intriguing journey of discovery – is the very thing to inject life into an arid literary situation. Additionally, the family tableaux it involves can't help but be touching. Burroughs himself had two sons and, although there doesn't seem any evidence that he loved Hulbert (born 1909) and John Coleman (1913) any more than his daughter Joan (1908), his patent fondness for his boys shines through the text.

Jack Clayton's age is not specified, but at the start of this book we infer he is in his early teens. He unnerves Jane because, despite having been told nothing of his father's jungle upbringing, he possesses a penchant for climbing trees and an obsession with Africa. He also has superhuman strength. The romantic notion that Jack would have somehow inherited the muscles and simian-like agility that his father acquired via conditioning has of course no basis in science, but such conceits are common even in today's more rationality-suffused culture.

A performing ape at a music hall transpires to be the captured Mangani Akut. After making secret visits to see Akut, during which he learns his language, Jack ends up with the ape's owner's hands around his throat. In a classic Burroughs example of unlikely coincidence, said owner is Alexis Paulvitch, former accomplice of Rokoff. (The latter ended up in Sheeta's belly in the previous story.) Akut kills Paulvitch to protect Jack. Jack then smuggles Akut onto a ship bound for Africa. Once there, Akut again resorts to killing to defend Jack when a man tries to fleece the boy at a sleazy hotel. To escape a murder rap, Jack flees with Akut into the jungle.

A relationship then develops that is reminiscent of that of Mowgli and bear mentor Baloo in *The Jungle Book* as Jack learns the ways of the wild. Although Burroughs shows Jack learning to recognise the smell of jungle animals and acquiring other survival instincts, he doesn't overdo it, depicting him chastened after cockily attempting to take on Numa before he is ready.

Ultimately, though, Jack becomes 'a creature of marvellous physical powers and mental cunning.' He is having such a ball with Akut that he only idly resolves to make his way back to civilisation at some hazy point in the future.

Jack loses in stages the pyjamas in which he has fled. He also loses his name, as Akut can't pronounce it. Instead, the ape dubs him 'Korak', which spelling is an approximation of the Mangani for 'killer'. Korak's first kill is a native who has committed no crime worse than being a member of a village that had made him and Akut unwelcome. This is a hallmark of a bloodthirsty and distinctly nasty strain to the book. Later on, Korak massacres the inhabitants of a village in the mistaken belief that they have eaten somebody he cares about.

Korak happens upon a beautiful, nut-brown girl his own age named Meriem, who is being held prisoner in an Arab stockade. Korak rescues the grateful girl and the two turn the jungle into a veritable Garden of Eden as they embark upon a love affair, communicating via the Mangani that Korak teaches Meriem. The love affair becomes sexual (or as close to sexual as the prudish Burroughs ever depicted anything) only after a passage of time we assume to be years.

In the second half of the book, Korak and Meriem are separated, with Meriem being cared for by a kindly couple who at book's end are revealed to be Tarzan and Jane, looking for their lost son. Before that revelation, one section sees Korak summon Tantor to rescue him from a burning at the stake, a scene that would feature in the movie adaptation of the book. The set-up would thereafter have all excitement drained from it by becoming a crushingly predictable staple of Tarzan films. At the novel's conclusion, Korak and Meriem are married on board the ship that is taking the Greystoke clan back to England, but not before arch-snob Burroughs has established the important fact that the new family member is no mere Arab waif but a princess.

Perhaps because of the above-mentioned diminution of physical perfection in the father that a grown son implies, after this book Burroughs did no more with Korak than feature him in a secondary role in a trio of novels in the middle of the series. Having said that, beyond this 'origin story', there wasn't much potential for the character, as demonstrated by Gold Key and DC Comics, who both later gave Korak his own regular title but failed to convey much more than an ersatz Tarzan. Burroughs himself only really differentiates Jack from his father by having him spurn the victory cry of the bull ape for a silent exultation. It must also be admitted that *The Son of Tarzan* relies for much of its appeal on being a rehash of the first Tarzan book. Nonetheless, it covers old ground adroitly and often charmingly.

The fifth Tarzan adventure was *Tarzan and the Jewels of Opar*, serialised in *All-Story Weekly* in November and December 1916 and published in book form in 1918.

This story showed Burroughs finally apprehending how he could prolong the ostensibly limited Tarzan concept. It also set the template for the series. With a few exceptions, ape-man novels would from now on involve lost cities, imported ne'er-do-wells, separate safaris with similar objectives but morally contrasting motives and a Tarzan who is the key to the relevant issue or – as a man in his element – the key to the survival of the good guys. Burroughs would in future years dot Africa with a most unlikely number of missing metropolises. Although these lost cities were sometimes marked by authorial ingenuity, and although Burroughs juggled and dovetailed quite impressively the stories of the separate parties seeking or stumbling upon them, in time this whole approach ossified into a rigid, groan-inducing formula, especially in its incorporation of the device of a man and a woman in the 'good' safari falling in love. *Jewels of Opar*, though, is one of the better examples, even if it does feature another of the tut-provoking elements of that formula in the shape of Tarzan temporarily losing his memory after a blow on the head.

The beautiful but deadly La is central to the proceedings in a tale that sees Tarzan looting Opar because – in an example of

Burroughs' penchant for depicting the ape-man as someone with a foot in both the jungle and high society – his African estate has become a bit strapped for cash. Also seeking Opar's treasures is a Belgian army deserter named Albert Werper, who is in cahoots with Arab villain Achmet Zek. (Burroughs also had a penchant for cosmopolitan villainy.) Zek decides to sell Jane to a harem (a common threat to Lady Greystoke in the Tarzan stories) but, when she is abducted, Mrs Clayton turns out to be feistily equal to the challenges she faces. Tarzan as ever manages to remain immune to La's lustful charms (surprisingly candidly drawn by the often moralistic author). That this time this is despite an amnesiac state that means he has no knowledge of having sworn marriage vows may provoke a response of, 'Mister, you're a better man than I.'

A dying witchdoctor croakingly predicting doom and a rhinoceros with attitude (he takes on seven lions) are amongst the thrills in a roller-coaster ride that has a whimsical twist in the tail.

In the autumn of 1916, a Virginia teenager named Herman Newman set up the first association relating to the ape-man. Newman explained in a letter to Burroughs that the impetus for the Tribe of Tarzan was that Tarzan had made a man out of him. The organisation had a tribe room for their meetings and played with grass ropes, hunting knives and bows and arrows. A delighted Burroughs obtained them publicity in *All-Story* and had bronze medallions struck for them to give out for achievement of tasks. (The medals were designed in imitation of the object Tarzan habitually wore around his neck: a locket containing photographs of his parents which he had found in the log cabin back in the first story.) Truthfulness, honesty, manliness, courageousness, health and cleanliness were among the values listed on the back of Tribe membership cards. In other words, a Tarzan-inflected variant of the Boy Scouts, itself then a very young organisation, having been formed in 1907.

The Tribes of Tarzan's code of honour might seem pretty

square, but this was several generations before questioning of society's mores was perceived as more admirable than steadfast adherence to them. Branches of the Tribe of Tarzan soon sprang up across the country, and 13 years later – long after Herbert Newman had grown up, joined the army, been demobilised and dropped out of the picture – it was going strong enough to be talking of striking out internationally.

All of this was significant because inspiring such formalised devotion after only five magazine stories/three books indicated that the ape-man already had the makings of a phenomenon.

Burroughs found another outlet for his Tarzan tales in the shape of *Blue Book*. It was that magazine which, from its issue cover-dated September 1916 through to the issue cover-dated August 1917, published new ape-man short stories at a rate of one per month. They were subsequently collated and published in book form as *Jungle Tales of Tarzan* (in the UK, *Tarzan's Jungle Tales*).

The word 'midquel' was not in currency in 1916/17 (and some lovers of the English language might suggest it shouldn't be today) but that is what the stories – and book – constitute, with Burroughs going back to the point in *Tarzan of the Apes* when Tarzan was an adolescent roaming the jungle, aware of the world beyond it only in the sense of what he had seen in the books in his parents' cabin. The author's opting at this juncture for Tarzan writing that was both fragmented and nostalgic may have been down to a combination of a repetitive strain disorder diagnosed as neuritis, a desire to pursue other projects, especially motion-picture adaptations of his properties, and an attempt to work around his uncertainty about how to continue the Tarzan franchise. However, constituting a holding action doesn't stop this book being a delightful entry in the Tarzan canon.

All these stories occur after the death of Kala but before Tarzan becomes king of his tribe by killing Kerchak. The 12 chronologically-presented stories are each technically self-contained, but the fact that they are interlinked – some subtly, some overtly – creates an episodic novel in all but name. Said novel sees Tarzan develop his first crush (on a comely Mangani), engineer his own rescue from threatening natives by calling on Tantor, win round a hostile mother in his tribe by rescuing her baby from danger, tussle with the notion of God, kidnap a young boy from a local village to father, compassionately return the homesick child, defeat the nefarious plans of an abhorrent witch-doctor, try in vain to teach his Mangani tribe to be vigilant of potential predators, confuse dreams with reality after becoming feverish through food poisoning, get rescued from peril in a roundabout way by bullets taken from his parents' log cabin, murderously torment the local villagers with both a lion skin and a real lion, and obtain a hero aura among the frightened Mangani for seeming to retrieve a disappearing moon that is actually in eclipse.

The lesson-learning against a wilderness backdrop, the short-form format and the title of the book (the phrase 'Jungle Tales' actually appears in Kipling) serves to strengthen the impression of the influence on Burroughs of the Jungle Books. Only the mean-spirited anti-black strain running through the stories diminishes the overriding air of sweetness and innocence.

When Burroughs had insisted on selling them only magazine publication rights to *Tarzan of the Apes*, a bewildered Frank Munsey Company had asked the author what other possible rights there might be. According to writer Gabe Essoe, Burroughs had seemed vague himself: 'I don't know. Maybe moving picture rights or something else.' Burroughs' inchoate hunch proved right for, successful though his novels already were, it was the new medium of the 'movies' that was the true making of both him and his ape-man creation.

Lost in the mists of time is how influential the first Tarzan movie was on the nascent medium of the moving picture. When *Tarzan of the Apes* (1918) was released, it was, apart from *Birth of a Nation* (1915) and *Intolerance* (1916), the longest cinema film up to that point. In an age when most movies were of two reels (each reel lasting between 13 and 15 minutes), this one ran to ten.

However, it wasn't just length that rendered *Tarzan of the Apes* remarkable. Although like so many pictures from the silent era it looks comical to modern eyes, it was at the time an amazing spectacle, innovative in both camerawork and production values. Its promotional campaign was a precursor of modern hype. There is even an argument for saying that it was the greatest cinematic cultural sensation up to that point for, grand and successful though *Birth of a Nation* was, its exposure was restricted by bans over its controversial content, while *Intolerance* was a commercial flop.

The National Film Corporation of America bought the film rights to *Tarzan of the Apes* four years after that aforementioned exchange between author and magazine publisher. The remuneration was a then-massive $5,000 advance, $50,000 in company stock and five percent of gross receipts. Their title was lofty, but the National Film Corporation of America was actually a start-up venture by a man with no cinema experience. Previously, William Parsons had been a life insurance salesman. He had inked a deal with Burroughs when the latter had been unsuccessful in persuading anyone to make a Tarzan picture after the idea was put into the author's head in 1913 by a New York play broker. Parsons raised the production money by selling stock in his newly-founded film company.

Parsons is listed as producer of *Tarzan of the Apes*, which was directed by Scott Sidney. Burroughs is, along with Fred Miller and Lois Weber, credited as a writer. Al Bohl, the producer of *Tarzan: Lord of the Louisiana Jungle*, a 2012 documentary about the movie, explains that this billing was more than just a courtesy credit: 'He was really part of the production at the start, but when they began to change the story a little bit he backed out … Burroughs just didn't understand that a book and a movie is two different things.' In correspondence with Parsons, Burroughs asserted that to change the first Tarzan narrative would be to 'ruin' it for the million or so people who he estimated had read it by then, even if 'the change made a better story of it.' Prior to the movie's release, a disgruntled Burroughs made enquiries about the feasibility of removing his name and even Tarzan's from the picture.

Bohl is fairly sure that *Tarzan of the Apes* was the first major American motion picture formally shot on location. 'By that time, film had pretty much settled into two coasts, either New York or California,' he says. 'At first they were just shooting *Tarzan* in California but they just felt like it didn't have that natural feeling. They couldn't go to Africa, because you couldn't get around like you can now.' (For the same reason, Bohl dismisses publicity of the day that suggested that an excursion had been made by the crew to Brazil.) Morgan City, Louisiana, fit the bill for a substitute Africa in being accessible and in having jungle-like greenery, a large black population and reliable transportation.

Ten-year-old Gordon Griffith was engaged to play the jungle lord as a young boy. Elmo Lincoln was the adult Tarzan, although not without a hiccup when his demand for a fee of $100 per week rather than $75 led to the studio re-casting Stellan Windrow in the role. The latter athletic vaudeville actor spent four weeks shooting jungle scenes in Louisiana, but, when America entered what we now call the First World War, Windrow decided to enlist in the Navy. A recalled Lincoln got his extra $25. Although Windrow agreed to waive a place in the credits for $1,000, Bohl reveals, 'Anytime they're high up in the trees, he's there. He did all the arboreal stuff. Down on the ground or lower limbs, you see Elmo Lincoln. Now they say it's because Elmo Lincoln was afraid of heights, but I've interviewed his daughter and she said he had never indicated to her that he was scared of heights at all ... It was probably that they'd fought so much of the elements – they had malaria – they probably thought, *Why shoot it all over again?*'

The film came in different running lengths. Explains Bohl, 'Originally the film was two hours and ten minutes. They had to cut it down.' Much of the footage excised from the longer version was non-jungle material. *Variety* complained in February 1918, 'The early sections are almost wholly devoted to planting the underlying theme of the story ... Much time is devoted to the reason for the parents of Tarzan going to South [sic] Africa, also a tremendous footage is held by the succeeding holder of the title of Lord Greystoke, his escapades, marriage to a barmaid (Bessie Toner) and subsequent heir (Colin Kenny) ...' Bohl: 'Most people enjoyed the jungle parts but not the rest of it, so they took out the English part and kept most of the jungle scenes and made it about 71 minutes long. They called it a digest version. Even though it was cut down to 71 minutes, the story still holds together.'

Sadly – and rather amazingly, considering hundreds, even thousands, must have been in circulation throughout the world – there is no surviving print of the first, 130-minute, version of *Tarzan of the Apes*. Bohl: 'They would melt them down to get the silver nitrates out and re-make film with. They just didn't really think about saving movies. It was so new a medium, they didn't really think much that it would survive.' Bohl adds that if any copy remains extant, it is highly likely that it will be severely corroded, but he does think one may turn up: 'It's very possible when they tear down some old movie houses or something throughout the world, they'll find it.'

The movie gets underway with a montage of shots of African wildlife that is indiscriminate about jungle dwellers and denizens of the plains but at least sticks to the fauna of the right continent. For the most part, the 'scenario' (as screenplays were then called) follows the plot of the first Tarzan novel, but the story for some reason starts two years before it does in the book, an apparently arbitrary refusal to adhere to Burroughs' date that would be a peculiarly consistent feature of Tarzan movies. After some English scenes featuring members of the Greystoke clan, we see the shipboard mutiny. Cut to the Greystokes hugging each other in fear against the backdrop of a departing ship. Binns, the sailor who saves the Greystokes from the same fate as the ship's officers, is unable to join them ashore as he wishes, because he is captured by Arab slave traders. A decade before talking pictures, these plot developments are, of course, helped along with title cards, some of which are quite literary ('Only the leopard outside the door hears the cries of the new-born heir of Greystoke'), and some colloquial ('I wonders if they died a thinking old Binnsey broke 'is promise to 'em').

In this narrative, Kala's baby isn't killed by Kerchak but dies of natural causes. This death sends the ape king into a 'frenzy of rage,' causing him to lead an invasion of the cabin, from where the Claytons' baby is stolen. The apes – described as merely that – are acrobats dressed in furry costumes, although the murky film quality and sepia tones of the era prevent them looking too risible. The men in suits alternate with baby chimps, used in close-up. Bohl: 'The way it reads to me, they saw if they wanted to have any interaction with apes, it would be best to use the men in costumes, because back then they didn't have animal wranglers like they do now.'

The name Tarzan is used in the title cards but its origin is not explained, at least not in the surviving condensed version. The boy Tarzan is shown swinging on handily situated and conveniently numerous vines, inaugurating a Tarzan tradition that movies just cannot seem to shake off and which contrasts with the ape-man's more plausible and exciting swinging from bough to bough in the books. Griffith is expressive and impressive, perfect in his mixture of innocence and animalistic guile. In an era before the censorship imposed by the Hays Code, the producers were relatively free of moral restrictions in capturing Burroughs' tale. As Bohl notes of Griffith, 'He probably has the longest – in a major feature film, not a blue film – nude scene of anyone in film history.' He adds, 'The females, the natives, they were nude to their waist.'

Griffith's unclothed state ends when the young Tarzan steals a loincloth after apprehending from the sight of his reflection in a pool that he is not an ape. Meanwhile, realising he is near the Claytons' cabin, Binns escapes his decade-long enslavement and heads for it. He discovers therein the skeleton of Lady Alice and swears to it that he will find her child and take it back to England. The boy Tarzan comes upon Binns asleep on the cabin floor. Binns teaches Tarzan to read while Tarzan in turn nurses him back to health. The returning Arabs thwart Binns' plan to take Tarzan home: the latter tells the boy to run for it and says he will look up his folks if he makes it back to Blighty.

Following another African animal-and-landscape montage, we are then introduced to 'TARZAN - -, THE MAN. ELMO LINCOLN.' Lincoln's screen presence is less conducive to the viewer's comfort than Griffith's. His build would be impressive in an urban setting, but a barrel torso does not seem the type of physique a lifetime spent in the trees would produce, and that's not even mentioning the strong suspicion that the actor is carrying a bit of ballast: one of the first shots of Lincoln finds him moving hand-over-hand along a horizontal creeper that is wobbling rather alarmingly. Having said that, in long-shot he is occasionally handsome, and the *Variety* reviewer – who was perceptive enough to snort at 'cut-ins of animal stuff' and who said of the apes, 'very foolishly a number of close-ups are shown which kill the illusion' – saw no shortcomings in Lincoln, whom she described as 'all that could be asked for.' 'The only [contemporaneous] criticism I've heard of Lincoln is that Burroughs didn't really care for him,' says Bohl. 'Even though they became friends eventually. The Stellan Windrow version of Tarzan was closer to what Burroughs envisaged Tarzan as being.'

Long hair on men in early cinema almost always looked ridiculous because – as society then frowned on growing out for real – it was represented by wigs. Lincoln's bushy-thatch-and-headband affair is no exception. 'It's so horrendous,' says Bohl. 'More a comical look. At that time, over-dramatisation was the way you did it, because they were still so close to stage plays, but that wig was so terrible.' It has been suggested that Lincoln was going bald, but Bohl says, 'Actually he had a really good head of hair.'

Bohl counted Lincoln playing at least six characters in *Birth of a Nation* and says, 'He plays two characters in *Tarzan of the Apes*. He's one of the mutineers on the ship. I don't think they really thought that films had that big an impact. It was almost like just having fun somewhat.'

Binns does indeed make it back to England, and a group of scientists and relatives of Tarzan's parents – Jane in tow – decide to set sail to check out his story of the jungle waif. It's rather ironic that this sort of tampering with the original story seems to have been what caused ERB to walk. The Tarzan movies would eventually build up a massive history of misrepresenting Burroughs' key character, but not only is this movie very faithful to the source, but the few departures from it make the tale far more credible. Bohl notes of Binns, a character not seen in the original novel, 'He was the glue that tied the story together ... He gave some plausibility to different things in the film. He escapes and comes back and finds Tarzan and teaches him how to read ... Then Binns leaves and goes to England and tells them that he's found the heir to the Greystoke fortune, and that prompts the safari to go find him, whereas in the book they're not looking for him at all, they're looking for gold.'

The safari discovers Tarzan's cabin and is presented with the same don't-touch-my-stuff note that the ape-man leaves in the book. Tarzan saves Jane from the aggressive amorous intentions of her fiancé, and Jane and Esmeralda from a lion trying to enter the cabin.

Some have dismissed as hype the legend that Lincoln killed the lion for real, but Bohl says, 'I do believe after hearing pros and cons that the lion was killed for the production of the film. [Lincoln] says that he did [kill it] and his daughter believes he did...' This is not as impressive as it might sound, for as Bohl points out, the producers used 'animals that were real old.' Although they would probably have been in a minority amongst the public a century ago, some people found the feat repugnant rather than impressive. Bohl: 'Lions breed really well in captivity, so they had a lot of them. The Humane Society, while it was a fledgling organisation, was against this, because Parsons announced that he was looking for six lions to kill for this film and some other things. When they found out about it they got all upset about it, and so he backed it down to just that one lion.'

Jane is kidnapped by natives, one of whose number has been shot dead by a fearful member of her party. Tarzan rescues her and carries her off before burning down the natives' village. The movie ends rather limply with Tarzan and Jane sitting on a log, the ape-man pointing out the delights of his jungle home. As *Variety* noted, 'The audience is left in the dark as to whether or not he has come into his birthright, whether he has won the girl or not, or, if he has, did he keep her in the jungle wilds...'

It's as easy for modern audiences to laugh at that uncertain ending (written at a time when screenwriters were still feeling their way with narrative film) as it is Lincoln's gurning expressions and peculiar hops off screen. On top of all that, the introduction of sound in the '20s made films like this, with their exaggerated, eye-rolling 'vocabulary', instant period pieces. Yet, for the era, this is often sophisticated stuff. The extremely high budget of $250,000 obtained exceptional production values. The sets for stately homes, ships and Tarzan's cabin are impressively believable. Meanwhile, we can just imagine the gasps of the picture-house audiences as lions, leopards, elephants and giraffes paraded across the screen. Although they can be naïve, the techniques are also sometimes imaginative (a cutaway to startled birds taking flight as Tarzan kills the killer of Kala could have come from any modern picture).

One is struck by just how similar is this movie to *Greystoke* (1984). Although this is inevitable on one level, for the latter is the only other Tarzan motion picture to closely follow the plot of Burroughs' first Tarzan book, it still seems remarkable that two movies, separated by 66 years and vast changes in film technology and societal mores, feel much the same.

With such a high investment having been made in this extravaganza, naturally the stops were pulled out promotion-wise, if mainly in New York, where the première took place on 27 January 1918. A symphony orchestra provided the accompaniment in the form of a specially-written jungle-themed score. Says Bohl, 'It was the first time – or any time – they've ever stretched [a banner] all the way across Broadway promoting a film. They say that they put the original stuffed lion in the lobby that they killed in the movie. They put a lot of fake foliage and stuff in the lobby and they released monkeys up in there. There's even one thing saying that they had a gorilla that was taking tickets. I don't know if it's true or not.'

Cinema had already developed the parasite of critics, many of whom had moved over from reviewing stage plays to the new-fangled 'photo plays'. Bohl reports that *Tarzan of the Apes* generally got good notices. More importantly, if probably related, it was also a hit with the public, becoming one of the first half-dozen movies to gross over a million dollars. Bohl: 'I believe they made more than that. I think that's a domestic [figure], but that film played all over the world. Most movie tickets of that time cost a nickel – that's why they're called nickelodeons – but *Tarzan*, they charged anywhere from a dollar to two dollars 50 cents per ticket, which was astronomical at that time. But the people paid it. There's even one advertisement I saw that said people stayed up all night just to see it. It was a little bit like *Star Wars* when it came out: people would just go see it, get back in line and see it again.'

Gordon Griffith succumbed to a heart attack in 1958, aged 51. Bohl: 'He was in two of the movies with Charlie Chaplin, so as a child actor he was really gaining ground, but like many child actors he fell out of favour. He stayed in the movie business and eventually became a producer. He directed some too.

'Enid Markey, who played Jane, was a stage actress, and after *Tarzan* it's my understanding from talking to her daughter that she didn't want to be stuck as being seen as Jane. Whereas Elmo never really broke away from Tarzan. She went on to New York and starred in a number of really well-known plays, and eventually she went into television and she made more films.' Bohl also says, 'As far as I know, no one from the production side did much of anything else.' This surprises him: 'It was just way ahead of its time. It's hard to believe that a guy like Parsons could pull something together so magnificently as he did.'

The link had been set in the public's mind between a Tarzan

picture and an enthralling spectacle. *Tarzan of the Apes* kicked off a film franchise that would be amongst the most successful of the first half of the 20th century and that continues, if in less all-conquering form, to this day. The transition to movies completed Tarzan's progress from merely successful product – one estimate has about 600,000 combined sales of the five Tarzan books in print at this point – to cultural sensation.

'The original film came out in January 1918 and by April they were making a sequel,' says Bohl.

News of the shooting of the sequel – which would be released in October 1918 as *The Romance of Tarzan* – incurred the ire of Edgar Rice Burroughs. Bohl: 'He said, "Why didn't you come to me and get a clearance to do that?" Well, they had the right to make the entire book but they only shot half of it and so they said, "Well, we're going to make a second film out of it." They rushed into production on this. They wanted to stay true to the original story, where there's a big forest fire. They were going to shoot that in California and they couldn't because of a burn ban. They used a lot of the original footage for Louisiana … that they'd already shot [for the first film].'

Lincoln, Markey and Griffith all reprised their roles in a movie that lasted 96 minutes and – according to the publicity – took four months to shoot. Although loosely based on the latter stages of the *Tarzan of the Apes* novel, it seems to have had more in common with the wild-man-in-civilisation concept of the book *The Return of Tarzan*. Flashbacks to the first movie explained who the ape-man was and how he came to be in California. Some critics mocked the sight of Tarzan in dress-suit, and Lincoln himself later said, 'They made a mistake when they put Tarzan in clothes. Tarzan is a wild man and he does not belong in a drawing room.'

Exhibitor's Trade Review described *The Romance of Tarzan* as 'a lively, romantic drama with thrilling situations accumulating at a breathtaking rate.' *Variety* was less charitable, dismissing it as 'a meller of the veriest sort' – 'sheer melodrama' in modern parlance. We are unable to adjudge who was right for, as Bohl explains of the film, 'There is no print left of it.' However, he does add, 'There's some belief that somewhere in Europe someone has an actual copy of the film.' Such are the vagaries of early cinema, though, that the one part of *The Romance of Tarzan* which is still extant is now part of the *Tarzan of the Apes* film. The producers belatedly rectified the feeble and inconclusive ending of the first movie by tagging on a scene from *The Romance of Tarzan* wherein Jane, having been delivered to the cabin by her forest god, calls him back when she sees him forlornly about to step into the jungle. Says Bohl, 'It was a better, more romantic ending, and people liked that.'

Although *The Romance of Tarzan* was less well-received and less commercially successful than its predecessor, as with the first Tarzan movie, it broke ground. Bohl: '[It's] one of the very first sequels made.'

Edgar Rice Burroughs was quite a war enthusiast. Politically conservative and intensely patriotic (although, almost conversely, anti-religion), he had no misgivings about America's entry in April 1917 into what was then known as the Great War. However hard-right some of his beliefs, though, one would hesitate to suggest that he saw the war as a godsend for the Tarzan series that he had been trying to manoeuvre out of a creative cul-de-sac since almost the moment the first instalment was published. Nonetheless, it can't be denied that said conflict gave a handy new sense of purpose to the ape-man.

Tarzan the Untamed was published in six parts in *The Red Book* from March to August 1919, and *Tarzan and the Valley of Luna* in five parts in *All-Story Weekly* in March and April 1920. McClurg collected the two tales in book form in 1920 under the title *Tarzan the Untamed* (the first time any Tarzan novel was published in the same year that any part of its story had been printed in a magazine; from hereon this would be the norm). It formed the longest Tarzan book there would ever be. This fat tome was full of barbarity and borderline fascism, most of it – surprisingly –

coming from Lord Greystoke. The war impinges upon Tarzan's world when, during his absence in 1914, the German army visits his estate in British East Africa. When Tarzan returns from a trip to Nairobi, he finds the dead body of his murdered wife. Tarzan incrementally goes insane, embarking on a quest for vengeance against not just the killers of his wife but all German soldiers, before turning to complete misanthropy.

While one can understand Tarzan's grief-stricken fury, and while allowances must be made for an era when dissent about the war was taboo, Burroughs' demonisation and degradation of Germans is still shocking. One of the book's scenes sees Tarzan forcing the Hun whom he thinks responsible for Jane's death to march for miles at spear-point, grimly unyielding as the German literally sobs and pleads his innocence, before leaving him to the mercies of a lion. We are invited to draw no adverse inference from the fact that it turns out that this man is indeed innocent and merely the brother of the real killer. Not only is this heavy, vicious stuff with a built-in sell-by date (albeit later temporarily given an unexpected extension by the Second World War), but Tarzan's aligning himself with the Entente powers is impossible to reconcile with what we know of the ape-man. Although it wouldn't be true to say he had never before killed for reasons of vengeance, no part of Tarzan's jungle upbringing would make him inclined to take sides in a conflagration that historians now consider a territorial squabble bereft of ideological differences. The only things that can be said for this bizarre out-of-character behaviour are that it at least creates a counterbalance to the similar treatment Tarzan doled out to blacks in most of the previous books and that the grim tone is an antidote to the 'soft' Tarzan later presented in the likes of the Weissmuller movies.

Such arguments, though, cut no ice with Germans. The first foreign translation of Tarzan was a 1918 Danish version of *Tarzan of the Apes*. It unleashed a highly lucrative revenue stream. In 1967, Burroughs biographer Robert W Fenton counted 26 languages into which Tarzan books had been translated, plus four Indian dialects. Although German was one of those languages, *Tarzan the Untamed* was deliberately not translated into Deutsch at the time. When outraged German journalist Stefan Sorel 'exposed' the book's contents, it caused a huge Teutonic backlash against Burroughs, destroying the market for his work there for an extensive period – somewhat ironically considering that the war was long over by the time either *Untamed* or the similarly Hun-baiting *The Land That Time Forgot* came out in book form.

In light of all this, how ironic that *Tarzan the Untamed* marks the start of the peak of the Tarzan novels. It is possibly the finest of all Tarzan books, even if it slightly betrays its origin as two separate stories, and even despite the presence of a bewildering unresolved episode in which Tarzan discovers on an ancient skeleton a cylinder containing a Spanish manuscript and a map.

While the first part of the book is taken up by Tarzan devising ingenious and cruel ways to help the British army kill Germans, the second follows his adventures in the lost city of Xuja, whose denizens arguably have an even greater rapport with animals than he but who are also completely loopy as a consequence of in-breeding.

The book version ends with the revelation that Jane may still be alive. While it was unequivocally her body discovered by the ape-man in *The Red Book*, the scene was altered so that Tarzan came upon a body charred beyond recognition but which he assumed to be Jane's because it was wearing her rings. Jane's death was almost certainly related to the problems in Burroughs' crumbling marriage to his wife Emma. Ironically, it was 'commuted' at the urging – according to their daughter Joan – of Emma herself, although some sources also cite the concern of Burroughs' editors. Either way, it makes even more unforgivable Tarzan's slaying of the alleged murderer's brother.

The large supporting roles for an English spy disguised as a Fraulein, Bertha Kircher, and a marooned RAF pilot, Harold Percy Smith-Oldwick, and the fact that they fall for each other, set the pattern for future Tarzan books in which the ape-man would play a diminished role that sometimes amounted to little more than a combination of *deus ex machina* and unwitting matchmaker. Also setting a pattern, *Tarzan the Untamed* is the first Tarzan novel whose title bolts a superlative to his name. These superlatives would come to seem arbitrary, then lazy, as the series sagged in quality, but this one was perfectly descriptive.

Silent movie actors did not need to know how to act as we would now define the term. In a field in which thespians were still prone to histrionics requiring little skill, it seemed perfectly natural that Joseph C Pohler, a New York fireman with no cinematic experience beyond bit parts, should be cast in the film adaptation of *The Return of Tarzan* when Elmo Lincoln had to decline to reprise the lead role for contractual reasons. The assumptions of the era ensured that the fact that Pohler was over six foot two and built like a tree trunk were the major requisites – although it's surprising that, even a hundred years ago, his cowlick and gormless expression don't seem to have raised casting-suite eyebrows. Some things, however, become comical only retroactively. For instance, an impetus for 'decency' in a society where men could be arrested for going topless at the beach saw the relatively skimpy outfits of Lincoln dispensed with in favour of an over-the-shoulder pelt – smirk-inducing ever since 1960 when the Flintstones were first depicted wearing similar apparel.

The movie was made by the Weiss Brothers, whose tender Burroughs liked the best. Symptomatic of the problem of pinning down reliable release dates for early movies, some sources state the picture started circulating from 30 May 1920, others 20 July. In any event, by then Pohler had been re-styled as Gene Pollar and the movie renamed *The Revenge of Tarzan*, the latter partly because it was feared that people would assume it was merely a re-release of the first Lincoln movie – understandable in light of the different versions of *Tarzan of the Apes* by now floating around. Not that the 'picturisation' by scenario-writer Robert Saxmar was that chronologically faithful to Burroughs' second

Tarzan tale, although most of its elements were ultimately deployed across its seven reels. (The nine-reel version shown at previews was cut down for wider release.) Harry Revier directed a production of which, once again, no print is known to survive. The film's publicity claimed that the three-month shoot involved location work in New York, Florida and California. This may even be true, but the trio of Weiss brothers – who set up a company called Numa to make this picture – were renowned for knocking off low-budget quickies. The contemporaneous testimony suggests that this showed on the screen, despite the usual panoply of wildlife, including lions, elephants and – puzzlingly – an example of the non-African ape the orangutan. For what it's worth, although notices were mixed Pollar was well-received and the film did
sufficiently good box office for Universal to offer him a then-princely weekly wage of $350 to make further Tarzan pictures for them. However, extortionate demands by Numa to release Pollar from his contract saw the deal collapse. Pollar – by all accounts a sweet-natured gentle giant – returned to his fireman's job. His Jane – Karla Schramm – turned up in the next Tarzan cinematic venture but eventually drifted back into her profession of musician and musical tutor. Burroughs later revised his politic contemporaneous praise for Pollar and *The Revenge of Tarzan* ('I have no criticism, and am very proud to be identified with the offering') to, 'As an actor, Gene was a great fireman.'

The franchise returned to the National Film Corporation for the next Tarzan movie project, a move facilitated by the recent death of William Parsons, whom Burroughs hated for reasons over and above disagreements regarding script. As if to underline its insubstantiality, *The Beasts of Tarzan* was skipped over for adaptation in favour of the fourth book in the series.

It was decided that *The Son of Tarzan* should be not a single motion picture but a serial, or chapter play – a form common then, now obsolete. The mathematics give an idea of the extra potential profit involved: audiences would have to attend 15 episodes of two reels each (around five hours of material) to see the whole story. Perhaps it was anticipation of high profits that caused National to agree to pay Burroughs a whopping $20,000 advance, approaching a quarter of a million dollars in today's coinage.

Manilla Martan, a popular singer of the day, was cast as the adult Meriem. P Dempsey Tabler was Tarzan. Gordon Griffith – the boy Tarzan in the first two Tarzan flicks – was cast as the young Jack Clayton. Ex-stuntman Kamuela Searle bagged the prize role of the adult Korak. The latter piece of casting, at least, was good: the toned Hawaiian was a fine figure of a man, something made easy to ascertain by the fact that this was the first example of Tarzan film to feature a loincloth. Moreover, Searle's long hair – unusually – seems real.

The serial took a reported cumulative seven months to shoot. Locations included San Bernardino, Pico Rivera, the San Francisco and Los Angeles coasts – and the Tarzana ranch. Without the existence of said ranch, it's possible that Burroughs would not have continued writing the stories of the character after whom it was named, for the financial burdens it imposed on him made a high workrate necessary, and of course the ape-man was by far the most lucrative of his characters. The photodramatist – another early term for scriptwriter – was Roy Somerville. Burroughs, smarting at some of the liberties taken with his stories by movie-men, made sure that he was guaranteed close involvement, visiting the sets regularly and consulting with Harry Revier, who shared directing duties with Arthur J Flaven. Despite the consequent faithfulness to the source, inter-title cards referred to 'Lord Greystone'. Meanwhile, Burroughs could do nothing about the pitiless gaze of the camera: although possible to sidestep in a book, the potential faults with a project involving Tarzan's progeny are painfully manifest here. Gordon Griffith is quite patently a child, making preposterous his character's overpowering of an adult Arab while rescuing Meriem. Meanwhile, Tabler's wig is idiotic beyond parody, as is his distended belly. The uncredited performer playing Akut looks absurd and almost offensive in his blackface, although that problem with convincingly depicting Mangani is admittedly not unique in this era. Nevertheless, there is some impressive stuff here, especially the scene where Tantor rescues Korak and trots off with him attached to the stake at which he was intended to burn.

The one unequivocal virtue of the enterprise is Searle, and it's difficult not to come to the conclusion that he would have assumed the lead role in the next Tarzan movie had he not been put out of action via an injury incurred during the filming of the Tantor rescue scene, and then been debilitated by the cancer to which he succumbed in 1924. Quite simply, he was the first adult actor to play Tarzan – which Korak here was in all but name – who didn't look ridiculous.

The serial started appearing in cinemas in December 1920 and did good business, recouping its costs within three months. Burroughs, though, was disappointed at its poor showing in the United Kingdom and said privately that he thought the film market had been flooded with Tarzan. Perhaps this is why he personally edited a two-hour movie version of the serial footage titled *Jungle Trail of The Son of Tarzan*, released in 1923. This still exists, but in partial and degraded form. Ten parts of the original serial, however, are extant and have been commercially released on DVD. There was an overdubbed European 'sound' release of the serial in the 1930s, although this now appears to have been lost.

There were some interesting innovations attached to *The Son of Tarzan*. Via tinting effects, the serial was given a form of cinema colour. It was also provided with what we now call multi-media promotion via the commissioning of a special song, 'Tarzan, My Jungle King', written by Norman Stackey and Osborne Tedman and sold as sheet music (although never recorded). Its most important innovation was something that had a profound influence on the serial form: by showing slivers of preceding episodes before each new one, *The Son of Tarzan* accidentally invented the soon *de rigueur* 'Previously ...' serial précis.

4 October 1920 saw the ape-man make his inaugural appearance in a further medium when the *Tarzan of the Apes* stage play opened in Britain.

Many will instantly find ridiculous the notion of a theatrical presentation of a tale largely set in the wild and involving inbuilt obstacles to credibility such as real people having to play animals. (The latter also applied to cinema, but camera trickery could at least ameliorate matters.) However, prior to television, radio and talkies, theatre was still such a huge part of people's lives that little if anything would have then been assumed to be beyond its parameters.

Methuen of London had been the first publisher outside the USA to publish a Tarzan novel and the ape-man was an English lord, so it was natural that the British should wish to mount a play about the character. Brixton was the location for Tarzan's entrée to the boards in a production that featured a prologue and four acts written by Major Herbert Woodgate and Arthur Gibbons. Elements of *The Return of Tarzan* were incorporated into the script. One doesn't know how seriously to take the report about the opening night sent to Burroughs by his UK agents Curtis Brown. As they had brokered the deal for the production, they could be said to have had a vested interest in not being critical. However, for what it's worth, they claimed, 'The jungle scenes were effective and proved distinctly to the taste of the audience. The parts of Tarzan and Kala were both played extremely well, Kala being particularly good.' A bit of gender switching was going on in the casting, with a man – Edward Sillward – playing Kala and a young girl named Gwen Evans depicting the ten-year-old Tarzan.

It was initially stated that the show had ten weeks' worth of provincial bookings following a fortnight's showing in Brixton. Reports are confusing as to how the tour progressed. Although Burroughs was notified at one point that it was to be curtailed in the week of 14 December, there are claims of sporadic stagings through to the following June. Adding to the confusion is American unfamiliarity with English geography. Irwin Porges stated in *Edgar Rice Burroughs: The Man Who Created Tarzan* that one performance of the play was scheduled for the capital on Boxing Day 1920 but that these arrangements fell through and '*Tarzan* was never staged in London,' him apparently unaware that Brixton is in south-west London and not, as he stated, 'in the provinces.' (This mistake was repeated by Taliaferro.) It would seem to be true, though, that the show never played the all-important West End. However, the fact that as late as February 1921 he agreed terms with Burroughs for a follow-up stage production in the form of *The Son of Tarzan* suggests Gibbons was happy enough with the takings, even if that production seems not to have been mounted.

Gibbons and his business partner Arthur Carlton also thought their property valuable enough to go to court to prevent one Dick Mortimer continuing to perform a sketch titled *Warzan and his Apes* consisting of Tarzan scenes done in 'dumb show.' Although the legal action failed – the judge's ruling mainly based on the fact that the sketch had been seen in music halls for six years – and although it might be viewed from today's perspective as unfairly attempting to suppress what was parody rather than 'passing-off', it is notable as possibly the very first civil case brought to prevent something that would be viewed by Burroughs and/or his licensees as an increasing menace in coming years: people jumping on a very lucrative, loin-clothed bandwagon.

Also suggestive of the idea that *Tarzan of the Apes* was a British stage success is the fact that the following year it transferred to Broadway, where it opened on 1 September. As he had in the English production, Ronald Adair – an actor with a boxing background – took the title role. Photographs of the time suggest he was well cast, possessing matinée-idol (if blond-ish) looks and a trim physique. Only his costume – looking more like leopardskin hotpants than an animal pelt loincloth – conforms to the comical patina overlaying so many Tarzan actors of the era.

As Woodgate and Gibbons' original script was adapted for the American market by the Broadway show's producer George Broadhurst, it's reasonable to assume that this version of the play was significantly different to what UK audiences had seen. Certainly, there was a new element in the form of live lions padding the stage. *The New York Times* felt Burroughs' source material posed 'almost insurmountable stumbling-blocks to the playwright' and that the story was told 'episodically and not always convincingly.' However both Adair's athleticism and his depiction of 'the gradations of the savage's education in the English language' came in for praise, as did the enterprise of Broadhurst and Mrs Trimble Bradley, the latter credited with having 'staged' the production: '[They] have lavished upon it a wealth of care, patience and attention to detail. They have created several jungle scenes that are striking in the extreme and have in general done their best to make this bizarre tale a convincing piece of theatre.' *Life* was far less generous, describing it as 'almost too bad to be true.' It ridiculed Tarzan being taught by Kala to wear a loincloth by the age of five so that the show could conform to civilisation's definition of decency, described Howard Kyle – head of an expedition from 'Greystoke Castle' to find the Claytons – as 'America's premier ham' and mocked the convenient coincidence that saw the Greystoke party arrive just as young Tarzan was in the vicinity. Having said that, it does seem as though the *Life* reviewer was almost looking for a target for his sarcasm: 'To those of our little band of condors who earn their living by making comical cracks about other people's plays it came like a visit from St Nicholas.' Reviews, incidentally, confirm that Adair spent some time on stage in trees, or at least approximations thereof.

The New York production closed after 14 performances, a paltry figure that justified Broadhurst's comment in a telegram to Burroughs that it was 'a complete failure.' Curtis Brown reported to Burroughs that Broadhurst was not going to pursue another course of action open to him – taking the show on the road to less merciless audiences than those to be found on the

Great White Way – because he felt the Broadway run had demonstrated it had little appeal to Americans. Burroughs seemed sanguine. He had taken receipt of a $1,000 advance and 10% royalties for the British production, and perhaps an advance for the American version, and all in all felt – according to his private correspondence – 'it will do the books no harm.'

Burroughs added, 'Most of the critics seem to think that the impossible has been attempted and I rather imagine they are right.' He opined that a stage Tarzan should be a 'real, honest-to-God Burlesque.' He would be proved wrong in his belief that it was impossible to mount a successful Tarzan stage presentation that was non-comedic – but not for eight decades.

By 1920, with several million copies of Tarzan books in print in the United States alone and the character the subject of an ongoing series of movies/serials, it would have seemed axiomatic to the public – especially those members of it left on tenterhooks at the end of *Tarzan the Untamed* by the revelation that Jane was almost certainly alive – that a new Tarzan book was high on the list of Edgar Rice Burroughs' priorities. In fact, Burroughs found the idea a deadening imposition and the execution a bore.

His recent correspondence had seen him confessing, '…for the last few years it has been a case of rearranging and camouflaging threadbare situations.' He admitted that he would never write another Tarzan story 'if it wasn't for the lure of filthy lucre' – also indicating that his weariness extended to the Mars tales, of which he had so far turned out four. In Autumn 1920, writing the follow-up to *Tarzan and the Valley of Luna*, Burroughs confessed to his McClurg editor Joe Bray that it was 'awful hard work' and that it was 'very possible that I shall never be able to finish this.' Hardly the most promising preamble to what became *Tarzan the Terrible*. Even the book's title seems a subliminal expression of the author's resentment at being chained to his most famous creation. Amazingly, it turned out to be one of the best and most ingenious Tarzan tales of all.

Published in seven parts in *Argosy All-Story Weekly* in February and March 1921, *Tarzan the Terrible* takes the Tarzan franchise fully into the realm of fantasy. Although this works to negate the merits of *Tarzan of the Apes* – whose events were broadly rooted in reality – it's difficult to argue with the fine result. In this thrilling, unique novel, Burroughs brings to Tarzan the incredible detail and invention that had always marked his Mars and Pellucidar universes, him describing as though witnessed in real life completely fictional customs, conditions and language (of which latter element a glossary is printed at the back 'from conversations with Lord Greystoke and from his notes').

Tarzan follows the trail of Jane, who, in escaping her German abductors, has ended up in a realm isolated by a huge bog. The realm is called Pal-ul-don – 'Land of Men' in the native lingo. The natives are the hairless, white skinned Ho-don and the hairy, black-skinned Waz-don. Despite their physical differences, the two races have in common the fact that they possess tails. The way Burroughs uses the philosophical and bodily differences of the 'dons' to mock racism would almost seem calculated to throw off the scent people who had begun to suspect the author himself of that offence were it not for the fact that he was operating at a time when there was no incentive to care about such things – which, confusingly, must mean he was sincere. The local wildlife is even more remarkable, including the jato, a lion-sabre tooth tiger hybrid (one of which the ape-man inevitably battles to the death), and the gryf, a carnivorous form of triceratops (which Tarzan learns to ride in a way he finds exhilaratingly reminiscent of straddling Tantor). A seized Tarzan so impresses his captors with his fighting prowess that he is given the title 'Tarzan-jad-guru' – Tarzan the Terrible. Jane has her own chapters, which show her being quick-witted and brave in the midst of religion-based skulduggery and intrigue. Tarzan leaves behind a trail of dead bodies as he works his way toward her, but he and his wife both seem doomed until the dramatic arrival of a mysterious rifle-wielding man glimpsed in previous chapters and now revealed to be Korak, who like a good son has been on their trail. The nuclear family depart Pal-ul-don on the back of a gryf.

Even leaving aside our contemporary knowledge of the way Burroughs snatched this artistic triumph from the depths of ennui, *Tarzan the Terrible* is a remarkable achievement. Although elements have antecedents in his Caspak series (itself, of course, indebted to Conan Doyle's *The Lost World*), one is left almost open-mouthed at ERB's creativity. Men with tails who live in cliffs honeycombed with caves reached by nailed pegs? Triceratops brought under control by a smart rap on the snout with a pole? A language thought through to an almost insane degree ('the names of all male hairless pithecanthropi begin with a consonant, have an even number of syllables, and end with a consonant')? Where does this stuff come from?

It all seems to show that sometimes it is not necessity but 'the lure of filthy lucre' that is the mother of invention.

'Picturised from the concluding chapters of "The Return of Tarzan"' read a poster for *Adventures of Tarzan*, the ape-man's cinematic appearance of 1921/22.

The Weiss brothers/Numa Films had decided to exercise their option to make a second film from the book upon which they had based *The Revenge of Tarzan*. When they learned that the Great Western Picture Company were not only keen to produce a new Tarzan project but had, via their associations with Universal to whom he was contracted, access to Elmo Lincoln, Numa agreed merely to distribute a product made by Great Western. Eyeing the success of the *Son of Tarzan* serial, Great Western decided to make the project a chapter play. The result was, according to some reports, the fourth highest-grossing cinema release of 1921 – quite extraordinary if true, for the first episode of *Adventures of Tarzan* apparently didn't play until 1 December that year. (The claim is more plausible if an alternative date – 1 October – given by Robert W Fenton, author of *The Big Swingers*, is the correct one.)

The fact that the first cinema Tarzan was restored to the role seems to have been the major reason for the big box office. At this point in history, Lincoln was still the definitive Tarzan to much of the public. That they appear to have welcomed him back with open arms was amazing for those – including Edgar Rice Burroughs himself – who thought Lincoln looked ridiculous. No less comical than his not-very-trim physique and noticeable double-chin is Lincoln's costume, which is a return to the just-one-nipple-please primness of the over-the-shoulder Pollar pelt. Moreover, the pelt is an elaborate two-part, trailing affair that is somewhat more feminine than Jane's leopard-skin dress. Sixteen year-old Louise Lorraine was a charming Jane. Lillian Worth played La. Robert F Hill and Scott Sidney directed.

The serial again consisted of 15 episodes. All were two-reelers except the first, which had an extra reel. There was also a ten-chapter 1928 version and a ten-chapter 1935 release, the latter with dubbed sound effects. The 1935 version is the only version known to be still in existence. For *Adventures of Tarzan*, the ante was upped with regard to on-set wildlife, particularly lions. As was by now standard, stories abounded of on-set lion-related fights-to-the-finish and escapes from maulings, which from this distance are impossible to separate into truth and publicity hype. The drawbacks of the serial format are sorely in evidence if the project is viewed in one or two sittings: manufactured cliff-hangers and a necessity for a quotient of thrills-per-episode make for a disjointed and frenetic experience.

Promotion-wise, the Weiss brothers recommended to theatre owners men dressed in ape costumes and jungle flora in the lobbies, while Lincoln went on a lion-wrestling supporting tour. Another interesting facet of the promotion is the fact that the script by Robert F Hill & Lillian Valentine was adapted for a newspaper serial. It has been said that segments of this print version, written by Maude Robinson Toombs, were published to coincide with each episode of the serial hitting the screen, but this doesn't seem consistent with the fact that it appeared in some places as early as March 1921. In 2006, with the Toombs serialisation long out of copyright, its chapters were collated in book form by ERBville Press (something said publisher also did with the Arthur B Reeve-written serialisation of the 1928 chapter play *Tarzan the Mighty*).

For various reasons, there would now be a six-year gap before Tarzan returned to the screen. This would seem to have played a part in the eclipse of the featured-actor career of Elmo Lincoln, who was too old to plausibly don the pelt again once the franchise resumed, and whose physique-oriented talent was dealt a further blow by the arrival of talkies.

Edgar Rice Burroughs had an answer ready whenever a journalist or correspondent (he replied to his fan letters) asked him about his literary abilities. It was a formula of words amounting to 'I'm a storyteller, me, and the public seem to love my stories.'

Behind that ostensible easy-going attitude toward the many reviewers and reporters who poured scorn on his purple prose, un-colloquial dialogue, pat *deus ex machina* and convenient plot coincidences was a simmering resentment at his art not being taken seriously. *Tarzan and the Golden Lion* – serialised in seven parts in *Argosy All-Story Weekly* from December 1922 to January 1923 – does rather suggest it is his critics who were right. However entertaining it (and much of the rest of his oeuvre) is, it demonstrates that Burroughs would always be a pulp writer.

The story literally begins where *Tarzan the Terrible* left off, with Tarzan, Jane and Korak making their way back from Pal-ul-don. The fact that they are strolling through the jungle as though Africa – Burroughs doesn't bother with country delineations – is a little principality in which home is a gentle amble away from any specific point is the first sign herein of Burroughs' irredeemable, if quite endearing, trashy sensibility. Also both ludicrous and charming is the little scene where the ape-man suggests to Jane – after winking at Jack – that he may have had simian parents. 'John Clayton, I shall never speak to you again if you don't stop saying such hideous things,' protests Lady

Greystoke. This exchange occurs after the trio discover an orphaned lion cub and Tarzan, by virtue of a rapport with wildlife that even the jungle-trained Korak admits he lacks, wins its trust prior to adopting it. The lion is christened Jad-bal-ja, Pal-ul-don for 'the Golden Lion', and will become Tarzan's equivalent of a Rottweiler: loyal to its master but enough to drive terror into the hearts of its master's enemies.

When Tarzan returns to his estate, he finds the Waziri – always depicted as showing him pretty much the same unconditional affection as Jad-bal-ja – rebuilding it. Because the war and the rebuilding have reduced his resources drastically, Tarzan decides to embark on another of his guiltless looting trips to Opar, whose denizens have neither appreciation of, nor use for, the treasures that surround them. Unbeknownst to him, also headed for Opar is a party that includes Flora Hawkes, a one-time Greystoke maid infected by money lust, and her partner-in-crime Esteban Miranda, a Spanish actor whom she has retained because his remarkable resemblance to the male half of her former employers will make easier her plans to plunder the lost city. That Miranda is the spitting image of Tarzan is unlikely enough: Burroughs has told us enough times of an amplified level of physical beauty about the ape-man (from *Tarzan of the Apes*: 'His face was very handsome – the handsomest, thought D'Arnot, that he had ever seen') that would make it nigh-impossible for him to have a *doppelganger*. Burroughs piles on the absurdity yet further by making Miranda such a convincing look-alike that he fools Tarzan's wife, the Waziri and even the animals of the jungle – with which, remember, even Korak doesn't have Tarzan's affinity. Then there is the unaddressed issue of the Spanish accent in which Miranda presumably speaks. Burroughs never disclosed to us the Mangani word for 'bollocks', but this is surely its definition. The literary writers with whom Burroughs secretly desired to be bracketed would never use such a comic-book device as a *doppelganger* even once but, astoundingly, this was far from the last time Burroughs would.

That La still carries a torch for Tarzan is demonstrated by her rescuing him (not for the first time) from the sacrificial altar when things go wrong at Opar. Meanwhile, it turns out that Opar has an adjacent site, the city of the Bolgani in the valley of the Palace of Diamonds. These Bolgani are not the common-or-garden gorillas we have previously understood this Mangani word to describe, but a mutant offshoot with the bodies of apes and the sensibilities of the more pretentious types of human. The narrative sees Tarzan take up arms on the side of the less developed Gomangani (another word retooling), whom the Bolgani oppress, and also restore La to her place as ruler of Opar, assisted by Jad-bal-ja and his formidable jaws. Esteban – whose portrayal by Burroughs as an actor ultimately not up to the job of depicting the ape-man may be his way of having fun at the expense of Elmo Lincoln – ends up a prisoner of cannibals.

Tarzan and the Golden Lion was the first Tarzan tale Burroughs did not physically write. A dictating machine became, after a few teething problems and a switch from his initial Ediphone to a Dictaphone, his 'writing' tool of choice.

Tarzan and the Ant Men appeared in seven parts in *Argosy All-Story Weekly* in February and March 1924. Burroughs wrote it in fits and starts. Once again he confessed that he hated the process, and once again he snatched inspiration from the jaws of lethargy.

Tarzan and the Ant Men gets off to an unpromising start with the reappearance of Esteban Miranda, who recurs – along naturally with the ludicrous *doppelganger* premise – throughout, albeit almost never on the same page as Tarzan. He wheedles his way out of captivity and stumbles through a series of adventures before winding up at the Greystoke estate, where Jane welcomes him as her husband and has to be disabused by someone less intimate with the real Lord Greystoke, Flora Hawkes.

Tarzan's own adventure begins when he disappears after going out in an aeroplane. In a scene on the veranda of his African bungalow involving him, Korak, Meriem and the latter pair's young son Jackie, we learn that Korak has taught dad to fly and that the trip on which Tarzan is about to embark is the ape-man's first solo voyage. Tarzan dips too low when inspecting the legendary Great Thorn Forest and his plane crashes into a mysterious land that has always been kept isolated by that impenetrable thicket. We are soon knee-deep in Minuni, another of the lost worlds that, according to Burroughs, pepper the African continent. There, Tarzan discovers the Alali, a primitive race whose women brutally dominate their men. Burroughs' own marriage problems seem to be manifested in this subplot. Although it – like indeed the ant-men premise – was the idea of his *All-Story* editor Bob Davis, Burroughs does seem to hammer out with inordinate enthusiasm a scene wherein a woman who has been struck with both spear and foot by a newly assertive Alali male hugs his legs as though in gratitude for putting her in her rightful place. Tarzan then encounters the ant men. The title is misleading, as the Minunians are up to 18 inches in height. Nonetheless, they and their society are as ingeniously thought through as Pal-ul-don and its residents, once again right down to the language, whose word constructions are completely different from those of Pal-ul-don's and involve some real tongue-twisters (two warring ant men tribes are called Veltopismakusians and Trohanakalmakians). If anything, Burroughs goes into too much detail, with page after page devoted to ant-man housing, history and dress. Certainly, it's difficult to imagine readers in their twenties and under – or those of any age merely seeking jungle-based thrills – finding much of interest in such dense pseudo-sociology. One would imagine that tiches like the Minunians would not be particularly aggressive, but their giant ant-hills are in a constant state of war with each other literally as a point of virtue. They ride nobly into battle on the backs of small antelopes.

Tarzan is temporarily shrunk to Minunian size in an experiment whose science is not defined sufficiently even to warrant the description questionable. Tarzan has advantages in his new size: he retains his normal strength and has a John Carter-like ability to leap over heads. Those who consider this tale a Lilliputian yarn are given some ammunition by another plot strand in which Burroughs depicts the Minunians as oppressed by taxation – although the knowledge that Burroughs was having money problems through over-reaching himself via the Tarzana ranch makes the passage seems less Swiftian satire than a profligate man's whinge.

For many fans, this event- and idea-packed work was the final aesthetically credible Tarzan. From hereon, with few exceptions, Burroughs' weariness with the character, his wife and even writing were often painfully apparent. If one subscribes to this supposition, it was at least a good way to go out. Learned Burroughs scholar Richard A Lupoff remarks in his book *Edgar Rice Burroughs: Master of Adventure*, 'If anything keeps *Tarzan and the Ant Men* from being the perfect Tarzan novel, it is perhaps the embarrassment of riches of the book…'

PART THREE: CONQUERING THE FUNNIES

There was little Tarzan activity over the following three years. That was not a symptom, however, of the world being tired of the ape-man. In 1927, he came back with a bang, with the first Tarzan cinema release for six years and two new Tarzan tales from Burroughs, one of which took the character into the uncharted territory of juvenile literature.

The hiatus in Tarzan pictures was partly due to the National Film Corporation, producers of *The Son of Tarzan*, going under following tax problems. Burroughs decided to take up the slack – as was his self-promotional wont – by agitating for a new picture himself. R-C Pictures – whose parent company was a precursor of RKO – took the bait and decided to film *Tarzan and the Golden Lion*, presumably adjudging the war content of *Untamed* dated and the otherworldly elements of *Terrible* and *Ant Men* unfilmable.

Burroughs was even responsible for the casting of the title role. At a party at Tarzana, his daughter Joan introduced him to her friend (and future husband) Jim Pierce, a football (American variety) coach and ex-player. Pierce was six foot four and very well-built, as the fact that he was in a swimming costume afforded Burroughs the opportunity to appreciate. Shooting took three months, although it's not clear if that includes a month in which Pierce was said to be recuperating after an on-set accident. Direction was by J P McGowan. Jane was played by Dorothy Dunbar. A then little-known Boris Karloff took several villainous roles.

In William E Wing's adaptation, Opar is excised – replaced by a diamond city – along with Flora Hawkes. That Esteban Miranda is played by Frederick Peters and not by Pierce demonstrates that the ape-man impersonation plot strand has been amended. Even Jad-bal-ja's Pal-ul-don name is changed to the all-American sounding 'Jab'. Tarzan is also given a sister, Betty. On the plus side, Pierce is the most impressive Tarzan yet, even if his distinctly '20s short blonde haircut with an emphatic parting is more reminiscent of F Scott Fitzgerald than a jungle man. (His over-the-shoulder leopard-skin pelt is an improvement on Lincoln's immediately previous feminine outfit, although still looks demure compared with a breechcloth.) The interior sets for the diamond city are lavish and exotic, as are its denizens' costumes. Jab is a magnetic presence: a pet lion sitting as calmly as a hearthside dog in the Greystokes' drawing room.

The six-reel *Tarzan and the Golden Lion* – variously stated as having been released in January, February and May 1927 – was a box office success but widely panned by the critics. In his '70s-published autobiography *The Battle of Hollywood*, Pierce said, '*Tarzan and the Golden Lion* hit a terrible market because "talkies" were coming in ... The studio considered dubbing in the sound-voice [sic] over the film and adding sound effects, but gave it up as too expensive ... The major chain houses had to turn it down as they were equipped for sound. However, many small towns and independent theatres had not yet wired up for sound, due to the great expense, and continued to screen silent films for two or three years after talkies. The picture proved to be a big hit on the B circuit.' Pierce also gave *Tarzan of the Movies* author Gabe Essoe some comments (which appear from their construction to have been written answers) in which he blamed the film for the end of his career as a featured player: 'Because of poor direction, terrible story treatment and putrid acting, the opus was a stinkeroo. I emerged with nothing to show for my strenuous effort except being typecast as Tarzan. I was out of a job.' That he was never again cast as the ape-man (at least on film) must have been particularly sickening for Pierce, as to play him he had passed up the starring role in the epic aviation movie *Wings*. Burroughs certainly seemed to think it was an injustice, and this can be put down neither to his usual public expression of support for a current cinema Tarzan nor loyalty to his son-in-law: in private correspondence long before Joan married Pierce, he wrote, 'We have found a man who really is Tarzan, and whom I believe will be raised to the heights of stardom.'

The fact that for several decades *Tarzan and the Golden Lion* was considered a lost film – although Pierce was informally told in 1976 that a print existed, one was confirmed as extant only in the '90s – gives reason to hold out hope that earlier Tarzan pictures gone astray may one day turn up.

Although Edgar Rice Burroughs was fairly used to book publishers declining to print stories he had successfully placed with pulps, up until October 1927 he never experienced the reverse. When the children's book *The Tarzan Twins* was published by P F Volland Co that month, it marked the unfortunate milestone of being the first Tarzan story that no magazine had deemed fit to publish, as well as being the first Burroughs book *per se* not to have appeared in a magazine beforehand. Admittedly, with a far smaller market existing for juvenile prose, Burroughs had few other places to go when *Youth's Companion* rejected the story.

The book was not the author's idea but that of J C Flowers, an employee of the company that owned Volland. Burroughs seems to have been enthused by the idea because it constituted new territory: although he had written whimsical stuff for his family that could be posited as juvenile fare, this would be his first book for children of any professional description. He certainly admitted to Volland president Theodore Gerlach that it was 'in the nature of an experiment.' However, Burroughs displayed no other humility in his venture into unfamiliar territory. He proceeded to ignore just about all the suggestions and requests of his publisher, aiming his story at 14-year-olds instead of the eight-to-12 age range originally proposed, declining to make one of his child protagonists a girl on the grounds that it would be indecent to have a female child running around a jungle half-clothed, and tetchily declining to increase the word count or make good the deficiencies Volland felt existed in his submitted manuscript.

Fourteen-year-old Dick and Doc, the twins of the title, are not really twins but cousins born on the same day who, different hair colour aside, look very much alike. The Tarzan part of their joint nickname came about when the kids at their 'excellent English school ... learned that Dick's father was distantly related to Lord Greystoke, who is famous all over the world as Tarzan of the Apes ...' It being the case that Lord Greystoke is famous all over the world as Tarzan of the Apes only via the sole place he exists – the media – means that Burroughs is breaking the fourth wall. Such post-modernism would increasingly be threaded through his Tarzan prose.

The plot of this slim read involves Dick and Doc being invited to stay at Tarzan's African estate, wandering off into the jungle after their train crashes, taking refuge in trees from hostile wildlife, being captured by cannibals who plan to cook them even despite Doc's awe-inspiring magic tricks, and escaping just before they end up in a pot. Tarzan and the Waziri arrive to rescue Dick and Doc when they are on the brink of recapture. The book's informal, paternalistic tone is quite sweet and actually appropriate for that eight-to-12 age range originally envisaged. It's not clear that Volland did target the book at an age as high as 14 – its heavily illustrated format and grinning cover illustration of the ape-man and the two protagonists suggest not – but the fact that it sold so poorly that it didn't even allow the publishers to recoup the author's small advance of $500 was probably more down to its surprising lack of local colour. The vivid jungle description at which Burroughs was usually so adept – and which would have been particularly appreciated by children, the world's most ardent zoo lovers – is mysteriously absent.

Perhaps the most interesting thing about this book is the cultural changes it reveals to have been engendered by time and tide. Burroughs' ambiguity on race issues is once again in evidence: 'Many other things they came to understand during the days of their captivity, not the least of which was a new conception of the Negro. To Doc, whose experience with colored people had been limited to a few worthless specimens of the Northern States, it came as a revelation. Even among the warriors of the cannibal Bagalla, he encountered individuals who possessed great natural dignity, poise and evident strength of character.' Another indicator of how mores have since changed is that many will be surprised to learn that there is any such thing as a designated Tarzan children's book. Tarzan novels are from today's perspective wholesome. At the point *The Tarzan Twins* appeared, their ornate prose and blood-splattered and occasionally sexually suggestive nature (especially the discussion of bestiality in the books featuring Opar) unquestionably made them adult fare.

December 1927 saw the ape-man's third media appearance of the year when *Blue Book* began their six-part serialisation of the new Tarzan story for adults, *Tarzan, Lord of the Jungle*.

Some might posit an unintended metaphor residing in the fact that the book starts with the ape-man lounging lethargically on the back of an elephant before being dragged against his will into other people's problems. (The lounging-on-Tantor opening and the unwilling adventuring would crop up again in the series.) However, although a reluctant Burroughs was, after a gap of three years, being forced through financial necessity to devise a Tarzan story, and although we are once more presented with a lost city peopled with intriguing and fantastical inhabitants as though his tested methods are now a veritable grid, the reader yet again can't help but admire both the author's inventiveness and his well-honed facility for storytelling. Even Burroughs' preposterous dialogue can sing. Additionally, the po face that Burroughs often wore for his Tarzan writing refreshingly gives way to a bit of twinkle-eyed merriment.

The comedy element comes from the scenes involving James Hunter Blake. This safari member wanders into a lost valley in which are located two castles containing rival factions of the Knights Templar who – like stranded Japanese soldiers still fighting World War II – are under the impression that the Crusades are still going on. Cue an amusing juxtaposition of Blake's wiseguy argot and low-born manners with the verily-

verily syntax and behavioural courtliness of the knights. However, as Blake is assimilated into the antediluvian society, wins friends – including an Arthurian princess – and engages in duels, one can't help but think that it is Tarzan who should be having these adventures. Intensifying the feeling that he is merely a supporting character in the book whose title bears his name – something that will afflict Tarzan stories more and more – are the chapters involving Arabs plotting to kill him. Impatience begins to mount at these characters for keeping Tarzan off the stage. There is also an emotional hole at the heart of the story, one that would be apparent in all Tarzan tales to a greater or lesser degree from hereon. Jane was at least fleetingly referred to in the previous book, but here she is not even mentioned. This, it has been surmised, is a symptom of Burroughs' desire for his wife to be similarly absent from his own life. Korak, Meriem and others who might provide a tender or human side to the ape-man are, and would henceforth be, absent, and the occasional presence of Jad-bal-ja – who appears at the end of this story – and Nkima – a mean little bugger of a monkey friend who would be first seen in *Tarzan and the Lost Empire* (1928) – hardly make up for this deficiency. In what seems a related matter, Tarzan himself is less likeable, compassion for his fellow man being replaced by irritation.

Incidentally, Burroughs' 'real' medieval book *The Outlaw of Torn* (magazine 1914, book 1927) featured a walk-on role for a character called Lord Greystoke, who is postulated by some at the more intense end of the fan spectrum as an ancestor of Tarzan.

When the first episode of the film serial *Tarzan the Mighty* appeared in the summer of 1928, a new actor inhabited the title role, but one whose potential the creator of Tarzan had long ago recognised.

Although Frank Merrill had appeared in previous Tarzan cinema ventures, his roles in *The Son of Tarzan* and *Adventures of Tarzan* were as stuntman and extra. It may have been *Adventures of Tarzan* from which director Jack Nelson remembered him when he had to re-cast *Tarzan the Mighty* after first choice Joe Bonomo had to pull out of the lead role after breaking a leg on the third day of filming. Burroughs himself had reputedly already noted Merrill's suitability about seven years before, remarking during a Hollywood set visit, 'That is the man to play Tarzan.' A weightlifter and national gymnastics champion, the six-foot, hard-bodied Merrill was in some respects the most convincing ape-man yet, with no hint of the flab, gormlessness, inappropriate hairstyle or effeteness that had detracted – singly or in combination – from the look of all previous cinematic Tarzans. (For the purposes of this Korak-less argument, Kamuela Searle can be said not to count.) He was let down only by his wardrobe, a knee-length over-the-shoulder leopard pelt. Adding to the impression of him being swathed in a ladies' dress were his leopard-skin headband and boots, the archetypal matching-accessory-and-shoes.

Tarzan the Mighty saw the franchise return to Universal. Jack Nelson and Ray Taylor directed – and reputedly contributed to – Ian McClosky Heath's script. Advance publicity stated that the serial was based on *Jungle Tales of Tarzan*. While some of the incidents and issues from that collection do crop up, the chapter summaries (no print of the serial is known to exist) suggest that, if *Tarzan the Mighty* was an adaptation of anything, it was *Tarzan of the Apes*. The details of the first book are recounted – and taken liberty with. It is Tarzan's uncle who comes looking for the lost Greystoke. Jane is excised from the scene, with the love interest for the ape-man now being castaway Mary Trevor (Natalie Kingston). Al Ferguson plays Black John, a pirate with a plan to pass himself off as the heir to the Greystoke fortune. Although the author himself had airbrushed Jane out of the picture in his last published Tarzan book, after a visit to the set he was furious at Universal's tampering with his creation and even contemplated legal action to stop the serial's release. The public, though, couldn't get enough. Like many serials, its first episode was distributed before filming of the series had wrapped, and box office was so good that its planned 12 episodes were extended to 15. It was an example of the process to which Burroughs would become wearily used: Joe and Jo Public loved Tarzan movies no matter how much they watered down or misrepresented his stories.

Although Tarzan had been shown swinging on tree vines in movies before, it was Merrill who properly installed it as a signature of the franchise. As someone who had done his fair share of high bar work and rope climbing, he had his own ideas about how Tarzan could be depicted making his way from arboreal a to b. A hidden loop he devised enabled him to swing with one-arm, with Kingston tucked under the other. Future cinematic ape-man Johnny Weissmuller was shown film of Merrill's swinging as an example of what we now call 'best practice'.

This serial inaugurated what would become a tradition in Tarzan films and TV shows. Mary Trevor's little brother Bobby (played by Bobby Nelson) provides Tarzan a junior but unrelated version of himself to protect and mentor, as would later Boy, Tartu, Jukaro, Jai and others. The reasons were presumably the studio's desire to appeal to a female demographic unmoved by derring-do and to provide a kiddie audience someone with whom to identify.

Although by 1928 writing Tarzan stories had long ago become a chore for Burroughs, the exercise must have struck him as even more unfulfilling than usual that year, for he had recently been alternating the jobs-of-work with projects that were of sentimental value and even, relatively speaking, high art.

In the latter category were his two Apache novels, *The War Chief* (written in the second half of 1926) and *Apache Devil* (written in the second half of 1927), almost certainly the most heavyweight stories for which he was ever responsible. In the former category was *You Lucky Girl!*, Burroughs' one and only full-length play. Written to try to advance his daughter's acting career, it's not the greatest drama in the world, but Burroughs must have enjoyed the fact that its creation brought a new dimension to his storytelling. Moreover, for the duration of its three acts, the author impressively goes against the grain of the chauvinism-cum-misogyny he betrayed elsewhere in his work as he places himself on the side of two showbusiness-inclined women whose traditionalist fiancés object to their careerist leanings. (The play was unproduced until 1997 and unpublished until 1999.) Come January '28, Burroughs was hunched miserably (it seems safe to assume) over his desk knocking out a sequel to *The Tarzan Twins* that wasn't even wanted (and would not find a publisher for eight years). His next formulaic adult Tarzan novel followed in March. The title under which it sagged said it all. *Tarzan and the Lost Empire* must surely have inspired many a sarcastic response of, 'Wot? Another one?'

There is indeed a strong feeling of familiarity about the events and situations: two cities at war, a time-bubble, a charismatic Western interloper who has to be rescued by Tarzan, a romance between two supporting characters, and a new set of exotic word constructions, in this case Latin. There are additional absurdities to overcome for the reader who doesn't easily suspend disbelief, over and above the fact that even an unexplored Africa in the late 1920s could not possibly be suspected of containing the number of isolated cities Burroughs posited. For instance, Tarzan becomes conversant in a new language (as characters frequently do in Burroughs fiction) in mere weeks. Moreover, despite being progressively kinder to black people, Burroughs' growing belief in eugenics rears its ugly head in a passage where a character advocates a bud-nipping approach to crime involving executing people simply for being related to wrongdoers.

Yet when that florid-but-fluid storytelling gets going and one becomes absorbed in the intrigues of rival outposts of a Roman Empire left behind by history, misgivings melt away. What schoolboy (or overgrown schoolboy) doesn't adore tales of centurions and gladiatorial arenas (where Tarzan startles the crowd by emitting the victory cry of the bull ape after taking out a lion)? Burroughs' impish humour can be easily missed amongst his general solemnity and occasional nastiness: how can one not love names like Dion Splendidus and Fulvus Fupus, or the fact that they are instantly recognisable as the handles of respectively a goodie and a baddie?

Tarzan and the Lost Empire was serialised in five instalments in *The Blue Book Magazine* from October 1928 to February 1929. When it made the usual graduation to book form, the publisher ident on the spine was not that of McClurg. The only time this had previously happened with an adult Burroughs novel was when Macaulay had published his Tinsel-Town exposé *The Girl from Hollywood* in 1923 after its magazine appearance the previous year. The setting up of Metropolitan Books was Burroughs' response to his growing financial problems. In 1923, he became one of the first writers to follow in the footsteps of Mark Twain by incorporating himself, but the implied financial canniness of this act needs to be set against the fact that although Edgar Rice Burroughs, Inc grossed $60,000 in 1928 – equivalent to over three quarters of a million dollars in today's money – most of this sum was swallowed up by taxes and such things as the expense of a large household staff at Tarzana. He had embarked on a convoluted method to retain a property he couldn't really afford that involved selling 125 acres to a country club – named El Caballero – of which he became a director. In 1928, Burroughs had to foreclose on the club, but that increased his problems, because Tarzana's other 350 acres were tied up in a bond the club had issued. It was a head-spinning mess and Burroughs had responded to it via increasingly desperate financial demands on those who published his work. Burroughs and McClurg had been good for each other, but the financially distressed have little time for sentiment. Burroughs was pleased by the fruits of a recently formed relationship with Metropolitan Newspaper Services, who had succeeded in selling a Tarzan newspaper strip. He was the only author Metropolitan Books would ever have on its lists.

By 1929, Tarzan had placed a foot upon the necks of the media of pulp magazine, book and film and let forth the victory cry of the bull ape over their conquered forms. His encounter with the stage had left him in the unfamiliar position of having to retreat to lick his wounds, but he was still in vigorous cultural health and ready to take on new challenges.

He had racked up more than one first in his 17 years, and when in June 1927 advertising man Joe H Neebe suggested to Tarzan's creator a daily newspaper strip, it seemed that the ape-man was now destined to constitute both the first example of a work from literature to be licensed for such exploitation and the first drama-based American strip. In the end, he had to share both honours, at least in the US, with *Buck Rogers in the 25th Century*, which strip – by a remarkable coincidence – debuted on the same date, 7 January 1929.

The well-known statistic (at least among newspaper strip and Tarzan buffs) that the Tarzan strip has been in continuous publication for over 80 years gives an inaccurate impression that it was a sensation from day one. Burroughs agreed with Neebe – an acquaintance of his brother Harry – a 50-50 split on any sales Neebe might manage to secure. The Hearst newspaper empire turned down the Tarzan strip because film rights weren't available as an adjunct, and an out-of-pocket Neebe had to bring in people with more experience in the field in the form of the Metropolitan Syndicate. Metropolitan artist Rex Maxon told Gabe Essoe that, once his company's president and general manager Max Elser had set a 7 January publication start date for *Tarzan*, 'He ... had to come through, but it wasn't easy to sell.' With no precedent for an adventure-based newspaper strip – all previous examples had been jokey ones colloquially referred to as 'funnies' – the market reticence was perhaps understandable. Britain was the only territory initially interested. Billed as 'A Serial Story in Pictures', the *Tarzan of the Apes* strip made its debut on 20 October 1928 in magazine *Tit Bits*. Three strips appeared in each weekly issue.

Maxon said, 'Finally Max made a deal with the North American Newspaper Alliance. If their papers would use the strip for ten weeks and then ask their readers if they wanted the strip continued, then Max would give them the entire ten weeks for what amounted to practically nothing.'

By that 7 January deadline, Metropolitan had sold the idea to 13 American and two Canadian newspapers. Despite those successes and the UK licence, there were no dividends that January of '29 to pay shareholders in Famous Books and Players, the incorporated company Neebe had set up to sell the strip. Possibly one of the reasons for the initial low take-up was that the strip started out with an adaptation of *Tarzan of the Apes* that was almost dogmatic in its faithfulness to the source. With the intrigues on board the HMS *Fuwalda* dominating the early days, and nothing resembling the Tarzan with which people were familiar appearing until into the third week, this would have been hard-going for fans of the thrill-packed films and serials.

Although the Tarzan newspaper strip didn't immediately reap Burroughs the dividends of the movies, it at least performed the role of pushing Tarzan's name and presence into a new quadrant of the mass media. Furthermore, Burroughs' close involvement meant that the results did not make him wince or consider reaching for his lawyers as the cinema Tarzan on more than one occasion had. Artist Hal Foster, a Palenske-Young Advertising Agency employee who had come to Neebe's attention, rendered Tarzan as the author had envisaged him, apart from the fact that his ape-man wore that ridiculous semi-singlet again. Although Foster's art was scratchier at this point than it would later become, it was stylish and evocative. Foster spurned speech balloons – some sources say at Neebe's request – for explanatory text and dialogue beneath the five panels of each instalment, something that added to a feeling of class. This format lasted for a decade, when in-panel captions were introduced. Speech balloons finally become a fixture of the strip in 1958.

The *Tarzan of the Apes* adaptation was concluded in 60 daily episodes (Monday to Saturday) and in August 1929 was anthologised in *The Illustrated Tarzan Book No. 1*. (There was never a No. 2.) Following that wrap-up, there was a three-month gap before the adaptation of *The Return of Tarzan* was ready. Foster withdrew from the strip to concentrate on his advertising work, replaced on 10 June 1929 by Rex Maxon. The 'continuity' – effectively abridgement – of *The Return of Tarzan* was handled, like the first adaptation's had been, by R W Palmer.

Maxon would draw the dailies almost continuously for the next 18 years, initially working his way through adaptations of the original Burroughs novels, although not always chronologically. The *Tarzan the Ape Man* strip that started in March 1933 was an adaptation of the previous year's Johnny Weissmuller movie of the same title, while *Tarzan and the Fire Gods*, beginning February 1935, was the first daily strip unrelated to either a Burroughs book or a Tarzan film. By 1938, the strip was adapting Burroughs manuscripts yet to appear in the pulps.

Like Foster, Maxon took a while to develop the style for which he is most famous, and his early work was not to everybody's taste: Tarzan's face often seemed like that of a waxwork in its expressionlessness, and Burroughs in particular took exception to Maxon's slapdash approach to figure drawing and research. Nonetheless, such was the power of the Tarzan name that a mass hypnosis seemed to occur, with people assuming that *ipso facto* the strip was good because it featured Tarzan. It proceeded to pick up increasing numbers of licensees around the country – 44 US newspapers were running it by April and over 70 by the second half of '29 – and around the world. The strips gained a second lease of life when reprinted in the long-running series of Tarzan Big Little Books.

On 15 March 1931, the strip made an important expansion with the advent of a Sunday edition. Sunday newspaper 'funnies' were more prestigious than the daily strips. Not only did they have their own sections, but each strip took up an entire page and furthermore was in full colour. In *Tarzan*'s case, the Sunday page consisted of 12 panels, plus a logo accompanying an additional illustration. (Unlike in the daily strip, captions appeared within frames.) Curiously, the first instalments of the

Tarzan Sunday strip featured the ape-man rescuing and proceeding to look after Bob and Mary Trevor, characters seen in the *Tarzan the Mighty* serial, although Mary here was not Tarzan's love interest but a child like Bob. Tarzan explained that he was taking them under his wing because he had 'lost a son whom I seek in the jungle.' This mash-up of literary and cinema Tarzan was not a good start after the daily strip's faithfulness to the books. Burroughs didn't get around to voicing his concern about this for a while because he was distracted by illness. He eventually complained, '...the only Tarzan story that I ever wrote which is a flop is a juvenile called *The Tarzan Twins*, written around two boys ... The thing that bothered me was the possible effect that the juvenile element in the colour pages might have on my book sales ... I am constantly endeavoring to impress on the public that the stories are primarily stories for adults and I am afraid that these Sunday colour pages are going to pull some of the pegs out from under my contention.'

Burroughs, though, was far more concerned by Maxon's art, and repeatedly stated his unhappiness with it. Some think that this is the reason why by 27 September 1931 Maxon was confined to the daily strip. Maxon himself implied a mutual-consent scenario, stating that doing the Sunday strip as well 'was too much work.' Whatever the truth, when Hal Foster returned to Tarzan to take up the reins on the Sunday strip mid-story, it inaugurated what many consider to be the first golden age of Tarzan comic strips. Foster's craft seemed to grow with his bigger canvas and with colour (even if the latter was added after he submitted his work). His lines became cleaner as his Tarzan became more credible and animalistic. He mercifully dispensed with that wretched circus strongman's leotard, even if its replacement more closely resembled leopardskin briefs than a loincloth. Foster's continuity was supplied by R W Palmer (March 1931 to November 1931), George Carlin (November 1931 to June 1934) and Don Garden (from July 1934).

Foster stopped working on Tarzan in 1937, but only because he was given the opportunity by the Hearst papers to write, draw and own the copyright on his *Prince Valiant* strip. An indication of just how beloved was Foster's ape-man is a recollection from Joe Kubert, a young fan at the time who grew up to become a Tarzan illustrator himself: 'I was reading this stuff when I was about eight or nine years old, and on a Sunday I'd wrap myself around that paper and I'd be in another world. The kind of work that Foster did in terms of telling a story really grabbed me out of wherever I was living in Brooklyn and took me to another place. The way he drew Tarzan made him live.'

When Foster's eight-year stint on the Sunday Tarzan strip came to an end, a replacement was found who was in some eyes even better. Although 26-year-old Burne Hogarth was two decades Foster's junior, his method was arguably more sophisticated, going in the opposite direction to Foster's quasi-impressionism to embrace a style almost overwhelming in its fine detail. Hogarth's first strip was published in May 1937. One of his amusing signatures was the way he would render Tarzan's very long (for the era) hair standing up almost in a cone as he descended from a height on an antagonist. Hogarth sometimes also wrote the scripts. He left the job in 1945 in a dispute over his lack of remuneration for book anthologies, but returned in August 1947 after being given a pay rise, even if conditional on supervision of the daily strip. Unable to balance his workload at his School of Visual Arts with the daily's obligations, he quit *Tarzan* again in August 1950. He would work on the ape-man's adventures in the future, but in the less restrictive parameters of comic books.

When Russ Manning took over the daily strip in December 1967 and the Sunday in January '68, it was an attempt by United Features Syndicate – who had been administering since March 1930 after buying out Metropolitan – to get a wayward strip back on track. (Tarzan had been given an orphaned child and the strip had featured an island called Tarzanland.) UFS had clearly been impressed by Manning's illustrations of Gaylord DuBois' faithful adaptations of Tarzan novels for Western comics and his work on Dubois' original stories in the same publisher's *Korak* title. Manning's dozen-year-stint – in which he employed a style even more burnished than Hogarth's – was marked by utter respect for the character's history. That he wrote as well as drew makes his seven-day workload even more impressive.

Manning was probably the last of the artists who made his name via the Tarzan strip, as opposed to being an artist drafted in because of pre-existing fame such as successors Gil Kane and Mike Grell. Gray Morrow became what looks like being the final *Tarzan* newspaper strip artist in 1983, when he took over both daily and Sunday jobs.

At its peak in the late '30s, the *Tarzan* strip was running in about 300 newspapers. For whatever reason, its appeal seemed to diminish significantly after World War II, with domestic sales dropping by a third between 1949 and 1959. Meanwhile, foreign sales peaked post-war at 55 countries. The handful of newspapers that take the Tarzan strip today are running reprinted material. However, this is enough to keep the strip's unbroken run staggering on and the hope burning in Tarzan fans that it will one day outpace the longest-running newspaper strip in the world, *The Katzenjammer Kids*.

Their other hope for the strip – a return to new work – looked as though it might have a chance through the aegis of Roy Thomas and Thomas Grindberg. In the early part of the new millennium, the latter well-known comic book artist approached United Features Syndicate with the idea of revivifying the Tarzan strip. Explains Grindberg, 'They actually thought it looked top-notch but they were more interested in one-line-gag strips and not action adventure. The continuity strips such as Tarzan are not big sellers like they used to be.' Not wanting the work he and Thomas had invested in samples go to waste, he agreed a deal whereby the two would produce a strip to be featured on ERB, Inc's website.

The Tarzan comic strip, incidentally, bequeathed an important part of the Tarzan universe. The distinctive Tarzan logo that is now a registered trademark of Edgar Rice Burroughs, Inc – upper case 'T', all other letters lower-case, all letters double-outlined, the tail of the two instances of 'a' melding into the next letter – first appeared (in a more primitive version) atop the opening instalment of the Sunday Tarzan strip.

When Burroughs set to the task of writing the next Tarzan novel, he may have decided to send the ape-man to Pellucidar because he thought that to have him stumbling upon yet another lost city or civilisation in Africa would be taking the mickey a little. Or perhaps it was mammon rather than plausibility behind his reasoning and he realised that if he dovetailed his jungle stories with his parallel tales of the world at the earth's core it would reap the financial double-whammy of appealing to fans of both series.

This sort of crossover – the only one of Burroughs' career, unless you count the likes of Tarzan's cameo in *The Eternal Lover* – was a precursor to the kind of thing that comic books practise *in extremis* today and that has seen the ape-man cross paths in that medium with the likes of Batman, Superman and cinema's Predator. Because such team-ups are the stuff of fantasy to the aficionado, it is to many Burroughs fans' chagrin that the author never wrote a tale in which the ape-man met his only other creation to approach his popularity, John Carter. Had Burroughs produced a Martian-set Tarzan story, it might have taken the ape-man's adventures too far into the realm of science fiction for the tastes of some – but perhaps Burroughs strayed over that line with *Tarzan at the Earth's Core* in any case. Whereas with a few exceptions the fantastical elements of previous Tarzan tales could be reasoned to be unlikely but just about plausible, by September 1929 – when *Blue Book* began its seven-part serialisation of *Tarzan at the Earth's Core* – the idea of our planet having a hollow, life-sustaining centre was already generally known to be not scientifically credible. Straining credibility further, insofar as it draws attention to artifice, the story's prologue contains an example of the breaking of the fourth wall: Jason Gridley – seen in the previous Pellucidar novel, which Burroughs had written immediately before this one – picks up a message on his radio set while in Burroughs' office in the real-life town established the previous year that was named after the author's most famous creation.

The message reveals that David Innes – hero of the Inner World novels – is in peril. Gridley travels all the way to Africa (the specific location in that vast continent identified only as 'Tarzan's country') in order to persuade Lord Greystoke to help him recue Innes, currently languishing in a dark dungeon in the land of the villainous Korsars. 'I believe that you are peculiarly fitted to lead such a venture as I have in mind,' Gridley explains when the ape-man's trained nostrils pick up the spoor of his safari and he goes to ask them what they are doing on his turf. The (unasked) question this raises is how Gridley has heard of Tarzan: as a figure in real life or as a cultural phenomenon that gave rise to the town of Tarzana (referred to three times in the narrative altogether). Although at this stage of the series Tarzan is usually reluctant to help people in trouble, he consents to travel in a dirigible all the way to the north polar icecap on the off-chance that a then-current theory that it contains a hole transpires to be true and will enable him to liberate a man he has never met.

The hole does transpire to exist and provides an ingress to Pellucidar for a party comprised of Tarzan, Gridley and groups of Waziri and Germans. Both latter groups are shown in a good light, as though Burroughs is trying to appease in one fell swoop those who had objected to his depictions of the indigenous population of Africa and the inhabitants of Deutschland (although, it should be pointed out that, at the time his treatment of black people didn't create anything like the furore surrounding his demonisation of Germans). When the party gets separated in Pellucidar, Tarzan isn't too perturbed, finding he loves this savage place and its outlandish wildlife. The fact that he comes across Sagoths – ape-like men who speak Mangani – makes him feel even more at home, although the havoc the eternal daylight wreaks on his usually impeccable sense of direction throws somewhat the perennial self-confidence that at other points sees him utter lines like, 'I am Tarzan – mighty hunter, mighty fighter.'

Gridley falls in love with one of the natives, the impetuous but beautiful Jana. The crushing predictability and banality of their romance is offset by less familiar Tarzan-novel components. The backdrop engenders a refreshing change from a predictable parade of Bolgani, Numa and Tantor wandering across Tarzan's literary landscape. Instead we are treated to a pteranodon swooping on Tarzan and carrying him off, sabre-toothed tigers laying waste to woolly mammoths and – a species from Burroughs' own brain – the Horibs, who despite their slightly comical, Roald Dahl-esque name are rather unsettling in the way they fatten up their prey in dank dungeons.

The Tarzan series might now be past its peak, but *Tarzan at the Earth's Core* sees Burroughs yet again pulling off his regular trick of subverting and defying impossibly limited narrative confines to create a compelling story.

Frank Hoban's *Blue Book* illustrations for *Tarzan at the Earth's Core* portrayed the ape-man in an over-the-shoulder leopardskin pelt. Other pulp illustrators had depicted the ape-man similarly. Although this apparel had never been part of his stories, Burroughs surprisingly had no objection to it. Hoban had previously put Tarzan in a leopardskin loincloth for *Blue Book* serialisations but made the switch, in the opinion of ERB scholar and chronicler Robert R Barrett, at Burroughs' suggestion. 'I have a piece of original art drawn by Burroughs [of] the various characters in *Tarzan at the Earth's Core* showing just how he thought they should look, and Tarzan is dressed in this same over-the-shoulder attire,' says Barrett. Courtesy of Hoban and fellow artist Herbert Morton Stoops, *Blue Book* would continue portraying Tarzan in this rather straitlaced way past the point when cinema had settled on the loincloth.

Tarzan the Tiger was the ape-man's introduction to 'talkies' – sort of.

The second 15-part Tarzan serial to star Frank Merrill boasted sound, but only in the sense that some audiences saw a version that was distributed with an accompanying record containing audio effects and music. Said record featured the victory cry of the bull ape. Those who had read the books must have been stuck by how feeble was Merrill's cry ('Yaa! Yaa! Yaa!') compared with the berserk ululation they had heard in their heads. The Johnny Weissmuller yodel soon to be unveiled to the world was more of an announcement of the ape-man's presence or a form of communication, but would have made a far more appropriate post-battle exultation.

    Tarzan the Tiger's first episode was released in October 1929. Direction was by Henry McRae. Ian McClosky Heath ('continuity') and William Lord Wright ('supervision') adapted the script from the Burroughs novel *Tarzan and the Jewels of Opar*. Both Merrill and Natalie Kingston reprised their roles from *Tarzan the Mighty*, although Tarzan's lady love was not Mary Trevor but once more Jane. While Al Ferguson took on the role of the villain again, it was in the form of the book's Albert Werper rather than the previous serial's pirate Black John. Kithnou played 'Queen La of Opar'. As the plot follows that of the novel fairly closely, it's mystifying why the serial wasn't given the book's title rather than the stupid name it was. After a bump on the head in the early chapters, Tarzan loses his memory and – we are told – 'reverts to his old life as Tarzan the Tiger.' There were plenty of other superlatives that could have been attached to the ape-man's name without rousing an army of pedants cognisant of the continent to which the striped big cat is indigenous. (Tarzan and friends are also aided by tigers in the serial.) Stupid too is the depiction of an ape being intelligent and dextrous enough to truss Jane.

    Although many are under the impression that it wasn't until the Weissmuller era that Jane was shown swimming nude in a Tarzan picture, in fact it was *Tarzan The Tiger* that first saw this occur; and, unlike that later instance in *Tarzan and his Mate*, the scene wasn't cut to appease the censors, even if the nudity is a distant shot of a dive. Another treat for the dads who accompanied their children to the picture houses was some exotic dancing by the bikini-clad women of Opar as La prepares to sacrifice Jane. Such sultry sights make Tarzan's modest leopard-skin dress look even more ridiculous. On a related note, a scene in which the ape-man descends from a vine and daintily and smilingly hops over to Jane in his bootees must surely have had even audiences of 1929 rolling in the aisles.

After Tarzan calls his animal friends to rescue him and Jane from peril, then plunders Opar to save his English estate, the serial ends with some kissy-kissy stuff between Lord and Lady Greystoke, dressed once again in the finery of civilisation.

Merrill had been pencilled in to appear in a third Tarzan serial – *Tarzan the Terrible* – but the sound era that he helped inaugurate was his undoing. He became one of the many silent-era actors adjudged to possess a voice that did not have the gravitas of his visual image. Merrill, however, indicated that he voluntarily bowed out of motion pictures for a career as Recreational Director for Los Angeles Parks because of his anxiety about the influence actors had on the impressionable. Either way, the decks had been cleared for what would be the most famous Tarzan actor of them all.

Tarzan, Guard of the Jungle was a pretty ungainly title for the story that was serialised in seven parts in *Blue Book* starting in October 1930. *Tarzan the Invincible*, substituted for book publication, seems little better, being a Tarzan title interchangeable with so many others. Or perhaps that's appropriate for such an identikit affair.

The furious but empty plot of *Tarzan the Invincible* doesn't bear repeating in depth, but the ape-man – once again rootless, with no family in sight – goes up against a group of communists in league with Arabs intent on looting Opar in order to finance their plans for global revolution. The feeling of over-familiarity is suffocating. Tarzan throws the same shapes we've seen him throw so many times before, whether it be lazing on the back of Tantor, following up his devouring of prey with a treetop snooze or fending off the advances of the throbbingly passionate La. Meanwhile, yet again a swell couple of kids fall in love against the exotic, hectic backdrop. Exacerbating that rigidly adhered-to pattern is staccato writing and didacticism. Burroughs had already written an anti-Communist allegory in the shape of *The Moon Maid* and this Tarzan tale is cut from the same red-baiting cloth. Despite having experienced poverty and despite a penchant for huge financial generosity towards friends and family, Burroughs was virulently anti-left, opposed not just to the cruelty of communism but the very principle of organised labour. The communists here are pantomime villains, with no suggestion permitted that any of them might be motivated by genuine concern for victims of social iniquity. The extremism and the soporific plot result in the first truly bad ape-man story since *The Return of Tarzan* 17 years before.

La and Opar would never be seen again in an adult Burroughs book. The author's increasingly desperate shoehorning in of the lost Atlantean outpost might make that a good thing on a surface level, but with La went passion and colour that the series desperately needed.

When this story appeared in book form in 1931, it became the first publication of Edgar Rice Burroughs, Inc. Financial returns on Burroughs' books had been disappointing of late – although this was true of just about every business in the Depression – and Burroughs was always looking for ways to increase his profit margins. He now cut out the middle man completely. Although Grosset & Dunlap continued in their role as distributors of his 'popular editions' – hardbacks bound in cloth that were the precursors of paperbacks – all Burroughs' first editions for the rest of his life would be self-published.

In October 1931, Edgar Rice Burroughs presented to the world just what it wasn't hungering for: another Tarzan story featuring a scheming communist, a lost race in the African jungle and a young couple who take time off from fighting peril to fall in love. Called *The Triumph of Tarzan*, it ran in six instalments in *Blue Book*.

Its title was changed to *Tarzan Triumphant* for book publication.

Although Burroughs almost always planted references to previous stories in his Tarzan tales (if not always chronologically consistent ones), *Tarzan Triumphant* is unusual in that its events occur as a direct consequence of its predecessor. Joseph Stalin, premier of the Soviet Union, is so enraged by Tarzan thwarting the Bolshevik plot in the story told in *Tarzan the Invincible* that he swears vengeance and sends an assassin Africa-wards. Tarzan, meanwhile, has taken up the case of the Bangalo people of Bungalo who hail from 'toward the north' and who have sought out the ape-man because *shiftas* resident in Abyssinia have come into their country and started seizing their people and selling them into slavery. Tarzan decides to help by accompanying a safari to the trouble-spot, him cunningly disguised as 'Lord Passmore'. On the way, Tarzan inevitably stumbles across a lost city full of intrigue and historical throwbacks. Midian is nestled in a dead volcano and its denizens are descended from a follower of the apostle Paul. Their Christianity has become perverted down the aeons into vicious puritanism of which human sacrifice is a component. A mixed-sex trio end up in this insalubrious environment and, as ever for Tarzan stories, the experience is the making of them and, as ever, one of them falls in love (in this case with a native named – yes – Jezebel) and, as ever, Tarzan makes sure they all get home safely. Also as ever, Burroughs throws in an unlikely coincidence: Tarzan's would-be assassin has fallen in with the *shifta* with whom he already has an appointment.

Just as *Tarzan the Invincible* began with a lot of waffle that suggested that what one was about to read was true, so the opening of *Tarzan Triumphant* is attended by similar whimsy, with Burroughs musing on the ripples spread through the generations by our ancestors.

Not for the first time in one of his novels, Burroughs scores points against religion. Ironically, many of the Soviet politburo would have applauded his ridicule of what they considered the opiate of the masses. They might also have had something to say, though, about the fact that Burroughs, in the supposed land of free speech, doesn't dare make the religion he condemns anything more than generic.

PART FOUR: HERE'S JOHNNY

With Burroughs' Tarzan books now having fully entered their long arc of decline and the Tarzan cinema franchise having lain dormant for three years in the new and uncertain age of talking pictures, the early 1930s is the point at which the ape-man could have died a cultural death. Although he wouldn't necessarily be forgotten today, Tarzan might easily have ended up occupying the same cultural backwaters as other figures with pulp origins like Doc Savage or the Shadow. Fortunately, Johnny Weissmuller was about to sweep – on a vine, of course – to the rescue.

There are conflicting accounts of how Metro-Goldwyn-Mayer (MGM) came to shoot the first proper Tarzan 'talkie'. Some sources state that the idea originated with the studio, who were anxious to find a vehicle in which to employ footage left over from their 1931 film *Trader Horn*, the first cinema drama shot on location in the 'Dark Continent'. Other sources state that ERB, Inc general secretary Cyril Ralph Rothmund approached MGM with the idea. It may even be that those two stories don't conflict. Initially, the film was actually intended to be a sequel to *Trader Horn*. A story outline depicted the eponymous character agreeing to lead an expedition to search for a lost tribe and *en route* encountering Tarzan, who kidnaps a female scientist in the party. Eventually the Trader Horn element was dispensed with.

The first choice to play MGM's Tarzan was weightlifter and shot-putter Herman Brix, but he was another prospective ape-man who had to pull out due to an injury, this one incurred on a prior job. (Unlike Joe Bonomo, though, he would get a second chance.) The replacement casting was inspired and crucial. Memories of him in later Tarzan pictures when he had gotten out of shape have blurred just how physically perfect was Johnny Weissmuller in the early years of his occupancy of the loincloth. He was as low in body fat and as toned of muscle as would be expected of someone who had won five gold swimming medals across the 1924 and 1928 Olympics. Importantly, unlike with all previous studios, MGM didn't hide this glorious bod. Although an artist depicted him as wearing an over-the-shoulder pelt in the movie poster of his 1932 debut *Tarzan the Ape Man*, the costume Weissmuller wore in the film was the diametric opposite of such modesty: not only did he sport just a loincloth but, slit as it was to the waist on both sides, it showed unprecedented amounts of flesh. On top of that was not just Weissmuller's handsomeness but his *appropriate* handsomeness. Unlike Jim Pierce, Weissmuller did not have urban good looks that made him appear as though he had just swapped a dress suit for an animal hide. Instead, he appeared genuinely wild. Yes, he had a side-parting, and early on even a hint of a blow-wave, but there was enough of an unruliness and greasiness about his barnet to make audiences believe that his domicile really was the jungle.

The casting came with an example of the type of serendipity that seems to confirm that something is just meant to be. The famous yodel that Weissmuller produced – never matched, let alone bettered, by any Tarzan actor – has been claimed to be his imitation of a product of MGM's sound department that melded the bleat of a camel, the howl of a hyena, the growl of a dog and the pluck of a violin string, each played a fraction of a second after the other. That the powerful, ululating and intrinsically human noise that emerged from Weissmuller's throat resembles none of those components instantly provokes the suspicion that this was the kind of public relations guff that in a less sceptical age tended to be reproduced unquestioningly by the media and lapped up by the public. Far more plausible is the theory that the yodel is a savaged-up version of the kind of thing that Weissmuller – of Germanic origin – was used to hearing in *bierkellers*. In private conversation unmoored to the requisites of publicity announcements, he told his daughter of yodelling contests at *schlachts* that pre-dated his film career, even if he acknowledged to her that he learnt to imitate a studio soup-up of his own holler.

MGM supposedly didn't even bother to screen-test

Weissmuller. Even if that claim is more hype, it is unlikely that the studio knew that Weissmuller possessed the capacity for such a vocal signature when they selected him. Yet his yodel – instantly imitated in school playgrounds around the world – would become the single most famous thing about the cinema ape-man. So much so that it has become a trademark in more than a metaphorical sense. The name 'Tarzan' was trademarked by ERB, Inc in 1965 for books and other paper products, and the trademark was extended to other items of merchandise at intervals thereafter. However, in 1998, ERB, Inc – at the urging of legal firm Fross Zelnick – trademarked the Tarzan yell preparatory to entering into a US licensing agreement for a Tarzan action figure toy with sonic capacity. Had he been alive, Weissmuller might have been amused – or possibly had some less benign emotion – to find that the relevant soundfile on Fross Zelnick's website was his own ululating voice.

Yet although the talkies gave Tarzan an instantly recognisable vocal signature, they also made him an idiot. In Tarzan pictures hitherto, the dual nature of a man who was jungle-raised but an articulate heir to the seat of Greystoke had been faithfully transferred over from the books. In the Weissmuller era, the character's origin went unexplained and his speech became pidgin English. The resultant innocent man-child persona was endearing to an extent, but it utterly traduced the source. Although he loved the money that began to pour in from MGM, Burroughs hated what they did to his creation: Joan Burroughs recalled her father shaking his head sadly in his seat after a cinema showing of a Tarzan picture by which the rest of the audience had been enthralled. Said Danton Burroughs, 'The producers always went in their own direction thinking they knew the character without reading the books. That frustrated him, but the money was good and he allowed the distortion. Every time he tried to get involved and steer these writers and producers in the right direction, they'd promise him something, then do something completely different.' Yet the traducing was a more complicated issue than that. As Bill Hillman says, 'Some of that is [Burroughs'] fault. He stipulated to some degree that the stories and some of the elements of the novels not be duplicated.'

Another change made to Tarzan by talking pictures was the pronunciation of his name. Burroughs' had always said 'Tar-zun,' but the makers of *Tarzan the Ape Man* had the actors enunciate the character's name as 'Tar-zaan.' The stress on the second syllable sounds less Western and therefore more appropriate, but it was the reach of cinema rather than logic that ensured that that pronunciation instantly and permanently became definitive. Stateside at least. British inclination was to stick to the short second 'a' – as was, strangely, Weissmuller's.

Trader Horn director W S Van Dyke was logically enough assigned *Tarzan the Ape Man*. The screenplay was 'adapted' by Cyril Hume (another alumnus of *Trader Horn*) with dialogue written by none other than Ivor Novello, a British thespian and composer now chiefly remembered through the UK songwriting award named after him. The plot sees explorer James Parker (C Aubrey Smith) on a quest to find the fabled elephant's graveyard. Daughter Jane (Maureen O'Sullivan), a flibbertigibbet with an incongruous deadly aim with a rifle, insists on accompanying him. The Irish O'Sullivan opted to play Jane as an Englishwoman, starting a tradition in Tarzan movies that has continued off and on to this day.

At 99 minutes, it is a long movie for the time, and things get off to a boring start. The only semblance of vitality in early sections dominated by family-reunion soap opera and a flat travelogue is, of all things, some weird, incestuous banter between Jane and her father. Meanwhile, even in its era it would have raised an eyebrow that, when a native bearer falls screaming to his death from a mountain, the 'Poor devil' uttered by Parker's employee Holt doesn't come until *after* he demands to know what was in the pack he'd been carrying.

If the leftover *Trader Horn* material was indeed the impetus for the film, it's somewhat ironic, because its use is risible: Jane and her father stand remarking on local customs in front of an

Tarzan's creator, Edgar Rice Burroughs (below), whose first published work (right) was set on Mars.

The first visual interpretation of Tarzan was a dramatic one (left). The ape-man's graduation to book form inspired an equally beautiful but more understated depiction (below).

A typically striking example of Tarzan cover art by J Allen St John.

McClurg US hardback (left) and Four Square UK paperback (below): same book, small title variation.

Edgar Rice Burroughs meets the first movie Tarzan, Elmo Lincoln.

Tarzan of the Apes (1918), the first instalment of a colossally successful movie franchise.

In 1920, Gene Pollar (above) was an unimpressive second Tarzan. Ronald Adair (right) played the ape-man on the stage the same year.

The Son of Tarzan (1920) offered a sublime Korak (Kamuela Searle, above) and a ridiculous Tarzan (P Dempsey Tabler, left).

Tarzan and the Golden Lion: P J Monahan provided the cover for the pulp publication (above), J Allen St John that for the book (left).

Jim Pierce in Tarzan and the Golden Lion (1927, above). The movie prompted a tie-in edition of the source novel (inset).

Tarzan the Mighty (1928) starring Frank Merrill, a fine ape-man but for his, ahem, dress.

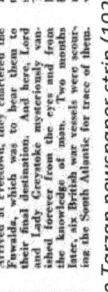

The first instalment of the Tarzan newspaper strip (1928).

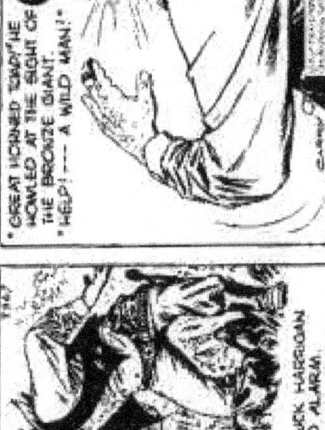

A 1950 Burne Hogarth strip.

The first Sunday Tarzan strip, 1931 (above). It bequeathed the official Tarzan logo, still in use 81 years later, as on the official Tarzan centenary emblem (right).

Different interpretations of the ape-man. Frank Hoban (right) vs J Allen St John (below); over-the-shoulder pelt vs loincloth.

This publicity shot for Tarzan the Ape-Man (above) more accurately represented Johnny Weissmuller's costume in the 1932 film than the demure outfit in the movie's poster (left).

Tarzan of the merchandise. Clockwise from top left: ice cream, jigsaw, assembly kit, trading card, nougat bar.

Weissmuller with Maureen O'Sullivan in *Tarzan and his Mate* (left), a celebrated 1934 film which boasted both action and flesh. Buster Crabbe was unimpressive in the previous year's *Tarzan the Fearless* (below).

Herman Brix appeared as Tarzan in a 1935 Burroughs production (above). Glenn Morris was the ape-man in Tarzan's Revenge (1938), whose poster emphasised the swimming celebrity of Eleanor Holm (below.)

By the time of his final outing in the loincloth, *Tarzan and the Mermaids* (1948), Weissmuller had to suck in his stomach for publicity pictures, but many still consider him the definitive ape-man.

Lex Barker as Tarzan (inset). His third ape-man outing, Tarzan and the Slave Girl (1950), produced an eyebrow-raising publicity shot (above).

Radio Tarzans: James Pierce (left), with his wife hiding his paunch; Lamont Johnson (below left); Carlton KaDell (below right). The Pierce show span off the hugely successful Signal Oil Tarzan Club, whose badge is depicted above.

obvious back projection of natives, while it was clearly acres of unused hippo material that compelled the producers to commission the writing of a quite distasteful aquatic slaughter section. Fourteen years on, things don't seem to have advanced much beyond the cut-ins employed in Elmo Lincoln's first film.

Apart, that is, from the technological leap of sound, one that enables the deployment of that yodel, first heard as an eerie, mysterious noise carrying to the safari from the depths of the jungle. Although wonderful, it is somewhat overused, ringing out in situations where the ape-man couldn't possibly muster sufficient lung power, such as when he is wresting a lion or executing a breaststroke.

Tarzan makes his first visual appearance around the half-hour mark. His acrobatics in the jungle canopy are quite impressive here and throughout – but is that a trapeze swing we discern in the treetops? Tarzan snatches Jane and carries her off to his tribe (men dressed as apes, apart from baby chimps portraying the young ones). One particular chimp makes his first of many appearances in the franchise. Tarzan's famous simian friend has variously been named in movie credits 'Cheetah', 'Cheeta' and 'Cheta', and variously implied to be male and female. The character has also been retrospectively claimed by often conflicting sources to have been played by animal actors in their care. No attempt will be made here to settle the issue of who the simian thesp was, but the spelling 'Cheeta' and the male pronoun will be used henceforth for the sake of convenience.

There is a funny tussle between Cheeta and the ape-man over Jane's handkerchief, while Miss Parker sits unamused between them. Tarzan then stabs to death an encroaching leopard. How a knife of forged steel ever came to be in his possession is not explained. As to his backstory, the closest it comes to being addressed is when Mr Parker remarks, 'I can't make it out – how did he get here?' Jane's response, 'Oh, what does it matter?' blithely dispenses with any necessity to supply an origin. Tarzan is none too gentle or polite to Jane, but does tuck her safely into a tree nest before chivalrously posting guard outside.

The next day, Tarzan frees an elephant from a trap before breakfast (freshly killed gazelle). Jane explores his vocabulary, which so far has consisted of 'Umgawa!', an instruction to his animal friends and foes as all-purpose as that yodel. The famous phrase 'Me Tarzan, you Jane' originates here, even though it is never quite said but rather is the media and general public's simplification of an exchange involving pointed fingers and repetitions of 'Me,' 'You,' 'Tarzan,' 'Jane' and various other words.

The safari catches up with Tarzan. In the ensuing battle, one of Tarzan's tribe is shot dead. A distraught ape-man starts taking revenge, picking people off one by one. Jane has begun to fall for Tarzan and defends him to his detractors. A bullet-grazed Tarzan fights a lioness to the death, after which her mate attacks him. Elephants respond to Tarzan's yodel for assistance. He is nursed back to health by Jane, who has been snatched by one of his tribe. The two frolic together, including a scene designed to show off Weissmuller's swimming prowess as he cuts through water faster than Jane can run parallel along the river bank. Jane starts to feel blissfully relaxed in the company of her innocent forest god, but she knows how important she is to her dad. There is a genuine moment of sadness when a forlorn-looking ape-man steps back into the bushes after returning Jane to her party.

Jane's party is captured by bizarre diminutive natives. 'Pygmies?' the question is asked. 'Dwarves,' comes the accurate reply – although 'in blackface' is left unsaid. Jane espies Cheeta and tells him to alert Tarzan, which Cheeta does, although he has his own mini-adventure on the way. Resorting to his yodel again, Tarzan rustles up a herd of elephants to help him, although on the way to fulfil the role of saviour he encounters a barrier of crocodiles, which he ultimately evades by scrambling onto a hippo's back. In the dwarves' village, the safari members are being thrown to the mercies of a giant, ferocious caged ape. The filmmakers' accomplishment of making this beast vaguely scary even though it is clearly a man in costume is undermined somewhat by the moment Tarzan throws his knife into the ape's face: the lodged weapon bounces about as only rubber can. The elephants invade the village and show savagery unheard of in real pachyderm life before carrying Jane, her father and Holt to safety. One of the elephants is fatally injured and, sure enough, immediately heads for the elephant's graveyard, where Jane's father expires in the realm of his dreams. Jane meanwhile decides to stay with her ape-man. She and Tarzan wave off Holt, who heads for civilisation astride an elephant.

From today's perspective, the film is very clunky in places, but at the time the miracle of synchronised sound was as awe-inspiring as 'moving pictures' had been at the turn of the century and would have provided *Tarzan the Ape Man* a real allure. Just when Western audiences had become blasé about the sight of African wildlife, now they could hear roars, grunts, growls and chatters accompanying it. While O'Sullivan's short hair means she is not yet possessed of the lustrous beauty for which she would soon become renowned, Weissmuller looks a million dollars.

Although *Tarzan the Ape Man* was one of the ten biggest box-office hits of the year, the cinema best was yet to come for a revivified icon.

Simultaneous with the première of *Tarzan the Ape Man*, *Argosy* magazine – in its issue dated 12 March 1932 – began a six-part serialisation of the latest Burroughs Tarzan story, *Tarzan and the City of Gold*.

Burroughs might have felt disdain for Tarzan movies but MGM's revitalising of the franchise – however cockeyed – was the kind of thing clearly beyond the character's creator, who turned in possibly the dreariest, stalest Tarzan tale yet. The lost cities this time are Athne (City of Ivory, whose inhabitants worship elephants) and Cathne (City of Gold, whose denizens bow down to lions). Tarzan seems strangely blasé about stumbling upon these places – but then maybe it would have been less realistic if Burroughs had depicted surprise on the ape-man's part. The queen of Cathne is Nemone. She resembles La in that she is fiery, half-bonkers and totally in love with Tarzan, who as usual with such temptresses is immune to her charms despite there being the now predictable Jane-sized hole in the proceedings. Tarzan once again learns the native language sufficiently speedily for easy story development but far too quickly to engender any sense of realism. Meanwhile, the spiritual aridity continues apace, with the increasingly aloof and superior Tarzan musing his most misanthropic thoughts yet, even if the conventions of the adventure story dictate that he shakes himself out of them long enough to assist people in danger, in this case a young woman called Doria who is due to be put to death by Nemone because she is prettier than she.

It's not all by-numbers stuff: just when we are expecting the sort of tussle to the death with a lion we have already seen 101 times in Tarzan tales, Burroughs provides a new spin by having a knife-less Tarzan turning and running away because he knows that Numa tires after a hundred yards. (His plan goes wrong because this is a lion specially bred for endurance, but a dramatic entrance by Jad-bal-ja saves the day.) Aside from such flashes of lateral thinking, though, this is clearly the product of a bored, uninterested author and an unhappy human being.

The next Tarzan story was serialised in *Blue Book Magazine* in five parts starting from August 1932. Despite its quick appearance after *City of Gold*, *Tarzan and the Leopard Men* is enveloped by sluggishness and inertia, perhaps symptomatic of which is the fact that it didn't appear in book form until *after* the following Tarzan magazine serial, *Tarzan and the Lion Man*, had been published as a novel, and this despite the fact that Burroughs wrote on the flap of the first edition of the latter book, 'Mr Burroughs believes this to be the poorest Tarzan novel he has ever written …'

In a sense, it's a surprise that *Leopard Men* doesn't work, for it sees Burroughs trying something a little different, at least in the sense that he appears to have decided (albeit temporarily) that any more lost cities would be just too much. Instead, he sets up an intriguing and potentially highly dramatic scenario involving the secret society of the title, whose fairly realistic activities – conducted in ceremonial robes and claws – involve cannibalism. Somehow, though, Burroughs manages to throw away the interesting concept, starting with the ostensible Ku Klux Klan metaphor of the Leopard Men: this book contains some of Burroughs' most racist material yet.

Back in 1915, *All-Story* editor Bob Davis had complained to Burroughs of *Tarzan and the Jewels of Opar*, 'You have introduced the old wallop-on-the-bean idea for the purpose of sidetracking Tarzan's intelligence.' A device that was hoary 17 years previously is here deployed again, and to no greater dramatic purpose than to have Tarzan fall in with the supposition of native Orando – who stumbles upon him after he has been knocked out by a storm – that he is a *muzimo*, or protective spirit. When Tarzan inevitably undergoes a second, process-reversing wallop, he is miraculously free of physical trauma. Meanwhile, with the exception of the contents of a cooking pot yielding up a grisly secret, the Leopard Men are a somewhat less scary (and active) proposition than we are at first led to assume by Orando, who persuades Tarzan to join him in his lonely resistance to their malign influence. Burroughs also throws in the obligatory fractured group of Westerners whom Tarzan is obliged to rescue from danger. The romance that predictably develops between two of them is as uninteresting as the revelation that one of the party is the long-lost younger brother of another. Philip José Farmer – the science fiction author and Burroughs fanatic who went as far as to proclaim himself 'the greatest authority on Tarzan' – described *Tarzan and the Leopard Men* as 'the dullest' of the Burroughs Tarzan novels. So leaden is the storytelling that we feel almost as though we are following in real time the drudgery Burroughs experienced as he wearily ground out another entry in the series he had long ago concluded was exhausted.

It's rather ironic that the deeper Edgar Rice Burroughs went into his rut with Tarzan, the healthier was the character elsewhere: on 10 September 1932, radio could now be added to magazines, books, films and comic strips as media conquered by the ape-man.

Because film is a 'fuller' medium than radio in that we use our main sense – sight – to experience it, the temptation is to assume that radio is a more primitive form to which cinema is the successor. In fact, radio is younger, with public broadcasts dating back only as far as 1920 (i.e. two years after the first Tarzan movie was released). Radio really took off in the Christmas of 1924 when the consumer buying trends came down on the side of the 'wireless' rather than the gramophone or the phonograph. Although music was radio's bedrock, performed drama became very important to the medium in an era in which it could otherwise be obtained only at the nickelodeon or theatre house. Radio dramas had originated in meaningful form in the late 1920s. *Little Orphan Annie*'s transference from comic strip to radio in April 1931 was pioneering, but the entry into the medium of a figure of such vast cultural recognition as Tarzan was more significant. It brought sorely needed income in bleak economic times: sponsors and advertisers were keen to attach themselves to ape-man broadcasts.

Burroughs had been considering for a while the idea of reading his Tarzan stories over the air, but Joe Neebe, who had first floated the idea of the Tarzan newspaper strip, was responsible for the ape-man swinging into radio, where Neebe was now employed. Neebe acted as Burroughs' broker in a deal with LA's American Radio Features syndicate for adaptations of Tarzan stories, starting with the first book. Burroughs had approval of the scripts and was able to veto the inaccuracies about wildlife about which he had been sensitive ever since being ridiculed for including tigers in the first version of *Tarzan of the Apes* and about which Rex Maxon's carelessness infuriated him. He was also able to prevent the ape-man becoming the kind of cartoon character into which MGM were turning him. It was presumably also the author who was responsible for the fact that each episode began with the quasi-advertisement, *'Tarzan of the Apes* – brought to you from off the pages of Edgar Rice Burroughs' thrilling book.'

Each show was 15 minutes long (ten without the commercials) and was designed to run three days a week. As with film and comic strips, Tarzan was in the vanguard of new methods. Radio dramas were usually broadcast live, but radio stations who subscribed to *Tarzan of the Apes* were circulated 16-inch transcription discs of the programme, an innovation that meant its reach was global: it was bought by stations in English-speaking nations across the world.

The publicity which claimed that a high-and-low search had been conducted for the radio Tarzan and Jane was somewhat eyebrow-raising, for after their supposed scouring of the country the producers decided to cast none other than Jim Pierce as Tarzan and Joan Burroughs Pierce as Jane – respectively son-in-law and daughter of the ape-man's creator. Ever loyal to his family, Burroughs had already gifted Pierce the right to appear in another Tarzan movie (something which was to later cause the author legal problems). Moreover, the Pierces worked not for the five dollars per show the other actors were paid but royalties, something that would ultimately make them a wealthy couple.

An unfortunate photograph was released to publicise the programme. Although still only 32, Pierce was now too rotund a figure to be stripped to a loincloth, and it was clear that the reason he carried in his arms a safari-suited Emma was to hide his (pre-) middle-age spread. However, this didn't matter too much with a product you couldn't see. What was painfully apparent, though, was that – while Joan was a trained actor – Pierce had got into the profession as a silent-era screen actor cast for his build. Moreover, Pierce's bull-ape victory cry was serviceable rather than awe-inspiring like Weissmuller's yodel. (It may have been dictated by Burroughs, for it seems to consist of an elongated version of the word 'Tarmangani'.)

Once again, though, the Tarzan brand name worked its magic. Moreover, although circumscribed by lack of visuals, the producers were conversely unhindered by the requirement to import or replicate animals, lost cities and weaponry, and could thus go to town on their panoramas. The listeners staring at their grilles were treated to all manner of evocative roars, burbles, gunshots and screams between the forceful (if a little pompous) present-tense description of Fred Shields. Ratings were excellent.

That the radio series began with an adaptation of the first Tarzan book, just as cinema, stage and newspaper strip versions had done, might seem like overkill on that story, but with the origin-less Weissmuller movie in circulation, perhaps now, of all times, such a reiteration was appropriate.

The publicity cross-fertilisation between Tarzans of different media was now at its apex. The ape-man was simultaneously to be found on screen, on radio, in comic strips and in prose. The consequences were predictable. When ERB, Inc claimed in 1936, 'Tarzan is the best known and best loved fictional character in the world today,' they were not exaggerating. Burroughs even had a feeling that he had reserved a space on a juggernaut that was going to make his novels obsolete. By 1935, he was writing, 'There is one factor that may have more effect on reducing book sales than any number of depressions, and that is radio ... Already, with two programs, we are netting more than we do from the sale of all our books, which, taken in connection with the fact that there are hundreds of similar programs on the air, suggests that people are taking their fiction this way instead of through books.' He was partially right: it would be the medium that effectively superseded radio – television – that decimated reading as a leisure activity.

Tarzan merchandise – or at least official Tarzan merchandise – went back to 1922 when Burroughs granted permission to New York manufacturer Davis & Voetsch to market toy simians with the ape-man's name attached. Perhaps the fact that Burroughs' royalty for the first year totalled just $120 is what initially made him relaxed about unauthorised merchandise such as the watermarked Tarzan bond paper that came to his attention in 1926: he wrote an unsolicited letter of forgiveness to the manufacturer in which he revealed he was using the paper for the manuscript of his latest novel. A Berlin café proprietor, a German chocolate manufacturer and an amusement park 'freak' all appropriated the Tarzan name without incurring more than bemusement from the author: he seemed to perceive them as involving the same sort of tribute implied by the fact of dogs and race horses (including one owned by the Prince of Wales) being named after his creation. He became more business-minded as he realised just how much money merchandising rights could generate.

The advent of the Tarzan radio show marked the point where ape-man merchandising truly took off. With merchandising, the Tarzan character was once again in the vanguard of a hitherto unknown phenomenon, or at least unknown on this scale. Acting on his own initiative, Burroughs commissioned statuettes of Tarzan characters from a company that had previously made figures based on the *Our Gang* film series. ERB, Inc sold these statuettes to sponsors of the Tarzan radio series, who in turn offered them as loyalty incentives to their customers. Although he had always been business- rather than art-orientated, it was the fact that half a million of these figurines had been shipped within the first 18 months of the Tarzan radio show that made Burroughs apprehend fully the need to protect his intellectual property. From now on, he would employ somebody specifically to license the Tarzan name, which was now so embedded in the language as a synonym for both strong and uncouth that it was in danger of being perceived as generic and public domain. (One synonym made the jump from colloquial to formal in the 1940s when Webster's dictionaries started defining the word Tarzan as 'a well-built, agile and very strong man.')

Burroughs had hit yet another goldmine. The Tarzan name appeared on commercial products in unquantifiable numbers. Some of these products were logical or at least semi-logical (Tarzan singlets, swimming trunks, chest expanders, action figures, phonograph records, posters, bubblegum cards, stickers, transfers, colouring books, board games, toy knives, archery sets, jungle helmets, animal jungle masks). Some were simply fatuous, examples of the way a brand name can lend allure to any random item (crockery, schoolbags, shoes, shirts, ice cream, chewing gum, bread).

The sponsorship of the radio programme by Signal Oil played a huge part in this process. Having hosted a première event for the show (Weissmuller was invited despite having nothing to do with it), the petrol company milked their connection to the ape-man for everything it was worth – which was plenty – via promotions like the Tarzan Jig-Saw Puzzle Contest (in which people could build up free of charge a four-colour Tarzan puzzle week by week by stopping into a Signal Service Station, with prizes awarded at the end). The pester-power factor was cranked up by the formation of the Signal Tarzan Club, a membership requirement of which was to bring a new customer to Signal. The club provided access to Tarzan badges, membership cards, photos and competitions, and awarded points redeemable against various consumer desirables for persuading others to buy Signal products.

Signal's blurring of the demarcation between cinema and radio Tarzans continued when in 1933 the company used its space on the radio programme to promote the new Tarzan picture, *Tarzan the Fearless*, and bought screen advertising and lobby A-boards at theatres to emphasise the link (which didn't exist) between Signal and the movie. The illogicality of all this was hardly going to bother Signal: within a year, the club's membership-card logo of a hollering Tarzan had been circulated to a reported 100,000. As well as the calculable financial benefit of causing so many people to fill up at Signal stations, there was the unquantifiable but undeniable benefit of the goodwill engendered by being associated with a brand that gave people a warm feeling. Signal furthered this goodwill by sponsoring baseball teams formed by Tarzan club members, creating another dimension to the Tarzan phenomenon that, although it might have been rooted in consumerism, actually ended up injecting a participatory and activist quality inherently absent in the consumption of art.

By 1934, Signal took the decision to end their sponsorship of the radio show. With them now having to administer a membership of 415,000, they may have thought that they had created a monster that was out of control. However, the severing of the tie may have had something to do with other factors.

In March of that year, the 130-episode adaptation of *Tarzan of the Apes* had finished and the show was part-way through *The Return of Tarzan*, which ran to 156 episodes. At that point, Burroughs decided not to renew his contract with American Radio Features. The suspicion must be that he wanted once again to cut out the financial middle man. There were other changes afoot. It was announced that Pierce and his wife would not be returning to their roles. Pierce later wrote, 'Toward the end of our contract, Joan became pregnant with Mike and the producer … was afraid that Joan would not have time to do justice to the job. I felt that we could get ahead a few episodes and Joan wouldn't be out long … They wanted me to continue with a new Jane, but I told them that Joan was just as important to the programme as I and resigned.' Burroughs felt compelled to write to the clients of the show emphasising that it would continue.

Tarzan and the Diamond of Asher, produced by ERB, Inc, debuted on 10 August 1934. There were 39 episodes of 15 minutes each written by Rob Thompson, who was personally chosen by Burroughs and whose chapter outlines the author would amend and approve before he went ahead and wrote a full script. Carlton KaDell played the ape-man. Jane did not appear. Unfortunately, the success Burroughs had had in publishing his own books did not transfer to the radio medium. Although the features of the story told in *Diamond of Asher* – a lost expedition and a missing man who is a Tarzan lookalike – may sound same-old, same-old, the KaDell show's execution and production values are generally considered superior to those of the Pierce show. Yet although it was pushed hard by Burroughs, who commissioned a glossy brochure to sell it, it found far fewer outlets than the Tarzan radio show was used to. A follow-up 39-part series, *Tarzan and the Fires of Tohr*, copyrighted in 1936, fared even worse. A Thompson-written Tarzan and D'Arnot adventure involving a lost expedition, ivory smuggling, a hidden city and a strange yellow race who engage in human sacrifice, it was bought by only a handful of domestic stations plus one each in Hawaii, Australia and Canada. More Tarzan radio scripts were commissioned and recorded but not broadcast: two chapters of *Tarzan and the Tower of Ho* by Rob Thompson and two chapters of *Tarzan in Pellucidar* by Jerry Cady.

Perhaps the public had simply got used to Pierce as the 'voice' of Tarzan. Whatever the reason, while the 1930s radio Tarzan flared sensationally, it quickly and quite dramatically faded.

In late 1931, a rather unseemly incident occurred on the doorstep of Edgar Rice Burroughs' home.

Jules Goldstone, a lawyer working for film producer Sol Lesser, handed the author $10,000. When Burroughs asked what this money was for, Goldstone explained that it was payment for a Tarzan movie to which Burroughs had previously agreed. Burroughs literally threw the money back at the lawyer and told him the relevant contract had lapsed. As the author closed his front door, Goldstone was left chasing thousand-dollar bills. That was the version of events of Lesser. Burroughs, in notes to himself, told a more sedate tale that also involved one Walter Shumway, comments about the nice weather and a polite but firm statement by the author that he knew what the two men were here to discuss and that he had no intention of engaging in that discussion. Somewhat unconvincingly – as though in preparation for a potential court case – Burroughs wrote, 'He did not show me any money nor any check.' Either way, a dormant contract had come back to bite the author on the backside.

It originated in a deal Burroughs had agreed in January 1929 – at a point between the two Frank Merrill Tarzan cinematic ventures – with a pair of producers, Jack Nelson and the aforementioned Shumway, who proposed a Tarzan movie or serial called *Tarzan the Fearless*. The agreement stipulated that the venture must be released within seven years. In what amounted to a wedding present to his new son-in-law, Burroughs also insisted on a clause that stated Jim Pierce be cast as Tarzan. Since then, the rights to the project had been bought by a third party, a consortium headed by Sol Lesser, responsible for the likes of an early *Oliver Twist* adaptation and *The Mine with the Iron Door*. Although Nelson and Shumway were in breach of the contract by not having paid Burroughs the $10,000 advance he was due to receive, Lesser's lawyer had discerned a legal loophole: Burroughs had failed to inform them of their breach, which itself could be made good by rendering payment to him. Hence the doorstep contretemps.

Burroughs' alleged refusal to accept the money made no difference to the contractual loophole. Both the author and MGM – shortly to start work on Weissmuller's first Tarzan picture, which had been assigned a very large budget – were now faced with a cinematic release that might queer their pitch. Although he might have acted in good faith – his cash advance was more than two years overdue, so he may have thought the project was dead – Burroughs must have felt more than a little awkward at the fact that he had assured MGM they had exclusive Tarzan movie rights. The most MGM could do – short of dropping their own film and suing Burroughs – was to grease Lesser's palm in order to persuade him to at least delay production of his own Tarzan project. Lesser agreed to the latter and, due to the subsequent box office success of *Tarzan the Ape Man*, by the time he was ready to exercise his option found himself in a much better position than he had been before. Some have posited the theory that it was Burroughs' mortification at this whole scenario that was behind his not objecting – at least in public – to the idiot MGM and Weissmuller proceeded to make Tarzan.

Although Lesser made his Tarzan different from the MGM version in that the romantic interest was not Jane but one Mary Brooks (Jacqueline Wells, later called Julie Bishop), he also stipulated that his Tarzan movie should portray the ape-man as the monosyllabic man-child seen by so many millions in *Tarzan the Ape Man*. That he cast an Olympic swimmer as Tarzan might also have been perceived as – ahem – monkey-see, monkey-do, but it seems to have been as much inspired by the fact that Clarence 'Buster' Crabbe – Gold medallist in the 1932 competition – had done very well in 1933 Tarzan rip-off *King of the Jungle*, portraying Kaspa the Lion Man.

The fact that Crabbe ended up in the picture was a saga in itself. When Burroughs had specified his son-in-law be cast in *Tarzan the Fearless*, Pierce was a fine figure of a man. As mentioned previously, Pierce had since been afflicted by a physical decline as shocking for its pace as its extent. Although, once the *Tarzan the Fearless* project was resurrected, Pierce gamely tried to shed the approximately 50 pounds by which he was overweight, it was clear to Lesser that it was a futile endeavour. In vain he tried to convince Burroughs to release him from the obligation to employ his son-in-law. Burroughs – who had the feelings of his own daughter to think about – refused, even when Lesser told him that with Pierce in the role his only option would be to make a comedy in which Jane was the dominant half of the pair and Tarzan a klutz. Although humourist Corey Ford was commissioned to write such a burlesque, this mocking scenario was not the one Lesser had envisaged when he bought the rights to the character, and eventually he paid off Pierce with $5,000, although not without what seems the deliberate humiliation of ensuring that a last-gasp screen test for Pierce was a Shakespeare soliloquy that he was bound to struggle through.

Crabbe had been part of the same 1928 Olympics team as Weissmuller and the two were pals, although the media inevitably now portrayed them as cinema rivals. Crabbe had also been screen-tested by MGM in 1931 for the role of the ape-man, if somewhat perfunctorily. His performance as the lion-raised Kaspa, incidentally, had seen him even more skimpily clothed than Weissmuller had been in *Tarzan the Ape Man*, with his buttocks on prominent display.

Lesser hired Robert F Hill – veteran of the Elmo Lincoln *Adventures of Tarzan* serial – to direct. Walter Anthony (dialogue), Basil Dickey and George H Plympton provided a screenplay which revolved around Tarzan agreeing to help Mary find her scientist father, who has been captured by the people of Zar, a treasure-bedecked lost city with a villainous high priest. A thousand-dollar bounty on Tarzan's head and a scheme to rob him of the Greystoke birthright he doesn't know is his add to the supposed intrigue.

Lesser attempted to have his cake and eat it by making both a 71-minute movie (released in August 1933) and a serial. His plans for maximisation of profits came unstuck when some theatres declined his two proffered options of running either 12 weekly instalments or an opening of an hour's length plus eight weekly chapters. Many instead ran just the 60-minute opener as though it was a feature, even though it had no proper resolution. However, the horrific reviews to which the feature was subjected were not just down to this confusion.

Right from the get-go, it seems almost as though Lesser is making the burlesque he once threatened: shots of Crabbe swinging on vines with pronounced hesitancy seem too silly to be meant seriously. Crabbe's floppy mop of dyed black hair and toothy smile seem more appropriate to a Marx Brothers movie, his thong-effect leopardskin loincloth looks painful, and what are we to make of his mock-spanking of his chimpanzee friend? In having Tarzan speak little more than two dozen words in the feature-film version, Lesser takes Weissmuller's verbal minimalism to absurd levels. Weissmuller's Tarzan had an edge even despite his innocence and taciturnity, but Crabbe plays the ape-man as an aw-shucks simpleton. Not only does he commit the cardinal sin of laughing – Burroughs' Tarzan might smile grimly but did not laugh, and the author made sure that Tarzan radio scripts depicting him doing so were amended – but he does so as gormlessly as an animated Disney character. Tarzan's battle with a rubber croc is as lame as his tussle with an uninterested lion. As with the MGM Tarzan, the deliberate annexation from the source novels creates problems. We are told Tarzan was kidnapped by a great ape when his parents were exploring these parts, but not why his name is Tarzan.

Crabbe never played the ape-man again but did carve out a successful career in serials, becoming particularly well-known for his roles as Flash Gordon and Buck Rogers. Meanwhile, despite such a substandard franchise entrée and his initially poor relations with Burroughs, Sol Lesser would become a lifelong friend of ERB and eventually enjoy a lengthy involvement with the Tarzan character.

From the ridiculous to the comparatively sublime. *Tarzan and the Lion Man* was the first, and indeed only, Burroughs Tarzan tale to break out of the pulp ghetto and be published in a slick. *Liberty* magazine serialised the story in eight weekly parts from the issue cover-dated 11 November 1933. That it was an unusually prestigious outlet for the ape-man was reflected in the fact that, for the first time, a magazine carrying a Tarzan story did not trumpet it on any of its covers. Perhaps it was *Liberty*'s classiness that made it willing to run this of all Tarzan stories, for in several senses it seems a mickey-take of a Tarzan industry that it might have felt to be beneath its readers.

When an author gets bored with a character, it becomes tempting for him to start being playful with him, and this seems to have happened here. Burroughs' flirtation in *The Tarzan Twins* with post-modernism could be dismissed as not really counting on the grounds that in a children's book the rules are somehow different, while the fame possessed by the ape-man referred to in *Tarzan at the Earth's Core* is not explicitly stated as art-related. In this story, however, Tarzan is proposed to be both a real person and as a cultural figure who is known from books and films.

Some parts of the book suggest another Burroughs motivation beyond playfulness: revenge on the Hollywood industry that had turned his noble creation into a fool. Yet Burroughs himself was not in too much of a position to carp about Tinseltown's creative leaden-foot. Herein we are treated – again – to a Tarzan double (the photogenic but cowardly film actor Stanley Obroski, cast as the ape-man), misanthropy (spirited stuntwoman Rhonda Terry is the sole likeable character, and Burroughs insists that only man evinces unnecessary brutality – which is scientific nonsense), a safari whose constituent parts get separated, and a hidden city.

Although Burroughs is not exactly a rapier wit, there is some amusement on offer in his apparent pops at both Buster Crabbe (*The Lion Man* of the title is a Tarzan rip-off movie being shot in Africa) and Weissmuller (it is remarked of the vaguely similarly-named Obroski, 'He don't have to act, but he looks great stripped'). Additionally, Burroughs depicts Hollywood movie types as philistine and clueless. (One of them even thinks there are tigers in Africa!)

Burroughs' latest hidden city rather tickles the funny bone. London, as it is called, was built by a mad scientist who styles himself 'God'. His experiments with transplanting cells from humans to gorillas have created a race of apes capable of talking and utilising tools (although Burroughs sidesteps the issue of how building an entire city is possible in the absence of fully opposable thumbs and the true precision grip). That the cells in question are from bodies interred in Westminster Abbey has led to simians with rather regal airs boasting names like Buckingham, Suffolk, King Henry the Eighth and Thomas Wolsey. They reside in antediluvian splendour, their living spaces numbering a castle. Tarzan gets the shock of his life when using the Mangani tongue to address one of these ostensible Bolgani: the gorilla has no idea what Tarzan is saying and responds in impeccable English. God, meanwhile, has gone in the other direction, sprouting hair as a gruesome consequence of planting gorilla cells into his own decaying body.

The final chapter is a sort of comedy coda that takes place a year after the other events and sees Tarzan – in his John Clayton civilisation persona – visit Los Angeles out of curiosity. He ends up being considered for a role in a Tarzan picture. However, the production manager nixes the casting with a curt, 'Not the type, at all.' Tarzan does get a consolation role as a white hunter – and then gets himself sacked when a lion goes out of control on set and he deals with it in his customary, blade-flashing fashion.

It's difficult to know how to take this story. On one level, it can viewed as slightly spoiling the escapism of the Tarzan series by deconstructing the boundaries of art and making the reader contemplate artifice. Moreover, one wonders whether those who love Burroughs for his stern-browed and resolutely heroic adventures want a Tarzan that, Carson Napier-style, skirts spoof. On the other hand, although *Tarzan and the Lion Man* is hardly a masterpiece, it is impressive that the author has found yet again a way to relieve the tedium of a rigid formula for an occasionally entertaining couple of hundred pages.

Although Buster Crabbe had been risible in the loincloth, it took Johnny Weissmuller's second appearance as the ape-man for the public to begin to perceive him as the definitive Tarzan.

The first Weissmuller picture had been important in establishing the parameters for the new Tarzan, but it had also been a movie that was feeling its way, something exacerbated by the fact that the methods of talking pictures were still being codified. *Tarzan and his Mate* was an altogether more confident enterprise. Although the result would not be palatable to the Burroughs super-purist – nor would any Weissmuller movie – it is considered by many the greatest Tarzan movie ever made.

Released in April 1934, *Tarzan and his Mate* has a screenplay by James Kevin McGuiness. Howard Emmett Rogers and Leon Gordon are credited with 'adaptation,' although this is certainly no adaptation of anything written by Burroughs. Still, the author could at least sometimes bring himself to dispense with his torment about such matters: he had recently shruggingly opined in correspondence that the character had 'survived' much traducing, plus he was being paid in the region of $45,000. Although nothing was shot in Africa itself, the film's staggering 1.2 million-dollar budget showed on-screen in a lush affair awash with extras and wildlife.

Surprisingly, considering the stature *Tarzan and his Mate* now possesses, the shoot was beset with serious problems. Filming was suspended for a fortnight without explanation. When it resumed, Rod LaRocque – originally cast as the character Marlin Arlington – had mysteriously disappeared, replaced by Paul Cavanaugh. The supposition is that LaRocque had become another of those silent-screen thespians whose voice didn't cut it in the world of the talkie. With over a third of the picture having been shot, much footage had to be discarded. Although he receives full directorial credit, not long afterwards Cedric Gibbons also disappeared from the set. Gibbons was an MGM art director. The chance Metro gave him to fulfil his ambitions behind the cameras transpired to be a costly indulgence, as 127,000 feet of footage was binned. He was replaced by Jack Conway. (That in his proper field Gibbons was talented is indicated by the fact that he designed the Academy Awards 'Oscar' statuette.) Additionally, an appendectomy for O'Sullivan necessitated her absence for over a month, with a double replacing her for some scenes. Then there was the unfortunate matter of Weissmuller suffering scraped skin in a sensitive place when astride a rhino. Nonetheless, when the shoot wrapped, the result was a picture that is now officially deemed 'culturally, historically or aesthetically significant' by the United States Library of Congress.

The events of *Tarzan and his Mate* take place nearly a year after those of *Tarzan the Ape Man*. Holt has returned with colleague Arlington to loot the elephant's graveyard discovered in the last (Weissmuller) movie. Unfortunately, Holt can't remember the way and needs Tarzan's help. Holt has the additional motive of wanting to return Jane – whom he loves – to civilisation, to which purpose he comes loaded down with tempting silk gowns, stockings and perfume.

Tarzan is not even heard until just under 21 minutes of the 95-minute movie, when his yodel rings out as the safari is attacked. When he does appear, Weissmuller is even more buff than in

Tarzan the Ape Man. He is living in a Garden of Eden idyll with Jane (who in the film is referred to as his wife, not the sexually suggestive 'mate' of the title). Jane (who is shown as having her own, more feminine yodel) comes into her own in this picture, which marks the point where her name and Tarzan's became synonymous in the popular consciousness. This is partly because she becomes a stronger character (faced with an advancing pride of lions, she quickly rustles up a barrier of flame) and partly because of the allure of Maureen O'Sullivan. The actress' beauty seems to blossom herein, her newly wild tresses tumbling about a chiselled, high-cheeked face into which glittering eyes seem set like jewels. This transcendent beauty is enhanced further by the skimpy two-piece outfit she wears in her new role as jungle housewife: audiences completely unused to screen flesh must have been maddeningly distracted by the creamy thighs and hips exposed by her high-cut loincloth.

Highlights of what would have been a mysterious, beautiful and scary spectacle on the pre-TV big screen are the scream- and drums-punctuated mass battle scenes between bearers and cannibals, and the veritable avalanches of big cats. At the climax, Tarzan calls on chimpanzees and elephants to save the day as the safari is deliberately exposed by natives to a shedload of lions. Counterpointing the thrills is much sweetness: Tarzan's teasing of Jane, Jane's leaps from high places into Tarzan's arms, Jane's excited trying on of the feminine attire brought by Holt, Tarzan's passing on to an eager Cheeta coffee he finds distasteful, and Tarzan exhibiting bewilderment at the music emanating from a gramophone. (A similar scene to the last appeared in the Crabbe movie, but disagreeably seemed to be inviting us to hold the ape-man in contempt.)

The treetop acrobatics are once more breathtaking, if again reliant on the fact that squinting audiences can't be quite sure, between the detail-obscuring monochrome and judicious long-shots, if Weissmuller's double is using a trapeze swing.

Although MGM were at least conscientious enough to affix large African-style ears to the more manageable Indian elephants they had elected to use, there is no realism here. What Tarzan and Jane might have in common when they can barely communicate is conveniently never explored. There's also lots of anthropomorphism, such as chimps kissing and holding hands, a hippo ferrying an injured Tarzan to shore and Cheeta navigating hazardous waters on a log. Showing Tarzan battling a crocodile is fair enough, but he also stabs to death a rhino, a more blameless and peaceable animal it's difficult to imagine. Meanwhile, Arlington is proved correct in his assumption that if he shoots an elephant it will realise it's a goner and instantly make a beeline for the elephant's graveyard. Despite the occasional bloody death, this is a celluloid comic strip, or even fairytale. However, it's a charming one. Or, as *Time* described it, 'A wild, disgraceful, highly entertaining orgy of comic, sensual and sadistic nonsense...'

The film could have been even better. In the original cut, Tarzan and Jane engage in a swimming scene in which Jane is nude. Excellent underwater cinematography and graceful, leisurely patterns by two Olympians – 1932 gold medallist Josephine McKim served as O'Sullivan's double – combine to create something exquisite. Even the notoriously prudish Burroughs adjudged it 'very beautiful and artistic.' Although audiences in more permissive American states and in some foreign territories did get to see it, the scene became the first major victim of the Hays Code, a list of rules designed to bring morality to the silver screen that were first properly enforced that year. The cut was a small tragedy. Happily, it has been restored for DVD releases.

Tarzan and his Mate was quite possibly the first cinema sequel of any description that was superior to its predecessor. It did according box office.

In the mid-1930s, the cinema-going public certainly had its pick of Tarzans. In early summer 1935, with the release of *The New Adventures of Tarzan*, Herman Brix became the third actor to portray the ape-man in as many years.

As was his custom with current movie ape-men, Burroughs had diplomatically enthused about Weissmuller to the media. Privately, he felt Weissmuller's Tarzan was a cartoon. Accordingly, in mid-1934, the author entered into a deal with businessmen Bennett Cohen, Ashton Dearholt and George Stout to form a company called Burroughs-Tarzan Enterprises, Inc, which would for the first time grant him total control over a celluloid Tarzan project. Added to the attraction of a cinema Tarzan that would for once be faithful to his original vision was, naturally, the welcome additional revenue stream it would bring to his financially overstretched world.

The project was beset with disaster throughout. Perhaps Burroughs should have foreseen this from the long sequence of misfortunes that had befallen his association with Tarzan cinema, whether it be his embittered departure from the very first Tarzan picture, having to pursue William Parsons for overdue monies or the potentially disastrous breach of contract he had ended up committing in regard to *Tarzan the Fearless*. The first misfortune to befall his own Tarzan cinematic venture was the fact that Messrs Cohen, Dearholt and Stout turned out to be the latest in a line of movie entrepreneurs who came up monetarily short: Burroughs had to guarantee a bank loan to them on the eve of shooting. As he had forgone an advance in return for equal profits and choice of leading man, this meant that Burroughs was effectively paying his supposed partners to make the film. The shoot itself was extremely challenging. The main part of it took place in Guatemala because, as independents, the producers had no studio and Dearholt, possessed of some experience of the Central American country, felt he could save a bundle. It ended up costing far more than it would have to film domestically. Guatemala had no film industry, engendering a complete 'location' shoot. The crew and actors had to endure primitive conditions, as well as the funny-tummy afflictions associated with unsanitary scenarios in tropical climes. They also had to put up with local corruption (the country's President secured a cameo in exchange for cooperation), wild storms and intense humidity, the latter of which destroyed film stock. The script was rewritten during the shooting. The budget ran out before the four-month shoot was over and the crew had to literally hide from creditors before they could return home.

That there were supposedly over a hundred candidates considered for the lead role sounds like Hollywood hype typical of the era. The loincloth went to Herman Brix, another man who had made his name in an Olympic sport (shot-putting). He had been in the running to play Tarzan for MGM but was ruled out when – you guessed it – he sustained an injury. Although not as muscular as Weissmuller, Brix was trim, solid, tall and looked good swinging on a vine. In fact, his physique is probably closer than Weissmuller's to what someone with Tarzan's jungle upbringing would realistically possess: it is only the visual shorthand employed by cinema that makes us assume the apeman's biceps should bulge. (Of course, *truly* realistic casting would see Tarzan played by a man with the freakishly over-developed forearms that would result from tree-swinging.) The handsome Brix additionally wore his hair in reasonably wild fashion, swept back off his forehead. Unfortunately, with many more lines to deliver than any previous sound-era Tarzan, he showed the drawbacks of casting an actor on the basis of his physique.

Contrary to some reports, Burroughs did not provide the basic story for what was originally entitled *Tarzan and the Green Goddess*. Correspondence between Burroughs, Dearholt and others involved in this production shows that Charles F Royal conceived the story told in his screenplay, which at some point acquired the new name *Tarzan in Guatemala*. As can be discerned, Guatemala was not serving as a substitute Africa the way that California and other locales had in previous Tarzan pictures. Although Tarzan had been seen in Paris and Algiers in *The Revenge of Tarzan*, this was the first cinematic Tarzan adventure to make an overt virtue of him visiting a foreign country, something that would in time become a tradition in the series. It may have been down to Burroughs, though, that the project followed the ill-advised template of recent novels in not featuring or mentioning Jane. The spirited 'feminine lead' Ula Vale (played by Ula Holt) would have been scant consolation to those cinemagoers charmed by the interplay between Weissmuller and O'Sullivan, especially those lucky enough to have seen the *Tarzan and his Mate* swimming scene.

The project ultimately became *The New Adventures of Tarzan* by way of *Tarzan and the Lost Goddess*. The story sees the ape-man travel Guatemala-way in search of the missing Paul D'Arnot. His path crosses with a father-and-daughter team with a dual mission of discovering jewels and a formula for explosives, both suspected to be hidden in the remnants of a Mayan city. A chaotic climax in a Mayan ruin sees Tarzan lift more than one native above his head and fling him to a bloody death.

The film explores fully the possibilities of the sound age. ERB purists will have been happy that the cinema Tarzan is heard to speak fluently and intelligently for the first time, even if this does begin another debate: why does the movie Tarzan have an American accent? Fidelity to Burroughs' novels is achieved in other ways as well. The name 'Lord Greystoke' litters the script and there are references to his English estates. Handily, Brix looks as good as a dickey-bowed Greystoke as he does a loinclothed Tarzan. His yodel can't match Weissmuller's, but that can be said of every successor to the swimmer. Brix tries gamely, with a yell that is a variation of (and in one example a possible straight lift from) the Jim Pierce radio Tarzan cry. Tarzan's primate friend is a strange combination of the MGM creation Cheeta and Burroughs' Nkima: although stated to be Nkima in the credits, Tarzan calls him 'Chkima' and the beast is played not by a monkey but a chimp.

Guatemala is depicted as having exactly the same wildlife as Africa. This is certainly ludicrous, but when the ape-man battles a lion, we for perhaps the first time in a Tarzan flick feel that someone has been saved from being eaten. This is because the direction (by Edward Kull) and cinematography (Kull and Ernest F Smith) is the best yet seen in a Tarzan movie. Even the 'cut-ins' are high-quality, with aerial photography impressively capturing herds of wildebeest and elephants (if in the act of running away from the aeroplane carrying the camera crew). The Guatemalan architecture and landscapes provide a welcome break from the now over-familiar African backdrops.

Unlike with *Tarzan and his Mate*, the production chaos was not a harbinger of commercial success. Even before the picture was in the theatres, Burroughs had lost faith in the venture, or at least its capacity to make him money. Had he not, Weissmuller would probably not have become the definitive Tarzan, for MGM's original deal with the author had been for just the two pictures already released. Burroughs agreed to extend terms with Metro in order to keep the cash coming in. The Metro deal in turn served to undermine *The New Adventures of Tarzan*, for MGM – far from being grateful to Burroughs for the chance he had provided them to add to the millions they had already made from his character – used underhand tactics to destroy its prospects. Movie theatres were warned that MGM's next Weissmuller Tarzan would not be offered to them if they elected to screen Brix as the ape-man. Consequently, *The New Adventures of Tarzan* was restricted to the smaller American theatre chains. There were even rumours that the unfavourable tone of the US reviews was down to pressure from MGM, then a mighty force in the land. Support for both theories is provided by the fact that MGM-immune overseas territories were as receptive to Brix as they had been to everyone else in a loincloth.

Burroughs-Tarzan, Inc responded to the MGM campaign by releasing the movie in three different ways, either undaunted by or unaware of the fact that such a strategy had simply sowed confusion with the Buster Crabbe *Tarzan the Fearless* feature-cum-serial. *The New Adventures of Tarzan* was made available as a 12-chapter serial, a 75-minute feature film and a combination of 75-minute feature film and 11 following serial chapters. No doubt the 'New' part of the title was also intended to add allure, but the corollary of such a designation is that, as soon as the release is succeeded by another, it becomes confusing. The poor domestic fortunes enjoyed by the venture may not have been the cause – some journalists had been stating that serials were old-fashioned even as far back as *The Son of Tarzan* in 1920 – but this would be the last Tarzan 'chapter play'. Despite MGM's alleged machinations, in summer 1938 Burroughs-Tarzan Enterprises, Inc edited a new 72-minute feature film from the last ten chapters of *The New Adventures of Tarzan*, inserting some unseen footage and releasing it as *Tarzan and the Green Goddess*. What was really another bite of the cherry was billed as an 'amazing sequel'.

Despite success in other serials, Brix was conscientious enough about his adopted trade to study acting and come back under a different name, Bruce Bennett. He was reasonably successful in his quest for credibility. Much the same could be said of *The New Adventures of Tarzan*. It wasn't anything like the flop MGM were hoping, but even had it been, it would still have served a useful function in notifying cinema audiences that the ape-man had an elevated hinterland not to be gleaned from the Weissmuller interpretation.

Burroughs-Tarzan Enterprises, Inc made three more films, but all were unrelated to Burroughs prose. Unfortunately, the problems encountered in the making and marketing of *The New Adventures of Tarzan* ended Burroughs' direct involvement in Tarzan movies and therefore any further possibility, at least in his lifetime, of the ape-man being represented on the big screen as he was depicted in his novels.

When *Tarzan's Quest* was serialised in six parts in *Blue Book* starting from October 1935, it was known as *Tarzan and the Immortal Men*. The bland final title was adopted for book publication. Its working title was more interesting: *Tarzan and Jane*.

Jane had been absent from Burroughs Tarzan prose for 11 years and nine stories. Some have surmised that her reappearance was a result of the author suddenly becoming less disenchanted with the female sex following the departure from his life of Emma Burroughs after 34 years of marriage and several years of domestic torpor. Burroughs divorced Emma while shooting of *The New Adventures of Tarzan* was taking place. By April of 1935, he was married to Florence Dearholt. A friend of his daughter Joan, as well as the recently divorced wife of one of his partners in Burroughs-Tarzan Enterprises, Inc, she was three decades the author's junior. Joan would later make clear to Burroughs biographer Robert W Fenton that she thought Dearholt had married her dad for money, but Florence seemed to bring Burroughs genuine happiness, at least for a while.

While the chronology supports the aforementioned theory about Lady Greystoke's revival, it actually seems more closely related to an attempt by Burroughs the previous year to assist his daughter in her career – one that, as with his play *You Lucky Girl!*, had come to naught. When Burroughs had declined to renew American Radio Features' contract for the Tarzan radio series, his three-page synopsis of his first intended story for his own Tarzan wireless venture had included a prominent role for Jane/Joan. Ultimately, however, Joan had not come back to the role, and the script had not been recorded. One is tempted to assert that someone whose recent work had shown he was desperately short of ideas for ape-man stories was bound not to let the contents of said script go to waste, but perversely ERB had declined the suggestion that he write a tie-in novel for the *New Adventures of Tarzan* serial. In any event, Burroughs now revived the radio storyline for what would be his nineteenth adult Tarzan book.

If Burroughs seems ambivalent about Jane's involvement in *Tarzan's Quest*, it is understandable if one considers that her personality – created long before he met his current wife – must have been informed by, or even based on, that of his first spouse. Jane greets her husband curiously formally when their parallel paths finally bisect ('Tarzan! Tarzan of the Apes'), while Tarzan doesn't speak to his wife once in the narrative. Neither would Jane be seen in the series again in anything other than passing, with Tarzan returning to his equivalent of staying down the pub with his mates: preferring to spend his time with the Waziri, Nkima and Tantor. On a related note, one wonders if the mission to resist ageing that forms part of the book's fabric stems from Burroughs' recent marriage to a woman in possession of energy levels far in his own past.

The plot of *Tarzan's Quest* revolves around a hunt led by Tarzan for the daughter of his Waziri friend Muviro. She has been abducted by the Kavuru, who are headed by the Greek God-like Kavandavanda. The latter estimates his age at a thousand years, the consequence of his tribe having discovered a formula that, when ingested monthly in the form of pills, can hold off the Grim Reaper indefinitely. As with anything in life that sounds too good to be true, there's a catch: in addition to pollen, plant roots and the spinal fluid of leopards, the pills' ingredients include 'the glands and blood of women – young women.' Consequently, the Kavuru regularly send out deadly scouting parties for females, having already worked their way through their own. Meanwhile, Jane has travelled over from the Greystokes' English estates both to visit her husband and to join pal Kitty and her friends in a hunt for a witch doctor who has 'an amazing formula for renewing youth and inducing longevity' – a curious, unresolved cul-de-sac in the tale that additionally betrays the frequent Burroughs flaw of a high level of coincidence. Inevitably, their plane crash-lands, inevitably the party includes a wisecracking man of the people (Neal Brown), inevitably Neal falls in love with another of the party (French maid Annette), inevitably Jane ends up in the clutches of Kavandavanda, and inevitably Kavandavanda is instantly smitten with Jane, despite his stated conviction that 'Man may only attain godliness alone. Woman weakens and destroys him.'

The reader doesn't blame him for being smote. Burroughs' *Tarzan and Jane* working title should have been adhered to (*Blue Book* changed it): this is as much Jane's book as her husband's. Burroughs' apparent sometime disdain for Jane/Emma/all womankind is rather ironic, because Jane as he draws her here is rarely less than likeable and admirable. No swooning damsel in distress, she copes pluckily with being surrounded by a hostile jungle (rendered in all its sweaty, sticky, scary glory, far from the cartoon projection of the wilderness of which Burroughs had sometimes been guilty) and the necessity to hunt for food (she despatches a lion threatening her intended quarry with some well-aimed arrows), and all done with a touchy-feeliness not in the frame of reference of her forest god.

At the end of an adventure that, despite its predictability, zips along smartly and contains a couple of shockers (murder and suicide among the jungle visitors), Tarzan puts paid to the Kavuru village by explosively crashing a plane into it.

Although the grotesquely evil Kavuru are white and although the Waziri are as usual depicted as noble, early on in the story the otherwise saintly Jane makes reference to 'smelly natives.' Perhaps we shouldn't be too surprised, then, that the close of the book sees the adventure's survivors dividing among themselves with inappropriate jollity the life-prolonging but blood-drenched pills.

The jacket and plates of the book version of *Tarzan's Quest* marked the end of an era. They saw the last Tarzan illustrations by J Allen St John. Although St John had been shunted aside before when Burroughs switched to Metropolitan and then started self-publishing, it had been because the writer felt he couldn't afford the artist's rates. Now it was more sentimentality that dictated a change as Burroughs' talented son John Coleman (Jack) became his regular illustrator. As St John had been drawing Tarzan interior plates almost without a break since *The Return of Tarzan* and covers since *The Beasts of Tarzan*, he had moulded the mental image of the ape-man for an entire generation of readers. (He also illustrated other Burroughs works, so had the same effect with John Carter *et al.*) St John may have been inconsistent in dressing Tarzan in a loincloth or a singlet but – perhaps partly due to a conscientiousness that meant he preferred to read a book twice before starting work – his art was usually stunning. He tended to favour two vivid figures centre-stage, although wasn't averse to colourful backdrops. Particularly memorable were his images of a giant eagle carrying off Tarzan on *Jungle Tales of Tarzan*, Tarzan almost forming an inverted comma with a lion he is battling on the cover of *Tarzan and the Jewels of Opar*, and the heaving wraparound battle panorama he provided for *Tarzan at the Earth's Core*. Many Burroughs fans cite one particular St John image of the ape-man as just as iconic as Clinton Pettee's immortal 1912 *All-Story* painting, even though it was unusually minimalist for him: his cover for the Grosset & Dunlap edition of *Tarzan and the Golden Lion*, on which the ape-man and Jad-bal-ja are seen in profile atop a hillock, a spear-carrying ape-man resting a hand on his wild companion as they both gaze at the horizon, all rendered in monochrome except, stylishly, for the gold-coloured cat. This striking, elegant image is now used as a logo by ERB, Inc and has even been turned into collectible statuettes.

From 1933, Tarzan featured in Whitman Publishing's Big Little Books and Better Little Books series. These were compact, sturdy hardbacks that featured novelisations of contemporaneous Tarzan movies and collections of Tarzan newspaper strips. Big Little Books also served another purpose in providing an avenue into print for the sequel to *The Tarzan Twins* on which Burroughs had precipitously embarked in 1928 and that had long lain in his metaphorical bottom drawer (in reality, probably his safe).

In 1934, with Volland gone to the wall, Whitman reprinted *The Tarzan Twins*. Evidently pleased by the sales, they proved receptive to the idea of a follow-up where Volland had not. *Tarzan and the Tarzan Twins, with Jad-Bal-Ja, The Golden Lion* was published in March 1936 (again, there was no prior magazine publication). As this was nearly a decade after *The Tarzan Twins'* original publication, much of the juvenile readership would likely have consisted of younger siblings of its readers. The sequel was designated a Big Big Book, and additionally served as a colouring book. The illustrations to which the readers were invited to apply their pencils were supplied by Juanita Bennett, who had provided the interiors for Whitman's edition of *The Tarzan Twins*. Unlike with that book, she also supplied the cover, and it was babyish even by Whitman's unthreatening standards, possessing that blocky style of much kids-oriented art of the era, as well as a technical naiveté (one of the twins has his back to the reader). When Canaveral Press issued the two Tarzan Twins books in one volume in 1963, things had moved on sufficiently for the publisher to commission a stylish cover from Roy G Krenkel that in no way condescended to the reader.

The story is stated as following on directly from that of *The Tarzan Twins*. A lionclothed and tooled-up (jungle-style) Dick and Doc leave the Greystoke estate in the company of Tarzan and Jad-bal-ja. They get separated from the ape-man when he goes off to investigate something in the jungle that is making his lion nervous. When a storm breaks, they also get separated from the golden lion (whose 'cruel, round, yellow eyes' make them fearful in any case). Trying to make their way back to the Greystoke estate, the 'twins' come across some outcast Oparians who are planning to set up an alternative to that city in which they have decided that 'Kla', a re-christened kidnapped missionary's 12-year-old daughter, will be their new high priestess. The boys decide to rescue her. This seems a presumptuous plan for a pair of tykes until a hidden Dick starts systematically slaughtering Oparian priests with his bow and arrows. Further sadism that it's difficult to imagine in a modern-day kids' book occurs when Tarzan arrives in the nick of time to prevent Dick dying on the sacrificial altar: he unleashes Jad-bal-ja on the high priest to deadly effect. The girl – real name Gretchen von Harben – is returned safely to civilisation.

Tarzan and the Tarzan Twins, with Jad-bal-ja, the Golden Lion was an absolute mouthful of a title but possibly not Burroughs' doing: his working title was *Jad-bal-ja and the Tarzan Twins*. It was at least not confusion-sowing like the title that Canaveral Press gave their otherwise useful '63 compendium: *Tarzan and the Tarzan Twins*.

No particular problems with chronology are caused by the

Tarzan Twin books. Because they are not meant for an adult audience, both are considered by Burroughs fans – to use a contemporary anorak phrase that would have no doubt made the author harrumph in contempt – 'non-canon'.

By the mid-1930s, Burroughs' ape-man-related energy levels were getting so low that he could muster only enough enthusiasm to write Tarzan novellas.

While *Tarzan the Untamed* had consisted of two separate magazine serialisations bolted together, it was a fat tome whose two constituent parts could conceivably have been issued as separate books. *Tarzan and the Magic Men* (published in *Argosy* in three parts from September 1936) and its sequel *Tarzan and the Elephant Men* (*Blue Book* in three parts from November 1937) would have been rather slim affairs if issued alone rather than combined in the novel *Tarzan the Magnificent*. Nor did they feature anything like the inspiration that marked the constituent parts of *Untamed*.

Of the two parts, *Magic Men* is the superior, even if it wanders again into the type of science fiction/fantasy and post-modernism that is such a far cry from the ape-man's original quasi-realism. Like several of the Tarzan tales of this period, it is set in Abyssinia (now Ethiopia), where the ape-man has journeyed at the request of an unnamed emperor 'to investigate a rumor that a European power is attempting to cause the defection of a native chief by means of bribery.' Considering the lethargic indifference Tarzan has shown toward the entire world of late, this mission seems a somewhat unconvincing and contrived way to manoeuvre him into a new adventure. Having said that, it is a blessed relief how agreeable Tarzan is in this story.

When Tarzan stumbles upon the Kaji and the Zuli, the author at least injects a couple of additional dimensions into his hoary old device of two marooned white settlements at war with each other, firstly in the form of a pair of magicians who hold great power in their respective communities via a form of telepathy and secondly by a motif of miscegenation – the warrior women of the Kaji have turned themselves Caucasian by kidnapping white men – that surprisingly seems to have an enlightened authorial motive. American writer Stanley Wood and his two guides are the compulsory interlopers from civilisation whom Tarzan has to rescue from danger. When he does – repeatedly – they all engage in discussion about who their bronzed saviour is. 'Say, he flits through the trees like a regular Tarzan,' remarks one, once again whimsically and self-indulgently placing the ape-man in a world betwixt fiction and reality.

Wood and his guides reappear in *Tarzan and the Elephant Men*, as does Gonfala, the Kaji Queen with whom Wood falls in love in *Tarzan and the Magic Men*. That this story is less inspired than its predecessor is demonstrated by the fact that Burroughs can't even be bothered inventing a new lost city but instead has the ape-man return to Cathne and Athne from *Tarzan and the City of Gold* for an adventure that in some respects is just a miniature rehash of that novel. A nice scene in which Tarzan generates favourable karma for himself via his good-natured rescue of a trapped Tantor provides one of the few moments of pleasure.

Jack Byrne, editor of *Argosy*, refused to publish *Tarzan and the Elephant Men* even though the novella to which it was a sequel had appeared in his magazine. He wrote Burroughs a long letter that constituted a polite but passionate critique of where the author was going wrong in his writing, condemning Tarzan's recent lack of motivation and the fact that, when he uninterestedly wandered into the affairs of others, those people were themselves uninteresting. He also suggested that Burroughs was descending into a stultifying style because he was too isolated from other authors and literary trends. Although Burroughs responded by selling the story to *Blue Book* and pointing out to Byrne that many publishers had been wrong about *Tarzan of the Apes*, he also conceded, 'I am rather fed up on the type of stories I have been writing for over a quarter of a century. I have said everything that I can think of saying about Tarzan, and said it over and over again.' Perhaps it was the weariness Burroughs revealed in this letter that explained why he had latterly been allowing editors to make the sort of changes to his writing that he would once have refused. Perhaps it was also because he felt he couldn't afford to make a fuss, with the rates paid by pulps continuing the downwards spiral into which they had been tipped by the Great Depression. Certainly, without the ancillary Tarzan profits – especially the $40,000 per picture he was being paid by MGM – it's difficult to imagine that Burroughs would have been able to support his lifestyle at this point purely with writing.

As with *Tarzan and the Leopard Men*, *Tarzan the Magnificent* was published out of sequence, collated and issued by Burroughs only after his next Tarzan story, *Tarzan and the Forbidden City*, had made it into book form.

Just when MGM were on a roll with Weissmuller – two strong films, two box office hits, an extension of their contract opening up the path to more bounty – they almost threw it away.

The origins of the failure of the third MGM movie, *Tarzan Escapes*, lie in the same sort of squeamishness that had seen the naked underwater ballet removed from its predecessor. This time, it wasn't the bare flesh that exercised the guardians of morality (O'Sullivan's no-way-is-she-wearing-knickers outfit had been replaced by a decorous raggedy dress), but gore and horror. In July 1935, MGM put into production a movie called *The Capture of Tarzan,* written by *Tarzan the Ape Man* screenwriter Cyril Hume. An apparently tough and sinewy proposition, it saw white hunter Captain Fry arriving in Tarzan's patch with the objective of capturing the ape-man and taking him back to civilisation to exhibit him like a beast in a cage. Jane's cousins are with him, although their aim is to help Tarzan's mate claim a fortune she doesn't know she has been bequeathed. Mass ritualistic slaughter by natives, bloodthirsty pygmies, vampire bats and gargantuan lizards were some of the perils faced by the interlopers and/or the ape-man against sometimes gothic, fog-wreathed backdrops. At the end, Tarzan despatched Fry with extreme sadism. It sounds like the best ape-man picture up to that point from any studio.

MGM's satisfaction over their second incremental improvement on the Tarzan franchise was short-lived. Preview audiences turned out to be hostile. One wonders how seriously to take the reports that children were terrified by such things as giant bats swooping out of the sky to carry off screaming porters: the fact that various leagues of decency formed some of the protesting parties suggests that adults were presuming to take umbrage on behalf of children secretly thrilled as they watched through their fingers. On the other hand, the Frankenstein and Dracula pictures of the same period that seem so tame to us today were never seen by the young then, so depictions of terror and bloodshed may have been genuinely unsettling to those of tender years. Although there is anecdotal evidence that the original edit – completed in late 1935 – was mistakenly shown on re-release as late as the 1950s, no copy of it seems to survive today.

The film's director Jim McKay – unenthusiastic about the cuts and reshoots ordered by the studio – was replaced by John Farrow, but the latter's changes were still not enough to please Metro. (Although Farrow, like McKay, received no formal credit, proof of the fact that he was on set at some point is the seven children he proceeded to have with Maureen O'Sullivan.) Richard Thorpe replaced Farrow, and indeed directed every other MGM Tarzan flick of that era. The family-oriented end-product saw the vampire bats excised, the ritualistic slaughter scenes toned down, much anthropomorphic chimpanzee behaviour introduced, jolly character actor Herbert Mundin flown in as a comedy foil and a somewhat familiar climax added that featured Tarzan summoning an elephant herd to save the day. Also in the spirit of 'Well, it worked before' was the inclusion of the crocodile fight from *Tarzan and his Mate* (yes, the exact same one). Even the title was made less hard-hitting, *Tarzan Escapes* being limp and puzzling.

It wasn't until November 1936, two years after the start of

production in an era when a movie would generally be in the theatres only months after filming began, that the 89-minute finished picture made the screens. MGM tried to brazen out the public knowledge of its troubled gestation by trumpeting on the posters '2 years to produce!' but, decades before the likes of *Ishtar* and *Waterworld*, *Tarzan Escapes* was a movie that had a pre-release bad smell hanging over it. Its jinxed reputation went beyond the production problems: producer Irving Thalberg died a week after completion and John Buckler (Captain Fry) perished in a road accident a week before release. Whether or not the bad portents worked to prejudice reviewers, the movie was panned, although *Variety*, for instance, could hardly be blamed for the 'derisive laughter' its reporter heard around him in the theatre.

It's an indictment of this picture's quality that the biggest impact it had on the culture is its apparent legacy to *The Flintstones*: *Tarzan Escapes* features a rope-and-pulley lift to Tarzan's treehouse operated by a docile elephant, an ape-powered fan, a baking oven constructed of mud and washing basins made of upturned tortoiseshells.

Although Sol Lesser had sold three of his remaining Tarzan options to MGM, he had astutely hung onto one. Seeing the ill fortunes of *Tarzan Escapes*, he decided the time was right to re-enter the game.

He was profoundly less astute in the man he chose to fill the loincloth. Although they had enjoyed mixed fortunes in the role, the last three men cast as Tarzan had been Olympic competitors. His plumping for Glenn Morris – gold medallist in the decathlon in Munich in 1936 – was therefore on the surface not a bad choice, especially as he was trim, muscular, 6' 2" and (a little-reported prerequisite for a movie Tarzan) smooth-chested. To those in the know – which didn't include much of the general public at a time when such things weren't widely reported – Morris' behaviour at those Olympics, when he ripped off the blouse of Nazi documentary filmmaker Leni Riefenstahl and kissed her breasts in front of 100,000 astonished spectators, made him even more natural for a role associated with animalism. Lesser's Jane-equivalent was also pretty wild: Eleanor Holm was well-known for a dissolute lifestyle, and not just as a result of having been kicked off the 1936 US Olympic swimming team for drinking and gambling. Possibly to capitalise on her wild-child image, Lesser gave Holm's character her own Christian name.

Although the Elmo Lincoln picture *The Revenge of Tarzan* was now nearly two decades in the past and marooned in the already antiquated silent era, calling the new picture *Tarzan's Revenge* seems a little lazy. However, that was in keeping with an enterprise that Lesser himself later admitted was a 'cheap quickie.' The script by Robert Lee Johnson and Jay Vann depicted the Reeds, a couple of big game hunters (one of whom, in another piece of gimmick casting, was played by famous gossip columnist Hedda Hopper) arriving in Africa with their grown daughter Eleanor and her fiancé. A turbaned, pipe-inhaling nawab takes umbrage when Eleanor declines to become the hundredth wife in his harem, and compels her to spend the rest of the picture evading his clutches. In the process of saving the day, Tarzan speaks a total of four words ('Tarzan' twice, 'Eleanor' and 'good'), not counting his yodel, which – as usual for a rival movie Tarzan's – sounds pitiful next to Weissmuller's. There are some good moments. The by-now *de rigueur* interludes featuring a chimpanzee engaging in play are undeniably cute. The picture also has an equivalent of the Johnny Weissmuller-Josephine McKim underwater ballet, with the two leads engaged in exciting synchronised water-cutting (clothed). Additionally, the warlike natives – all facepaint, feathers and nose-rings – are fearsome, while the photography captures nicely the nabob's opulence. However, D Ross Lederman's direction is plodding and the fact that three of the main actors are not trained thespians inevitably shows, no matter how likeable the spirited Holm.

Although the scriptwriters find room in a rather short picture (70 minutes) to provide another ostentatious display of Holm's swimming prowess, Tarzan is on screen for just ten minutes. Maybe this is because Lesser realised he had made a terrible casting mistake. Pictures of Morris hurling javelins in his previous life show his muscles straining impressively, but such sights apparently blinded Lesser to the drawback of his face. Once again, he has cast as the ideal of male beauty someone who looks like a Marx brother, in this case Harpo, the silent lunatic of the four famous film brothers, something exacerbated by his hills-and-dales hair. When he doesn't look too silly, Morris simply looks too nice. Having said that, there was no call for Weissmuller's wife Lupe Velez to kick him in the shins at a Hollywood party with the cry, 'You are not heem!'

Neither Morris nor Holm ever acted again (many unkind critics disputed they had done so in *Tarzan's Revenge*) and the film was a flop upon its January 1938 release. Having emerged from the jungle in a mauled state twice in a row, one might imagine Lesser would have left well enough alone, but he would be back in the vicinity again.

Controversy and confusion has raged about the Burroughs book that was published in late 1938 as *Tarzan and the Forbidden City* but serialised in *Argosy Weekly* in six parts starting in March 1938 as *The Red Star of Tarzan*.

Well before that serialisation, its storyline had formed the basis of the 1934 radio serial *Tarzan and the Diamond of Asher*, whose writing was credited to Rob Thompson. Also before the magazine serialisation, Burroughs wrote a continuity storyline of it for the Tarzan newspaper strip that, deemed unacceptable, was rewritten by one Don Garden. Derivation wasn't the only issue. When the *Argosy* serialisation started, the fact that Paul D'Arnot was referred to as 'Pierre' and that several Mangani language terms were incorrect led some to assume that it was a ghost-written work. The fact that it contained slapdash and stereotyped writing that was of a parodic level only strengthened this impression. In fact, the reality was less sinister and perhaps more depressing: overzealous sub-editing by *Argosy*'s Ben Nelson and Burroughs Mitchell was responsible for the mistakes and inconsistencies, while Burroughs' complete lack of interest accounted for how awful was the writing.

The book version follows closely Burroughs' semi-rejected script continuity. It features a Tarzan lookalike yet again in the shape of adventurer Brian Gregory, although even Burroughs seems bored with the hackneyed and implausible device, because he ceases to make play with it a short while in. Gregory has gone missing while on a quest to find the lost city of Ashair, which reputedly hosts the legendary Father of Diamonds. D'Arnot, in his last appearance in a Burroughs Tarzan tale, is assisting Gregory's father in his search for his son. (In a parallel of Burroughs' real-life infatuation with a woman 30 years his junior, D'Arnot has the hots for Brian Gregory's 19-year-old sister Helen.) Tarzan displays no inclination to remove himself from the back of Tantor, where he is found lolling, until he is informed his old friend is in the area.

Ashair is one of a pair of warring cities – the other being Thobo – located in an extinct volcano. We are left to infer from sketchy details that the cities are descended from ancient Egypt: unlike with his previous lost settlements, Burroughs can't be bothered devising a detailed backstory. Nor, with the exception of the appearance of some giant sea horses, can he be roused enough to make anything special of the potentially intriguing fact that parts of the plot are set underwater. Burroughs musters the energy to throw in a baby Tyrannosaurus Rex, but not to explain its presence. The contrast is painful between such authorial lethargy and the incredible enthusiasm and inventiveness behind that dinosaur-bedecked lost city Pal-ul-don.

One of the few moments of inspiration comes when Tarzan is confronted not by the customary single lion but by a pair of Numas: he escapes from the predicament by lifting one above his head and hurling it at the other. The lions fight, leaving Tarzan to vanquish the tired victor. Meanwhile a twist in the tail that seems a nice touch falls apart when one starts to think about it. Atan Thome, Brian Gregory's rival in the hunt for the Father of Diamonds, opens the casket containing his object of desire only to find it contains – a lump of coal. Er, but how would the primitive Ashairians have acquired the geological knowledge of how diamonds are formed? By now it was obvious that Burroughs couldn't give a toss about such internal contradictions.

Perhaps allowances should be made for the fact that the story was originally intended for radio, which medium doesn't have the nuances of prose. However, an author of Burroughs' vast experience could surely have made good such inherent problems. The argument could even be made that his work as author was this time made easier by an existing plot.

Not that Burroughs was completely without authorial pride. When he published the story as a novel, he reinstated his original manuscript, jettisoning all the changes that his correspondence shows he acquiesced to *Argosy* making. The magazine version's title derives from a Tarzan-less prologue in which a witch doctor babbles about a red star that will lead to unimaginable riches. The fact that the prologue was not included in the book and that *Argosy* was part of the Munsey 'Red Star' line suggests that the prologue was contrived self-promotion written by Burroughs at their behest, or even written by *Argosy* without Burroughs' knowledge. Incidentally, by means not easily fathomable, the magazine version did leak out into book form: for instance, it was printed in the UK New English Library paperback of *Tarzan and the Forbidden City* in the 1970s.

Two novellas followed by a novel based on an already-broadcast radio series unambiguously marked a trajectory of diminishing enthusiasm. It was one that would continue. From here, Burroughs' Tarzan work slowed to a crawl.

Although *Tarzan Escapes* had had its problems, a proposition as strong as the Weissmuller Tarzan franchise was not to be thrown away on the basis of one flop, nor even the bombshell dropped by Maureen O'Sullivan that she wanted out. Accordingly, in June 1939, after a gap of two-and-a-half years, MGM came back with a Tarzan movie that reinvigorated the series.

Weissmuller's contract with MGM forbade him taking other roles between Tarzan pictures. The happy-go-lucky Weissmuller filled his days by throwing himself into a glamorous lifestyle and taking part in aquacades, a then-popular form of entertainment in which people who had made their name in competitive swimming, such as Weissmuller, Eleanor Holm and Buster Crabbe, would wow the crowds with water-based feats. O'Sullivan, however, was a serious actress for whom the Tarzan franchise was a limited and increasingly limiting quadrant of her career. She was also beginning an epic series of pregnancies. Added to that was her hatred of the chimp playing Cheeta, which for some reason insisted on trying to tear chunks out of her. Accordingly, she asked to be given the traditional no-way-back exit. The studio acquiesced to her character's death, and shooting started in January 1939 on what was originally called *Tarzan in Exile*.

MGM – perhaps mindful that one of the reasons for the failure of rival Tarzan pictures was that a lone ape-man had no one to play off – decided to fill the hole O'Sullivan's departure would leave in the Tarzan family. Just as the fourth Tarzan novel had resorted to the canny device of providing the ape-man a son – as had the fourth Tarzan cinema venture – so the fourth Weissmuller film gave the ape-man male progeny. However, 'Boy' was no Korak, although he was a Greystoke. The screenplay by Cyril Hume depicts a plane crashing in Tarzan and Jane's territory. It carries the nephew of one Lord Greystoke, his wife and his infant son. The latter is the only survivor in the wreck and Jane is keen to adopt him, over Tarzan's initial objections. This set-up was deemed necessary in light of the fact that, unlike in the books, the MGM Tarzan and Jane had never been shown to be formally married: the Hays Code banned either depiction or overt suggestion of pre-martial intercourse.

Tarzan quickly comes to love the child he and his mate have prosaically named Boy, even running down female antelope to provide him with milk. This was mirrored by the real-life affection between Weissmuller and Johnny Sheffield, the seven-year-old from Pasadena over whose casting as Boy Weissmuller had final say. Their chemistry shines through in the traditional scene showing off Weissmuller's swimming prowess. The two perform their own lengthy underwater ballet, one that culminates in Tarzan grabbing hold of a giant turtle while Boy clings to Tarzan's ankle. This and other examples of a loinclothed-but-happy nuclear family can't help but be endearing. Jane, incidentally, is sometimes seen behind furniture, baskets of fruit and other handy means of masking O'Sullivan's swollen belly.

After a gap of several years, the inevitable snake enters the Garden of Eden when a search party comes looking for the heir to the Greystoke fortune. The slimy Austin Lancing (Ian Hunter) is particularly keen on reaping the benefits that go with power of attorney. Jane doesn't know this and is persuaded that Boy will be better off brought up in London. She has to cruelly deceive Tarzan to enable Boy's whisking away to civilisation.

As originally scripted, Tarzan's hurt at that was to be nothing compared with his devastation when Jane received a fatal spear injury from the Zambeli tribe who captured the departing safari. Ironically, considering the fact that she had already made her last appearance in his novels, Edgar Rice Burroughs was furious when he heard that Jane was for the chop. MGM responded to his I'll-sue telegram by pointing out that their contract banned them from compromising Tarzan's character, not anyone else's. However, although Jane's creator was not able to stay the studio's hand, public opinion was. The outcry that erupted when details appeared in newspapers of Jane's intended fate motivated Metro to ask O'Sullivan to shoot an alternate ending wherein she recovered and she, Tarzan, Boy and their chimpanzee allies made for home atop a trio of elephants.

There is a sense of *déjà vu* attending some of the 82-minute film: Tarzan once more calls upon a herd of elephants at the climax to enable a rescue from a hostile village, while the footage of him killing that poor rhino is resurrected from *Tarzan and his Mate*. *Trader Horn* wildlife and scenery stock is also poured in (the only location shooting done for this picture was in Florida, so as to take advantage of its crystal-clear waters). However, *Tarzan Finds a Son!* provided a Tarzan picture with a very different, warm tone, and furthermore increased the appeal of the series to kids. Those who didn't like the new direction – an American family set-up transplanted to a forest treehouse – would have to get used to it: Boy would appear in all but one of the remaining eight Weissmuller Tarzans.

'Rather fed up' with his writing, Tarzan in particular, he may have been, Burroughs seemed to feel no fatigue when it came to promoting the ape-man and widening the character's markets. In mid-1939, he was busily trying to stoke up interest in his new idea, the Tarzan Clans of America. For this proposed organisation, Burroughs wrote privately of an aim of two million members. A project that sought to rival the Boy Scouts, even to turn every boy in the United States into a miniature Tarzan, wasn't as presumptuous or over-ambitious as it might seem. When at this juncture a leading American magazine declared Tarzan to be 'the best-known literary character of the 20th Century,' it was not exaggerating. Who at that point in history had not been repeatedly exposed to Tarzan via books, magazines, cinema, stage, radio, comic strip or a combination thereof? What child had not fantasised that he was the ape-man? (And indeed what adult had not fantasied something else about Johnny Weissmuller or Maureen O'Sullivan?)

The Clans could be viewed as being in the Burroughs tradition of cutting out the middle man: just as he had become involved in making Tarzan films and radio programmes and had begun publishing his own novels, so he was now seeking to oversee personally an equivalent of Signal Oil's Tarzan Club, which itself had been a commercialised variant of Herman Newman's Tarzan Tribes.

For a membership fee of one dollar, kids (girls were allowed to join at the discretion of the male Clan members and with the permission of their parents) would get a membership card, the latest Burroughs novel and the Clans' Official Guide. Although Burroughs made a big mistake in putting an illustration of a Waziri, not Tarzan, on the cover, thus rendering it instantly less covetable, the Guide was quite substantial: Burroughs was responsible for all of its 32 pages of text, which was like a version of the minutely detailed notes he habitually wrote on the planets and lost cities traversed by his novels' protagonists. It contained instructions on Clan formation, ranks (chief, sub-chief, medicine man, scribe, high priest, etc), conduct of meetings, initiation, Clan songs, Clan dances, construction of weapons and dismissal and demotion of members. It was rounded off with an ape-English dictionary.

Yet for all the energy put into it by this man approaching his sixty-fifth birthday, for all the value-for-money of the membership fee (sending members his latest novel would have resulted in a net loss for the author) and for all the success of the movies of Weissmuller – whom Burroughs obtained MGM's permission to name 'Chief of Chiefs' – the Clan project got nowhere. The reason seems to be that Burroughs did not have a large organisation like Signal Oil behind him, with its easy access to vast numbers of potential recruits. He had envisaged MGM as fulfilling this role, hoping they would distribute leaflets and information about the Clans in the lobbies of theatres showing *Tarzan Finds a Son!* (This was before anti-trust rulings stopped movie studios owning the venues in which their products were screened.) When MGM disappointingly requested only 60 copies of the Official Guide, it was clear that they were not planning on providing the huge promotional springboard Burroughs had thought they might.

That their booklet is now an incredibly rare collector's item is a stark measure of the Clans' failure. Whereas Signal Oil had 415,000 members at its peak, it is estimated that only around 200 copies were ever distributed of the Official Guide of the Tarzan Clans of America. Teenager Herman Newman had done far better back in 1916.

*

At the end of the 1930s, Burroughs wrote to magazine editors about a new idea he had for Tarzan: to turn him, in a series of short stories, into 'a jungle Sherlock Holmes.' The ape-man would deploy his wilderness nous to solve mysteries like the murder of a colonial official, the kidnapping of a woman by white slavers or the disappearance of a big-game hunter.

On the surface, this notion was an intriguing one, suggesting a fresh impetus for the ape-man. The format ERB proposed also seemed wise: after all, the author had previously employed the short-story form to work his way out of a narrative impasse to fine effect with *Jungle Tales of Tarzan*. Perhaps the latter is why across the course of 1939 Burroughs started on fulfilling his vision of Tarzan short fiction despite the fact that the response his idea received from editors was not exactly overwhelming enthusiasm, and despite warnings from at least two editors of the low remuneration he could expect per story. When he did submit the results of his endeavours, Burroughs sometimes allowed extensive rewriting by his unimpressed clients. Humility is always an admirable quality, but it seems rather sad that a man presiding over a million-dollar industry like Tarzan whose track record as a successful author was unassailable should so readily acquiesce to his art being tampered with by anonymous sub-editors for the sake of pitiful sums like $250.

Following the first story, Burroughs abandoned his jungle detective plan, if not the short-story format. 'Tarzan and the Jungle Murders' (published in *Thrilling Adventures* in June 1940) apparently quickly apprised him of the fact that his hero being able to follow spoor with his keen sense of smell hardly rivalled the dazzling deductive armoury of the man at 221b Baker Street, and that his own particular narrative strength did not lie in the incremental reveal. Following the second story, 'Tarzan and the Champion' (actually the first of the stories to be published, appearing in *Blue Book* in April 1940), Burroughs abandoned the idea of short ape-man fiction. In the first two months of 1940, he wrote a new novel (*Tarzan and the Madman*), then turned his attention to his other franchises until the following November, when he embarked on a novella he called 'Tarzan and the Castaways' (serialised in three parts in *Argosy Weekly* starting in August 1941 with the second-hand and nonsensical title 'The Quest of Tarzan'). The two short stories and the novella were somewhat ghettoised in Burroughs' lifetime, with the author not bothering to collate them into a book. They saw the light of day again only in 1965 via the compendium *Tarzan and the Castaways*, when – a decade-and-a-half after his creator had passed away – the world was suddenly hungry for literary Tarzan once more.

It's difficult to assess the only version of 'Tarzan and the Jungle Murders' to have seen print, as, according to Irwin Porges, it is just as much a *Thrilling Adventures*' sub-editor's work as Burroughs'. (Had he still been alive, Burroughs would never have allowed the magazine version, rather than his own, to be printed in the *Castaways* compendium.) It's a mixture of Poirot and Tarzan, with the ape-man solving a murder mystery by his jungle wits but gathering everybody together to unmask the culprit in classic drawing-room whodunit style. Unfortunately, Burroughs can't write in the whodunit style. Not only is the mystery a no-brainer, but he fails to drop any hints along the way and engages in the ultimate cheat by referring to a crucial clue for the first time right at the end. 'Tarzan and the Champion' sees Tarzan's jungle invaded by heavyweight boxer 'One-Punch' Mullargan, who has come with his manager to hunt game, if hunting is what one calls machine-gunning zebra. Mullargan and the ape-man engage in a bout of formalised fisticuffs that Tarzan inevitably easily wins, although the two then join forces to rescue the boxer's manager from a tribe of genuinely scary cannibals. The story culminates in Mullargan responding to the suggestion that Tarzan possesses the fighting ability to take his championship away from him, 'Who? Dat bum?' This brief story is amusing and serviceable.

Tarzan and the Madman, Burroughs' return to ape-man novels, was written over the first three months of 1940. It is a groan-inducingly bad Tarzan *reductio ad absurdum* featuring the nth Tarzan double, the nth sinister safari that irritatingly serves to keep Tarzan offstage and the nth warring lost city containing the nth high priest keen on human sacrifice. Colin T Randolph Jr (or 'Rand', also known – slightly confusingly for those who had read *Tarzan and the Lion Man* – as 'God') doesn't actually possess Tarzan's looks, but it is risible enough that the author has him mistaken for the ape-man and – due to the amnesia and delusion hinted at in the title – has him believe he is him: Tarzan's identity is one not possible to step into without exceedingly uncommon strength and heroism. Apart from the evocative or powerful scene or two to be found in every Burroughs book, the only thing to be said for *Tarzan and the Madman* is that it's short.

Magazine editors had put up over the years with a lot of substandard plotting and unlikely scenarios from Burroughs. However, in 1940, 28 years after *All-Story* had bitten Burroughs' hand off to publish *Tarzan of the Apes*, the pulps had finally had enough. Despite the allure of Tarzan's name and his continuing popularity in the media of comic strip and film, *Tarzan and the Madman* was the first adult Tarzan story that Burroughs failed to place with a magazine. In their replies to Michael S Mill – Burroughs' rep-cum-agent, eight years in his employ – some magazine editors added withering criticism to the rejection, one lamenting, 'Tarzan doesn't seem to be Tarzan anymore.' ERB clearly knew the work wasn't up to much. Significantly, he didn't bother putting it out as a book, unlike a subsequent Tarzan story also rejected by magazines.

'Tarzan and the Castaways'/'The Quest of Tarzan', written at the end of 1940, actually indicates that Burroughs was on the right path in reducing word count. Although it contains absolutely nothing new, the fact that it is about half the length of an average novel leads Burroughs to dispense with disjointed capture-chase-recapture and safari in-fighting scenarios. He distils everything to its essence. The brisk pace and lean prose mean that our patience isn't tried, even despite us being presented yet again with such staples as an ape-man who has lost his memory through a blow to the head, a young couple who fall in love, a lost city that practises human sacrifice and a fight to the death with a lion. Something else that assists the energised feeling is a change in backdrop. Following a shipwreck, the action takes place on the uncharted Pacific island of Uxmal, although the fact that the ship has a cargo of African animals that Tarzan compassionately frees helps give the wildlife a familiar look. The lost city this time is of Mayan descent, which enables Burroughs to indulge his wont of providing an interesting historical nugget or two. One doesn't even have to buy into Burroughs' love of societal hierarchy to delight in a passage wherein a snooty woman bad-mouthing Tarzan is astounded when another character icily puts her right with the comment, 'Madam, "that creature", as you call him, is John Clayton, Lord Greystoke, an English viscount.' The chief villains of the story, incidentally, are Germans. With the Second World War now raging beyond America's shores, Burroughs seems to be insisting 'I was right after all' about his depiction of the Hun in *Tarzan the Untamed*.

In fact, America's entry into the war in December 1941 was the main reason Tarzan – and indeed fiction – shortly disappeared off Burroughs' agenda. Once the United States entered the conflict, Burroughs – aside from his war journalism and two unpublished (non-Tarzan) scraps – wrote nothing until June 1944. Paper rationing also brought to a halt the printing schedules of Edgar Rice Burroughs, Inc. Considering the unproductive and rejection-strewn nature of Burroughs' Tarzan writing recently, the war may have come to him as a welcome intervention.

Despite his recent artistic failings, Burroughs found while fulfilling his new role of America's oldest war correspondent that Tarzan's impact on the culture was both inescapable and positive. He was frequently surrounded by journalists half his age and younger who had been weaned on Tarzan films and, in some cases, had learnt some of their writing chops from his ape-man novels. He rarely had to carry his own bags as he travelled the world.

*

Tarzan made his phonograph debut in 1941 in the form of two Decca record sets which contained ERB, Inc-produced ape-man sound adventures that utilised the same production crew as the radio show. Elliott Lewis was the man picked to voice Tarzan.

Meanwhile, should they have been left in any doubt despite the way he had seen off all pretenders so far, the public would be caused no more confusion during Weissmuller's remaining occupancy of the loincloth about who was the real movie ape-man. Film studios, producers and Janes were subject to change, but all eight Tarzan pictures released between 1941 and 1948 featured Johnny. His position was further underscored by a doubling of the rate of new releases. In contrast to its impact on Burroughs' Tarzan writing, the Second World War was a period in which the cinematic Tarzan industry was cranked up, seeing the release of no fewer than five Tarzan flicks, even if the production of the first of these predated America's entry into the conflict.

Tarzan's Secret Treasure was a minor and short (81 minutes) offering. Despite MGM trotting out the 'two-years-in-the-making' spiel again, shooting wrapped two months after its June 1941 start. It was released in December 1941, the very month of the Pearl Harbor attack. (John Coleman Burroughs' comic strip *John Carter of Mars* debuted on that historic 7 December itself.) An early script outline by veteran Tarzan screenwriter Cyril Hume had revived the idea of Jane being killed off, this time to enable the ape-man to take up with a glamorous big-game hunter. However, MGM had only recently agreed to a salary hike to retain Maureen O'Sullivan. Myles Connolly and Paul Gangelin subsequently devised a concoction with less of a sizzle factor. Their story involved the revelation that Tarzan's area of the jungle is awash with gold, which of course is of no use or interest to Tarzan, his mate and son, but of vast intrigue to nefarious elements of a group of scientific explorers. The bad guys kidnap Boy in order to compel Tarzan to lead them to the gold, but they wind up in peril in a native village before – what else? – Tarzan calls an elephant herd to the rescue. In other words, nothing new whatsoever – unless Tarzan being introduced to whiskey counts. The second-hand feel was aggravated by budget cuts that took place after the death of producer Irving Thalberg, ones which necessitated the re-use yet again of the crocodile fight from *Tarzan and his Mate* and further airing of *Trader Horn* travelogue.

There are plenty of the now expected underwater scenes, for which Florida was utilised once more. Boy – already more articulate than Tarzan, albeit with an inexplicable American accent – gets his own interludes in which he is seen going off exploring on his own and playing with his native pal Tumbo (Cordell Hickman). Comic Cheeta passages are featured more heavily. This and the ever more ludicrous treehouse all mod cons – this time we see an egg-timer (Cheeta holding an hour glass) and a fridge (a bamboo trough that constantly pours water on perishables, which include caviar) – make it unmistakable that the studio is aiming, if not exclusively at kids, then at a family demographic. Burroughs put his foot down when he became aware of a scene in which Tarzan laughed uproariously, and it was excised. The author's thoughts on the way that Weissmuller was noticeably thickening are not recorded. It's an indicator of just how popular Weissmuller was that he would appear in seven more Tarzan movies when his best days, physique-wise, were already behind him.

Coming up to the next Tarzan picture, MGM apprehended a problem that Burroughs had discovered a long time before: that a jungle backdrop provides limited opportunities for fresh storylines. With *Tarzan's New York Adventure*, released in April '42, the studio decided to address this difficulty by making the ape-man's jungle a concrete one.

Burroughs had put Tarzan in the developed world as far back as the close of the first novel and *The Return of Tarzan*, but MGM succeeded where those works failed and created intriguing and amusing juxtaposition.

In the screenplay by Myles Connolly and William R Lipman

from Connolly's original story, the action starts with the Tarzan-Jane-Boy underwater jungle swimming scene from *Tarzan's Secret Treasure* and the crocodile fight from *Tarzan and his Mate*. This however is where the familiarity – if not the re-use of old clips – ends. When Tarzan and Jane are attacked and left for dead in a forest fire, it is assumed by some visiting circus-owning trappers that Boy has been orphaned. The youngster is taken back to civilisation – if that is what one can call New York. In fact, the ape-man and his mate are alive and well. They follow the trail back to the Big Apple, paying their way with gold ingots. There, Tarzan has to deal with new experiences like cantankerous cab drivers, pompous hotel desk clerks, shower stalls, telephones, radios, smoke-filled nightclubs and courtroom cross-examination as he and Jane seek to wrest legal custody of Boy from circus owners Rand and Sargent. The latter have had a lucrative foreign offer to buy the child and the animal act he has developed while under their care and are therefore reluctant to let him go (although hardly enthusiastic about admitting this as their reason).

Cheeta gets plenty of his usual light-hearted screen-time, but the comedy potential of Tarzan's bewilderment at what he calls the 'stone jungle' ensures he has his own scenes of a not dissimilar tone. The ape-man is seen yodelling fully clothed in the shower and remarking of a wailing radio singer, 'Woman sick! Cry for witch doctor!' However, he is never ridiculed by the filmmakers. In court, the fact that Tarzan continues to have trouble with conjunctions proves less important than the power of his homespun wisdom ('Teach Boy where to find water when thirsty, where to find food when hungry. Tarzan teach Boy to be strong like lion and happy like bird ... Wise man need little ... Boy grow up to be brother of sun and friend of rain. Hurt nobody, want nothing people have. Grow old like cedar tree. Boy will be good man. Happy man'). It impresses the judge and amuses the public gallery. However, a legal setback resulting from it being pointed out that he and Jane are not Boy's natural parents sees Tarzan go, as it were, ape. After assaulting the defending attorney, he escapes by climbing up the outside of the building and making his way across rooftops by means of ladders and flagpole ropes, the chase culminating in a spectacular 200-foot dive off Brooklyn Bridge. The climax provides a new spin on the elephants-to-the-rescue plot device when Tarzan calls upon circus animals to come to his aid. When the eagerness of Rand and Sargent to retain their money-spinner ends in murder, Tarzan and Jane are awarded guardianship of Boy.

It doesn't seem to have been a production motivation, but that Weissmuller is clothed for much of the proceedings (a double-breasted cream suit) is a handy diversion from the fact that he is getting out of shape. It's rumoured that the chance to be a clothes-horse was a reason for O'Sullivan agreeing to make the movie. She certainly cuts a dash in the fashions of the day topped by an elaborate hair-do. Original movie ape-man Elmo Lincoln makes a cameo as a circus roustabout.

This movie was the shortest of all MGM Tarzans so far – not much more than an hour and ten minutes – but the best since *Tarzan and his Mate*.

The main reason for the step up in the rate of Tarzan movie releases in the early '40s would seem to be that the production baton was wrested from MGM – who had demonstrated a penchant for two-year gaps – and handed instead to Sol Lesser, whose career had revealed a philosophy of striking while the iron was hot.

After *Tarzan Finds a Son!* Metro-Goldwyn-Mayer had given Weissmuller a new contract. That it was one for seven years (albeit with option caveats) at a juncture where they had no guarantee of making more than two further ape-man pictures suggests that their decision to pull out of the market was not voluntary. *Tarzan of the Movies* author Gabe Essoe theorised that the war's decimation of the foreign markets so crucial to the franchise's bottom line prompted MGM to re-evaluate Tarzan's financial worth to them; but, in apparent contradiction, he also said that Burroughs decided not to renew the studio's right to the character after those aforesaid two pictures were made.

If the latter is true, it may have been because Burroughs knew that Sol Lesser was waiting in the wings. The man who had bludgeoned his way into the Tarzan movie business by buying out that dangling Walter Shumway/Jack Nelson/Jim Pierce film contract had somehow endeared himself to the author, possibly because he was, like Burroughs, a man with his eye permanently on the main chance. In 1943, Lesser finally became the producer of the official Tarzan series, as opposed to a day-trader occasionally putting out pictures in competition with the 'real' fare. Few of the public will have understood or cared about the reasons for Tarzan movies being attached to a new three-letter studio acronym – RKO financed and distributed Lesser's independent productions – but it marked the start of a new era in Tarzan cinema that would ultimately last 15 years. That period saw the release of 15 movies featuring a total of three different leading men and straddled the transition to colour stock. Lesser, incidentally, later claimed that during his time as Tarzan producer a healthy proportion of the grosses continued to come from foreign countries (75% in his estimation).

At first, not much visibly changed. The absence of Jane precipitated by O'Sullivan finally bowing out lasted only a couple of pictures. In the meantime, the insurance policy MGM had sought against O'Sullivan's departure was now cashed in as the series temporarily became a Tarzan-and-Boy double act, starting with *Tarzan Triumphs*, released in the first two months of 1943.

The picture opens with Boy – having presumably been taught literacy by his unseen step-mother – reading a letter from Jane, who is visiting her own mother in London. Jane imparts the news of the World War. Tarzan is no more interested in this than in the beseeching of the beautiful Princess Zandra (Frances Gifford) who wants him to come to the aid of her Palandryan people, whose lost city has been invaded by Nazis intent on looting its valuable oil and tin. In a quite transparent geo-political metaphor, when the war impacts directly on his own world in the form of Boy being kidnapped by the Nazis in pursuit of a stolen communications radio, Tarzan concludes that he cannot continue to pursue a policy of isolationism. The co-opting of Tarzan for wartime propaganda – the fate of many pop-culture characters of the day and requested of Lesser by the US State Department – was handy for Tarzan's new producer in one sense. Not only did it give Tarzan a fresh foe and a variation on the usual jungle intrigue, but it provided another way for the ape-man to endear himself to the public. A scene in which Tarzan shrugs off his neutral stance with the furious declaration, 'Now Tarzan make war!' reportedly caused moviehouse audiences to erupt into cheers. The picture was so enormously successful that in his long production tenure Lesser never managed to replicate its commercial impact.

Despite the Hays Code, the ape-man's pursuit of Germans is almost as bloodthirsty as that seen in the book *Tarzan the Untamed*. However, it's doubtful that this provoked the sort of moral qualms that would have been felt by some back in 1916 over the fact that Tarzan Tribes were helping to sell so-called Liberty Bonds. With their death-skull insignia and wholesale slaughter, the Nazis were the sort of villains that few were going to object to the ape-man despatching by tricking them into a lake filled with flesh-eating fish, instructing an elephant to push them off a cliff or (in a scene similar to one in *Tarzan the Untamed*) leaving them to be eaten by a lion in a pit. In a body-strewn 78 minutes, even Boy and Cheeta get in on the bloodshed. The chimpanzee emits one of his characteristic shrill laughs after having filled a Nazi full of machine-gun lead. As with so many Weissmuller Tarzan films, the ending features a comic Cheeta scene, this one involving the chimp accidentally reaching Germany on a radio and being mistaken for the Führer.

With the switch in producers and studios, Richard Thorpe was absent from the director's chair for the first time in four (MGM) pictures, replaced by William Thiele. Also changed, if only slightly, was Tarzan's yodel, Lesser/RKO not owning the

MGM recording of it. Higher production values were evinced by the fact of a Tarzan picture for the first time being provided a proper musical score. Roy Chanslor and Carroll Young contributed the screenplay from a story by Young. Burroughs had cause to be incredibly grateful to the latter two men. As if the enforced cessation of his publishing activities wasn't enough, the war had cut off his royalties from many foreign territories and even reduced his income from the Tarzan comic strip, as their lowered pagination had caused some newspapers to cease licensing it. Only six months after its premiere, *Tarzan Triumphs* had earned Burroughs $100,000 in royalties on top of his $25,000 advance.

The fact that he had finally helmed a successful Tarzan picture seemed to go to Sol Lesser's head. Within months of the release of *Tarzan Triumphs*, he put into production *Tarzan's Desert Mystery*, another Jane-less, Nazi-bashing affair. Not only was the formula the same but its appearance in December 1943 marked an inordinately short gap between two cinematic Tarzan ventures from the same studio. Although not a flop, it was almost predictably far less successful than its predecessor, both commercially and artistically.

Thiele directed again, while the script was by Edward T Lowe from a story by Carroll Young. The sand dunes of Olancha, near Lone Pine, doubled as the Sahara. Jane's absence is explained this time as the result of her tending to wounded soldiers in England. A missive from her requests that Tarzan send a malaria serum for jungle-stationed troops she is nursing. The letter-home-to-the-treehouse device was used again partly because Lesser was still holding out hope that O'Sullivan could be persuaded to change her mind about retiring. However, as with Princess Zandra in *Tarzan Triumphs*, he ensured that the distaff side was represented prominently. In fact, perhaps too much so, as Connie Bryce (Nancy Kelly) occupies a disproportionate amount of screen time in contrast with Tarzan, who languishes unseen in a prison cell for long stretches of a picture that itself runs to only 70 minutes. Even when he is on screen, Tarzan speaks just 40 words or so, a pronounced taciturnity that would be a feature of Lesser's term, with the resolutely commercial producer determined to make things as uncomplicated as possible for non-English speaking markets.

Connie is a jive-talking American magician whom Tarzan saves when on a desert journey with Boy and Cheeta to find the plants needed for the vaccine. (Her breasts, incidentally, aren't that much bigger than the increasingly plump Weissmuller's.) She is not what she at first seems, having a secret mission as soon as the party reach the Arab city of Bir Herari to expose one Hendrix as a Nazi called Heinrich. There is lots of swirling sands, Arab and Nazi villainy and frenetic horse-riding, and no lions or crocodiles in sight (nor, indeed, any of the mystery promised by the title). This could be seen as a worthy attempt to vary the jungle formula, yet the film was panned partly because of the un-Tarzan-like environs. The scenario becomes even more unfamiliar in the film's final act, where Tarzan – who has finally reached the location of the vaccine plants – is pitted against dinosaurs. Well, is shown stepping away from back-projected footage of dinosaurs filched from the 1940 picture *One Million B.C.* If studio audiences who would not live to experience computer-generated imagery (CGI) didn't know enough to find this comical, nor the inclusion of an oversize man-eating plant, the reports are that they did crease up at the sight of a giant spider munching on a Nazi.

The latter science fiction scenes appear to have been added in the reshoots and re-jigs that Lesser authorised when he adjudged the first cut unacceptable: they are not mentioned in early press briefs. There is nothing necessarily wrong with the idea of them. After all, Burroughs had successfully deployed such fantastical elements in his work, and the technical know-how existed for it to be done credibly, as in 1933's dinosaur-bedecked *King Kong*. Such material could even have made a decent Tarzan picture on its own. What it helps result in here, however, is a mess, and by common consensus the poorest of the dozen Weissmuller Tarzans.

*

In 1944, Lesser finally bit the bullet and recast the role of Jane. He picked Brenda Joyce to be O'Sullivan's successor. Joyce was a former model who had made a transition to actress in pictures like *The Rains Came* and *Little Tokyo, U.S.A.* Although Joyce was blonde and spoke with an American accent, audiences accepted her readily enough, and in fact she outlasted Weissmuller in the franchise.

Joyce made her debut in Spring 1945 in *Tarzan and the Amazons*. Kurt Neumann was appointed to direct a screenplay by John Jacoby and Marjorie L Pfaelzer. By the time the movie was in production, World War II was clearly in its endgame and the impetus for a propaganda picture was no longer present, not least because the public were heartily sick of war. Accordingly, the third RKO/Lesser Tarzan went for a story more in keeping with Burroughs' own lost-city bent.

On their way to pick up a returning Jane, Tarzan and Boy rescue from a panther a young Amazon woman. Of course, the Amazons were, as the name implies, from South America, but as mis-locating animals by a continent was a Tarzan movie tradition there was no reason to stop at humans. The ape-man returns the girl to her home city of Palmeria, which with its occasional human sacrifices and immensely plunderable reserves of gold is rather Opar-like. Before departing, he promises to her queen that he will not divulge the city's hidden location to anyone who might for some reason have cause to ask. Cue the entry of a safari of scientists who, by an amazing coincidence, have heard of this forbidden paradise ruled by beautiful women. They recognise jewellery stolen from it by Cheeta as bearing its hallmarks. Although Tarzan keeps mum, Boy is fooled into thinking the scientists have good intentions and takes them where they want to go. Boy is sentenced to death by the Palmerians for his troubles, but Cheeta luckily alerts the ape-man to his peril.

Despite having hit 40, Weissmuller has noticeably lost a few pounds since the previous picture and demonstrates the probable way how with an impressive blurred swimming segment that culminates in a crocodile battle that shows the benefits of switching studios: unable to re-run the MGM-owned musty croc fight from *Tarzan and his Mate*, Lesser authorised the filming of a new one which turned out to be superior. Another memorable scene involves Tarzan allowing two of the villains to die in terror in quicksand, illustrating that, although often cartoonish, the Weissmuller Tarzans were not exclusively kid-stuff.

Tarzan movie titles were beginning to resemble Tarzan book titles again, but just as *Tarzan Triumphs* had nothing to do with Burroughs' *Tarzan Triumphant*, so *Tarzan and the Leopard Woman*, a 72-minute feature released in February 1946, did not consist of an adaptation of the author's *Tarzan and the Leopard Men*.

However, a Burroughs flavour definitely infused this new venture, written by Carroll Young and directed by Kurt Neumann. High Priestess Lea (played by an actress with an even more exotic name, Acquanetta) is not only one letter away from La but similar to the Opar *femme fatale* in her homicidal sultriness. The cult she leads is reminiscent of the Leopard Men of Burroughs' book, although their motives for slaughter while dressed in ceremonial skins and claws are a cross between a form of Satanism and anti-colonialism. Tarzan ends up tangling with them when a young boy from the cult named Kimba (Tommy Cook) infiltrates his household. The brother of Lea, he has been sent to spy on Tarzan, who has been looking into the cult's activities at the behest of a local commissioner, but the boy has his own mission in mind: bringing back Jane's heart to prove his manhood. This all makes for a rather sinister, brooding Tarzan picture, especially as the leopard cult are given their own throbbing dance numbers.

A trim Weissmuller peels back the years as he defeats one Tongolo the Terrible in a wrestling bout, tussles with big cats and simultaneously fends off leopard worshippers and crocodiles. Almost symbolic of his revived physique is the fact that he destroys the leopard cult by bringing the roof down on them, toppling pillars in a Samson-like finale. Not that he doesn't receive some help: once again Cheeta makes a crucial intervention when doom seems inevitable, an inclusion with which Lesser seems to have been as obsessed as his predecessors were with getting Tarzan to yodel for the intervention of Tantor. The growing Johnny Sheffield, meanwhile, is beginning to rival Weissmuller himself, even if he is not yet quite as tall as his screen father. Accordingly, he is given a fight scene with Kimba.

This feature received unusually extensive advance publicity. Little wonder when Lesser was in the franchise for the long haul: the previous January he had issued an announcement that he had a 20-year exclusive deal to make Tarzan movies.

Although Tarzan had been a pioneer in several media, including adventure newspaper strips, he was a Johnny-come-lately to the field of what the British call 'comics' and the Americans 'comic books'.

By 1937, comic books had been established in America as artefacts separate from newspaper supplements, but it wasn't until February 1947 that an original Tarzan title hit the stands. Indeed, the ape-man had been beaten to that format by adaptations of considerably less popular Burroughs creations John Carter (who became a feature in Dell Comics' *Funnies* in April 1939) and even the Inner World (*Pellucidar* appeared as a one-off strip in Hawley's *Hi-Spot Comics* in 1949, drawn by John Coleman Burroughs, as was John Carter from his fifth Dell appearance).

The hardcover reprints of Tarzan newspaper strips that appeared in *The Illustrated Tarzan Book* and Whitman books don't quite count as comic books. *Tip Top Comics* – in which Tarzan appeared from April 1936 off and on through to 1954 – and *Comics on Parade* – which saw ape-man appearances from April 1938 to August 1940 – were recognisably comics, but the Tarzan material consisted of reprints of the newspaper strips owned by United Features Syndicate, the titles' publisher. Although Dell were famous as a comic book publisher, Tarzan's appearances in the late '30s in the likes of their *Famous Feature Stories*, *Popular Comics* and *Crackajack Funnies* were text stories with accompanying illustrations. Dell's *Large Feature Comic, Series 1 #5* (1939) again featured reprints of the Foster strips, but its card/paperback covers, and the fact that all of its 76 pages were devoted to the ape-man, makes it arguably the first proper Tarzan comic book. However, for the purists, still not the real deal.

The fact that, unlike *Large Feature Comic*, its original artwork wasn't restricted to a few splash pages gives *4-Color* #134, cover-dated February 1947, the accolade of first Tarzan comic book proper. It was Western who had secured the American comic book rights to the ape-man, although – slightly confusingly – the logo attached to their product was that of licensees Dell. Despite mixed artistic results, Western would hang on to those rights for exactly a quarter of a century and therefore define the comic book Tarzan for more than one generation of children.

'Tarzan and the Devil Ogre', the all-new story featured in *4-Color* #134, demonstrated many of the problems that would become associated with the Western Tarzan. The cover of the publication is simply embarrassing, a smiling Tarzan waving from atop an elephant with only the fact that he is wearing leopard-skin briefs denoting anything remotely savage. The artist responsible was Jesse Marsh, who also provided the interior illustrations. It would be unfair to judge Marsh's abilities on the basis of this comic or any other published over the next few years: this was an era characterised – presumably because comic books were such a new medium – by child-like, scratchy art by young men who had been given their chance before they were quite ready. Many of them – including Marsh, Batman's illustrator Bob Kane and Superman's original artist Joe Shuster – grew up in public, blossoming in technique in front of their readerships. Suffice it to say that in 1947 Marsh – a long-term Disney artist but unfamiliar with comics – had a rudimentary method laughable by today's standards. Particularly risible are

Tarzan's expressionless face and page-boy haircut.

The writing is of far greater interest. This comic, in common with all the films (presumably by contract), states this to be 'Edgar Rice Burroughs' Tarzan'. Unlike with the films, it's the truth. The story was written by Rob Thompson, based on his unbroadcast radio scripts for *Tarzan and the Tower of Ho*. That the story provides an explanation of the name 'Tarzan', includes Paul D'Arnot, mentions the Waziri, utilises the Mangani language and depicts the ape-man as a cultured, articulate and occasionally imperious individual suggests a writer steeped in the original novels. (As with the radio Tarzan, the victory cry of the bull ape is 'Taar .. maan .. gah .. nee .. ee .. ee!!') The 50-page story takes in a lion fight, a beautiful female explorer on a search for her missing father, a treacherous safari member, a cache of gold and a battle between the ape-man and a white gorilla. A limp ending notwithstanding, it's not half bad and certainly doesn't condescend to the readership. Few adults read comics in those days, but those who did and who were also familiar with Burroughs' work must have been heartened. Their happy state wouldn't last long.

Six months on from 'Tarzan and the Devil Ogre' came the appearance of the second all-new Tarzan comic book when *4-Color* #161 ran a Thompson-written adaptation of his radio serial *Tarzan and the Fires of Tohr*. After this apparent two-issue experiment, Western inaugurated an ape-man comic book with a regular schedule, the 36-page *Tarzan* appearing bi-monthly after its cover-dated January-February 1948 debut. The story in the first issue borrowed elements from Burroughs' *Tarzan the Magnificent*, while the one in the second issue was entirely new. In both cases, it was still Burroughs' Tarzan being portrayed. As early as issue three, however, Dell capitulated to the ape-man as defined by Johnny Weissmuller – treehouse, Boy and all – stopping only at making Tarzan speak in the films' staccato style. By issue 13, the comic was regularly featuring photographs of the latest screen Tarzan on the covers (admittedly to striking effect).

The decision to conflate the movie and novel Tarzans would seem to have been the publisher's. Although like Marsh he was not formally credited, the writer of Western's Tarzan comic from its second issue, with few exceptions for its entire life, was Gaylord DuBois. The latter told a Burroughs fanzine that he had been a Burroughs reader and fan since the 1920s and added, 'If I'd consulted my personal taste alone, I would have held faithfully to ERB in all my Tarzan comic scripts – but if I'd done that, I'd have been promptly fired.' Perhaps that gave DuBois a get-out for his rather stolid writing style, although it should be pointed out that, however maligned, the Western Tarzan title was popular enough to step up to a monthly frequency with the issue cover-dated July 1951.

As he had in every other medium, Tarzan replicated his comics success across the Atlantic. The UK's *Tarzan Monthly*, published by Donald F Peters, Ltd, made its debut in 1950 and lasted for 19 issues by publishing reprints of American Sunday newspaper strips. In September 1951 came a title from Westworld variously called *Tarzan: The Grand Adventure Comic* and *Tarzan Adventures* that originally appeared fortnightly before switching to a more traditional UK-comics weekly schedule. Those stats aside, of somewhat more historical importance is the involvement of a young man named Michael Moorcock. He started out as a contributor (features and short stories) before taking on its editorship. Later, he would become a major and very much Burroughs-influenced science fiction author. The phrase 'young man' is not used loosely here: incredibly, Moorcock was just 16 years old when he became assistant editor and 17 when he assumed the editor's position.

Moorcock says, 'I learned to read long before I went to school and my father, who had left my mother, left a few books behind, two of which were ERB titles – *The Son of Tarzan* and *The Master Mind of Mars* – which I loved. I could get the others from a little commercial lending library near where I lived, so it's fair to say I was reading Burroughs since the time I could read ... I produced an ERB fanzine from the age of 14 and continued to produce it at

15 when I left school. I worked as a messenger for a shipping company, then as a junior consultant for a firm of management consultants. While there I produced a vast number of fanzines, because they gave me permission to use their printing facilities. I interviewed the then editor of *Tarzan Adventures*, who didn't like the published piece but his colleagues did. It turned out he wasn't popular. He was fired and his assistant wrote to me suggesting I write some features and maybe some text stories *a la* John Carter. I started doing those and a bit later he suggested I apply for the job of assistant editor – letting me know that he was leaving shortly and that I would then get his job. That's what happened. Full-time job.'

Moorcock took over *Tarzan Adventures* with Volume 7, No 25 (21 September 1957). 'It had been running for years, always featuring some text pages,' he says. 'It began as an offshoot of the Mondadori Italian/French large-size comic, which simply reprinted the Sunday pages ... The Mondadori company, who published rafts of magazines, had eventually stopped doing it, so Donald Peters, my boss, had changed the format to US comic-book size, so that it would get better display on the racks, and added text features and stories, because in those days schools didn't ban comics which had some "educational" content ... Alastair Graham, the previous editor, had wanted to take it in a different direction, which was why he commissioned so much stuff from me. I went further because I had writers and artists standing by, all of whom were ERB fans. The mag became a sort of junior science fantasy pulp, with departments etc ... I had an 80-year-old assistant who wasn't up to much. Sammy Samuels came in twice a week to help on press days.' Moorcock describes his editorship role as, 'Normal duties. Commissioning pieces, getting everything together on time ... There's a bit more about this routine in my novel *The Whispering Swarm*, which is semi-autobiographical ... I commissioned a lot of John Carter-style stuff, white hunter stuff and so on.' Moorcock 'absolutely' endeavoured to inform *Tarzan Adventures*' readership of the fact that Burroughs' Tarzan was not the ape-man of the films.

Although Moorcock wrote 'frequently' for *Tarzan Adventures*, including many serials, he says, 'I didn't ever feel the urge to write Tarzan and so never asked ERB, Inc.' It has been stated that amongst its reprints of US newspaper strips, *Tarzan Adventures* occasionally featured British-originated Tarzan strips, which would have made them the first of their kind. However, Moorcock says, 'All our Tarzan stuff came from UFS, from whom we leased the strip.' However, he adds, 'I rewrote some of the Hogarth strips when we couldn't find plates in English. They had all been burnt up in a big [German bombing] raid on London, which destroyed so many books and publications in 1941.'

Moorcock says his adult colleagues were able to take him seriously despite his tender years because, 'sales figures rose sharply; they went from around 7,500 to 25,000.' Westworld ran a Tarzan Club through the publication. Joining brought a large plastic badge, a membership card and the ability via the decoder on the back of said card to read messages printed in the magazine. Although members don't seem to have been getting much for their one-shilling dues above and beyond the thrill of being in the exclusive ranks of a notional club, the venture appears to have been quite successful. When Burroughs bibliophile Vern Coriell joined, his membership card stated that he was member number 8,522.

Although he would continue to be an occasional contributor, Moorcock's editorship of *Tarzan Adventures* ended with Volume 8, No 17 (26 July 1958). 'I went to work for *Sexton Blake Library*,' says Moorcock. 'When I left, Sammy took over, but the circulation began dropping badly and it didn't last much longer.' The publication died right at the end of the '50s.

Moorcock says editing *Tarzan Adventures* was not instrumental in his becoming a novelist ('I was already writing fiction long before'). In 1975, he co-wrote the screenplay of the movie adaptation of *The Land that Time Forgot*, but some are surprised that he did not follow in (or even precede) the footsteps of the authors who have been licensed to continue

Tarzan's adventures in print. 'It never occurred to me,' he says. 'I felt the first three Tarzan novels said all there was to say, and while I read and enjoyed all the others, up to *Tarzan and 'The Foreign Legion'*, I didn't want to add to sequels.' If he were offered the chance now, would he take it? Perhaps answering with the nonchalance that can come only from having himself created iconic characters like Jerry Cornelius and Elric of Melniboné, he says, 'I wouldn't write a Tarzan book. I generally don't use others' characters.' However, he also says that if he did write a Tarzan novel, 'I'd leave out the racism. I noticed how well the books lived without it when BBC radio read *Tarzan of the Apes* as a serial. They abridged it slightly and omitted the racial prejudices of ERB's day. When I came to reread the novel, the racism jarred as it had not when I first read it.' However, Moorcock also observes that *Tarzan Adventures* 'had quite a few black African subscribers from most parts of Africa, so perhaps we're over-sensitive to the racist issue.'

Tarzan returned to British comics in the Swinging '60s in *TV Tornado*, published by City. The Tarzan strip illustrated by Harry Bishop that started in its first issue on 14 January 1967 was given justification in a gogglebox-themed weekly by the first Tarzan television series, then on the airwaves. In a milestone for UK Tarzan comics, the strip was all-new. Another TV-themed British weekly, *TV Comic*, and its associated annuals, featured both Tarzan strips and text stories in the 1970s.

There were also UK reprints of Western comics material, starting in May 1967 via World Distributors. From 1970 onwards, Top Sellers published Tarzan and Korak comics in American format: 6x10 inches with colour-interiors. They were popular enough to move from a monthly to fortnightly schedule. Dez Skinn, who edited both, says that the Western work 'formed the backbone' of the Top Sellers titles, but adds, 'We also ran European strips sometimes, not just the wonderful Russ Manning work ... The way that Tarzan worked, if you got the right in your territory to doing Tarzan or Korak, you became part of the pool. When you created material, your material could then be reprinted by Sweden, by America, by France, by anybody else who was a member of this Edgar Rice Burroughs licensed pool ... The American material was often so much better than the European material that we ended up reprinting the American material, but we could have equally reprinted the Spanish material. The Brits were part of the pool, but a minor part, because if you've got thousands of pages of material out there you never will convince your boss that it's worth having a bigger budget to create new material.'

Williams, like Top Sellers, was an element of the publishing division of Warner Brothers. It was Williams' name that appeared in the indicia of a fondly remembered ape-man product from the early '70s: *Tarzan – Giant Book*. The publication lived up to its title in its nigh-A3 dimensions, card covers and thick spine. Originally shrink-wrapped with five free Western reprints, it featured articles on Edgar Rice Burroughs, the movie Tarzan, the Mangani language and African flora and fauna. The three stories it extracted from *Jungle Tales of Tarzan* would have been many young people's introduction to Burroughs ape-man prose. The heart of the book, though, was four wonderful Gaylord DuBois-Russ Manning adaptations of Burroughs Tarzan novels. These were Western reprints (blown up colossally in size) dating from the 1960s when an earthquake in the world of ERB in general and Tarzan in particular caused DuBois to be granted his wish of sticking closely to the Burroughs boilerplate.

Tarzan and the Huntress, the third ape-man movie in a row with a quasi-dominatrix allusion in its title, appeared in Spring 1947. Despite his youth, the sprouting Johnny Sheffield was beginning to look far more the part of Tarzan than Weissmuller, who could now only be said to be trim for his vintage.

Kurt Neumann directed the 72-minute picture, which was a surprisingly strong entry in the series. The script was provided by Jerry Gruskin and Rowland Leigh, although the Saint's creator Leslie Charteris gets an enigmatic 'Screenplay Constructor' credit. The plot exploits the real-life fact of the shortage of exhibits in zoos following World War II, with freelance hunters – one of whom is female – coming to the kingdom of Farrod (a monarch friend of Tarzan and Jane) to bag some lucrative wildlife. They are given royal permission to capture just two of each species, but against a backdrop of palace intrigue they renege on that agreement, much to the displeasure of Tarzan, who, despite hitherto being always ready in movies to kill a lion or even a rhino, is posited as a defender of jungle animals. The plot gives more opportunity than usual to show off wildlife footage, which is sweeping and beautiful and – in the case of the crocodile-infested pool seen at one point – chilling. As is Tarzan's cold-blooded despatch of three of the invasive hunters. They may have been collectively complicit in the death of Farrod, but the ape-man's vigilantism is not so palatable when directed against villains somewhat less diabolical than Nazis.

Lesser wasn't big on sentimentality in Tarzan pictures, but he authorised some extended kissy-kissy stuff between Weissmuller and Brenda Joyce and a lovely new underwater ballet with Tarzan, Jane and Boy almost enough to put Olympic synchronised swimmers to shame. However, the sentimentality was purely for the screen. Tarzan's comment to his step-son 'Boy man now' turned out to be bad news for Sheffield, as did a general view summed up by the *Hollywood Reporter*'s comment, 'It is no longer possible for him to do cute things.' After eight films and eight years' service, Sheffield was dispensed with by Lesser on the grounds that he had outgrown the role.

Edgar Rice Burroughs seems to have enjoyed his time as a war correspondent, despite few of his field stories seeing print. However, such adventures as climbing aboard ships via cargo nets and coming under ack-ack fire on bombing missions were not the ideal prescription for a man who had suffered more than one heart attack before taking up his role. In early 1945, he confided in a letter to a friend that he felt so weak that he didn't think he would ever regain full strength.

He had, though, one last Tarzan-related triumph ahead of

him, and it emerged from his war-correspondent days. Burroughs wrote *Tarzan and 'The Foreign Legion'* from 10 June to 11 September 1944 in a period during which he was formally stationed on Hawaii, his home since April 1940. (A sort of exile, as this was two decades before Hawaii was absorbed into the United States.) By then, paper restrictions were easing sufficiently to enable him to reactivate his publishing house. *Land of Terror* – a Pellucidar novel dating from 1938 and rejected by all of the magazines to which it had been offered – appeared in April '44. His first post-war publication was *Escape on Venus*, a quartet of stories that had previously appeared in *Fantastic Adventures* in 1940 and 1941. *Tarzan and 'The Foreign Legion'* was published by Burroughs in August 1947. Not only was it the first Tarzan story for six years and the first Tarzan novel for eight years, it would transpire to be the last Burroughs Tarzan tale of the author's lifetime. It ended things on a high note.

That is, if you can ignore its vicious racism. Having had his fingers burnt over *Tarzan the Untamed*, Burroughs had held off involving the ape-man in the Second World War. He changed his mind at the prompting of George Carlin of United Features Syndicate, who suggested his hero take on the Japanese. The face-off was, for an English peer, somewhat illogical. Although the British did confront their forces in that conflict, the Japanese were always far more of an enemy to the country off which Pearl Harbor was based. In the resultant book, Burroughs proceeded to make the Japanese as one-dimensional and unambiguously evil as he had the Germans in *Untamed*. He also portrayed them as cowardly, which might surprise any Allied soldier or seaman who had to endure the Japanese armed services' remarkable capacity for self-sacrifice, up to and including suicide.

Yet just as World War I and *Tarzan the Untamed* had reinvigorated the Tarzan franchise, so the Second World War was a blessing in the way it provided the means to inject fierce drama into the ape-man's world, as well as to open it out. That was all a writer of Burroughs' abilities needed to produce a fine novel. The stultifying situation that Jack Byrne had suggested existed in Burroughs' life and writing back in the mid-'30s had ended with the attack on Pearl Harbor. Burroughs had gone out into the world, seen a lot, learned a lot and no doubt read a lot. Possibly just as importantly, he had taken a break from the Tarzan treadmill he had seriously begun to resent. He returned to the Tarzan series older, wiser and refreshed. Testament to this is the fact that, its absolutism about the enemy notwithstanding, *Tarzan and 'The Foreign Legion'* is a surprisingly understated affair. The persona of Tarzan, for instance, is not referred to until nearly a quarter of the way into the book, up to which point we get instead more than a hundred references to Col John Clayton, who is working quietly as a humble observer on a reconnaissance and photographic mission over the island of Sumatra in the Japanese-occupied Dutch East Indies. Similarly unexpected is the fact that Burroughs has the supporting characters debate with each other the nature and validity of hatred.

It is only when Clayton's plane is shot down over Sumatra and his party is threatened by a tiger that we are back in familiar territory. (It's rather amusing, even sweet, that in his last Tarzan story, Burroughs finally finds a way to give the ape-man a legitimate encounter with the striped big cat.) The colonel places a foot on his vanquished adversary and unleashes the victory cry of the bull ape, at which point his companions apprehend that this is none other than Tarzan of the Apes. Although once again Burroughs is distractingly melding fiction and reality – 'Is dat Johnny Weismuller [sic]?' one of the crew asks – there's a touching valedictory subtext to a post-modern scene when one of the characters observes, 'And there's the scar on his forehead that he got in his fight with the gorilla when he was a boy.'

Being stranded in Sumatra creates a set-up similar to that of 'Tarzan and the Castaways'/'The Quest of Tarzan' insofar as the ape-man has to act as guardian for a group cut off in a non-African wilderness. However, the differences begin with the fact that the land is teeming with hostile Japs (as they are almost uniformly called). The island also turns out to play host to a young woman called Corrie van der Meer, last survivor of a Dutch family slaughtered by the invading Japanese who has been living on her considerable wits. Dutch guerrilla fighter Tak van der Bos is also waiting to join the narrative, as is Sarina, a Eurasian female pirate. The three American soldiers with whom Tarzan was flying are of mixed racial parentage – leading to various ethnic bantering – but also possessed of a salt-of-the-earth quality that is no less affecting for it being clichéd. This motley crew are dubbed 'The Foreign Legion' by the local guerrillas. (Note the inverted commas in the book's title to denote that it's a nickname, not always reproduced by publishers, some of whom seemed to think Tarzan had somehow become a new Beau Geste.) The action is somewhat back-and-forth, full of captures and rescues. However, this is more in the order of an exciting and suspenseful story than a disjointed one, and it all culminates in an impressive ocean chase as the party head for the safety of Australia.

Burroughs doesn't stop short at demonising the Japanese. He goes so far as to have Tarzan and his friends threatened by the indigenous (and, it turns out, Mangani-speaking) orangutan, a gentle simian as underserving of such a malevolent portrayal as that poor old rhinoceros that Weissmuller slaughtered. Another misstep is Burroughs portraying Tarzan as fashioning a loincloth from a parachute. The drama of a scene meant to convey a reversion to the savage persona in which John Clayton always feels more comfortable is somewhat undermined by folk memories of British women in World War II procuring their frilly undies in the same way. The faults are easily outweighed by the plusses, though. It's not just the change from the African backdrop and the undeniably interesting/exciting situation of war that give the book its power. Burroughs turns back time to the 1910s and '20s when his writing was at its keenest, shrugging off that torpor and cynicism that had afflicted his output in recent decades. The characters are believable and, most significantly, the dialogue – Burroughs' perennial weak spot – consistently feels real.

For all of that, this was another adult Tarzan story that Burroughs failed to place with a magazine. *Tarzan and the Madman* was one thing, but the fact that editors were now turning down even a high-quality Tarzan showed how the pulp industry was becoming a thing of history. Still, at least we consequently know – unlike with 'Tarzan and the Jungle Murders' – that this is unadulterated Burroughs and not the amended version of a sub-editor.

There is one rather odd element of this book. The 'Legion' begin discussing a people who are reputed to have discovered the secret of eternal youth. Tarzan weighs into the debate. 'I have twice seen absolute proof that perpetual youth can be achieved,' he says. One of those occasions we know about from *Tarzan's Quest*: the longevity pills with a grisly secret behind them manufactured by the Kavuru and shared out by the principals at the end of that novel. The other is something to which Burroughs has not previously referred. Tarzan explains, 'When I was a young man ... I saved a black from a man-eating lion. He was very grateful, and wished to repay me in some way. He offered me perpetual youth.' Tarzan was sceptical but was told by the man's elderly chief that he had known this man – visually in his twenties – all his life, '...so I let the witch doctor go to work on me.' Tarzan himself – who it was established in *Tarzan of the Apes* was born in approximately 1888 and who of course had fought in the last World War – seems to be in his twenties to his companions. It is implied that the witchdoctor is the reason for this, because, from what Tarzan says, he did not partake of the Kavuru immortality pills as we had previously been led to believe.

Why, though, did Tarzan fail to bring up during the course of *Tarzan's Quest* that he had no need of the longevity pills? Burroughs seems to have decided to revise the ape-man's past after suddenly realising that, if Tarzan stories occurred in real time, the ape-man would have been in his mid-forties when the events in *Tarzan's Quest* occurred, and the pills' benefits commensurately smaller. But why would his thoughts stray in this direction when the general public – especially in an era well before anorak fandom – barely spent a minute wondering why popular-culture icons were ageless? Was it perhaps the discomfiture of a near-septuagenarian at the thought of his own mortality?

Tarzan and the Mermaids, released in March 1948, made it four Weissmuller ape-man pictures in a row in which his character shared billing with an exotic female.

However, 'mermaid' is a misleading description of Mara (Linda Christian), a young woman with two standard legs – no tail – whom Tarzan literally catches in his fishing net. She transpires to be from the isolated island of Aquatania, from which she has fled because the high priest of her homeland is trying to force her into a marriage she doesn't want. When Mara is forcibly taken back to her homeland, Tarzan and Jane – who it has been established have sent the absent Boy to be educated in England – determine to aid her. Not only does he return Mara to the arms of her true love, but Tarzan demolishes the superstitious religion of the Aquatanians based around their imposter god Baloo, whom he hurls to a grisly death. Along the way, Tarzan performs an astonishing dive off the Acapulco cliffs – stuntman Angel Garcia died in the execution – and battles an octopus.

The 68-minute movie – written by old trouper Carroll Young – is not top-notch ape-man fare but is often intriguing. The lush scenery results from the fact that this is only the second Tarzan cinema venture shot on location in a foreign country. Said country is not Africa – where the movie is set – but Mexico. Acapulco, the Aztec ruins of San Juan de Teotihuacán and the studios of Churubusco and Mexico City provide a pleasantly unfamiliar texture, even if director Robert Florey is sometimes too anxious to present a travelogue. Also exotic is the score from Dimitri Tiomkin, which enables some quasi-spiritual temple singing and includes a solo spot for minstrel postman character Benji (John Laurenz).

Weissmuller's comical full figure is not helped in any way by the bizarre decision to put him in sandals. Although he might have been sleeker than most men in their mid-forties, a useful comparison is Jock Mahoney, who was in his mid-forties when he stepped into the loincloth yet – whatever his deficiencies in the role – had zero body fat. The fact that he was aware of how he had thickened was demonstrated by Weissmuller sucking in his stomach in publicity photos.

Weissmuller had repeatedly complained about not receiving a share of the Tarzan films' grosses. The promise he alleged Lesser made that he would receive this when his contract was renewed after *Mermaids* seems the stalling action of a producer who knew that the actor's time was up. (Burroughs had mocked Weissmuller as a 'poor old soul' to Lesser as far back as 1944.) There was no new contract. The film sees Weissmuller one last time effortlessly lifting an adversary above his head before hurling him to the ground, the method by which he had always implicitly insisted that great strength continued to underlie his increasing bulk. At the end of his 16-year reign as the ape-man, this consummate aquatic Olympian also gets a final opportunity to show off his prowess in the water.

Both Sheffield and Weissmuller immediately found gainful employment after their separate exits by playing characters inconceivable without the existence of Tarzan, something which provided another example of how widely the ape-man had fanned out into society. Sheffield assumed the role of Bomba, the Jungle Boy. Bomba was a corporate creation by the Stratemeyer Syndicate dating back to 1926. The company used their in-house pseudonym Roy Rockwood for the tales they sold to publishers Cupples & Leon. There were 20 Bomba novels through to 1938, split evenly in location between the Amazonian jungles and Africa. The series ultimately relocated to the latter continent as though the parties concerned could no longer be bothered with a fig-leaf denial of Tarzan imitation. Bomba was white, spoke both English and ape and was a ferocious fighter. He was on a quest to discover his origins, to which clues were discovered in each book. Bomba being an adolescent, Sheffield was perfect for the role when the character made the transition to the silver screen. Sheffield appeared as Bomba 12 times up to 1955. The fact that the last of the Bomba films was titled *Lord of the Jungle* rather seems to be taking the piss, as indeed does the television pilot Sheffield's father then produced for him featuring another jungle character, *Bantu the Zebra Boy*. After that show was not commissioned, Sheffield obtained a business degree, armed with which he subsequently pursued a variety of professions.

Weissmuller, meanwhile, played Jungle Jim between 1948 and 1956. This character was based on a comic strip that debuted in 1934. Illustrator Alex Raymond – co-creator of the character with writer Don Moore – had something of a history of taking his cue from Burroughs, having re-tooled John Carter of Mars as Flash Gordon. As with Bomba's anonymous creators, Raymond and Moore did what was requisite to evade a plagiarism suit, locating their action in Asia rather than Africa and clothing their hero in khaki, not a loincloth. Jim was a hunter (cum adventurer) but had both a rapport with the beasts of the jungle and a pet simian. The Jungle Jim character was popular enough to jump media, appearing in film, on radio and in comic books (some written by Gaylord DuBois).

Already on $50,000 per movie by the end of his Tarzan run, Weissmuller became even wealthier via Jungle Jim, where he got that percentage he had unsuccessfully sought from Lesser. Bizarrely, the last three of his sixteen Jungle Jim features dropped the character's name and made out that Weissmuller was playing himself, the reason being that the rights to it had been lost to the producers of a new TV series – in which Weissmuller was starring.

In between latter-day Tarzan pictures, Weissmuller had tried with scant success to expand his horizons as an actor. The fact that he was associated with nothing but jungle-related action put paid to his acting career when the Jungle Jim TV series finished after one season. After that, Weissmuller traded on his swimming career and on his name in public relations work and commercials, and was gleefully unembarrassed about doing so, as is the way of American celebrities when their time in the spotlight is over but their affection amongst the public is not. An illustration of that affection is the fact that he appears in the celebrity montage on the front cover of The Beatles' *Sgt. Pepper's Lonely Hearts Club Band* album. Weissmuller dictated that his Tarzan yodel be played at his funeral, which occurred in 1984.

It should be noted that in Burroughs' lifetime the author himself showed little inclination toward litigation regarding either parody or rip-off. Although he had misgivings about a wrestler calling himself Tarzan and a murderer being dubbed Tarzan by the media, neither Buster Crabbe's *King of the Jungle* nor Bomba nor Jungle Jim nor Sheena, Queen of the Jungle (a glamorous distaff Tarzan who starred in comics, pulps, films and TV starting from 1937) nor a single one of the veritable 101 Tarzan pulp and movie imitations – as opposed to passing-offs – inspired a writ from him. Ditto the plainly John Carter-inspired *Flash Gordon* strip. The most logical inference for his inaction is a fear that witness-stand cross-examination might have led to questions about Burroughs' own debts to predecessors. For instance, some claim he got a lot of his Barsoom ideas from obscure novels *Journey to Mars* (1894) by Gustavus W Pope and *Lieutenant Gullivar Jones: His Vacation* (1905) by Edwin Lester Arnold.

Separate from but adjacent to the issue of media characters who would not have existed without Tarzan are those of piracy and plagiarism. Over the course of more than a decade straddling the Second World War, an Argentinian publishing house issued 30-odd Tarzan books credited to J C Bovirio. In Cold War Russia, Burroughs' Tarzan novels were immensely popular, but he did not receive a penny from their huge sales because the Soviet government viewed the concept of royalties as a capitalist irrelevance.

Although the author lost – or at least failed to gain – a fortune because of such matters, it was the movie Tarzan that was subject to the most piracy and plagiarism. This process was assisted by the fact that, in a more fragmented world than we have today, the Berne Convention on copyright was easier to circumnavigate even where ideology didn't prohibit governmental goodwill. When, for instance, news of the 1940 production *The Adventures of Chinese Tarzan* by the Hsin Hwa Motion Picture Company of Singapore attracted the (no doubt belated) attention of Burroughs, the prospect of litigation in an unknown legal system in a foreign language in that then-mysterious land would have been a daunting one. India, another vast and densely populated country with a then-casual attitude toward intellectual property, was responsible for a trio of illegal Tarzan movies in the 1950s – bizarrely, for distribution in Nigeria. In a rare act of competence, ERB, Inc's Cyril Ralph Rothmund obtained an injunction against their continuation. Back in 1944, Sol Lesser's task in stopping the dissemination of a similarly unauthorised Turkish Tarzan film was made somewhat easier when the distributors informed him they wanted to sell him the rights to it. Already aware that they were infringing his live-action privileges, at a screening Lesser found himself looking at his own production *Tarzan's Revenge* with close-ups of a Turkish actor spliced in. He exercised his legal prerogative to confiscate the print.

PART FIVE: EXIT WEISSMULLER

At the end of the 1940s, it must have seemed inconceivable to some that anybody other than Johnny Weissmuller could portray Tarzan on screen.

The role having been his for more than a decade-and-a-half, and exclusively his for nine years, any new actor risked looking presumptuous by taking it. The world, however, moves on. Sol Lesser wasn't going to abandon his lucrative franchise because of some airy-fairy notion of definitiveness, nor was any ambitious would-be star about to spurn the opportunity of a lifetime because there was a chance the public would not warm to him quite as much as it had to dear old Johnny. Enter Lex Barker.

Although he had a hinterland of American football and track excellence, his summer stock and movie contract work meant that Barker was arguably the first real thespian to be cast as Tarzan. RKO director Lee Sholem claimed he interviewed over a thousand actors and athletes after Lesser set him the task of re-casting the ape-man but gave the job to Barker without an audition when the latter came up to his office to make enquiries about it. The actor was handsome, six foot four and possessed of a barrel chest and a rippling, toned physique. Barker later claimed previous contract status with Fox and Warner Brothers had yielded little work because of the fear he would physically outshine the leading man, which status he was considered to be too much of an unknown to be granted himself.

He certainly looked every inch the part of Tarzan, although some might quibble about a couple of things. Although deriving from refined stock was a fundamental aspect of Burroughs' noble savage, the all-American pucker of Barker's face that betrayed his prep-school-and-Princeton background was incompatible with the movie image of Tarzan. Meanwhile, the way his hair was swept up and back raised questions about out-of-place grooming that Weissmuller's increasingly unkempt mane hadn't for a long while.

Tarzan's Magic Fountain, Barker's entrée, directed by Sholem, was released in January 1949. Barker was one of those young American men who had been weaned on Tarzan, and he was so thrilled to be given the role that the 29-year-old was to be heard publicly chattering about playing it until he was 50. Perhaps Elmo Lincoln – given a bit-part in the film by a publicity-canny Lesser – had thought the same thing back in the second decade of the century. Presumably on Lesser's instructions, Barker rang the changes insofar as his Tarzan was taciturn rather than incapable of fluent English. He was also different in that he seemed to be versed in martial arts. Familiar elements included Cheeta and Jane (Brenda Joyce becoming the second – and to date last – actress to play opposite two different Tarzans). The glossy locales of the previous Tarzan picture were missing, replaced by the old make-do venues of the LA Arboretum and Encino Ranch.

The film's title was incongruously feminine and an unwise switch from its no-nonsense original, *Tarzan and the Arrow of Death.* Scriptwriters Harry Chandlee and Curt Siodmak would seem to have read the latest Tarzan novel, for the fulcrum of the movie is the secret of immortality, in this case one obtained from the titular fountain, located in the hidden Blue Valley, which has kept downed female aviator Gloria James (Evelyn Ankers) the same age for 20 years. When she emerges from the valley, Gloria finds that the effects of the fountain are not permanent, and experiences a transformation more to be expected in a horror movie. This prompts her return to the refreshing waters. Naturally, avaricious interlopers are intent on profiting from this phenomenon of nature regardless of the disruption it will cause the natives who call the Blue Valley home, and naturally Tarzan is having none of it. In the grand set-to that follows, people meet grisly ends via rolled boulders, flaming arrows and an avalanche. Gloria and her new husband stay in the now fully sealed Blue Valley, there to remain forever young.

The 73-minute film was nothing spectacular and Barker would never have a unique yodel – Weissmuller's RKO-era one was overdubbed – but it was a decent enough effort to set the newcomer on course for, if not portraying the ape-man 'til he was 50, a respectable tally of five movies.

Barker's second outing was originally announced as *Tarzan and the Golden Lion*. Upon its May 1950 release, though, it had the non-Burroughs title *Tarzan and the Slave Girl*. However, the script of the 74-minute movie – written by Arnold Belgard and Hans Jacobyit – contained a strong strain of the ape-man creator's style.

A lost white tribe descended from ancient Egyptians who worship lions and who come to Tarzan's attention because they abduct young women is a set-up clearly derived by mixing together elements from two or three of Burroughs' latter-day Tarzan novels. The Lionians bring not just terror but a deadly disease, the fatal effects of which motivate their abductions: they seek to repopulate their declining society. Tarzan fetches a doctor who has a cure for the disease. Said doctor has in his employ an attractive nurse named Lola (Denise Darcel), who becomes the slave girl of the title when she, along with Jane, falls into the Lionians' clutches. When the serum is lost, it imperils one and all. That Barker's type of youth and power hadn't been seen in Tarzan films for several years is made explicitly clear in a muscular and frenetic film, directed again by Sholem. Tarzan is seen breaking open crypt prisons with brute force and fighting to the death kidnapper Sengo.

Brenda Joyce had bowed out of the series to raise a family. The problem that this created with Jane would never really be resolved in Lesser's time. If she had never become embedded in the public's mind as Tarzan's mate in the way O'Sullivan had, Joyce had done well enough in the role to last five pictures that spanned two different leading men. Now, however, there would be a bewildering succession of Mrs Tarzans, as Lesser – who around this time reputedly turned down a young Marilyn Monroe for the part– chopped and changed with every picture. That is, when the actress herself didn't jump ship. The ridicule of what she called her 'intellectual friends' put paid to Vanessa Brown, the brunette who took the role in *Tarzan and the Slave Girl*.

Not that she was exactly done a service by the script: depicting a jealous Jane engaging in a catfight with a Lola who has ambitions to burrow beneath Tarzan's loincloth may have been in the spirit of increasingly informal times, but was undignified and out of character. The suspicion that the catfight might have been designed to entice an older demographic was strengthened by a curious publicity picture for *Tarzan and the Slave Girl*: the sight of the ape-man standing with feet planted apart and knife ready to take on adversaries was expected enough, but not Lola kneeling beside him clinging fearfully to his leg, her head pressed against his hip.

According to an unsourced quote in *Tarzan – Giant Book*, Burroughs approved of Barker, adjudging him 'the real Tarzan,' and adding, 'Of all those hundreds of men whom I've met who have wished to play Tarzan, he is the only one who has had something more than muscles between his ears.' Perhaps fitting, then, that Burroughs' last public appearance was on the set of *Tarzan and the Slave Girl*, where he and Barker posed with the author's daughter, grandson, daughter-in-law and Vern Coriell, who three years earlier had started the first of what would become a wave of Burroughs fanzines.

In the resultant photographs, it is notable that Burroughs is the only one seated. The author had become increasingly debilitated by heart attacks and the onset of Parkinson's Disease. Before he had started losing his physical capabilities, he had effectively admitted that his mental capacities were less than they had been. In January 1941, he wrote to his son Jack, 'I can't squeeze out a single new plot,' surmising that a writer 'is born with just so many.' He recovered from this lack of confidence sufficiently to turn out some Venus and Mars novelettes, the scraps mentioned previously and two above-average novels, *I Am a Barbarian* and *Tarzan and 'The Foreign Legion'*. His final published volume was *Llana of Gathol*, a compendium of four previously-published Mars novelettes issued in March 1948.

Writing-wise, *Tarzan and 'The Foreign Legion'* was his swansong. For the remaining six-and-a-half years of his life after its September 1944 completion, he simply never found the energy or interest to complete anything but letters. He roused himself enough to write 83 pages of a new Tarzan novel in September 1946 before abandoning it. The following year, he had another go at chronicling the ape-man, with even less successful results.

By now, Burroughs was living frugally, having at the end of 1945 bought a two-bedroomed house in Encino, Los Angeles, around the corner from ERB, Inc and virtually in the shadow of the mansion over the border in Tarzana that he had forfeited during the Depression. His letters suggest he settled happily enough in these final years into the role of retiree and old man. In the last year of his life, he re-read his *oeuvre* to, as he put it, 'see what I had said and how I'd said it.'

It has been reported that Burroughs died reading the Tarzan Sunday newspaper strip. More accurate would be to say that the funnies were spread before him when he was discovered dead in bed by his housekeeper on 19 March 1950. Journalistic penchant for myth, symmetry and sentimentality seem to have done the rest.

Whatever the exact circumstances, it brought to a close a life that, it has to be said, appears to have been for most of its 74½ years unhappy, unfulfilled or both. Burroughs never seemed to like or be satisfied by his pre-writing employment, and suffered extreme financial hardship when his family was young. There was a glorious period in the '10s and '20s of the 20th century when he was charged up with the new thrill of being a famous author and a wealthy man at a point where he still had good relations with his wife and had a young family on which he doted. Although it would be absurd to suggest that he experienced no happiness from thereon, that which he did seemed almost predestined to be followed by disillusion. It is striking how quickly writing became just another job to him, an increasingly resented means to finance the economic folly of the Tarzana ranch. Then came disillusion with his marriage. While his second marriage did seem to provide him genuine domestic bliss for a short while (like a love-struck teenager, he planted a secret message to Florence Dearholt in the mid-'30s Barsoom novel *Swords of Mars*), that union formally ended in May 1942 after just seven years and at a point where the couple had been living apart for more than a year. Its termination created yet more financial burdens. Burroughs also had to endure the humiliation of increasingly frequent rejection letters from magazines and the ever-dwindling financial returns from those that did deign to publish his writing.

Yet Burroughs had triumphed on many levels, with three adored and adoring children, massive success in his chosen field and, despite many artistic failures, continued inventiveness in his Mars books and writing that increasingly evinced stylistic evolution. Above and beyond all that was something that few writers in the history of literature can boast: the creation of a character so iconic and enduring that his name has entered both the language and the dictionary.

Although the early 1950s saw television beginning to become a phenomenon, in 1951 radio still dominated the American hearth. The return of Tarzan to that medium was therefore a big deal.

The idea was that of Walter White Jr, who operated Commodore Productions and Artists, Inc. Having previously achieved considerable wireless success with *Hopalong Cassidy* and *The Clyde Beatty Show*, in the second half of 1950 White contacted Cyril Ralph Rothmund to broach the idea of licensing Tarzan. With a go-ahead from Rothmund secured, White commissioned some scripts. Budd Lesser, David Chandler and the team of Robert Schaeffer & Eric Freewall are known to have been responsible for some of them, although poor documentation by Commodore – a very small outfit – means that it can't be said for certain that they were the only scriptwriters. The show was titled *Tarzan, Lord of the Jungle*. Although each episode had an introduction that included the line, 'Transcribed from the immortal pen of Edgar Rice Burroughs,' with the exception of two episodes partly based on latter-day Burroughs novels, all the scripts featured original plots.

Considering the proprietorial care he had taken over the previous radio programmes, it's doubtful that Burroughs would have allowed the producers of the new series to take some of the liberties with his character that they did. He would have approved of the fact that Tarzan spoke fluent English, but the author would have raised an eyebrow at the fact that, as an adult, the ape-man for some reason lived in the log cabin built by his doomed parents, that he laughed loudly, that he hung around with natives who somehow knew Mangani terms for animals and that his frequent aloofness was replaced by something approaching gregariousness.

Having said which, the series recalls the idea Burroughs himself had back in the late-1930s to reinvent Tarzan as a jungle detective. The episodes were kicked off by a visit to the hut by either a native or one Captain Stanley Lawrence, who presented the ape-man with a mystery or problem that he then set off to solve like a one-man, loinclothed FBI. Tarzan was played by Lamont Johnson, who possessed a stentorian all-American voice that no Burroughs fan would have found *bona fide* but had the sort of authoritativeness that the average listener would have associated with Tarzan's physical strength and power. Dramatic-toned narrator Charles Arlington linked well-written and evocative scenes, which featured incidental music and, where appropriate, animal background noise. Each weekly half-hour episode began with a fairly respectable yodel.

Although decent stuff, the show started slowly, making its debut on a single Los Angeles station – KHJ – on 4 January 1951. Before long, however, it occupied a spot on 45 Western state stations. From 22 March 1952, it made the jump to national broadcasting, having been picked up by the CBS network. It performed creditably, managing to break into the ratings top ten to nestle alongside the likes of *Amos 'n' Andy*, *Lux Radio Theatre* and *Gene Autry*. Yet this apparently highly promising situation evaporated quickly. CBS stopped broadcasting the show after 27

June, supposedly for a summer break of 13 weeks. It never broadcast any further editions. After that, it was back to local radio, plus a few foreign sales. White produced 75 episodes in total.

Around this time, Artransa in Sydney, Australia began producing a daily 15-minute Tarzan show. Transmitted Monday to Friday at 6 pm, *Tarzan, King of the Apes* saw the ape-man played first by future Hollywood star Rod Taylor, then later by Ray Barrett and Lloyd Berrell. Jane was also played by three different actresses: Marcia Hathaway, Pamela Page and Joan Landor. It is estimated that over 1,000 episodes were broadcast. The few that remain are high quality and more faithful to Burroughs than the Commodore series.

The royalties from the Australian show had to be ceded by ERB, Inc to Walter White when he pointed out that he held the rights to Australian Tarzan radio broadcasts. This act of incompetence by Rothmund was not untypical: in the early '40s he had publishers who wanted to issue cheap editions of Burroughs books virtually tearing their corporate hair out over his penchant for simply not responding to letters or, when he did, engaging in counter-productive brinkmanship. Another consequence of his incompetence was that three Tarzan books – including, insanely, *Tarzan of the Apes* – were out of print even before Burroughs died.

It was with Lex Barker's third flick that a film producer finally took the plunge and decided to shoot a Tarzan film in Africa. Sol Lesser didn't intend to do it by halves either: possibly mindful of those who had noted what a waste it had been shooting the spectacular Mexican landscape in black-and-white in Weissmuller's swansong, he also determined that this would be the first colour Tarzan film. Almost all of his efforts went to waste.

Shooting began at Mount Kenya and its surrounds in July of 1950, the height of summer – in the States. In Africa it was winter, and Barker found his bronzed tone fading. This was only the start of a series of calamities. The imported chimps played up and Kenya transpired to be short on simian acting talent with which to replace them. Consequently, Cheeta was absent from a Tarzan picture (competing Tarzan films excepted) for the first time since 1932. Half of the footage was lost in an accident. The weather got so bad that, in late August, cast and crew retreated to the safety of California locations, at which point the production lost its director, Phil Brandon. His replacement Bryon Haskin had scriptwriters Samuel Newman & Francis Swann (John Cousins is credited with additional dialogue) rework the story. Just as the crew had retreated from Africa, so the producers retreated from the concept of a colour film. The monochrome picture made it to the cinemas in March 1951 as *Tarzan's Peril,* although the tradition of Tarzan sharing the billing with a glamorous female continued in the UK, where American working title *Tarzan and the Jungle Goddess* was retained. Despite Lesser's ambitious intent of widening the scope of Tarzan pictures, what emerged was merely a serviceable ape-man flick, although it could be argued that even this was an achievement in the circumstances.

The story revolves around Ashuban Queen Melmendi (Dorothy Dandridge) who declines the offer of marriage to King Bulam of the Yorango tribe. Bulam joins forces with a thoroughly nasty gun-runner called Radijeck (George Macready), who provides Bulam with the weaponry to take Melmendi's village. Radijeck also slaughters police commissioners, leaves one partner-in-crime to die in the jungle and murders the other before turning up at the treehouse to demand Jane lead him to civilisation. Jane is saved in the nick of time by her returning mate, who has already turned in a good afternoon's work by freeing Melmendi's people and despatching Bulam. Radijeck is thrown to his death.

Jane is here played by Virginia Huston, although the soon-to-be renowned actress doesn't get much of a chance to shine in the role. In the few sections of the 79-minutes in which she is present, she is done no favours by either a strangely luxurious white pelt costume or a functional housewifely hairdo that contrasts badly with the memory of O'Sullivan's tumbling curls.

The history of Tarzan reveals a creative tendency to turn to the concept of a junior ape-man to reinvigorate an ailing franchise. Sure enough, this is what Lesser did with *Tarzan's Savage Fury*, released in April 1952.

Apparently to this purpose, Lesser hired Cyril Hume, the scriptwriter who had introduced Boy in *Tarzan Finds a Son!* Hume collaborated with Hans Jacoby and Shirley White. The trio's script saw an attempt to incorporate some of Burroughs' books into the movie-Tarzan landscape, although the results are compromised by the requirement to stay within the parameters already set for the celluloid ape-man. We learn that Tarzan is a Greystoke heir and was raised in the jungle by his father. We are introduced to a tribe called the Waziri, although they are not under Tarzan's command. Continuing the garbled translation of Burroughsonia is the fact that there is a villain called not Rokoff but Rokov (Charles Korvin).

Rokov and companion Edwards (Patric Knowles) are seeking valuable industrial diamonds to which they know Tarzan can lead them. Rokov murders Tarzan's cousin Oliver, Lord Greystoke, and Edwards assumes the dead man's identity. Oblivious of their machinations, the ape-man is busy being a father to Joey (Tommy Carlton), a white boy made an orphan by lions and whom he has rescued from the fate of becoming native crocodile bait. Jane enjoys playing mother to Joey, who naturally is loinclothed-up to become a miniature of his new step-father. Dorothy Hart becomes the first redheaded Jane, although only readers of the more luxurious fan magazines would know this, as the film was in monochrome again. She is, though, by no means the first Jane to persuade Tarzan to do something against his better judgment for visitors who she belatedly learns are up to no good. In this case, she persuades her mate to lead his supposed cousin and Rokov to the diamonds they say are necessary for British national security. Cantankerous hippos and hungry cannibals bar their path. When Rokov steals the diamonds and murders a Waziri witchdoctor, Jane is marked by the tribe for execution. Joey, meanwhile, gets over his understandable lion-phobia the hard way. Tarzan fights Rokov and flings him into a lion pit before dashing to the Waziri village to make an eleventh-hour intervention in Jane's sacrificial ceremony.

This picture finds room for some of the location footage from the ill-fated African excursion for *Tarzan's Peril*. Endfield's direction is strong in a pacy 80 minutes whose action is leavened with nice sentimentality.

Barker got to speak an unusually high number of lines (137) in *Tarzan's Savage Fury*, but this upward dialogue gradient – for which the actor had agitated – was considered by Lesser to be the reason for the picture's lacklustre box office performance, and he determined to reverse it with the next one. (He presumably also adjudged the experiment with Joey a failure: the boy promptly disappeared from the series as though he had never been.) It's not known whether Barker informed Lesser he would not be signing a new long-term contract – which had one more movie on it – before Lesser made the dialogue decision. Barker was too much of a Princeton gentleman to publicly say anything other than, 'It's time for a change ... although I have nothing against playing the part.'

Lex Barker had done well in his tenure in the loincloth, looking credible in films that were mainly high quality. He still looked a million dollars in his June 1953 swansong *Tarzan and the She-Devil*, but as well as not being given many lines (a record low for him of 83), he was not, as he had previously been, furnished with a good script or much action. Consequently, he departed the series not with a triumphant yodel but a whimper.

Not only did Joey disappear from the franchise as soon as introduced, but Dorothy Hart – whose pre-Raphaelite beauty would have been ideal for the forthcoming colour age – also failed to return. Barker's fifth Jane in five movies is Joyce

MacKenzie. In shades of the book *Tarzan the Untamed*, the ape-man spends much of this movie in a distraught state when he discovers the burnt-out remains of his home and believes his beloved to be dead. However, where that dramatic set-up gave *Untamed* its impetus and power, here it drags the proceedings down, as the ape-man spends a large chunk of the 76 minutes moping apathetically in the cell to which he has been consigned by Lyra – she-devil of the title – and Vargo, her accomplice in ivory poaching. Future Perry Mason Raymond Burr plays Vargo, while Monique Van Vooren as Lyra convinces us that she is indeed deadlier than the male. There is a return to the Tantor-to-the-rescue climax, but with the twist that the ape-man has been forced upon pain of Jane's death to call up the elephant herd by the tusk-desirous villains. Naturally, Tarzan turns the tables on the khaki-clad ne'er-do-wells. Kurt Neumann directed the Karl Kamb & Carroll Young script. The Arboretum and RKO Encino Ranch were the backdrops not provided by footage from 1934 movie *Wild Cargo*.

Although he was a little typecast for a while, Barker had more acting chops on which to fall back than Weissmuller. He also had a more refined intellect. Subsequently, he became a multi-linguist thespian who made movies all over the world but was particularly successful in West Germany. That success bought him homes in Geneva, Rome and Barcelona and a 50-foot yacht, but not a long life. As if to prove that a magnificent physique is a guarantor of nothing, Barker died in 1973 of a heart attack at the shockingly young age of 54.

In the 1930s, Burroughs had suggested to Tarzan movie producers that they make an ape-man picture a dependable annual event. In the following decade, his dream came true, to such an extent that it was noteworthy when 1954 marked the first year without a new Tarzan feature in the theatres since 1944.

Part of the reason for that hiatus was the necessity to find another man to fit the loincloth. As with Lex Barker, the official story, which might even be true, is that serendipity provided the actor where auditions hadn't. Despite the testing of many prospective Tarzans – 200 was the customarily implausible figure quoted this time – 27-year-old Gordon Werschkul was found working as a lifeguard in a Las Vegas hotel by a holidaying Hollywood agent. Six foot three and good-looking, he had a torso shaped like a 'V' and a chest that was, amazingly, even broader than Barker's. If his bodybuilder's physique was technically not the type that would be created by a life in the trees, only the fanboys – as they then weren't called – were going to cavil. Also inappropriate was his elaborate pompadour – although there was a hint of wild man in the fact that his hair was almost shockingly abundant for the time. That long hair may have been a sign of changing times, likewise the fact that the new Tarzan's loincloth was the skimpiest yet. As was then common in showbusiness, Werschkul's name was de-ethnicised: he became Gordon Scott.

Yet with *Tarzan and the She-Devil* not having done appreciably better than *Tarzan's Savage Fury*, Lesser decided to debut his new ape-man as cheaply as possible rather than make an investment in him. Scott's entrée, *Tarzan's Hidden Jungle*, was released in February 1955. With movie audiences becoming ever more sophisticated, its extensive use of mismatching stock footage held the franchise up to ridicule. Complicating matters was the fact that distributor RKO was in severe trouble. In fact, so strapped for cash was the studio that a married couple turned out to have more wherewithal, even if that couple were *I Love Lucy* stars Lucille Ball and Desi Arnaz, who bought them out in 1956.

Although Cheeta is present, Jane does not appear. This seems to have been less to do with Lesser wearying of casting new actresses in the role than a desire to inject into the proceedings as much spice as was possible for the era: there is a sexual frisson attending Tarzan flinging into a pool the beautiful United Nations nurse Jill Hardy (Vera Miles) after she notes that she needs a wash, and in the way he watches her nude bathing. However, the ape-man remains as chaste as he does in

Burroughs' Jane-less novels. Instead, his passions are channelled into saving his beloved jungle from Burger (Jack Elam) and DeGroot (Charles Fredericks), big-game hunters who care not a fig for the fact that they are trampling all over the sacred animal-exalting beliefs of the local Sukulu tribe and are not above fooling United Nations employee Dr Celliers (Peter Van Eyck) into helping them in their quest for ivory, hides and animal fat. As a consequence of them leaving a trail of havoc and mischief, Tarzan has to nurse a baby elephant back to health and rescue Jill from a python. Additionally, he is sentenced to death by a witch doctor. Burger and DeGroot meet a grisly end beneath the feet of elephants stampeding at the ape-man's behest. Tarzan then saves Jill and Celliers from lions. Presumably, the limp way he does this – a few 'Umgawas' making the animals back down – is because a tussle to the death was deemed inappropriate at the climax of a movie in which he is posited as the friend and protector of wildlife.

Harold D Schuster directed the 73-minute film, whose script was furnished by William Lively. The Sukulu chief was played by Rex Ingram, who'd had a bit part in *Tarzan of the Apes*, 37 years and ten Tarzan actors previously.

Inevitably after the death of the author of a long-running, popular series of books, the issue of succession is raised by his fans. This fact was illustrated by Stuart J Byrne's *Tarzan on Mars*.

Pulp author Byrne, who often wrote under the *nom de guerre* John Bloodstone, was flattered by the suggestions of admirers of his work that he might be able to take over the Edgar Rice Burroughs mantle. He overcame his initial scepticism to write as a sort of exercise a novel in which the ape-man travelled to the red planet to rescue both Jane and La. The text showed how steeped Byrne was in Burroughs by attaching the high priestess of Opar to a loose thread of the author's published Barsoomian history. Ray Palmer, editor of *Other Worlds Science Stories*, so loved what he read that he wrote an article in the November 1955 edition of that publication enthusing over Byrne's manuscript –

whose author's name he did not reveal – and encouraging people to write in with the vague pledge, 'I'll back you up on Tarzan!' With an ambition that wasn't too outlandish in the days of mass circulation print products, he aimed for '100,000 names on my desk within the next 60 days.' Byrne later claimed that Hollywood began sniffing around, that famous science fiction author and Burroughs devotee Ray Bradbury gave his blessing and that Palmer had a potential 20,000 worldwide orders for the published book. Street & Smith Publications, Inc then made a formal overture to Edgar Rice Burroughs, Inc, guaranteeing a 25% royalty upon a go-ahead to publish. Cyril Ralph Rothmund's refusal instantly collapsed the tower of hope and intrigue that had suddenly sprung up in Burroughs-world.

Byrne was convinced that the pitch was wrong: his agent and Street & Smith had tried to sell him as a successor to Burroughs rather than promote the manuscript on its own merits. From thereon, *Tarzan on Mars* existed only in a twilight world of mimeographed copies circulated amongst Burroughs fans through the post. (It was joined there in 1972 by *Tarzan at Mars' Core*, a spiral-bound book by one Edward Hirschman whose alleged private print run of 2,000 was high for such enterprises.) In the modern age, of course, *Tarzan on Mars* is easily available, whizzing around the world as e-mail attachments and even viewable in full online, where the threat of legal action that previously prevented its wide dissemination seems not to be a factor because nobody is making money from it. It was also serialised in a hard copy fanzine across three years in the 1990s.

Yet Byrne may have been wrong about ERB, Inc's reasons for blocking publication. He had a vested interest in not perceiving his manuscript as over-long (at well over 100,000 words, it outstrips all Burroughs Tarzan novels except *Tarzan the Untamed*), his action plodding, his character motivation impenetrable (Tarzan literally waits years before setting off in search of the missing Jane), his exposition interminable and his knowledge of previous encounters between Tarzan and La surprisingly sketchy (especially considering his attempts elsewhere to show off his familiarity with Burroughs with obscure references to minor characters from each series). For all these reasons, *Tarzan on Mars* is really little more than a grand precursor to the 'fan fiction' with which it nowadays shares space online.

Following *Tarzan's Hidden Jungle* there was once again a two-year gap between ape-man pictures. When *Tarzan and the Lost Safari* was released in March 1957, it inaugurated the new era that Scott's first film might logically have been expected to.

In need of a new distributor, Lesser approached MGM. The studio that had had such great success with the character in the 1930s was understandably amenable to renewing its association with the ape-man. With Metro's big bucks behind him, Lesser was finally able to fulfil his ambitions relating to widescreen and colour that dated back to the beginning of the '50s. Colour film was technically around at the dawn of cinema, but it had truly taken off in the 1930s. Although even by the mid-'50s plenty of cinema releases were still in monochrome, if any film series was ideally suited to colour it was Tarzan. MGM cranked up the lustre by approving filming in British East African locations. Furthermore, for the first time, African location shooting consisted not just of establishing shots but of primary sequences. Even the non-jungle shooting was far-flung: the cast and crew decamped to Elstree Studios in England. Just as importantly, a high-quality script was procured from Montgomery Pittman and Lillie Hayward.

The action starts when Tarzan spots a 'sky-bird' crashing in the jungle. Having rescued the passengers just prior to their aircraft sliding over a cliff, he agrees to lead them to the coast. Lost safaris of around half-a-dozen people were a speciality of Burroughs, and the crashed crew are reminiscent of his writing in their disparateness: wealthy couple Dick and Diana Penrod, gossip columnist 'Doodles' Fletcher, blonde bombshell Gamage Dean and bored playboy Carl Kraski. Another ERB trait emerges in the way that romance blossoms between two of them, even if they are a former couple who begin to regret their split. Diana is captured by inhabitants of the village of Opar. Although Tarzan rescues her from the prospect of the sacrificial altar, the Oparians are on the party's trail for the remainder of the proceedings, assisted by hunter 'Tusker' Hawkins, who desires both Diana and the ivory bounty that is the Tusks of Opar.

H Bruce Humberstone's pacy direction and the lustrous colour are almost enough across the 84 minutes to make us not miss Jane. (The ape-man shows no interest in the beautiful women he encounters, although they certainly take an explicitly stated interest in him.) Cheeta, who for once isn't deployed to overly comic effect, plays a crucial role by using Doodles' lighter to set Opar on fire. The climax occurs on a burning rope bridge, on which Tarzan battles Hawkins while dodging Oparian arrows.

Although the Opar village here bears little resemblance to Burroughs' city of that name, there are more elements of the author's original ape-man than usual, including Tarzan explaining a backstory that involves being raised by apes after his parents perished in the jungle. (The scriptwriters get Kerchak and Kala mixed up in this recounting.)

With reviews of the picture being good, the validity of the new Tarzan era was confirmed. There would never be another black-and-white Tarzan movie.

Lesser was clearly feeling confident about Tarzan's viability. *Tarzan and the Lost Safari* hadn't even wrapped before he turned his attention to bringing the ape-man to the small screen.

The rise of television had been rapid indeed. The US networks began broadcasting in the late 1940s. By the mid-'50s, half of American homes had a TV set. It was presumably the fact that it was already clear that cinema had a huge rival – one that, at the time, nobody had any way of knowing would not be the death knell for movies – that caused Lesser to exercise his Tarzan rights in that direction.

Or, rather, try to exercise what he imagined to be his rights.

Walter White Jr had already been granted such rights in December 1950 by the bungling Cyril Ralph Rothmund. A brace of legal tussles followed. ERB, Inc – who understandably wanted Sol Lesser to apply his considerable live-action expertise to an ape-man TV show in preference to the shoestring operation of Commodore Productions and Artists – instituted a suit against Commodore to get it out of its obligations. When ERB, Inc lost, White issued proceedings against Lesser, who during the shooting of *Lost Safari* had formed a Tarzan TV company and then publicised an agreement he had reached with NBC. The latter network promptly pulled out of the deal until such time as the dispute with White was resolved. Lesser opted for the ploy of conceding the first-refusal of which White's rights consisted, knowing White did not have the wherewithal to mount an expensive TV production. The predictable upshot eventually occurred of Lesser buying White out.

When Lesser was finally in a position to authorise production of the ape-man's TV debut, he did it as a job lot with the next Tarzan cinematic venture. Three Tarzan TV pilots were filmed back-to-back alongside the movie *Tarzan's Fight for Life*. All four projects featured Scott in the lead role, the wholesome, fair-haired Eve Brent as Jane and another reincarnation of Boy in the shape of Tartu, the couple's ten-year-old adopted son, played by Rickie Sorenson. Incongruous with the ambition Lesser had lately poured into the ape-man, all four projects betrayed a pedestrianism largely responsible for their collective failure, which itself was ultimately responsible for Lesser bowing out of the Tarzan industry completely.

Tarzan's Fight for Life was not shot in Africa – or even Elstree – but at MGM's Culver City studios. It was a puzzling step backwards, one for which the intercutting of African footage garnered on the location trip for *Tarzan and the Lost Safari* was not compensation, not least because the screenplay left much to be desired. Perhaps Thomas Hal Phillips was genuinely trying to do something refreshing by spurning the time-tested device of Western interlopers with sinister plans, but he failed to come up with anything of comparable inherent dramatic possibility: the film could actually have been titled *Tarzan's Fight to Get Jane an Appendectomy*. Aside from Mrs Tarzan's burst appendix, the action – directed by Bruce Humberstone – revolves around the difficulties encountered by one Dr Sturdy (Carl Benton Reid) in bringing modern medicine to a jungle where witchdoctors and their potions hold sway. Tarzan – an unlikely champion of medicinal enlightenment – is on more comfortable territory when he battles an 18-foot python. When the film was released in July 1958, much was made in publicity of the fact that the year marked the fortieth anniversary of Tarzan cinema. The reviews, however, concentrated on the 86-minute film's dullness and it did relatively poorly at the box office.

At least, however, it saw the light of day. The first of the Tarzan TV pilots revolved around a battle between the ape-man and a trapper, the next a hunter with the ape-man in his sights, the third a treasure-oozing lost city. With Tarzan having proven his on-screen popularity with the public via what was already the second longest-running franchise in cinema history, it might be assumed that Lesser and NBC would readily obtain a sponsor for the show. In fact, none proved interested – then the kiss of death for a prospective American TV series with a high budget. Apart from footage included in two travelogue TV shows called *Bold Journey* that aired in 1956 and 1957, the public did not get to see any of the Gordon Scott Tarzan TV series until 1966 when a 74-minute TV movie was compiled from the three pilots and broadcast as *Tarzan and the Trappers*.

Charles F Haas and Sandy Howard are the credited directors and Frederick Schlick and Robert Leach the writers. The telefeature is palpably different from big-screen Tarzan because of a family-oriented tone that sees the provision of separate, sex-thoughts-banishing treehouses and a rather large loincloth for Scott hoisted right up over the navel. Being an artificial construct, it's doomed to be episodic, as well as difficult to assess aesthetically. Its backdrop would have made it exotic fare for mid-1950s TV (what den would not have resounded with joy at such sights as Tarzan chasing villains on the back of a commandeered giraffe?). Additionally, its nuclear family set-up – a sort of Jungle Family Robinson – would have chimed with the cornball tone of the broadcast drama of the era.

Back in '58, With *Tarzan's Fight for Life* bringing in disappointing returns and the TV episodes sitting uselessly on a shelf (their monochrome would have made them seem somewhat old-fashioned had they been released in the cinemas), Lesser became disillusioned. Producers Sy Weintraub and Harvey Hayutin found him when he was vulnerable (he'd also recently suffered a heart attack) and he accepted their offer of two million dollars for his production company, which of course included the rights he held to the ape-man.

Lesser had started as an interloper in the franchise and an irritant of Burroughs but had become the dominant force in screen Tarzan, which in terms of exposure was – for better or worse – the most culturally important manifestation of the ape-man. His departure from the stage after 15 features and a serial was truly the end of an ape-man era.

PART SIX: THE WEINTRAUB ERA

Although Harvey Hayutin was originally his business partner, Sy Weintraub bought him out after two pictures. It was therefore Weintraub who became the public face of a new Tarzan-film era, albeit one not as long cumulatively or even contiguously as Lesser's.

Weintraub was a TV man whose career included devising *The Late Show* and being vice-president of the largest supplier of films to American television. He felt that he could modernise Tarzan and return the movie series to the spirit of the books. Although his results in that were mixed, he turned out high-grade films while updating the character for people weaned on James Dean, Elvis Presley and Marilyn Monroe, a generation whose values were not as conventional as those of Lesser, Edgar Rice Burroughs or, come to that, Lord Greystoke.

No sooner had Sy Weintraub assumed control of the Tarzan franchise than he found himself facing competition from an 'unofficial' picture when MGM announced that they were to embark on a re-make of Weissmuller's entrée *Tarzan the Ape Man*. Weintraub naturally protested, but MGM had every legal right to shoot the movie, as at the time re-make options were written into their contracts as standard. Metro paid a heavy price for their re-make that would not even have been compensated for had it been a box office hit: Weintraub initially did not allow his ape-man productions to be distributed by them.

Had Weintraub been of a mind to immediately replace Gordon Scott, buying out his contract at this point would probably have been prohibitively expensive. However, starting with his first effort, *Tarzan's Greatest Adventure*, released in July 1959, Weintraub changed the character Scott had hitherto played. Weintraub decreed his Tarzan speak intelligently, conjugations and all. He also ordered some spice, dispensing with Jane to this purpose. In 1960, he would explain, 'The kids of today want action and adventure, and a bachelor figure is more exciting than a jungle suburbanite swinging home every night to tell his little woman what happened during the day.' Jane would not appear in a Tarzan film again until 1981. In the pursuit of his object of action and adventure, Weintraub authorised more realistic – and sometimes harrowing – violence.

Weintraub also paid close attention to quality. Key to that was production values: the combination of Kenyan location shooting and British technicians that was deemed to be behind the success of *Tarzan and the Lost Safari* was replicated for *Tarzan's Greatest Adventure*. On top of that, the script by Berne Giler and John Guillermin, from a story by Les Crutchfield, is mean and lean – something probably inadvertently helped by the minimal presence of Cheeta due to the imported American chimps being frightened by jungle noises. In the same spirit, Tarzan displays nary a trace of playfulness or humour. Guillermin maintains the tautness with quickstep direction. He also beautifully photographs the lush, teeming landscapes, often with imaginative camera angles.

It's presumably on this picture that Weintraub learnt of the sound problems inherent in Tarzan pictures: he developed a *modus operandi* of silent shooting because post-dubbing (usually in London) was the best way to get around the issues created by passing aeroplanes, noisy natives, the cries of indigenous fauna and the commands of animal wranglers.

The plot is propelled by the deeds of a party of white villains which is led by an old Tarzan adversary named Slade (Anthony Quayle) and includes a man named O'Bannion (a young Sean Connery). Slade's sassy blonde aviatrix girlfriend Angie (Sara Shane) starts out as a member of said crew but defects to the side of light when she sees the extent of her companions' ruthless venality. *En route* to a diamond mine they intend to plunder, the group murder hospital staff in a quest for dynamite. Tarzan follows their trail, enduring the attentions of a crocodile and a poisonous spider in between attacks from Slade's party, although is provided inadvertent help by the members of the latter turning on each other. When villain Dino is helplessly trapped in quicksand, his mauling by a panther epitomises the new edginess of the franchise. An exciting 90-minute feature climaxes with Tarzan and Slade fighting to the death on top of a cliff. Even the poster art is powerful: a long shot of Tarzan unleashing a victory cry, fists clenched, from the precipice from which Slade has just fatally plummeted. The only black mark is the way Weintraub chickens out of fully sexualising Tarzan: a scene wherein the ape-man and Angie sucked face was unwisely excised, even if audiences were left in little doubt as to what happened immediately after the cut.

After all that care, and despite glowing reviews, *Tarzan's Greatest Adventure* ended up a relative flop due to half-hearted promotion and poor distribution on the part of Paramount: this film was hardly designed to be playing two-fers with Jerry Lewis comedy *Don't Give Up the Ship*.

Tarzan's Greatest Adventure was the sort of superlative-packed title common in Hollywood at the time, but on this occasion it was more than hype. Not even just a superior Tarzan picture, it for some remains the best even to this day. More remarkably, it's difficult to see Burroughs doing anything other than unequivocally approving of it.

The man MGM chose as their competition for Gordon Scott was a 24-year-old contract player named Denny Miller.

He was an unusual Tarzan, but – he points out – not unique: 'They keep saying I was the first blonde, but Buster Crabbe was a blonde.' (In fact, the first was technically Jim Pierce.) Physique-wise, though, Miller fit the template of Burroughs' forest god. Miller explains, 'My father was a physical educator. He was on President Kennedy's and President Eisenhower's Council for Youth Fitness. He bought me a set of weights when I was in eighth grade.' Miller's muscle mass and Greek-god looks ultimately attracted the attention of movie talent-scout Bob Raison.

Miller's acting roles before being cast as the ape-man included *Some Came Running* with Shirley MacLaine, Dean Martin and Frank Sinatra. He didn't consider Tarzan his big break, having a rather matter-of-fact approach to his roles. 'I took the work that they told me to take,' he shrugs. 'I was a misplaced basketball player.' That notwithstanding, he originally told the studio that they might be looking in the wrong direction: 'I recommended Bill Smith, the actor, because I had worked out at the same gym and knew that he had a better build than I did. However, they screen-tested Bill and myself and several others, and for some reason I got the part.'

Of his screen test, Miller recalls, 'Believe it or not I walk out of the jungle and Jane is sitting on a log and I'm soaking wet – obviously, it's either rained or I've been in the water – and I sit down with her and recite the 23rd Psalm. They kept telling me that they were going to make this version of Tarzan a much more educated and more intelligent variety than they had before. I said more in that screen test than I did in the whole movie.' Regarding the issue of his movie being frowned on by Weintraub, Miller says, 'I was happily ignorant of all that going on.'

Miller took the trouble to sit down and watch several of the previous Tarzan movies: 'I enjoyed Elmo Lincoln very much. I'd seen most of the Johnny Weissmuller ones and a couple of the Gordon Scotts.' Miller also boned up on the yodel. 'They gave me a recording of one of the yells,' he says. 'I don't know which one it was, but it was the one that they used in the film. They gave it to me way before the shooting started and I was living at the beach and at night I would go down and yell at the waves so as not to be arrested. I did never come close. I sounded like a wounded yak when I yelled. I did a yell and then they just snipped it out in the sound department and laid in the other sound. Carol Burnett does it much better. I officiated at some Tarzan yell contests. Usually little girls and women [win].'

Miller had to go through the bizarre-sounding process of attending a loincloth fitting. 'As a matter of fact, I have one of them,' he reveals. 'They had two of them, because when one was wet and they wanted it dry it was better to have one waiting instead of trying to take a hairdryer and dry the one off. I don't think I ever had to change, so I don't think that happened due to scheduling.'

Miller received instruction from a stuntman on how to swing on a vine. He was told to 'start off with your arms extended and not in a right angle so that you didn't panic when you get to the upside of the swing. Some people panic when they can't hold their arms at a right-angle because of the added gravity.' His training didn't prevent swinging mishaps, though. 'My stunt double was a very good stunt double [but once] he was on another job and I did a swing that he would have normally taken that was quite a long one,' he explains. 'I swung out from a tree house. They had erected a stand for two guys to stand on about 30 feet high to catch me when I got there. The person that tried the swing before me was considerably less weight than I and he was much shorter. He got there just fine. When I went out on my swing I knew that my chest was going to hit the top of the thing and I curled up and took the collision with the bottom of my feet. That kind of tipped the thing and the two guys that were supposed to catch me were reaching for something to hold on so they wouldn't fall off of the stand, so I just went backwards and bounced off the side of the bamboo house, which cut my leg a little bit. I got in smaller and smaller arcs until I was still and I was holding onto the vine – it's a rubber-coated rope with a leaf here and there sticking out so it looks somewhat real – and they got a ladder and came up and let me down. But I didn't ever fall off of a vine.' This was fortunate for, in the days before workplace health-and-safety regulation, there was no trampoline to break a fall. Not that there was no protection at all for the actor. Miller: 'If it was a very high swing, they usually give you a leather loop that was attached to the rope and covered with leaves so it wouldn't be seen, so I could have hung there for quite a while before they came and got me.'

The conscientiousness detailed above on the part of MGM in preparation for the 82-minute film, shot over six weeks on their backlot in Culver City, West Los Angeles, makes it all the more curious that the studio in most other respects treated the new

Tarzan the Ape Man – and its potential audience – almost with contempt. 'MGM had done other low-budget films, but I don't think ever that low,' says Miller. A case in point was a scene shot with Joanna Barnes, this movie's Jane, on a cement-bedded river on which some of Johnny Weissmuller's swimming scenes had been filmed. The budget didn't extend to heating the set. 'Her teeth were chattering so much they couldn't understand what she was saying,' says Miller. 'So they gave her several drinks of brandy and that warmed her up enough to be able to say the lines.' It was understandable that a re-make should follow the plot of the original Weissmuller movie fairly closely, but not so much that the footage should include parts of that and other Weissmuller movies. Also featured were sections of *King Solomon's Mines* (1950). Miller notes, 'I was amazed that they had so many wildebeest charging across the screen. It was a piece of stock footage. We didn't do that scene for sure on the backlot.' The crowning piece of the farce is the fact that nowhere in the movie is Miller's character referred to as Tarzan.

The tone of the production was set, albeit inadvertently, with the first scene Miller filmed. 'Sound stages and outdoor stages are full of hazards for people who are running around barefoot,' he explains. 'Nails and splinters and twigs and glass. So they took an impression of my feet, then they made me rubber or Styrofoam soles for my feet and glued them on. The first shot of the show was me swinging on a vine from behind the camera, over the camera, letting go and dropping with my back to the camera and stopping and putting my hands up and telling Jane and her father that we got to go hide because there's going to be a stampede. Well, they rolled the camera, I swung out, I dropped where I should have been and hopped just a little bit. Those soles were right where I'd landed – they came off. I never saw them again.'

Although it would be over-dramatic to suggest that this film was cursed – filming a Tarzan picture is hazardous almost by definition – the shoot does seem to have been afflicted by pratfalls and misfortunes. Miller: 'When I showed up [one] morning there [was] a 30-foot wire fence around the indoor set. They had a little old lady there and a guy with a shotgun. I found out later my stunt double wasn't there; a new guy was there. They asked me to go in there. It would be an easy thing: "You just wrestle around with this house pet." It's a cheetah. A little old lady had hold of him by a leash and they had painted over the muzzle on his mouth. I said – very wisely afterwards, I thought – "I'd like to see the stuntman do it first." So they got the stuntman up on a tree limb, and he was supposed to drop down when the cheetah went under him. Well, they got a live goose and they held the goose by the neck and showed the goose to the cheetah and they held the cheetah behind a bush. They let the cheetah go and the cheetah crouched down like he was going to get that goose for lunch and as soon as he was under the branch, the stuntman just moved about an inch and the cheetah heard him and now they can't get the cheetah to go under the limb. So they asked the stuntman to just stand in front of the cheetah and they unleashed him and they started to film it and the cheetah lay down on its back and rolled over like a big kitten and wanted to play. They tried slapping the cheetah in the face and there was a blur. The stuntman was bleeding from his shoulder, down his chest, along his left side, down his thigh. After that happened, I said, "I won't go in there." So they got this stuffed animal. And it looks like a stuffed animal.'

Not that this prevented Miller from having teeth sunk into him. 'A chimp bit me on the hand once,' he says. 'The trainer had told me, "If he bites you, hit him, because he'll take a part of you with him." It wasn't the chimp's fault, really. He was a nice little chimp. Marvellous. They're so intelligent. They had a shot where the camera shows me walking away and the chimp has come to get me to go back to help Jane. He is instructed by his trainer to run up to me and reach out for my hand, and he wants to pull me back. Well, after I get ahold of his hand, the trainer is behind the camera and yells to the chimp to come his way, and I won't let him go. Naturally the chimp is going to go where he gets his food and his instructions, so I felt his teeth on the meaty part of the outside of my left hand. I lifted up my hand and the chimp came with it. I punched him in the nose and he let go and he went up in the rafters, and it took us half an hour and a BB gun to get him back down.'

Meanwhile, the crocodile Miller was supposed to fight to the death was in no fit state to bite anything. Miller: 'They tried to use the same mechanised 20- or 30-foot alligator [sic] that Johnny had fought in one or two or more of his films. It turned into a fiasco. I jumped on its head as they were pulling it by wire because the mechanism didn't work anymore. It'd been sitting out in the sun for 20 years or more. When I jumped on it, I went down to the bottom and came out, I thrashed around and I got up, and when I was tired I stood up, and everyone was on their hands and knees on the shoreline, laughing. The camera had been on a boom and the operator had laughed himself right out of the chair. They told me that the tail went up and it sunk like a submarine. They never could use it.' Instead, the crocodile fight from *Tarzan and his Mate* was used yet again. This recycling had been risible enough the first few times, but now it was little short of desperate: *Tarzan and his Mate* had been in black-and-white whereas the new *Tarzan the Ape Man* was in colour. Miller: 'They tinted it, and it looks like tinted black-and-white film. It's kind of a terrible green.' Moreover, in places Weissmuller's face is clearly visible.

Riding elephants was a happier experience for Miller: 'It was fun.' However: 'They don't like chimpanzees on their back so it took us all about half an hour to get up there. They handed the chimp from behind the elephant so he couldn't see.'

As for his Jane, Miller says of Joanna Barnes, 'We got along fine,' despite revealing a painful piece of improvisation on her part: 'In one scene where we were fighting and she's frightened to death, she tried to bite me on the knee, which wasn't in the script, but it made the fight look realistic.' Barnes has gone on to become a successful novelist.

Tarzan the Ape Man – released in October 1959 – was written by Robert Hill and directed by Joseph M Newman. MGM's bizarre decision to give the film a low budget was exposed as an archetypal false economy when it proceeded to be derided for its shoddiness. Inevitably, there were no more unofficial Tarzans made by MGM, at least in that era. 'I heard at the time that they had the rights to do two more, and I was not against having to do those,' says Miller. 'But I never heard again it mentioned.' Not that he was waiting around to hear anything: 'I was off on many other projects. I've been very lucky. A long career in Hollywood is ten years. A career of over 50 years [like mine] is not unique, but it's very [rare] ... I've never brooded overmuch and certainly not whether I get a job.'

Miller didn't take in *Tarzan the Ape Man* until two or three years after its premiere. 'I didn't see anything that I did for a very long time because it made me so nervous,' he explains. 'I would say that there are more than half of [my roles] I haven't seen ever.' His reaction when he did see the film? 'Like I always did with other roles, I would get involved with thinking, "Oh my goodness, I don't walk that way." It was all physical – there was no mental piece to it: "I wish I had done this" or "I wish I had done that."'

Miller's film boasts a dubious accolade: 'It's listed in *Tarzan of the [Movies]* under a chapter heading "Tarzan the Worst".' Miller is philosophical: 'I laughed at that and I've talked to [the author] Gabe Essoe since. He says, "It was not you, it was the production."'

Unlike many actors who are better regarded for their ape-man portrayal or who had longer reigns as Tarzan, Miller has enthusiastically embraced his place in history as one of the select few to don the loincloth. 'I've been to at least ten or 15 Dum-Dums,' he says of the conventions of Burroughs devotees. 'Only on two occasions did I ever see another Tarzan attend. Ron Ely has never been at one I've been to. I've spoken at several of them. My licence plate is "X-Tarzan" ... I know of people who consider playing the role of Tarzan to have ruined their acting career. Bruce Bennett changed his name. His autobiography, written by a friend of mine, the title of it is *Please Don't Call Me Tarzan*. I know Mike Henry thought that whatever career he had being a second banana to Jackie Gleason, he thought Tarzan didn't help him out. I have never had the feeling that I didn't get a part because I had played the role of Tarzan. On the contrary. I played one called Tongo of the Jungle on *Gilligan's Island*. It was one of the most fun. When I go to film festivals, people ask for pictures of Tongo more than any other part that I've played, and I've played hundreds of parts ... I did enjoy everything in the film. I've enjoyed it ever since. It's fun being a cartoon.' Miller even goes so far as to say, 'There's been no negative aspect of playing the role of Tarzan. I've had it described as one of the longest-living hero figures in fiction, at least in the United States, that has entertained more little kids ... It's grouped together with Superman, Batman and Mickey Mouse all over the world ... It was a unique job. It was like being in a circus: go ride that elephant, play with that monkey, swing on that vine, jump from that right into the water ... What's more fun than that?'

The effect of *Tarzan the Ape Man* on Miller's other career as a physical instructor has been 'delightful.' He says, 'It's helped me get into offices of doctors at hospitals and places to talk to fourth-graders about too much violence on television.' Messianic about physical education, Miller is the author of the fitness book *Toxic Waist? Get to Know Sweat!*, as well as the autobiography *Didn't You Used To Be ... What's His Name?*

'Having played Tarzan is probably one of the biggest joys of my life,' summarises Miller.

Weintraub may have been trying to improve Tarzan films, but on one level he was just as much the cliché of a movie mogul as Sol Lesser: for his second venture, he tried to repeat the formula of his previous film, seeking to re-recruit *en masse* the actors who played the four villains in *Tarzan's Greatest Adventure*, even though their characters had all met a grisly fate therein. Perhaps luckily for the growing integrity of the series, only Al Mulock was available to come back to portray a different interloper.

Tarzan the Magnificent, released in July 1960, was 88 minutes long and, as with the previous film, distributed by Paramount. It's not related to the novel of the same name, although does share something with Burroughs' writing style in the shape of a narrative that alternates Tarzan's escapades with the adventures of a safari comprised of disparate types: a black engineer, a pompous ass (played by British character actor Lionel Jeffries), the latter's bored high-society wife, a doctor and a smouldering sexpot. The safari members are passengers on a boat blown up by the family of Coy Banton, a villain whom Tarzan is transporting to Kairobi [sic] to be punished for a number of murders, including that of a policeman friend of his. As the ape-man is indirectly responsible for their plight, he reluctantly allows the group to accompany him. Banton's brothers remain on his trail, led by their father Abel (John Carradine).

Tarzan fans could live with the non-appearance of Jane and the reduced role of Cheeta, but a refinement too far for some was the absence for the first time since talkies began of a Tarzan yodel. However, Robert Day's able direction, the Kenyan location shooting and the reversed-chase nature of the screenplay by Day and Berne Giler all make for an evocative, taut and exciting picture similar to its (Weintraub) predecessor, if not quite as good. With one exception. Just as *Tarzan's Greatest Adventure* had a set-piece mano-a-mano battle between the ape-man and the chief villain atop a cliff, so this picture culminates in Tarzan and Banton fighting to the finish. The scrap is a corker, starting on a bluff adjacent to a waterfall, descending into a river and winding up on rocky shore. It's a rumble in the jungle that is vicious and spiteful for its entire five-minute duration. Scott had always prided himself on doing his own stunts and the fact that his adversary was played by top Hollywood stuntman Jock Mahoney only added to the scene's power.

And Scott's reward for this? To lose his job to the actor who played the man whom he subdues and drags off to state justice. Although Scott's technique had blossomed as his character's vocabulary had widened, his producer had decided he wanted a leaner, more agile man in the lead role. Scott subsequently made some sword-and-sandals pictures in Europe before his career sputtered to a halt in the mid-'60s. Although Weintraub must have paid off the remaining two years on his contract, and although he was able to milk the convention and signing-booth circuits, his death in 2007, aged 80, found Scott penniless and – having left a trail of wives, children and debts behind him – pretty much friendless.

Scott not only made two of history's best Tarzan pictures, but is unique on a couple of counts: he straddled monochrome and colour Tarzan movies and he portrayed the ape-man as both a pidgin-English speaker and an articulate individual.

With both Harvey Hayutin and Gordon Scott dispensed with, Weintraub now pursued a new vision for Tarzan over and above the significant changes he'd already made to the franchise.

He explained in an interview, '...50 percent of our profits are made abroad ... I want to stress the international aspect, make Tarzan somewhat of a world traveller ... I'd like to do something in Peru, or India, perhaps ... He's international; every country thinks he belongs to them.'

As for the leaner, more agile man Weintraub recruited for the lead role, Denny Miller says, 'Jock Mahoney was one of the best stuntmen in the history of stuntmen in Hollywood. He was an athlete. I've heard people say he could vault over three horses from the side and not touch them other than the middle one and just the saddle. He could stand in the saddle and ride at full speed. He had all those wonderful attributes because he had a strong, agile, coordinated body.' Mahoney wasn't merely a stuntman, though. Graduating to *bona fide* actor, he appeared in many action films and became famous by playing the title character in the early-'50s TV Western series *The Range Rider*. Weintraub of course had become cognisant of Mahoney's physical qualities when he saw the rushes of *Tarzan the Magnificent*. Having lost out to Lex Barker over a dozen years previously, Mahoney was in a long Tarzan-movie tradition of actors who got the ape-man role second-time around. With all this and the fact that he was six-foot-four and devoid of body fat, he was ostensibly perfect for the role.

Weintraub plumped for India as the first of his international locations, recruiting John Guillermin to direct Robert Hardy Andrews' script. *Tarzan Goes to India* sees the ape-man called to the sub-continent by his friend the Maharajah (played by Murad) and his beautiful daughter Princess Kamara (Simi) because they are very concerned about the construction timeframe of a power plant and dam: it is so tight that it will not enable the shipping to safety of a herd of 300 elephants whose home ground the plant is to be built upon. Bryce (Leo Gordon), the man tasked with erecting the plant, is an old adversary of the ape-man, having run into him on Tarzan's home turf when he was poaching ivory. Naturally, he is left cold by Tarzan's pleas to postpone the construction long enough for him to save the elephants by driving them through a mountain pass. Ultimately, not only does Tarzan save the elephants, he then uses his pachyderm friends to assist in the finishing of the power plant.

Tarzan is assisted by a Mowgli-like boy named Jai, played by an actor of the same name. As well as serving as a point of identification for a great wedge of the intended audience, Jai is a crucial buddy-figure for Tarzan in the absence in this outing not just of Jane but also of Cheeta. Everything ape-man-related Weintraub did from hereon would feature a character similar to Jai.

Evident on screen are the fruits of a two-month location shoot in places like Bangalore, Bombay and Madras. They are enriched by this being the first Tarzan film shot in the widescreen technique of CinemaScope and underlined by noted Indian musician Ravi Shankar contributing to the exotic soundtrack.

Although he sanctioned Tarzan tussling with a rogue elephant, a leopard and a cobra, Weintraub neglected to take advantage of the perfect opportunity afforded by the location to depict the ape-man battling a tiger. At least Tarzan's yodel is reinstated.

Having evidently forgiven them for the Denny Miller picture,

Weintraub granted MGM distribution rights to *Tarzan Goes to India*. Said studio – who released the 86-minute film in March 1962 – rewarded him with the highest Tarzan grosses to date. Even if no doubt greatly assisted by the vast audiences in the titular sub-continent receptive to this particular picture, this was quite a feat.

So what's not to love? Well, both the international aspect and Mahoney's casting create problems. The internationalism is a perfectly valid idea and a good way to inject variety but, when Burroughs had Tarzan visiting far-flung locales in 'Tarzan and the Castaways'/'The Quest of Tarzan' and *Tarzan and the 'Foreign Legion'*, he set up the relocation properly. Robert Hardy Andrews does not. We are mystified as to how Tarzan and the Maharajah are friends, why the ape-man is well-known on a different continent, and – because the screenplay does not explain the character's Lord Greystoke hinterland – how he has the wherewithal to charter a plane. (The film begins with the ape-man dropping into a lake in the titular country, having needed only to dispense with his flying helmet and goggles to be in traditional Tarzan costume.)

As for Mahoney himself, he is in great condition for a man of his age – but that age is 42, only one year younger than Weissmuller when the latter was belatedly pensioned off. In many scenes, his vintage is painfully apparent, especially ones involving that beneath-the-chin angle that is so unforgiving for anyone over forty, no matter how well-preserved. His non-chiselled features are also incongruously, almost farcically, ordinary. His lank, swept-back hair only adds to the impression of looking at your uncle. Moreover, his body might be fat-free but it also teaches us the value of the cinema shorthand that the muscular physiques of previous Tarzan actors had constituted. Yes, our brains tell us that a man brought up in the treetops would more likely have a physique like his than Gordon Scott's, but our eyes insist that Mahoney as Tarzan is a joke.

Although Tarzan had always been popular, *Tarzan Goes to India* was released into a world that was unexpectedly newly receptive to the ape-man.

A school employee in the Los Angeles suburb of Downey was the reason. Her profession was librarian, a breed with which Edgar Rice Burroughs had had an edgy relationship. In March 1922, for instance, the *Wisconsin Library Bulletin* featured an article by one Professor Noble that condemned his books both for harmful moral effects on children and unlikely plots. Burroughs later stiffly declined a request from a library in Tarzana for a set of his books on the grounds that the main Los Angeles Public Library had banned his works because they supposedly had no literary value. Not that the author didn't receive nice feedback from library staff: an English librarian copied him in on a letter he had written in rebuttal to Professor Noble, while a Syracuse, New York librarian, in denying to the author a rumour that had reached his ears that a ban was about to be enacted, pointed out that his books were so popular that they had problems keeping 'them from being stolen from the shelves.' However, Burroughs' hurt and hostile feelings on librarians in general can be gleaned from this passage of a letter from 1928: 'I, too, have noticed how my name is always ignored by literary writers, librarians and other members of the intelligentsia ... I wonder why they dislike me so much.' The Los Angeles ban outlasted Burroughs himself by two decades.

The issue relating to the Downey school librarian was of a nature that Burroughs had actually encountered while he was alive. A priest had once contacted Sol Lesser and threatened to denounce Tarzan from the pulpit over the fact that the ape-man and Jane were living in sin. As he was clearly talking about the films, the holy man was actually on firm ground, but when Lesser passed on to the priest Burroughs' message that he should check out the wedding ceremony in the book *The Return of Tarzan*, he was placated. In removing from shelves two donated Tarzan books on similar moral grounds, the Downey librarian – who perhaps mercifully remained anonymous – found herself publicly referred to in terms like 'spoilsport.' She was acting on a complaint by a parent, but of course there was no reason why she should have meekly surrendered in the face of it.

A scandal of minuscule proportions ensued. The Downey ban became public knowledge on 27 December 1961, when newspapers across America picked up an Associated Press story. That the district's imposition of a similar ban on Zane Grey titles was mentioned only in a footnote indicates that editors were printing the story not because they were taking it seriously but because they were rejoicing in the opportunity to run headlines like 'Librarian Trees Tarzan on Morals Rap' and humorous references to the jungle drums beating out the rumour that Tarzan and Jane had been living in sin in their treehouse, et groan cetera. As Supt Bruce Moore of the Downey Unified Schools District said that he and his colleagues were opposed to any ban, and as Sol Lesser was responding to reporters' phone calls with the line about *The Return of Tarzan* that he had trotted out to the clergyman several years previously – and as the inevitable Burroughs fans, ostensibly outraged but secretly pleased to be able to show off their knowledge, were sending corrections into newspapers – this hardly had obvious potential to develop into a media storm. Two days after the story broke, papers were running headlines like, 'Are Tarzan and Jane Wed? South of NC Nobody Cares,' and, in a turn of events that would no doubt have infuriated Burroughs, a different librarian opined that he only objected to ERB's books on literary grounds. The issue was dead before the year was.

Fate, though, works in peculiar ways. With the subject of Tarzan books suddenly all over the newspapers, it reminded people of an almost forgotten pleasure. It also prompted some weaned on that pleasure to consider passing on their childhood partiality to the kids they themselves now had. Additionally, it steered fans of the Tarzan movies to ape-man adventures to which they had paid little attention or even of which they had not been previously cognisant. Demand for Tarzan novels shot through the roof, and continued to do so into 1962, a publicity boon marking Tarzan's half-centenary that could not have been more advantageous if it had been planned. The only problem was, that demand could not be met.

Here was where the haughty ineptitude of Cyril Ralph Rothmund had categorically backfired. The general manager of ERB, Inc had in the dozen years since Burroughs' death presided over a shocking decay in the business with whose profitability he was charged. Not only had he allowed every single one of the books published by ERB, Inc – which included nine Tarzan titles – to fall out of print, but he had refused to license their release as paperbacks by other publishers. Although that format had existed as far back as the 1930s, Burroughs himself had been wary of paperbacks and their potential for eating into his profits. He permitted in his home country only the publication of a 1940 paperback abridgment of *Tarzan in* [sic] *the Forbidden City* and editions of the first two Tarzan books that were distributed by the government free of charge to troops during the Second World War. In recent years, though, paperbacks had begun a big growth in popularity and Rothmund had failed to move with the times. The fact that it was later estimated that worldwide paperback sales of Burroughs books between 1962 and 1968 totalled 50 million – more sales than in all the previous years combined in all editions – gives an indication of how costly this was. In 1961/62, the only Burroughs ape-man adventures still orderable at bookstores and libraries were some Grosset & Dunlap budget editions licensed from McClurg, sales of which now increased by 25%. In his usual style, Rothmund didn't bother affording New York booksellers Jack Biblo and Jack Tannen the courtesy of an answer when they wrote to ERB, Inc – they estimated 'several times' – about Tarzan books, requests for which they found themselves swamped by in the wake of the newspaper reports.

This latter discourtesy cost ERB, Inc even more money, for Biblo and Tannen evidently made the assumption that ERB, Inc's apparent indifference indicated that it no longer had a financial interest in the character's prose adventures. They instigated a copyright search at the Library of Congress. US copyright law at that time dictated that copyright on works expired after 28 years unless renewed. To their amazement, the pair found that ERB, Inc had not renewed the copyright on approximately half of Burroughs' published books. This meant that they could, if they so wished, re-publish these books themselves and – as would be the situation with any other public-domain work – pocket all the profits. They quickly set up Canaveral Press, and by April of 1962 were soliciting orders for 21 Burroughs books, three of them Tarzan titles. Even so, they were beaten to the punch by Dover Publications, who released ten Tarzan novels in four paperback compendiums. Paperback publisher Ace also joined in the ERB free-for-all. ERB, Inc, meanwhile, belatedly struck a deal with Ballantine Books for an official paperback line. Chaotic and confusing though the situation was, it at least meant that the demand for prose Tarzan could now be met. By November 1963, *Life* magazine was reporting that the ERB re-releases had 'sold something more than 10 million copies, almost one thirtieth the total annual sales of all paperbacks in the US.' Ace and Ballantine had ordered second printings of 300,000 and 110,000 respectively of each of their Tarzan titles, of which Ballantine had already issued a dozen and were scheduling the remaining ten. The 'Tarzan of the Paperbacks' *Life* special report in which that statistic appeared was – *Life* being one of the States' most iconic magazines – itself a boost to the tsunami of publicity on which the books' sales were riding. *The Wall Street Journal* and *The New York Times* reported on the Burroughs revival too.

Playwright, screenwriter, journalist and soon-to-be novelist Gore Vidal – a boyhood ERB fan – was prompted by the boom to re-read several Burroughs books. He delivered his verdict in the December 1963 edition of men's glossy *Esquire*: 'Though Burroughs is innocent of literature and cannot reproduce human speech, he does have a gift very few writers of any kind possess: he can describe action vividly.' He concluded on a note of intellectualism of which the concurrent Burroughs retrospectives were innocent: 'James Bond, Mike Hammer and Tarzan are all dream-selves, and the aim of each is to establish personal primacy in a world which in reality diminishes the individual. Among adults, increasing popularity of these lively inferior fictions strikes me as a most significant (and unbearably sad) phenomenon.'

The free-for-all didn't last long. Lawyers working for ERB, Inc discovered that the copyright on the magazine versions of the Burroughs books had been renewed. The subsequent book versions were therefore automatically protected. It would seem that ERB, Inc were an unintended beneficiary of a conscientiousness on the part of the magazine publishers that the Burroughs estate lacked. Canaveral were allowed to continue publishing Burroughs hardbacks, while Ace and Ballantine shared the paperback rights. However, publishers all around the world were now on notice to cease and desist.

The Ballantine paperbacks came with the pointed banner slogan 'Authorised Edition,' but their dull typography and boring cover illustrations made them somewhat less covetable than the Ace books, which had dynamic cover layouts and exciting art by Roy Krenkel and Frank Frazetta. Because Frazetta was also used by Canaveral for covers and spot illustrations, and because he provided some new Ace covers in the early 1970s, his vision of the ape-man became by default as important and defining for a certain group as St John's had been for the readers of his era. Interestingly, most Frazetta fans think the artist was not working at the top of his game when rendering Tarzan. His pictures certainly weren't as lushly erotic and vibrant as either his own celebrated Conan paperback cover paintings or Boris Vallejo's Tarzan paperback covers of the 1970s. Nor were they as dynamic as Neal Adams' covers for the same Ballantine series that Vallejo's pictures graced. The possible exception, not intended for book publication, was a watercolour (date unknown, but judging by its explicitness, much later than the '60s) called *Tarzan meets La of Opar*, in which a bound ape-man is being presented to the High Priestess by two naked women. La is herself proffering her naked pudenda to the captive. At the insistence of the gallery buying the piece, Frazetta painted out the erection he had given Tarzan.

There were also 'new' Tarzan books on the back of the Burroughs boom, something assisted by Rothmund's departure. (Robert Barrett: 'He was asked to retire.') Almost symbolically, when the three Burroughs children assumed control of the company and investigated its safe, they found within it half a million words of unpublished Burroughs prose that nobody had known existed, among them several complete novels.

Back in 1950, *The New York Times* had claimed that the just-passed Burroughs had left behind 'approximately 15 incompleted Tarzan tales.' This intriguing figure has been scaled back by subsequent archive research to two, plus two humorous playlets, *Tarzan & Jane: A Jungleogue* (1933, a 16-page distillation of *Tarzan of the Apes*) and *Tarzan's Good Deed Today* (circa 1940s, a three-page play for children). However, there was some complete Tarzan material that had never been published in book form and one complete novel that had never been published in any form. In the new atmosphere of hunger for Tarzan prose, *Tarzan and the Madman* was transformed from a Tarzan self-parody considered unfit to print by both the pulps and ultimately Burroughs himself into a myth-shrouded 'lost' ape-man novel. Either that or ERB, Inc sanctioned its release because they thought at that point that it might well be the only Tarzan work to which they unambiguously held exclusive publication rights. Its appearance in June 1964 from Canaveral rather spoiled the dignified end to the series that *Tarzan and the 'Foreign Legion'* had constituted. Things were redeemed a little when in December 1964 the only other completed Tarzan prose material that had not appeared in book form – the magazine-published Tarzan short stories 'Tarzan and the Jungle Murders' and 'Tarzan and the Champion' and novella 'The Quest of Tarzan' – were mopped up and issued together through Canaveral as the reasonably solid *Tarzan and the Castaways*. It was still a slightly flimsy coda, though.

In a sense, most of the Tarzan books published from the Burroughs boom onwards were new. In 1962, the '60s may not yet have been a swinging proposition, but it was already clear that times and values had changed profoundly since the apeman's entrée. Burroughs fans will swear blind that the author was not as racist as some make out. They have some ammunition insofar as many Negros – as society was then beginning to feel uncomfortable calling them – were depicted by him as noble, intelligent and brave. But more were depicted as brutish, stupid and vicious. This in itself was not completely damning – it would be absurd to have white baddies but ban the depiction of black villainy – but there is no getting around the fact that some of Burroughs' writing portrays the very state of being black in pejorative terms. In the era of John F Kennedy and Martin Luther King, this would have repulsed much of the public – and no doubt many publishers – in a way it would not have only a decade before. (It's interesting that no parent seems to have been reported as demanding Tarzan books be removed from library shelves on the grounds of racism over the previous 50 years.) Ballantine's versions of the Tarzan books cut out many of the racial epithets and toned down colloquial speech that might be interpreted as insulting, such as Esmeralda's 'Lawd-a-mighty' dialogue in *Tarzan of the Apes*. Even innocuous references to skin colour were sometimes altered. Canaveral meanwhile completely removed anti-black comments from their compendium *Tarzan and the Tarzan Twins* on the grounds that the book's child demographic did not know enough to be able to recognise and reject bigotry. Both the Ballantine and Canaveral alterations were made with the blessing and, in some cases, encouragement of ERB, Inc. Inevitably, over the years the situation became one wherein many readers – and, one suspects, some reprint publishers – didn't even know that the books in their hands were bowdlerised.

There were also new ape-man tales Burroughs had nothing to do with. 'Today's great interest in the adventures of Tarzan and some of the many other exciting characters created by the master storyteller Edgar Rice Burroughs has brought a demand for new, fresh Tarzan stories.' So read a blurb on the second page of a series of five Tarzan novels published in 1964/65 and credited to one Barton Werper. The name was a pseudonym (derived from a character in *Tarzan and the Jewels of Opar*) for married couple Peter and Peggy Scott who, along with their publishers Gold Star, were taking advantage of the confusion over whether Tarzan was in the public domain. This was arguably reasonable, and the assertion of an interest in new Tarzan stories would transpire to be demonstrably true, but the execution was somewhat questionable. *Tarzan and the Silver Globe, Tarzan and the Cave City, Tarzan and the Snake People, Tarzan and the Abominable Snowmen* and *Tarzan and the Winged Invader* reveal the Scotts to be not Burroughs aficionados like Stuart J Byrne (*Tarzan on Mars*) but merely jobbing writers. It shows in their lack of knowledge not so much of names but of established details and modes of behaviour: Kala is portrayed as a mother of many when in fact she bore only one child; the Mangani – stupid and easily distracted in Burroughs' books – are given almost human-level intelligence; Tarzan, Jane and La are unrecognisable as the characters we know: the first immature where we had always known him as noble, the second stuck-up where Burroughs' version exuded warmth and the third crudely strumpet-like in comparison with the subtly sensual template. The Scotts take it upon themselves to create a new backstory for La, which would be a bloody cheek even if it were not ludicrous (she's now a 300-year-old Venusian). Over and above the unfamiliarity with the territory, their writing is sloppy, full of inconsistencies and repetition and guilty of such bad pacing that they throw away what could be entire chapters in a page or two of blurred action. The Scotts also directly lift passages from Burroughs books, and if we can forgive that legally – at the time it appeared it was safe to do so – we can hardly extend the same understanding on aesthetic or moral grounds. Burroughs was mocked by many for his formulaic style but it is pastiche as bad as this that makes one see just how nuanced – and therefore difficult to emulate – that style was. Not that readers seemed to care overmuch: that Tarzan was once again a licence to print money was demonstrated by the fact that Gold Star only refrained from issuing further Tarzan books because of legal action by ERB, Inc.

The number of pirated and plagiarised Tarzan films had diminished in recent years as reliable and quick global communication had made it more difficult to trade in unauthorised work without it coming to the attention of legally interested parties in the First World, and as Third World countries anxious to avail themselves of the benefits of cooperation with the developed world began submitting to their standards regarding policing copyright. However, the confusion over the issue of Tarzan's copyright status created a new rush to make ape-man pictures, all of which – whether the makers knew it or not – were illicit. Early-to-mid 1960s Italian, French, Russian, Jamaican, Czechoslovakian and Indian Tarzan productions were either planned or finished before ERB, Inc and/or Sy Weintraub put the relevant parties right.

Most of these productions were the usual laughable, tacky and lost-in-translation Third World fare. One Indian production had Christine Keeler of the Profumo sex scandal taking a role. An American production (possibly with some West German involvement) was to have featured Brick Bardo in an adaptation of *Jungle Tales of Tarzan*. The scriptwriter was one Ron Haydock, who as 'Vin Saxon' had just started on a literary career studded with books rejoicing in titles like *Perverted Lust, Sex-a-Reenos* and *Pagan Lesbians*. Joe Robinson took the lead in the Italian production *Tarzan Roi de la Force Brutale*. After legal activity, it was released with Tarzan's name changed to 'Taur'. The Jamaican production *Tarzan and the Jewels of Opar* had an imported New York crew and, playing the ape-man, Olympic pole-vaulter Don Bragg.

More legal action from ERB, Inc caused Charlton Comics to cease publishing the Tarzan title they had started in December 1964, but this story was one that involved as much love as avarice and, furthermore, had a positive outcome.

In 1962, Western had parted company with their former client Dell and begun publishing a Tarzan title in their new Gold Key line, although the fact that they continued the numbering and employed the creative staff from the Dell publication meant that, for readers, it was the same comic, even if it changed its title to *Tarzan of the Apes* from November '63. Apart from its beautiful painted covers (a custom begun in the latter days of the Dell title), it was the same staid proposition it had always been. Western's comfortable world, however, was shaken up by the appearance of the first issue of Charlton's *Jungle Tales of Tarzan*.

Charlton had decided to adapt that particular book because it was one of those whose copyright status was then in question. The comic book's editor Pat Masulli stated inside its first issue that 'the true flavor of Tarzan as created by Mr Burroughs has rarely been tasted in comic books. We intend to change that.' The four issues of the title published through to July 1965 – written by Joe Gill and drawn by Sam Glanzman – certainly succeeded in that objective of authenticity and were surely the best Tarzan comics published to that date. ERB, Inc managed to get them off the shelves on the grounds that, public-domain questions about the parent book aside, Tarzan was a registered trademark, a tactic that would stand them in good stead. Nonetheless, the artistic gauntlet had been thrown down, and Western were prompted to, as it were, ape Charlton's strategy of being faithful to the original texts. Enter the third famous Tarzan comics artist, Russ Manning. Already responsible for Western's *Korak, Son of Tarzan* title, he now set about illustrating, in an elegant style a universe away from Jesse Marsh's early scratchy naïveté, a series of Gaylord Dubois-written adaptations of the original Burroughs Tarzan novels that for many provide the definitive comics depiction of Lord Greystoke to this very day. The only element of Manning's beautiful work to which anyone could object was the colour he made Tarzan's loincloth: what jungle animal gives rise to a crimson pelt?

That jump in quality of Western's Tarzan comics, although high, was probably the least significant of the massive changes that had been wrought in the Tarzan landscape since December '61. History no more records the name of the Downey parent who demanded that the supposedly immoral Tarzan books be removed from the shelves than it does the librarian to whom s/he made that demand. Said parent, however, had an effect akin to a publishing earthquake – proving, some might suggest, that history is written by the whiners.

While the Tarzan publishing business was going through its turmoil, Sy Weintraub was preparing the follow-up to *Tarzan Goes to India*.

With both his choice of actor and his concept of a globe-trotting Tarzan apparently vindicated by box office returns, he now decided to send Mahoney to Thailand. Although the country depicted in the resultant 92-minute film *Tarzan's Three Challenges* was a nameless generic Oriental kingdom, full use was made of Thailand's breathtaking backdrops, including jungles, temples, giant Buddha statues, elaborately decorated elephants and an army of exotic dancing girls. It's rather unfortunate that the man playing Tarzan doesn't match up to such splendour.

Once again, the ape-man's presence is requested in a faraway land in which he inexplicably has contacts. When arriving by parachute, he is observed by a child who – of course – runs to him with an excited cry of recognition. His mission is to protect a young spiritual heir named Kashi (Ricky Der) from the machinations of one Khan, brother of the dying spiritual leader Tarim, both latter roles played by Der's real-life uncle Woody Strode. In order to prove his worthiness to be Kashi's protector in the dangerous jungles that form the path to the Crown City where the succession ceremony will occur, Tarzan must face Khan in three trials, two physical, one cerebral. Although Cheeta is again absent, anthropomorphic comic relief is provided by a baby elephant named Hungry.

The script by Berne Giler and Robert Day is reasonably good and Day's direction also satisfactory, but Mahoney is once again a problem. That he is now the oldest Tarzan ever is painfully apparent in places, especially during the challenge in which he has to endure buffalos pulling on his arms from opposite directions: as he grimaces in agony, there seems no end to his chins. Matters were further complicated by a dramatic drop in Mahoney's weight when he picked up amoebic dysentery, dengue fever and pneumonia. Never powerful-looking in the first place, by the end of the film he seems farcically tired, frail and aged. For the viewer, accepting that Tarzan has bested Strode in a hand-to-hand battle (engendered by Khan exercising his right to challenge the succession) is simply impossible.

This would be Mahoney's last Tarzan film. The talk afterwards was of mutual agreement, but the realities of contract law are such that Weintraub almost certainly paid the actor off, even if an exhausted Mahoney – who took 18 months to regain his lost weight – was probably glad to divest himself of the role. Weintraub doesn't seem to have shed Mahoney because he concluded that he had made a mistake. Even before *Tarzan Goes to India*, he had been talking about taking the Tarzan franchise to the small screen. With these plans now lain, and with them being by definition long-term ones involving arduous week-in, week-out shooting, he needed somebody younger than the 44 that Mahoney was upon the June 1963 release of *Tarzan's Three Challenges*.

Some Burroughs aficionados had always thought rippling, bulging muscles were not the likely outcome of a simian rearing. With Mahoney, such Burroughs fans learned the wisdom of the adage, 'Be careful what you wish for – it may come true.'

The two years and 11 months between *Tarzan's Three Challenges* and the next entry in the series was the longest gap between Tarzan flicks since 1927, but it was not the consequence of inertia.

The hiatus is partly explained by the fact that a new Tarzan actor had to be chosen, partly by the fact that Weintraub was working out an elaborate plan to use the film series to piggy-back the new actor into a TV show and partly by the fact that Weintraub was stockpiling productions shot back-to-back. Partly, also, it was because he was busy shaking up the Tarzan concept, or, for younger readers, rebooting the franchise.

The usual stratospherically high number of candidates interviewed to be the new Tarzan was given out (400 this time), but, as is common in the cinema Tarzan story, possibly even standard, the lucky man was actually approached by the producers rather than vice versa. Mike Henry was a 28-year-old footballer (again, American variety) of seven years' standing. In addition to thrilling the fans of the Los Angeles Rams with his exploits as a line-backer, he had a smattering of experience in small TV and film parts. He also had a brain: Weintraub got the idea of trying out Henry when he watched a TV documentary that the latter had produced about the team. Weintraub signed him up after a screen-test, although stipulated he lose 20 pounds. Henry made another sacrifice of his own volition, retiring from football.

He may have been a little stiff as an actor, but Mike Henry was probably the best-looking Tarzan so far. His six-foot-four frame was a study in physical perfection, packed with rippling muscles where Weissmuller had been merely trim and toned, yet not tending towards the over-solidity of Scott, while his handsome face not only seemed to have come straight from the pencil of Hal Foster but was devoid of Barker's rich-boy softness. This well-'ard Michelangelo's David was to appear in Tarzan movies like none before, even if they were on the same update-and-toughen gradient Weintraub had inaugurated seven years previously.

That his entrée – distributed by American International – was originally named *Tarzan '66* (posters with that title were prepared) indicates how anxious Weintraub was to make Henry a Tarzan for a new age. Although the original title was abandoned in favour of *Tarzan and the Valley of Gold*, the content of the movie, released in May 1966, screams out the zeitgeist. It asserts that, jungle man though he might be, Tarzan inhabits the same world that has recently been transformed by the Beatles, James Bond and sexual liberation. There is some wacky credits lettering and modishly jazzy soundtrack music. Meanwhile, 007 (then defined by Sean Connery's portrayal) is poured in by the bucketload: Tarzan is seen with short, neat hair, wearing a suit, carrying a briefcase and boarding planes and helicopters. That Henry is the first film Tarzan allowed a hairy chest seems another nod to the hirsute Connery. As per usual, Tarzan doesn't get up to hanky panky with the film's *de rigueur* smouldering sex bomb, but there is a deliberate frisson of eroticism in the record skimpiness of his loincloth. (Although, as was now standard with cinema Tarzans, it is a loincloth with a gusset, an illogicality required to preserve decency in the event of the kind of 'upskirt' shots inevitable for a hero who has brawls and climbs trees.) There's even a little Bondian humour, such as when Tarzan kills a baddie by toppling a giant decorative Coca Cola bottle on him, or when he cracks when preparing to turn from civilised gent to ape-man, 'I'll need a good rope, a hunting knife and a soft piece of leather.' In a press statement, Weintraub himself said of the new Tarzan, '…he is the embodiment of culture, suavity and style, who is equally at home in a posh night club or the densest jungle.'

The ape-man's adversary, Augustus Vinaro (David Optashu), is slavishly in Bond movie-villain tradition: a rich madman who covets gold, he blows people up with elaborate time-bombs and employs an Oddjob-like goon (Don MeGowan) whose very name – Mr Train – is of Ian Fleming-esque parodic formality. Even Vinaro's death – being buried under an avalanche of gold – is tangentially reminiscent of the gold-paint sprayed demise of Jill Masterson in *Goldfinger*. Although scriptwriter Clair Huffaker had a grounding in Western material rather than the young medium of espionage pictures, he had clearly been employed because of the vast knowledge of pacy adventure he had gained on TV shows like *Rawhide*, *Bonanza*, *Lawman* and *The Virginian* and movies like *Seven Ways from Sundown* and *The Comancheros*.

Tarzan also got nasty under Henry, whose extraordinarily bloodthirsty trio of films saw Weintraub take full advantage of the relaxation in recent years of rules on movie violence. However, although the grown men in the theatre audience had plenty of realistic bloodshed to entertain them and the grown women plenty of Henry's body to occupy them, Weintraub's estimation of the age group and gender of a large proportion of the demographic was made clear by the fact that he again gave Tarzan a boy sidekick, in this case ten-year-old Ramel (Manuel Padilla Jr). Meanwhile, should hilariously lugubrious and wizened old Incas need someone with whom to identify, Manco (Francisco Riquerio) does the honours. His crown looks like it weighs more than him, although not more than his bottom lip.

Despite the changes, Weintraub perseveres with his Tarzan-as-globetrotter strategy. The action takes place in Mexico, with Weintraub's Banner production company showing off the splendour of the Acapulco-adjacent jungles, Chapultepec castle, Plaza de Toros bullring and Aztec ruins, all in full colour. The ape-man is summoned to the country by Ruiz, an old friend. When he gets there, he finds himself tasked with the objective of preventing Vinaro – who has murdered Ruiz – looting the ancient treasures of an Incan people whose chief, Ramel, he has abducted. Tarzan is assisted by Vinaro's ex Sophia (played by Nancy Kovack, but originally intended to be portrayed by Sharon Tate, who turned it down), a chimpanzee (Dinky, not Cheeta), a lion and a leopard. Although Tarzan has the expected hand-to-hand fights, he is also shown in more high-tech combat: from grounding a helicopter with bolas (the crash immolating the crew) to commanding a tank. Like all the Henry Tarzans, the 90-minute, Robert Day-directed film is entertaining without being great.

Viewers unfamiliar with the more cosmopolitan ape-man of Burroughs' books must have felt that Tarzan as a global adventurer was a totally contrived device. Had they read the new film's Ballantine paperback novelisation by Fritz Leiber – which joined the dots between the prose and screen Tarzans – it would have made more sense.

'It was Ballantine Books who contacted Hulbert Burroughs, Ed's son, about continuing the Tarzan series, because they were reprinting the Tarzan books,' says Robert R Barrett. Whitman had published a 282-page novelisation for young readers of the *Tarzan and the Lost Safari* film, believed to have been written by Frank Castle (Burroughs' is the only name on the cover). However, a brand-new, authorised Tarzan novel for adults was something more elevated – the type of thing about which many 'ERBivores' had long fantasised. That Leiber was a celebrated author in a field adjacent to Burroughs', and an ERB fan to boot, was additionally exciting. That *Tarzan and the Valley of Gold* was conferred by ERB, Inc prestigious canon status was indicated by the '25' the book featured on its cover – it continued the number sequence from *Tarzan and the Castaways*.

Although the movie Tarzan had moved back toward the prose Tarzan in recent years, a novelisation of a Tarzan picture written in a Burroughs vein is something of a contradiction: the two are often conflicting beasts to say the least. Then there is the fact that novelisations are even more the bastard offspring of literature than pulps. Leiber – an award-winning author in the fields of science fiction and sword and sorcery – would have understood the latter point. It was presumably eagerness to fulfil a longstanding ambition to follow in his author hero's footsteps that led him to agree to take on the job.

Leiber approaches the task at hand seriously. The book is a solid 300-plus pages. Moreover, he doggedly strives to maintain continuity with Burroughs' books via numerous footnotes, and to reconcile where he can the traduced/simplified screen version of Tarzan with the prose original. On the debit side, he is also anxious to show off his research in other areas: his wodges of Brazilian history and travelogue are the kind of action-interrupting waffle Burroughs would never have included in his fiction. (His sometimes mildly boring detail about the customs and landscapes of imaginary places don't count.) Meanwhile, as it's inconceivable that he hasn't read *Tarzan's Quest* and *Tarzan and 'The Foreign Legion'*, one is not quite sure what point Leiber is making by portraying the ape-man as puzzled by his own agelessness.

Throughout, Leiber provides additional backstory, motivation and symbolism, thus enriching without contradicting or obstructing the narrative created by the Huffaker screenplay. He also impressively displays discipline in dispensing with his usual post-modern style for a straight-ahead adventure yarn in Burroughs' spirit.

Sales of the book were not encouraging, although some have suggested that this might have been because Ballantine confused potential purchasers by utilising a cover illustration that had already been seen on their edition of *Tarzan and the Golden Lion*. Hopes harboured by ERB fans for further Tarzan books included more Leiber stories, perhaps even original ones, Leiber being authorised to finish the unpublished Burroughs Tarzan tales whose existence was publicly known of if not their correct number, and John Coleman Burroughs – a writer as well as illustrator – taking on the task of continuing his dad's character's adventures. Because of those poor sales, however, such hopes had to remain in the realm of dreams. There would be no new ape-man novels for two decades. The Burroughs boom, it would seem, had already bumped up against its natural ceiling.

Although Mike Henry's tenure in the loincloth spanned exactly two years in theatrical release-date terms, in reality his duration as Tarzan was more fleeting.

He filmed his three Tarzan movies one after the other – a process lasting about 12 months – and handed in his notice not only before the third was completed but prior to the first's cinema release. The second, *Tarzan and the Great River*, was shot in Brazil while *Valley of Gold* was in the editing suite. There was supposed to be a hiatus between that and *Tarzan and the Jungle Boy*, a rest period particularly necessary in light of the imminent commencement of filming of the TV series, but Weintraub instead decided to take advantage of good weather and get the third movie in the can. In addition to the arduousness of Henry contiguously shooting three feature-length films whose physicality was by definition already greater than that of the average Hollywood production, he suffered an endless series of misfortunes: a chimp bite-induced fever, dysentery, an ear infection and a liver infection. The third movie turned into a nightmare when torrential rain reduced production to a crawl. Henry informed Weintraub that he was done not just because he was emotionally and physically exhausted but because he was – courtesy of the television series – facing what seemed like eternity far away from home.

Henry pursued a $875,000 civil action for maltreatment, abuse and working conditions detrimental to his health. That the legal notion of 'duty of care' was then not as established as now, and that Henry had indicated that in principle he was game for danger by insisting on doing his own stunts, would have raised interesting points of law had the suit proceeded to hearing stage, but as Henry explained to *Filmfax* magazine in 2011, 'We amicably settled the whole thing out of court.'

In the meantime, Weintraub was bereft of a leading man for a series that was due to start filming in a month. Ron Ely was a 28-year-old with just a few scattered acting credits. He had already secured a part in one of the new *Tarzan* TV episodes as an ape-man imposter. Weintraub hurriedly upgraded him. Some reports have posited Ely as yet another actor to have secured the Tarzan role at the second attempt, but he claimed in a later newspaper interview that he had decided, after auditioning for the job Henry eventually obtained, that he didn't want it: 'Tarzan was nothing more than a muscle man, which I'm not.' With his good looks and his imposing six-foot-four height, Ely had two of the attributes associated with the ape-man. Although he didn't have the third – a mass of rippling muscles – Weintraub decided that his lean body would work. Unlike in the case of Jock Mahoney, he was right: Ely may not have possessed bulging biceps or a chest like a beer barrel, but he was still visibly nobody's pushover.

That the *Tarzan* TV series even made it to the airwaves was a small miracle for, such were the production's travails, the crew became convinced it was jinxed. When filming started in

February 1966 not far from Rio, torrential rains washed away specially constructed sets, then washed them away again when they were rebuilt. Mosquitos, dysentery and fraught misunderstandings with locals were rife. After five-and-a-half months, only five episodes had been filmed and the show was half a million dollars over budget. Co-producer Jon Epstein bailed. In May '66, filming was relocated to Mexico, where Weintraub spent close to $200,000 building new sets. The productivity went up a little, with five more episodes completed in two months, but lest the demoralised and battered crew think the curse of the programme had evaporated, a panicked elephant killed a trainer on set. Not long afterwards, Epstein's replacement, Leon Benson, himself left. Weintraub's hair is reported to have gone grey by the eight-month mark, by which time 11 episodes had been completed. There were 20 still to be made for the first season.

Ely performed his own stunts, although he insisted in a 2012 interview with latimes.com that, contrary to what has been said, this was not at his own insistence: 'I wound up doing everything before I knew I was doing everything ... We just didn't have a way to hide a stunt guy. He would have had to have been almost identical to me physically and that just wasn't around at the time.' This situation had the inevitable consequences. A now well-known publicity photo of Ely covered in bandages and plasters demonstrated the 17 injuries he accrued during filming of the first season – lion bites, broken shoulder and cracked ribs among them – with numbered indicators. Although this photo was clearly over-the-top – he couldn't have had all the injuries at the same time, and the criss-crossing of some of the plasters was cartoonish – advertising the perils of playing Tarzan was perhaps a rather dangerous move by Weintraub considering the Henry litigation. Ely had his own problems with the photo. 'I resented it terribly,' he lamented. 'They didn't begin to chronicle the things that happened to me ... I was injured constantly, and was always recovering from an injury. Some of them were quite serious ... There was a helluva lot that they didn't even touch on, broken bones that they didn't know about. I don't even remember all of them. And I don't want to.'

'Sixty-six was a bonanza year for live-action Tarzan, with three different actors being seen by the public in the role. NBC decided to transmit in part the Sol Lesser TV Tarzan project they had abandoned nearly a decade before. The three Gordon Scott pilots edited into a feature-length movie aired on 5 May 1966, the same month as *Tarzan and the Valley of Gold* reached the big screen. Either that Henry film had prompted NBC's move or else it was the imminent arrival of the Ely series. If the latter, it was a curious way for the network to herald its own show. Not only was the Scott vehicle poor quality, but its monochrome looked dated: Ron Ely's *Tarzan* was one of the first action-adventure television series transmitted in colour. The latter show made its debut on 8 September, one week earlier than originally planned following some scheduling skirmishes between NBC and ABC. Considering how behind was Weintraub production-wise, bringing it forward was not a wise move, but even less judicious was NBC's decision to invite all the remaining living movie Tarzans to a reunion in Mexico to arouse interest. Three showed up to meet Ely, and although Jock Mahoney was still in reasonable shape, the resultant publicity photos of him and Ely standing on a branch preparing to swing on vines beside the similarly loinclothed but profoundly out-of-shape Johnny Weissmuller and James Pierce were not a pretty sight.

The *Tarzan* TV series was the most intensive ape-man project ever assembled: the 57 hour-long episodes provided across its two seasons by a team of over a dozen writers equated (minus adverts) to nearly 30 Tarzan cinema features. Even the serials had not come close in screen time. It was also the widest exposure for the ape-man there had ever been: no matter how many millions of books were in circulation and no matter how many screenings there had been of Tarzan films at the cinema or on TV, nothing could match the character's regular weekly presence in living rooms across the planet. Which leaves the question: was the show any good?

American television in the second half of the '60s was a limited medium, squeaky clean cum socially conservative, tending toward morality tales and conforming to a square-jawed Hollywood paradigm of heroism in which the irony, playfulness and ethical doubt common in screen drama today did not feature. This combined with the severe restrictions on depictions of violence that then existed – especially in a show with a 7.30 pm transmission time – meant that this Tarzan wasn't even going to be as savage as his cinema incarnation, let alone the prose original.

The show depicts a Tarzan who is loved by some, feared by others, but known by all. Wandering a jungle country never identified by name, he is either called upon for help or else stumbles into conflicts in which his conscience insists he must provide assistance. Princesses, poachers, witch-doctors, diamond smugglers, gun-runners, missionaries and revolutionaries all cross his path. The problems experienced or caused by them are, with a combination of a rather all-American politesse and fisticuffs, wrapped up by Tarzan in a neat little bow by episode's end (except with two-parters). In one episode, assisting the forces of good even necessitates the ape-man entering a jungle Olympics. Tarzan's warning cry is Weissmuller's classic MGM yodel, to which the astute Weintraub had clearly somehow secured the rights. Another inheritance from the movies is Cheeta.

Each episode of the Ely series would start with the spoken précis: 'The dark land of the jungle is the country of the unknown, of savagery, terror and peril beyond the imagination of men. Here in the forbidden tangle of the jungle, a child was found and raised by the great apes. The boy took the name Tarzan and later was educated in civilisation. But then, Tarzan returned to the deadly land he knew so well, and everywhere in the jungle from the great falls to the huge mountains, to the land of ghost men and the limitless rainforest, the cheetah has grown to know one who is swifter, the lion knows one who is braver: Tarzan. The strength of Tarzan no man can say. Deep in the jungle, Tarzan continues to enforce his law ... the law of right. Tarzan's awesome warning cry is known to every living creature in the jungle. Hearing that cry, the antelope knows he is safe, the lion pauses, the crocodile seeks the safety of the water. The elephant comes to his friend ... Tarzan of the Apes.' It's an exercise in providing a background that doesn't necessarily chime with Burroughs' original but doesn't quite contradict it either: 'great apes' are mentioned but not Mangani; the genesis of Tarzan's name is only partly explained; the means by which he was both found by apes and educated in civilisation are left opaque.

By now, Burroughs fans were long used to the trade-off with authenticity that commercial reality, practicality and technical limitations always imposed on live-action depictions of the ape-man. Inevitably, though, there were fundamental tamperings with the source material destined not to go down well with the purists. Perhaps in light of her absence from many of Burroughs' books, the non-appearance of Jane can't be strictly counted as an example of such. However, even the best Tarzan books and films without her had proven a little emotionally arid, and this series is afflicted by the same problem, one for which the presence of an adopted orphan son doesn't compensate. Jai was always a curiosity. The character's name was stolen from the Indian boy actor in *Tarzan Goes to India*, while, for those bothered to think about it, his ethnicity was puzzling: he was played by Manuel Padilla Jr, a Californian of Filipino heritage who had appeared as an Incan in *Tarzan and the Valley of Gold*. In the TV show, although his character's caste was not specified, it was obvious that he was a geographical anomaly. Other source-deviation issues include the fact that Tarzan doesn't tangle much with wild beasts, making him at times almost just a cop without trousers. As for Tarzan's original noble lineage, Weintraub commented in December 1967, 'We dropped the English lord business because of Ron Ely's American accent.'

Many Burroughs fans were relatively happy with the balance struck between lowest-common-denominator fare and authentic

Burroughsonia, especially toward the end of the first season as early aesthetic fumbling gave way to slicker production and more adult-oriented scripts. Of course, the show was designed not for ERBivores but for Mr and Mrs Average and their two-point-four children, many of whom had never heard of Burroughs. Although ratings started out shaky – it initially didn't break the top 50 – by December *Tarzan* was top 20. The pulsating theme music, the urgent baritone of the opening-credits announcer and the way that the series' logo gradually appeared across the screen in the wake of Tarzan's body swinging on a vine, as well as its wildlife montage, made for the kind of title sequence that creates viewer goodwill even before the action starts. It should also not be underestimated just how novel the series was in the way it provided a window on the spectacular natural landscapes of what were then parts of the world little seen on television, let alone in glorious colour. *Tarzan* also genuinely seems to have succeeded in its aim of being a family show. While men and kids liked it as much as anticipated, the allure of Ely's scantily clad form also seems to have drawn in the ladies: *Tarzan's* first season had the highest proportion of female viewers aged 18 to 34 of any prime-time show.

The second, and weakest, of the Mike Henry ape-man triptych saw release in September 1967. Distributed by Paramount, it was originally proposed by Weintraub as a feature called *Tarzan, Spain*, but as well as ending up set in Brazil was renamed *Tarzan and the Great River*.

The ape-man is once again summoned by one of the friends he mysteriously has dotted around the globe and, as before, makes the journey looking like a Madison Avenue exec before stripping down to a hardly-there breechcloth. The script by Bob Barbash, from a story by Barbash and Lewis Reed, sees Tarzan's friend the Professor (Paulo Gracindo) alert him to the activities of the Jaguar Cult, who are led by Barcuma (Rafer Johnson, a former Olympic decathlete) and have as their twisted mission the enslavement of local villagers for work in diamond mines.

Those who resist are liable to suffer death by poisoned jaguar claw. The cult predictably make things personal for the ape-man by killing the Professor. Tarzan sets off after them in the company of a lion (Baron) and a chimp (Cheeta) that he had previously given to the Professor for his menagerie. What might seem a reasonably clever way to justify the inclusion of fauna familiar from Tarzan flicks is later completely undermined by Tarzan encountering, with no explanation, lions in the Brazilian jungle and hippos in the Amazon river. On his travels, the ape-man runs into the comedic character Captain Sam (professional funnyman Jan Murray), and his cabin boy Pepe (Manuel Padilla Jr again). The now traditional feisty eye candy to whose charms Tarzan is strangely immune is Dr Ann Phillips (Diana Millay), to whom the Captain delivers medical supplies and whose jungle hospital comes under attack by the cult for encroaching on Barcuma's patch.

Robert Day directed an 88-minute film that is an awkward mixture of plodding and frenetic, sweet (there is plenty of levity involving Captain Sam, Pepe, the lion and the chimpanzee) and sadistic (Tarzan slaughters enemies willy-nilly, including a group he burns alive without bothering to find out if they want to surrender).

There are a couple of blasts from the past: Weissmuller's classic yodel was dubbed in and the ape-man's high dive into a river was spliced from *Tarzan's Greatest Adventure.*

Three days after the release of the second Mike Henry film, the NBC Tarzan series returned to the screens. Famous faces had speckled season one, including Jock Mahoney, Woody Strode, Don MeGowan and Julie Harris (some of whom were of course familiar from Tarzan flicks), but it was in the second season that the guest stars got really impressive: the Supremes, Ethel Merman and Helen Hayes were among those who put in appearances. Weintraub explained that this was so as to ensure a large adult audience. The ante was also upped with regard to backgrounds: it was planned for episodes to be shot in London,

Guatemala and Mozambique. Ratings continued to be pleasing. Three months into the second season, Weintraub was publicly saying, 'We think – and NBC thinks – the series is good for ten years.'

Which begs the question: what on earth happened in the two months between that confident prediction and 21 February 1968? On that latter date, with six more episodes of season two still to air, the announcement was made that *Tarzan* did not feature in NBC's plans for the next TV season. Weintraub airily spoke of the show returning on the grounds that it was one of the highest-rating shows ever to be dropped from the schedules. He also said, 'We will continue production to meet our present obligations.' That the second season ended up being five episodes shorter than the first suggests that he was told by the network not to bother with those obligations, and that scripted *Tarzan* episodes remained unfilmed. Certainly, the London edition (where, according to Gabe Essoe, the title 'Lord Greystoke' was finally due to be enunciated) didn't materialise.

Some sources have cited the inordinate expense of making the show as the reason for its cancellation. Whatever the reason, the '66-'68 *Tarzan* series burned brightly but briefly. Yet it had a disproportionate impact. Because it was being repeated well into the '70s, it comprised the major readily available live-action ape-man fare at a point in history when the character was not represented on cinema screens. Consequently, Ron Ely was the only Tarzan actor many '70s kids knew.

Mike Henry cited May 1968's *Tarzan and the Jungle Boy* as his favourite of his three ape-man movies. His reason was that it was the one that dispensed with the 'Bondage' and moved back toward the character's true nature. Although filmed in Brazil, it also moved the character back to his home country. The only thing Bond about the picture is Steve Bond, the youngster who plays 13-year-old Erik Brunik, aka Jukaro, the jungle boy of the title, whom journalist Myrna Claudel (Alizia Gur) and her husband decide to try to track down after he is spotted by an aerial photographer.

The boy has survived by his wits in the wild for six years after the death of his father in a boating accident. (Even more impressively, he has managed to retain a mop of hair that looks like it's just been shampooed.) Tarzan decides to find him, although won't help Myrna in her mercenary pursuit of a story. While on his quest, the ape-man interferes in a battle for succession between the sons of a dying native chief, with the inevitable frenetic consequences. Bad son Nagambi (a returning Rafer Johnson) bears a grudge against the ape-man for preventing him cold-bloodedly killing his sibling Buhara (played by Johnson's real-life brother Edward). Meanwhile, Myrna has defied Tarzan's orders not to follow him, with the inevitable life-threatening upshot. When Tarzan finds Erik, he naturally strikes up a rapport with his vine-swinging, loinclothed mini-me. Counterpointing this warmth and the comedy of Cheeta is more of the protracted bloodshed endemic to the Henry trilogy.

Steven Lord wrote and Robert Gordon directed the 90-minute film, distributed by Paramount. It was a good way for Henry to bow out. He subsequently had a long acting career that lasted into the 21st century before it was curtailed by Parkinson's Disease.

A short clip from this production showing Steve Bond walking through the jungle with his leopard was used to represent Tarzan as a young boy in the opening credits of the Ron Ely series.

In the month before the second season of the Ely series started airing, Sy Weintraub ceased to be the owner of the live-action Tarzan rights. He acquiesced to a buy-out by National General Corporation, although he continued to head the Banner production company NGC had gobbled up. The airing of the second season disguised it at first, but it was the end of another era for the ape-man, and in more ways than one.

In the same interview in which he predicted the cancelled *Tarzan* show would be back, Weintraub said that there might be

Tarzan feature films starring Ely. In the event, the only cinema releases featuring Ely as the ape-man were spliced two-parters from the NBC series that were given a theatrical outing in 1970: *Tarzan's Deadly Silence* and *Tarzan's Jungle Rebellion*. Ersatz though these exercises were, without their respective releases, there would have been no new *bona fide* Tarzan cinema in the '70s whatsoever.

ABC responded to the cancellation of the Ely show two days later by broadcasting a 60-minute edit of Denny Miller's *Tarzan the Ape Man* as a pilot for a possible new series. It would be unwise to infer too much from the fact that the series didn't happen – the reason could as easily have been that movie's poor quality as a lack of public interest in the ape-man. However, although the Tarzan live-action rights Weintraub had sold ran until 1972, and no doubt could have been easily extended, they were not exercised.

The only person who seemed to be interested in shooting Tarzan pictures was Manuel Caño, who helmed two Spanish-Italian projects, *Tarzan En La Gruta Del Oro* (*Tarzan in the Golden Grotto*), released in 1970, and *Tarzan Y El Arco Iris* (*Tarzan and the Rainbow*, but probably better-known as *Tarzan and the Brown Prince*), released in 1972, both starring Steve Hawkes, a former Mr Canada, as the ape-man. It's perhaps unfair and patronising to immediately tag as quasi-bogus movies that, although filmed in English, secured no general release in the UK or US. Nevertheless, farce seems to have surrounded both productions, and in discussions of cinematic Tarzans they have tended to be lumped in with the likes of *Tarzan Roi de la Force Brutale*. Yet in an interview with the website tarzanmovieguide.com, Hawkes insisted that rights were properly sought and obtained from ERB, Inc – up to a point. Of the first picture, he said, 'The American producers, in the middle of the film, ran out of the money due to the flood in South America. They lost all the equipment and almost all the footage. The company was unable to pay the Edgar Rice Burroughs fees and they negotiated a lesser amount by changing it from Tarzan to Zan ... The second movie,

Tarzan and the Brown Prince, the rights were paid in full. I was present when the contracts were signed. I'm not sure whether the Italians paid their dues or not.'

That the second movie became the 'proper' ape-man film by virtue of being able to use the Tarzan name is something of an irony, as it is considered the weaker of the two, with Tarzan – an impressive crocodile fight aside – taking almost a passive, observer's role. The first picture was well-made, albeit in an over-archetypal Tarzan style. The solidly-built Hawkes is an impressive figure in both films. Also known as Steve Sipek (he was born Stjepan Šipek in Croatia in 1942), he has since run a big cat sanctuary in Florida, a career direction inspired by his life being saved during the shooting of his second ape-man picture by a lion that he claims dragged him from a fire and ripped off his bonds. He bristles when his films are described as unauthorised. At one point, clicking on his name on his website unleashed a Weissmuller Tarzan yodel.

That the Caño/Hawkes films were all the Tarzan movie franchise could muster at this point in history demonstrates how shockingly rapid was the debasement of its currency. Although Weintraub had modernised the live-action Tarzan, he had apparently taken the character as far as it could go in a changed world. The '60s had been a questioning decade, one in which relatively upstanding and conventional characters like Tarzan had begun to lose their attraction to a youth who wanted their heroes cut from more rebellious and gritty cloth. Even Mike Henry's mass-murdering Tarzan would have seemed broadly unhip to fans of *Bonnie and Clyde* and *Easy Rider*. Meanwhile, the Burroughs Tarzan bought into all the assumptions about privilege loathed by the emergent counter-culture. There was also an ever-increasing trend toward realism in art: jungle escapades couldn't help but seem a little florid set against urban grit, while, in what were ideologically-charged times, the production of escapist fare seemed to some – especially the young – a conservative, even regressive act. There were no doubt other reasons why the ape-man came to be perceived by financiers as a less viable option after *Tarzan and the Jungle Boy*, the decreasing exoticness of Africa in a more connected planet among them. Whatever the precise truth, although Tarzan would continue to be visible in the culture during the '70s in comic books, an animated TV series, merchandise and that never-ending comic strip, as well as in the pastiches and spoofs that had always been intertwined with the character's life, of the crucial, most prestigious, most profitable stuff – i.e. live-action drama – there was none. After more than half a century, the days of Tarzan bestriding popular culture like a colossus were drawing to a close.

Tarzan: The Biography

PART SEVEN: THE LEAN YEARS

Although historical perspective now enables us to see that 1968 marked the end of the glory days of live-action Tarzan, at the time Burroughs fans continued to foster grand dreams in that direction. Two mooted Tarzan cinema projects became for them a Holy Grail, although also something of a running joke.

The first was a Gene Roddenberry picture. Roddenberry had helmed two seasons of *Star Trek*, the series he had created, but, anxious to make the jump into 'features', he in 1968 left the show and signed a contract with National General, current owner of live-action rights to the ape-man. The National General deal – according to Roddenberry's private correspondence – involved 'a Tarzan feature and getting a contract for a second feature of my own choosing by doing so.' If this implies a cynical motive for making an ape-man film, Roddenberry seemed to disprove this with his next sentence: 'Actually, the Tarzan thing does interest me since I have long felt the subject has never been handled properly on film and that the only right way to do it is to return as much as possible to the original Burroughs concept.' On 7 June 1968, Roddenberry detailed his thoughts to Sy Weintraub about 'a new approach' to the character. His 14-page letter spoke of his having viewed Tarzan films from different eras and concluded that Tarzan should be presented as an intelligent man in a romantic and mysterious period, but should depart from Burroughs' template in dispensing with Jane: he wanted Tarzan to be a virile free agent.

As *Star Trek* was massively popular and inventive, and as it had a crossover in demographic with Burroughs' SF works, Roddenberry seemed an ideal figure to rekindle Tarzan's cinema flame. In newspaper interviews with headings like 'How I'd Film Tarzan,' he dangled the mouth-watering prospect of a movie true to the source, but one that wasn't rooted in the now comical techniques of a previous era, like the 1918 *Tarzan of the Apes*, nor botched, like *The New Adventures of Tarzan*. Plans were made to shoot the picture in Kenya and Italy. An excursion was made to the Olympic Training Camp in Lake Tahoe to find a leading man.

However, the project never got anywhere. Explanations differed. Some sources claimed that the budget Roddenberry was offered by National General would cover only a TV movie when the small screen was a ghetto he was seeking to escape, and some that the sexual explicitness he planned was problematical. Symptomatic of the differing recollections, even Roddenberry's authorised biographer David Alexander wasn't quite sure whether Roddenberry thought he was embarking on a production meant for cinemas or for the small screen. Roddenberry's production colleague Morris Chapnick told Alexander a few things about the project, among them that Roddenberry wanted to portray Tarzan as racist by having him clinically watching a native being tortured but intervening when the same thing happened to a white man, and casual about sexual mores, asking a woman, 'Do you want to mate?' (Tarzan was rebuffed.)

Philip José Farmer had a different perspective on the then-prevailing assumption that Roddenberry was a Tarzan fan and steeped in Burroughs lore. He later disclosed that Roddenberry had given him a copy of his freshly-written Tarzan script and asked him to look it over. 'I didn't think much of it,' Farmer wrote, 'although some parts did have merit. My judgment may have been influenced by some inexcusable errors re names and events in the Tarzan canon.' Farmer claimed that he found out later that Roddenberry didn't really know the books: 'He'd sent out a man named Hank Stein to research Tarzan for him. Stein spent an afternoon in the library and handed in his notes to Roddenberry.'

Although Roddenberry's work – titled simply *Tarzan* – features La, D'Arnot and the Waziri, and presents Tarzan as articulate, in its own way it strays as far from the Burroughs template as MGM and Sol Lesser had, and possibly further. Roddenberry's script is closer in tone to a Robert E Howard sword-and-sorcery tale, what with its mysterious cylinder that can unleash deadly heat and a revived ancient alien that Roddenberry describes as 'Half-manlike, half some strange animal.' Roddenberry also adopts a comics-character tradition in seeking to make Lord Greystoke the mild-mannered secret identity of his superhero alter-ego Tarzan. That Roddenberry unburdens Tarzan to be a fornicating bachelor by having Jane killed, and that he sets the action in 1890 so as to portray an Africa un-demystified by industrialisation, are matters of taste. Had it been made at the time, however, it's difficult to see this movie not being ridiculed as the effort of a man trading on a character he did not understand, and whose tenure on *Star Trek* had blinded him to the fact that not every story needs an extra-terrestrial.

In 1970, Burne Hogarth retired from teaching comics at the School of Visual Arts that he had co-founded in 1947. One consequence of his retirement was that he returned to illustrating Tarzan after a break of more than two decades.

There are many candidates for first graphic novel but the 1972 Watson-Guptill publication *Tarzan of the Apes*, written and drawn by Hogarth, is definitely one of them. Tarzan's popularity and consequent ripeness for adaptation had caused him so many times before to be in the cultural vanguard, and here was another example. This was comics on a whole new level. That it was a beautiful, large-format, full-colour hardback of 122 pages at a time when comics were seen as disposable kid-stuff was just the half of it. The book saw Hogarth take full advantage of the fact that he was now free of the restrictive stylistic and size parameters of newspaper strips: his dynamic layouts on his new, larger canvas saw his characters literally bursting through conventional, regular panel shapes. He also exploited his freedom from the Comics Code Authority (moral watchdog of the US industry, but only with regular-sized comics) and the family orientation of newspapers. The boy Tarzan had been seen nude in comic strips and comic books often enough, but here the only concession Hogarth made to decency was convenient obstruction of the view of his genitals. Hogarth added to the classy air by not using speech balloons.

As his book adapted only half of *Tarzan of the Apes*, many were naturally hoping Hogarth would finish the job. Some were disappointed, then, when his next Watson-Guptill book was *Jungle Tales of Tarzan* (1976). Even worse, these adaptations of four of the stories in that Burroughs collection were rendered in monochrome only. However, what transpired to be Hogarth's farewell to the character was still very worthy. Hogarth rose to the challenge of black-and-white magnificently, layering so much detail into his already pleasantly florid style that the effect was almost dizzying. Furthermore, the philosophical and existential conundrums Burroughs had explored in the chosen stories – 'Tarzan's First Love', 'The Capture of Tarzan', 'The God of Tarzan' and 'The Nightmare' – made for an unusually quiet and thoughtful Tarzan comics experience. In both Hogarth books, there was much symbolism and hidden imagery for those who cared to look.

Another great Tarzan artist, Russ Manning, was also responsible for Tarzan projects that can be termed graphic novels, if not on quite the same deluxe scale. When he ceased work on the daily newspaper strip in 1972, it was to write and draw the comics that ERB, Inc were providing for European publishers. Amongst this work were such large-format paperback publications as *Tarzan in the Land that Time Forgot*, *Tarzan and the Beastmaster* and *Tarzan in Savage Pellucidar*. As with Hogarth's material, Manning's beautiful art was equal to his love for the character.

While standard comics could not hope to match the prestige of such enterprises, in 1972 that quadrant of the Tarzan universe saw an upgrade when the Tarzan franchise was transferred to National Periodical Publications. This company was the home of DC, which, if it did not produce the best comics, was the biggest name in the business, chiefly because it was the home of the iconic triumvirate of Superman, Batman and Wonder Woman.

With the exception of just half a dozen of its 52 issues, the DC

Tarzan comic became synonymous with one man. At various points, Joe Kubert handled everything on the title: writing, drawing, cover illustration, editing and even briefly lettering. 'My understanding was that one of the prime reasons the Burroughs people gave the character to DC was because they had seen my work and had me set to do it,' says Kubert. However, he does admit, 'I've heard another story to it. My friend Carmine Infantino, who was the boss at the time, tells me that he had to convince them to permit me to do it.' If ERB, Inc were apprehensive about Kubert working on Tarzan, they perhaps had some justification. He was probably best known at this time for his artwork on army character Sgt Rock. He also admits he was a writer only 'off and on.' However, Kubert says of the corporation's reaction to his Tarzan work, 'From the outset, the people up at Burroughs were more than happy with it.'

'I loved his books,' Kubert says of Burroughs. 'My conscious attempt when I started doing the Tarzan was to perhaps capture that feeling that I had when I first read the books and to try to convey it in the work that I was doing. For that purpose, I re-read all the books again.' As mentioned previously, he had also adored the depiction of the character by Hal Foster. 'One of the reasons I think that I became a cartoonist in the first place was because of the beautiful work that was done originally, especially by Hal Foster when he was doing it through the newspapers,' Kubert says. 'It was a living, believable character. That's what I was trying to do. I re-read all the Foster material.' Although Kubert had also enjoyed Burne Hogarth's work, he was not very familiar with Russ Manning's: 'I really hadn't followed or seen the Tarzan as it was published in other magazines.' As for the movie Tarzan, Kubert says, 'I loved Johnny Weissmuller. He came probably closest to what I envisioned as what Tarzan should look like and Tarzan should be. The others I was not too crazy about. The tendency with a character like a Tarzan – so popular, so successful – is try to twist the damn thing any way to Sunday to try to make it a little different, a little bit more personal, and in the process tear away pieces rather than add to it.'

DC's book premiered in early 1972, the inaugural issue cover-dated April. At first its title (according to logo, rather than indicia) was *Tarzan of the Apes*, but would eventually mostly be just *Tarzan*, though for a spell it was *Tarzan, Lord of the Jungle*. It would also change depending on what novel adaptation was currently running in its pages. The debut's cover featured the words '1st DC issue' in a prominent yellow circle, but directly across from that was the information 'NO. 207,' which must have been confusing to some. Presumably, DC were continuing the numbering from the final Gold Key book because they thought this would engender the inheritance of its readership.

Spread across the first four DC issues was an adaptation of the novel *Tarzan of the Apes*. A four-part story was unusually long in American comic books at the time, especially at DC. 'They gave me complete freedom in what I was doing,' Kubert says of his employers. He notes of the process of adaptation, 'You are definitely encumbered. There are perhaps dramatic effects that might be slightly different, compositions for panels, but essentially you have to follow that story as the story was written. It doesn't mean that it was a chore. I love it, because I felt that, despite the fact that the story was going to be the same, perhaps there was something I could add to it, perhaps something I can do just a little bit differently than was done before ... What I concentrated on was to get the sense of the character, the feelings, the credibility that I felt when I was a kid.' Kubert set the beginning of the story in 1888, just as in the Burroughs book, but he adds, 'More important than the timeframe was to get the sense, the feeling of the character, the nuances, the characterisation – not some large muscle-bound guy running around in a loincloth but somebody who was believable and credible.'

Of course, Kubert was by no means the first comics writer to adapt Tarzan books. 'Strangely enough, that didn't intimidate me as much as it did invigorate me,' he says. 'It gave me something to shoot for. I have been influenced by every good piece of work that I've seen. Nevertheless, I've never felt that I was competing with those artists, trying to do a better job than they did. I don't try to emulate them as much as I try to learn from them.'

Tarzan of the Apes, The Return of Tarzan, Jungle Tales of Tarzan and even *Tarzan and the Castaways* were logical choices for adaptation, although Kubert's decision to also tackle *Tarzan and the Lion Man* – one of the weaker ape-man books – is less explicable. These DC adaptations alternated with new Tarzan stories. Kubert doesn't recall why but suggests, 'Perhaps it was the tediousness of going through the whole story and then digesting it – there were no more four-parters – into a 30-page or a 32-page magazine.' The science fiction and fantastical elements of some of the newly-written stories – for instance, the snow ape and dinosaurs the ape-man battled in issues 227 and 228 respectively – suggested to some that Kubert was trying to compete in the sword and sorcery field with Marvel's *Conan the Barbarian*, which was the darling of comics fandom at the time. Kubert: 'No. I wasn't reading a lot of the other books. I did not have a hell of a lot of time. Just as a change of pace, I would try to vary the stories as much as possible. There are certain directions you can take in doing a jungle story, but then you're limited to the jungle and the backgrounds, so trying to get a little magic into a story, or histrionics or anything to make it look a little bit different, would be a plus.'

Although he divested himself of lettering duties, Kubert continued to write, draw and edit Tarzan, as well as contribute covers. Asked if he should have reined back in some areas, he says, 'Perhaps, but the writing didn't take an incredible length of time because I would have had to lay out the stories anyhow to make sure that they were told the way I envisioned them. And the way I write, I write and do the rough layouts at the same time.' He does concede that editing his own work created a potential conflict of interest: 'That third eye is something that every artist and every writer has to have.'

That first DC *Tarzan* issue had featured not only the debut instalment of Kubert's *Tarzan of the Apes* adaptation, plus a Hal Foster newspaper strip reprint, but also the start of an adaptation of *A Princess of Mars* – evidence that DC were interested in Edgar Rice Burroughs properties across the board. Two months after the *Tarzan* title started, the company began their own *Korak* book, which also continued the Gold Key numbering. As well as the exploits of the son of Tarzan, *Korak*'s first issue boasted strips featuring Carson of Venus and Pellucidar. Three months after the Korak title's debut came *Tarzan Presents Edgar Rice Burroughs' Weird Worlds*, which featured, at least for its first seven issues, Barsoom and Pellucidar strips. Its issue cover-dated November '75 saw *Korak* morph into *Tarzan Family*, a reprint-dominated anthology. Kubert drew covers for all of said books, and was editor of *Korak*. He says of Korak, 'Frankly I didn't feel that the character had any kind of personality or background or reason other than it being just another Tarzan.' However, the Korak book was differentiated from its Tarzan stablemate a little by the fact that it featured a quest (Korak's search for Meriem) spanning multiple issues.

On the main *Tarzan* title, the ERB butter was spread even thinner from the April-May 1974 issue when it became a 100-page book. 'The responsibility of putting it together was given to me, so I did it,' shrugs Kubert. 'This is above and beyond doing the kind of work, especially with the drawing, that I've continued to love. It is a business besides an artform. I kind of separated myself from involvement or even asking questions.' Kubert adds that there was no difficulty filling those pages, but does acknowledge the tenuousness of the connection of some of the strips – Bomba, Congo Bill and Detective Chimp featured – to the title character: 'As happens very often in my business, it becomes almost a helter-skelter kind of an operation. You just drown the original idea.'

Pragmatic though he was, Kubert was distressed at his inability to maintain the quality of Tarzan's adventures. 'I was editing about half a dozen different books at least, and doing I don't know how many different covers, and I found that I just couldn't maintain the schedule,' he explains. 'I had to call on other artists to help me with the work. Despite the fact that the artists I had were incredibly good, incredibly talented people, and I laid out all the stories – I would rub them out on 8½ x 11 stationery and send it to them in illustrated form in addition to the text of the script itself – still it wasn't the thing that I had envisioned.'

Almost farcical measures were resorted to in order to help Kubert keep up with the publishing schedules, including an artificial collaboration with his hero Hal Foster on 'The Stone Sphinx' (issue #237). 'I incorporated things that perhaps were printed years and years ago,' Kubert explains. 'I even used a Burne Hogarth story from the daily strips or from the Sunday papers and converted it into the comic books in a vain attempt to meet some sort of schedule with the book. The set-up for the Sunday pages – the grids, the panel sizes themselves – very often did not fit into the design of the page that I was using, so I would add some drawings of my own to pre-existing work in order to make it feasible and complete the illustration. I took great pride in at least making an attempt to keep up with those masters.'

On the front cover of issue 221, Kubert seemed to be paying homage to another master: his illustration of Tarzan astride a lion, about to plunge a knife into its flank, is very reminiscent of Clinton Pettee's classic depiction of the ape-man on the front of *All-Story* in 1912.

The conclusion of his adaptation of 'Tarzan and the Champion' in issue 249, cover-dated May 1976, was Kubert's last original contribution to the DC *Tarzan* book, barring front covers and a pair of 'Balu of the Great Apes' back-ups. He recalls the reason for his ceasing to work on the title as, 'The sales did not warrant continuing to publish it,' although he admits that he has no idea why an adaptation of *Tarzan the Untamed* in the following six issues was contributed by Gerry Conway and Denny O'Neil (scripts) and José Luis Garcia-Lopez and Rudy Florese (art).

'I'd always been a huge fan of Tarzan, and the opportunity to work on the title after Joe left was irresistible,' says Conway. 'But I think we were all aware that the book hadn't been selling well and that in all likelihood it was doomed to be cancelled. So it was a bittersweet experience.' The final two issues were half-hearted, given over to reprints of Kubert work from the first year of the title's existence.

The DC *Tarzan* comic book had existed for two months shy of five years. Both Kubert's scratchy and impressionistic artwork and his deeply knowledgeable scripts are fondly remembered by ERB aficionados.

March 1972 saw the publication of a rather bizarre book called *Tarzan Alive*, sub-titled *A Definitive Biography of Lord Greystoke*. Written by science fiction author Philip José Farmer, it posited Tarzan as a real person whose adventures had been fictionalised by Edgar Rice Burroughs.

Of course, Burroughs himself had said as much in the introduction to *Tarzan of the Apes* ('I had this story from one who had no business to tell it to me'), but plenty of the novels of the era carried similar tilts at authenticity and it was understood that they were as much fiction as what followed them.

Farmer wasn't actually the first to claim that Tarzan was real. In their issue cover-dated March 1959, the New York-based *Man's Adventure Magazine* published a feature by one Thomas Llewellan Jones titled 'The Man Who Really Was ... Tarzan'. Although the article of over 3,300 words conceded, 'There never was a Lord "Greystoke". That particular name was made up; pulled right out of the air,' it also baldly stated, 'But the actual character, the person on whom the entire series was based, did live. There really was a man, an English nobleman, who, shipwrecked on the jungle coast of Africa, was cared for by the apes, grew up with them and eventually survived a thousand adventures before returning to London to assume his rightful title and position. The man was William Charles Mildin, 14th Earl of Streatham. For 15 years, between 1868 and 1883, his life was the prototype of Tarzan.'

What is striking about the article is its verisimilitude. It smacks of truth partly because it *doesn't* precisely follow the Burroughs story, while its deviations from it are sufficiently convoluted that one wonders why a fiction writer would bother. Mildin, it is claimed, ran away from home aged 11 in a boyish fit of anger and obtained a berth as a cabin boy on the African-bound *Antilla*. He was the only survivor when a storm wrecked the vessel and washed him ashore. He made friends with a hideous but unexpectedly friendly group of apes of an unspecified species and lived with them for six years. Although he did not become king of this tribe of apes – he was far too physically puny – his knowledge of fire and the advantages provided by his greater dexterity with his hands made him a fondly regarded member of the group. Nor did he learn the ape language, but he did pick up the meanings of various simian sounds. His ape name was (phonetically) 'Okhugh'. From there the story departs wildly from that of Burroughs, involving Mildin making friends with black tribes, polygamously marrying women of 'coffee-colored skins and high, firm breasts' and having several children. Hearing of a nearby trading post manned by whites, he ultimately made a 22-day trek to civilisation. Back in Britain, with him having resumed his seat and inherited his fortune, war-fever and English libel law kept his extraordinary tale out of the newspapers even beyond his death in 1919. His one (white) son died in 1937 and the latter's will stipulated his papers be sealed for 20 years after his own death, upon which time his father's handwritten account of his jungle adventures was discovered and then just as quickly buried lest its revelations of far-flung offspring jeopardise the bequests the son had made to charities or cause legal headaches based around succession.

It all makes for a more plausible story than *Tarzan of the Apes* because it side-steps the questions the latter raises, such as how a man raised from infancy by simians could be so 'normal' and how a child who had only heard English as a baby could teach himself to read it. Yet the issues of *The Times* that Jones claims verify the existence of Mildin and the edition of Lloyd's *Register* that he says confirms the wreck of the *Antilla* have proved to contain no such information. The sheer depth and believability of the article begs the question why – aside from money – Jones made up such a story. Or perhaps the fact that within it he confesses to having been a Burroughs fan answers that question. We'll apparently never know: Thomas Llewellan Jones itself seems to have been a pseudonym, for no other article with that by-line readily comes to light. Philip José Farmer was sceptical of the article in an afterword he wrote to it when he reprinted it in his collection of writing on feral children, *Mother Was a Lovely Beast* (1974), but he was clearly being wilfully provocative: *Tarzan Alive* is like a grand version of 'The Man Who Really Was … Tarzan'.

In *Tarzan Alive,* Farmer claims to have tracked down Lord Greystoke through a 'close study of *Burke's Peerage* and another source I am not free to divulge.' Courtesy supposedly of conversation with the ape-man, he then takes the reader through each and every published Burroughs Tarzan story and explains what happened in the real-life equivalent adventure. (Tarzan revealed that a surprising number of the lost civilisations succumbed to dysentery; meanwhile Farmer informs those readers who hadn't already apprehended it that the known scientific facts ruled out the events of *Tarzan at the Earth's Core* as having taken place.) Farmer reproduces what he claims is the Greystoke coat of arms, gives Jane Clayton née Porter's recorded vital statistics (38-19-36) and includes a bizarre section in which he invents what became known as the Wold Newton Universe. In the latter, it is stated that nominally fictional characters like Tarzan, Doc Savage and Sherlock Holmes are real and gained their powers via the fact that their forebears were exposed to genetic code-changing ionisation in 1795 when a meteorite crashed in the Yorkshire village through which they were passing. This all sounds the domain of mimeographed fanzines – the means of distributing fan effusions before the internet cut out the need for paper – but the book ran to over 300 pages and was published by the mainstream Doubleday.

In 2001, the present author asked Farmer whether *Tarzan Alive* was a spoof or if he was serious in claiming that the ape-man really existed. He replied, 'I get asked that question quite often. I said, "Well, if you can believe in God, you can believe in Tarzan – and vice versa."' He then laughed heartily. The prosaic reality is that Farmer's conceit of Tarzan being a real person was possibly a ploy to enable him to legally publish a book with 'Tarzan' in the title. The period was littered with Farmer-penned works in which he effectively sought to inherit the mantle of Tarzan scribe without seeking the permission of the Burroughs estate, who – due to his earthy style – would almost certainly have withheld it. Usually, he avoided legal action via implicitly invoking pastiche and not using the actual Tarzan name.

In *A Feast Unknown* (1969), Farmer depicted characters called Lord Grandrith and Doc Caliban, a thinly disguised Tarzan and Doc Savage, who share a common father in the shape of Jack the Ripper. Both men get aroused by engaging in acts of violence. It spanned two sequels – *Lord of the Trees* and *The Mad Goblin* – printed literally back-to-back (in the Ace Double series) in 1970. Each book in the latter volume told the same story through the eyes of a different one of the pair. It was published in the same year as *Lord Tyger*, which depicted a young boy of noble birth named Ras Tyger growing up in a jungle with ostensible ape parents who repeatedly answer 'because it is written' (or 'not written') when he enquires about aspects of his life that puzzle him. It turns out that the written things in question are in Edgar Rice Burroughs' *oeuvre*. Boygur, a mad millionaire ERB fan (i.e. someone like Farmer only with a lot more money), has arranged for young Ras to be given an upbringing as close as possible to that of Boygur's ape-man hero. When Tyger learns the truth of his false life, he unleashes hell. In *Time's Last Gift* (1972), a group of people from the far future travel back in time to prehistoric days. Burroughs fans will spot the clues indicating that one of them – John Gribardsun – is another of his disguised Tarzans. It spawned two loosely related sequels, *Hadon of Ancient Opar*

(1974) and *Flight to Opar* (1976), both of which, as their titles imply, flesh out the lost civilisation of ERB's Tarzan stories. The Farmer Opar books were given approval by ERB, Inc, but with *The Adventures of the Peerless Peer* (1974) the corporation finally took action against the man who had for so long been writing veiled Tarzan adventures of whose tone Burroughs would most certainly not have approved. As with so many Farmer books of this ilk it was intriguing – positing Tarzan and Sherlock Holmes teaming up to defeat evil, their adventures related as usual with Holmes books by Dr Watson – but the fact that the peerless peer was actually named Greystoke (even if he was never referred to as Tarzan) was clearly considered to be taking the piss. The book disappeared from the shelves, and when the story reappeared as 'The Adventure of the Three Madmen' in the compendium *The Grand Adventure* (1984), Mowgli (from the now public-domain *The Jungle Book*) had taken the place of the Tarzan figure. Farmer was again pushing the boundaries of copyright in *Mother Was a Lovely Beast* by including a supposed part of the autobiography of Lord Greystoke. This and a verbatim alleged interview with Tarzan 'conducted' by Farmer for *Esquire* in 1972 were later included in a 2006 Bison Books reissue of *Tarzan Alive*.

Some Burroughs fans were intrigued by Farmer's works but others were literally disgusted, not least because Farmer stayed true to the fascination with bodily functions and naturalism that had made him a groundbreaking SF author, the first of which undermined the glamour of the Tarzan character, the second of which undermined his entire premise. Farmer's love for and expertise on the Burroughs Tarzan books was obvious. (As touched on previously, in one essay, he modestly disavowed one person's claims that he was the world's foremost ERB expert but did concede that if the same person had '…said I was the greatest authority on Tarzan, he'd have been right.') Yet he could not, or at the very least did not, write like ERB. Burroughs sought at all times to shield the reader from the sexual act and bodily exigencies. Farmer veritably rubbed them in the reader's face. Whereas Burroughs depicted people mesmerised by Tarzan's awesome beauty, in *A Feast Unknown* Farmer showed a smitten man raping him. In a fight scene at the end of the book, the Tarzan character has his erect penis ripped off by the Doc Savage character (which, unbelievably, is not the most sickening depiction of violence in the narrative). Whereas in *Tarzan Alive* and *Mother was a Lovely Beast* Farmer displayed signs of obsessive-compulsive disorder in attempting to rationalise internal discrepancies in Burroughs' Tarzan work and explain away facets of it that cannot have stemmed from real life, *Lord Tyger* goes in the opposite direction, seeming to be a cathartic admission that the entire Tarzan series is comic book-level bunkum. Its protagonist behaves in ways far more logical for someone of his extraordinary upbringing: he eats like a pig and is sexually predatory toward African girls, a visiting European woman and pet monkeys.

Tarzan Alive includes what is effectively a Tarzan short story, one that is both impressive and rather poignant, with the ape-man wandering through a devastated, deserted Opar forlornly calling out 'La!' Farmer must have felt at the time that this was the closest he was ever going to get to what was clearly his fantasy of writing a 'proper' Tarzan tale, but toward the end of his life fate would transpire to have a trick up its sleeve in that regard.

Tarzan Alive got surprisingly respectable reviews from upmarket newspapers, whose reviewers had clearly decided to show they were good sports by being willing to join in the pretence of the ape-man's existence. Meanwhile, the stone that this book dropped into the pool of literature created an altogether unexpected ripple.

The subject matter of his previous novels had established J T Edson as the British equivalent of Zane Grey. A Derbyshire man, his Wild West was nothing more than an aggregation of the mythologised versions he had read in print and seen on screen, and he cheerfully admitted this, but he compensated for it with compelling storytelling that owed much of its power to his meticulous attention to mechanical and geographical detail (although not to internal series continuity). So popular were his tales of the likes of Dusty Fog, Mark Counter and the Ysabel Kid, and so prolific was his workrate, that by the mid-1970s he was well on his way to publication of his one hundredth book. Leading up to that 1979 milestone, he embarked on a quite unanticipated Tarzan-esque side-turning in his career.

Edson had read and clearly been tickled by *Tarzan Alive*: little nods to its theory of a genetic link between the world's army of fictional heroes would crop up regularly in his books. He went a stage further, though, in picking up on an assertion in Farmer's work that Korak was not Tarzan's real son but adopted (a typically anal Farmer way of explaining the discrepancies in Burroughs' books regarding Korak's age). To Farmer, Jack Clayton was instead John Drummond-Clayton, the biological brother of pulp hero Bulldog Drummond. Edson approached both ERB, Inc and Farmer for permission to expand upon this nugget of an idea. Their respective go-aheads for his creation of a second adopted son of Tarzan gave him a legal way of getting into print the adventures of a jungle hero on which he had worked even before his cowboy writing career began. The result was Bunduki.

James Allenvale Gunn was orphaned in the Mau Mau uprising (1952-1960) and adopted by the Greystokes at the age of three. He is also the adoptive cousin of Dawn Drummond-Clayton, granddaughter of Korak and Meriem, who – in an example of how Wold Newton universe machinations can easily skirt incest – becomes his 'mate'. Nicknamed Bunduki after the Swahili word for firearm, Gunn works as the Chief Warden of the Ambagasali Wild Life Reserve. One day, both he and Dawn plunge over a gorge in a Land Rover, but instead of crashing to their deaths awake in an alien land. They have been transported to the planet Zillikian in order that, should he so wish, Bunduki can become Chief Warden of this jungle world, which is populated by tribes from other planets and a hodgepodge of Terran wildlife from all continents. (Said wildlife includes

Mangani, which, we are informed, Bunduki's 'father' told him became extinct back on earth in the 1950s). When Bunduki and Dawn ask the 'Supplier' why he brought them to the planet, they receive the reply, 'It has long been our wish to do so with a pair from your family. But we are not permitted to remove any life from its natural habitat unless it is on the point of dying. Every time we saw one of your family in danger, we computed that ... they would contrive to escape.'

It's rumoured that the alien planet conceit was a sop to ERB, Inc because the corporation was anxious that the series not encroach too much on its intellectual property (although it's a mystery how that squares with Edson taking it upon himself to claim that Tarzan and the entire Clayton clan – made homeless after Kenya gained independence – now live in Pellucidar). The alien planet premise immediately poses a problem with the perils the hero faces: the author is free to make up his own physiological and geographical rules rather than adhere to the ones of whose dangers the reader is cognisant. Moreover, the aliens stripping Bunduki of his warden's outfit and placing him in a leopardskin loincloth possesses no logic but instead feels like a form of Tarzan fetishism. In any case, the Supplier received a bad hand. Neither raised by apes like his step-father, nor even the beneficiary of a Korak-style relocation to the jungle as a boy, James Allenvale Gunn is merely tall, strong, good with weaponry, adept with languages (including Mangani) and – because of the household in which he grew up – both trained a little in following trails and in possession of pill-assisted longevity. Truly, a second-rate Tarzan.

Another problem is Edson's prose, which reads like he typed it with his lip bitten. His pages are stuffed with interminable description of weaponry and his action is repeatedly interrupted by irrelevant conversations and pedantic footnotes. There are occasions where his obsession with footnotes bisects an anal mentality as pronounced as Farmer's to insufferable effect (e.g. 'At no time in his 24 biographical books on the life of Lord Greystoke does Edgar Rice Burroughs suggest that Tarzan made use of vines when travelling through the trees'). Edson seems to think this is all compensated for – rather than exacerbated – by his habitual use of exclamation marks. This clunkiness is emphatically not Burroughsonian, even if Edson's distaste for depicting sex and printing obscenities is (an example of the author's puritanism is provided by the fact that we are told that Bunduki chose to attend a Kenyan university because he was 'disenchanted with the so-called permissive society in England').

However, the series was made viable by a combination of Edson's large fanbase, book-starved Tarzan fans and the fact that the Seventies was a boom era for casual purchases of men's action novels. As well as *Bunduki* (1975), Britain's Corgi published the sequels *Bunduki and Dawn* and *Sacrifice for the Quagga God* (both 1976), all with the strapline 'Adopted Son of Tarzan'.

Edson then hit a snag. Marion Burroughs was an ERB family heir through marriage to Edgar Rice Burroughs' son Hulbert. Hitherto an absentee chairman, in 1976 she assumed active control of the company. She proceeded to adopt a rather hardline approach to ERB, Inc's intellectual property. Not only did she vigorously pursue alleged breaches of it, she also decided to rein back on co-operation with projects that she felt blurred its margins, including Edson's. She became a hate figure among fans, who could understand why she might launch a suit against blue comedy *Jungle Heat* on the grounds that it denigrated the Tarzan character, but not why she sought to obstruct Edson, Farmer and John Eric Holmes (author of a Pellucidar novel published with the corporation's blessing), writers who adored Burroughs and his creations and were satisfying a public hunger that ERB, Inc hadn't seemed inclined to.

Either way, it left Edson in a bit of a pickle, especially as he would seem to have stockpiled Bunduki novels. He got around it by dropping any use of Tarzan's name in his next Bunduki book, *Fearless Master of the Jungle* (1980), and hoping that the characters, backgrounds and precepts he had established in what was by now a franchise of its own would see him through commercially. However, although he included in compendiums published between 1979 and 1990 four Bunduki short stories set on earth before the character's alien transportation, there would be no further novels featuring the character, and the completed Bunduki book *Amazons of Zillikian* remains unpublished to this day.

What is most peculiar about the whole Bunduki affair is that, although ERB, Inc were (originally) prepared to authorise this series, they apparently would not do the same with new Tarzan books. If, on the other hand, the absence of new ape-man tales on the shelves was due to the reluctance of publishers, one would have imagined that the success of Bunduki might have made those publishers think again. It so happened that the year Bunduki made his debut was also the centenary of Burroughs' birth, which accrued the author's creations some measure of publicity. That there was no new Tarzan novel in 1975 to exploit this was negligence on the part of someone.

Michael Heseltine's collar-length, un-parted blonde hair had already made the Member of Parliament a bizarre figure in the House of Commons, let alone his own Conservative party, before the moment in 1976 where, in a heated debate about nationalisation, he furiously swung the Commons' ceremonial mace. The combination of that intemperate gesture and his unruly thatch saw him acquire forever the nickname 'Tarzan'. The bestowing of that title was proof positive that the ape-man's name was still an instantly understood byword for wild and untamed.

Meanwhile, August of that year saw the arrival of a musical titled *T. Zee*, one of what turned out to be several futile attempts by Richard O'Brien to match the success he'd scored with *The Rocky Horror Show*. Although it was more a parody of comic-book culture than of Tarzan itself, the show featured an out-of-shape monosyllabic muscle man searching for a Jane-esque mate. For anyone unsure about to whom this alluded, the title provided a further clue.

Spoof and parody attend any successful artistic creation. Indeed, both are a litmus test for a work or franchise's societal impact and both count amongst the greatest compliments that can be paid to the success of the creation so mocked. Except that the nature of mocking means that it doesn't always come over as a compliment, hence the frequent sensitivity of copyright holders to mickey-takes. To be mocked is bad enough, but to be aware that the person doing the mocking is making money from it can be infuriating. In addition, there is sometimes a genuine belief on the part of copyright holders that the parody might cheapen the commercial worth of the original property by making the pubic perceive shortcomings on which they had not hitherto focused.

Since Arthurs Gibbons and Carlton tried to put the kibosh on Dick Mortimer's skit *Warzan and his Apes* back in the 1920s and failed on the grounds of their lack of promptness, legal rulings and changes in legislation in various countries have put such ventures beyond the reach of the law by declaring parody a legitimate means of artistic expression distinct from passing off (a form of deception involving tricking the consumer into believing that he is purchasing something involving someone else's creation) or plagiarism (blatantly lifting other people's work or concepts). In any case, it's difficult to imagine the Burroughs estate, or even Burroughs had he been alive, finding anything but hilarious the early-'60s Peter Cook sketch 'One Leg Too Few' in which a massively optimistic monopedal actor auditions for the role of Tarzan. (The casting director famously observes, 'I've got nothing against your right leg. The trouble is – neither have you.')

However, there arises a question of when parody becomes either damaging or a form of free-riding. A 15-minute preview of the X-rated French-Belgian animated motion picture *Tarzoon: Shame of the Jungle* went down a storm at the 1974 Cannes Film Festival, but somewhat less well with the Burroughs estate, who tried to prevent the full movie's release. A French court upheld the makers' right to parody. The knife was twisted further by the American distributors, who in 1978 cannily hired Johnny

Weissmuller's son, also called Johnny, to voice one of the parts for its American distribution. They also commissioned a movie poster from Don Martin, whose style was instantly recognisable to that considerable part of the US public who devoured *Mad* magazine. The Burroughs estate in the meantime had alighted upon a US law about degradation of trademark, and a domestic judge, ordering that their intellectual property not be further damaged, forced the producers to remove the 'Tarzoon' part of the title – with measurable financial damage to the picture. As mentioned, ERB, Inc also took action against the '90s movie *Jungle Heat*, a parody whose porn ingredient could be argued to be hazardous to a wholesome franchise. Its occasional presence on cable TV demonstrates that the estate ultimately failed to do little more than contract its circulation. They did, though, manage to shut down 1978 comic book *Hoverboy*, published by American independent Vigilance. This parody of the Tarzan story involved the titular hero becoming as one with animals when his plane crashes into a jungle. Vigilance might have gotten away with it had they not decided to include a cover sunburst declaring, 'Because you people seem to like Tarzan,' with the ape-man's name rendered in that unmistakable and trademarked double-outlined Tarzan logo.

Tarzan Presley, a 2004 novel by Nigel Cox, was a literature-reality mash-up featuring the story of a man raised in the forests of Wairarapa, New Zealand, who becomes rock 'n' roll's first major icon. It was critically acclaimed and a bestseller in the author's native NZ. However, ERB, Inc prevented it being sold in any other country and ensured that all Tarzan references were removed from future editions in the author's homeland, where it is now known as *Jungle Rock Blues*. The author said in justification, '...what was I going to do, write a letter to ... whom, I couldn't imagine ... saying, "I think I might be going to write a book in which a character from one of your books might appear, though in radically changed form – is that okay?"' Sympathetic journalist Steven Price offered, 'Burroughs never asked Kipling's permission to write his Tarzan stories.' Publisher Fergus

Barrowman even went so far as to say, 'Tarzan is so much a part of the general culture and discourse that I believe it ought to be part of the public domain.' Such airy comments make one inclined to forgive the corporation for being possibly a little too cynical in their knowledge of the fact that parody is less well-defined and protected outside the United States.

When an emotionally and physically shattered Mike Henry handed in his notice to Sy Weintraub in 1966, he made an interesting career choice in signing up to play the lead in a TV pilot called *Taygar, King of the Jungle*. Recalls Denny Miller of the title character, 'He was a klutz. He was always falling into natives' traps and he was always taking the wrong vine. My ex-wife Kit Smythe was the Jane part, which was Ruthie. The first shot of the pilot is her making a salad in the treehouse and the whole wall caves in and she turns to Mike, who has crushed the side of the house in, and says, "That's the third wrong vine you've taken this week." It was a delightful show.' Miller was in fact one of the few people who saw the pilot, because Sy Weintraub's Banner Productions instituted legal action to stop both its broadcast and the production of a putative series on the grounds that it was a deliberate attempt to burlesque and ridicule the Tarzan character. Yet the similarly-themed *George of the Jungle* animated TV show made it to the airwaves in 1967 without legal ramifications, and in 1997 became a successful live-action motion picture. Perhaps this dichotomy can be put down to personal issues between Weintraub and Henry, while *Taygar* failing to find a sponsor and hence a buyer can probably be ascribed more to a lack of appetite for legal tussles *per se* than proof of the legitimacy of Weintraub's objections.

Adding to legal cloudiness about when spoof becomes denigration is the leeway permitted Tarzan mickey-takers back in the 1930s by the then-owners of Tarzan live-action rights. In 1933, MGM allowed the Hal Roach studio to portray the ape-man as a wimp with glasses in *Nature in the Wrong*. In 1934, MGM produced *Hollywood Party*, in which Jimmy Durante riffed on a similar theme by personating 'Schnarzan'. This must surely have played a part in making those inclined to parody and mock Tarzan consider they had permission so to do, or had a get-out if challenged.

Considering the ape-man's presence at the forefront of so many new media, it's something of a surprise that it wasn't until the late '70s that anybody seems even to have considered adapting Tarzan into the format of animation.

In the 1960s and 1970s, Filmation were the kings of American Saturday-morning cartoon action series. Headed by Norm Prescott and Lou Scheimer, their *modus operandi* was not to create new franchises like competitors Hanna-Barbera but to acquire licences for the adaptation of existing intellectual properties. More than one generation was weaned on their animated takes on Superman, Aquaman, *Journey to the Center of the Earth*, *The Hardy Boys*, *Sabrina the Teenage Witch*, *Gilligan's Island*, *Star Trek*, et al. As their offices were virtually within walking distance of those of ERB, Inc in Tarzana it was perhaps inevitable that Filmation would license the ape-man. Yet the very fact that in the mid-'70s the Burroughs estate gave the go-ahead for a Filmation Tarzan cartoon is a measure of the falling stock of their property. Robert Kline, storyboard supervisor and storyboard artist on the Filmation Tarzan show, candidly concedes, 'When Lou finally got the rights to something and was able to put it on the air – and this was often commented on by critics and so forth – it's kind of the last gasp of a property. They wouldn't put it on Saturday morning as a limited animation TV series until they figured, "Well, we can't really do much else with this." An awful lot of what Filmation produced were knock-offs of extinct properties. It was rare that they would be able to do a show that had any kind of name recognition if that property was really hot at the time.'

Certainly no great cachet was going to attach to 1970s US Saturday morning fare. The allure of the familiar characters and properties Filmation licensed was sometimes necessary to blind kids to the shortcomings of their rather basic product. Their animation was cheap-and-cheerful and its trademark was the overuse of the 'stock' shot. Kline: 'They insisted that we use as much repeat footage or same-as footage as possible.' Kline also reveals, 'It was rare that you were able to test the footage before it went into full-colour production, so often a scene would be animated without really knowing how it was going to turn out. The animator would just have to base his decision on previous experience. Even at the time, studios like Disney would look at pencil tests and so forth and re-work it. There was no such luxury at Filmation or Hanna-Barbera.'

Of his company's contact with the ERB estate, Kline explains, 'We worked with Danton Burroughs. I don't recall meeting Marion Burroughs. As it was, we did not spend a lot of time interacting with them, although I do recall Danton did the Tarzan call that's used in the Filmation version. I think he had worked on it for years and years and got it down, and Lou Scheimer wanted him to do it.' This certainly tallies with Denny Miller's recollection of ERB's grandson's prowess in that department: 'He was the best at it that I have ever heard ... We were on a talk show, six of us together: Gordon Scott, Johnny, Buster Crabbe, James Pierce ... Danton Burroughs hid behind a partition and any [of the six] that wanted to, they'd put their hands up and he'd do the yell so that the live audience didn't know that they were faking it.'

Kline points out that although Filmation did things as cheaply as possible, that doesn't mean they operated inexpensively in an absolute sense: 'We had over 350 people working on the shows at different points: you had storyboard people, layout people, designers. The layout people would draw the scenes in detail: the background and the characters, where they were going to be positioned. Then you'd have the animators that would move the character, the assistant animators, the clean-up people that would do the final lines, background painters. There was a recording studio there, there was editing facility there, everything that was needed to make the film except processing ... It was only in terms of re-runs and merchandising and other benefits that the show could even show a profit.'

Filmation titled their show *Tarzan Lord of the Jungle*. Because it was kids' fare, violence was reduced to, er, cartoon level. Says scriptwriter and associate producer Len Janson, 'As writers, we had access to all the Tarzan books, read them all and used what we could. They were great books, but the violent aspects inherent to the stories could not be used because of the hard line of CBS' Broadcast Standards. I remember one fight with the censors that underlines the frustrations of doing that show: they refused to let the ape-man carry a knife despite our promises that he would never use it. There were many battles like this and we lost probably 90 percent of them.' The weaponless Tarzan sent threatening animals packing with an 'Unk!' (Mangani for 'Go'). If he had no option but to engage in physical contact, it would be done via bland methods, for instance, tepid wrestling or the disablement of a dangerous snake by wrapping it in a knot and depositing it on the ground, with the animators even going to the length of making sure the viewer saw the snake was not left in distress by depicting it untangling itself and slithering to safety. Moreover, says Kline, 'Lou Scheimer was concerned about what he put on the air for kids. He didn't want to put anything on that didn't have a good moral attitude.' That *Tarzan Lord of the Jungle* tended to morality tales might not have made it any different to the Ron Ely live-action series but, considering that several of the episodes were direct adaptations of Burroughs stories, this sometimes meant shoehorning. Then there was the effect of something that had not existed when Burroughs created his character. What the world had not quite yet dubbed political correctness dictated that black Africans be seen nowhere on the show. Says Kline, 'That would have been too controversial. It would have been too difficult to show them in a way that wouldn't create some kind of critical backlash, so it was just avoided by not having any and dealing with Burroughs' lost cities and those kind of locations.'

Filmation were not a purely mercenary company. Their *Star Trek: The Animated Series*, for instance, used the voices of the actors from the original live-action series and featured mature scripts by well-known SF writers, while their *Fat Albert and the Cosby Kids* had a significant educational content. Accordingly, despite the constraints, *Tarzan Lord of the Jungle* was a reasonable product that had several worthy components.

The show began airing on the CBS network on 11 September 1976. It consisted of episodes of half-an-hour each (including the interludes that followed the 'We will return after these messages' announcements). Tarzan's lines were spoken by Robert Ridgely, who seemed to have almost a monopoly on heroic voiceover parts at the time, him also vocalising animated series *Flash Gordon* and *Thundar*. That Ridgley's stentorian American tones were most certainly not the kind of thing heard wafting across the benches of the House of Lords mattered less than their combination of authority and drama. Each episode's opening titles featured a Ridgley-voiced introduction: 'The jungle – here I was born, and here my parents died when I was but an infant. I would have soon perished too had I not been found by a kindly she-ape named Kala who adopted me as her own and taught me the ways of the wild. I learned quickly and grew stronger each day, and now I share the friendship and trust of all jungle animals. The jungle is filled with beauty and danger, and lost cities filled with good and evil. This is my domain, and I protect those who come here. *For I am Tarzan – Lord of the Jungle!*' The opening credits ended with an in-profile Tarzan delivering a facsimile of the Weissmuller yodel, which froze into a title card, emblazoned naturally with the double-outlined Tarzan logo.

Quite unexpectedly, this show was amongst the most faithful adaptations of the Burroughs books there had yet been. Kline points out, 'It was only a few years before that there had been the big paperback renaissance of the Tarzan books and the John Carter books, so for those of us who were in our twenties or early thirties, we'd gotten familiar with Burroughs through that renaissance.' The main credit here seems to be due to Len Janson and his fellow associate producer Chuck Menville, who co-wrote all of the first two seasons. None of the seven other writers brought in for the third and fourth seasons managed to write more than four episodes each, either singly or in combination, and the credits show that, even at that point, Janson and Menville were still masterminding the series and sometimes contributing odd scripts or turning other writers' storylines into teleplays. The first season of 16 episodes and assorted episodes thereafter reveal an astonishingly detailed knowledge of the original books: portraying Jad-bal-ja and Pellucidar was one thing, but references to and words from Pal-ul-don, Opar and the Mangani are used in remarkably layered and sometimes almost mischievous detail.

The animation was actually a cut above the usual Filmation fare. The studio may have been continuing its money-saving repeat use of the same scene-shifting shots, while their curiously stately action sequences were no doubt a symptom of their policy of employing as few frames per second as feasible. However, their decision to use rotoscoping – the tracing over of live-action footage – added a slightly more realistic feel. ERB, Inc loaned Filmation copies of Weissmuller films – *Tarzan the Ape Man* and *Tarzan and his Mate* – for this purpose. Kline: 'We rotoscoped live-action footage for some of the scenes in the series that were used over and over again where Tarzan is swinging or landing on a branch or where a lion runs at the camera and jumps over it – those kinds of things. In those cases the timing is right off of live-action footage.' Also helpful in achieving a degree of class is Tarzan's resemblance to Burne Hogarth's handsome, noble vision of the ape-man. Kline: 'Herb Hazelton was responsible for designing the Tarzan character. He did the original model sheets from which other people drew the character. It was Hogarth's way of drawing Tarzan that was being emulated on purpose.' Dramatic music and atmospheric jungle noises added to a reasonably rich feel.

Although Filmation's Tarzan endured for four seasons in total, only the first was a dedicated ape-man series. Kline, though, denies that this was because the studio lost their nerve about the character's appeal. 'If you track any of the other shows, the same thing happened with all of them,' he reasons. 'Very rare was a show in its initial form allowed to do new episodes season after season after season. Even with *The Flintstones*, they still had to re-think how they were presenting [it] – it couldn't just be another season of *The Flintstones*. The kids would have to feel like they're watching something that they hadn't seen before.' Thus, when the ape-man returned in 1977 for his second animated season, it was as part of *The Batman/Tarzan Adventure Hour*, not a team-up between the pair as might be assumed but merely a shared billing. Six new Tarzan episodes alternated with repeats of first-season episodes, a somewhat unwise juxtaposition considering that the quality was now on a downward gradient. The Burroughs content was also diminishing. There was additionally an increased science fiction element, with the ape-man having adventures with a whale in Atlantis and winged men, one of whom – Argus – was a refugee from a Dell comic for copyright and motivational reasons unknown. Then there was the giant robot... 'This wasn't my idea of the right way to approach it, of course,' says Kline, 'and yet it was so common to the thinking then that it seemed like it was perfectly safe to proceed in that way. When you talk about the absence of any authentic Burroughs-style conflict involving action and violence, you've got to replace it with something.'

For the third season (1978), the ape-man was part of a show billed as *Tarzan and the Super 7* and his segments were now just 15 minutes long, which meant that the repeats that alternated with the six new episodes were severely edited. Burroughsonia was again in short supply. Additionally, the moral messages were now being laid on with a trowel.

Just when the show seemed to be in an unstoppable tailspin, the fourth season, incorporated in the second run of *Tarzan and the Super 7* in 1979, saw the ape-man's sections brought back up to the quality level of the first season. Tarzan's episodes were of 30 minutes' duration once more, Burroughs' world was again represented by more than scattered Mangani speech, while the African wildlife that had been curiously missing lately began reappearing. Making an appearance after a complete absence hitherto was Jane ('Look Nkima – it is three men and ... a young lady! How beautiful she is'). The inaugural credits had always shown a smouldering cabin and Kala picking up a helpless human babe, but that and the opening voiceover was as far as an explanation of Tarzan's origins went. The episode *Tarzan and Jane* was a loose (and naturally seriously telescoped) adaptation of *Tarzan of the Apes* in which the ape-man filled in more hinterland details. Talking in the log cabin to Professor Porter and his daughter, he said, 'This house was built by my parents, who were marooned on these shores much like yourselves. When my parents died, I was adopted among the great apes, but I later returned to this house, rebuilt it and from these books taught myself the language of men ...' The ape-man goes with a giggly Jane on a rather suggestive sight-seeing tour of his 'strange' but 'not forsaken' wilderness home. Following an adventure in a lost city, Miss Porter and her father decide to defer their return to civilisation. Tarzan promises he will visit them often.

That fourth season was the last hurrah for the Tarzan cartoon, which, when it re-emerged in 1981, consisted only of heavily edited repeats in the *Tarzan/Lone Ranger/Zorro Adventure Hour*. A brief afterlife was provided by 1984 re-runs.

Kline has misgivings about the quality of the *Tarzan Lord of the Jungle* episodes he has revisited on YouTube: 'It's pretty dull by today's standards ... The original [Burroughs] stories have such a different quality to them, they're so exciting from an action standpoint. That had to be cut back so much. You can see the results of that creative handicap. Plus there was so little time to accomplish whatever had to be done for it. The best way to demonstrate that variance is to compare the Filmation Tarzan TV series with the Disney feature film ... It was just so infuriating to us as kids in our twenties that we had to work under those economic and time restrictions, because we really wanted to do great things. Our biggest influence at that time were the Superman cartoons that the Fleisher studios did back in the '40s. We were never able to even get close.' Janson has equally harsh memories about what was his first-ever writing job: 'We felt that the show was watered down to the point it had little to do with the original vision. But that was and still is the realities of kids' TV, and one reason most of it is so bad.'

However, asked if *Tarzan Lord of the Jungle* was considered a success and an endeavour with which Filmation were pleased, Kline at least says, 'Oh yeah. Absolutely. I do believe it was quite popular. I remember one of the major creative people at Hanna-Barbera, Bob Singer, going out of his way to compliment us on what a good job we had done. He was very impressed with how well we had put that together. If you go back and you look at what was on television at the time, it's a bit of a stand-out in terms of the quality.'

Joe Kubert and Gerry Conway may have obtained the impression that it was poor sales that caused the DC Comics Tarzan title to be cancelled, but that was not the story circulating elsewhere.

In *Eerie* magazine #79 cover-dated November 1976, journalist Joe Brancatelli cited what he termed a reliable source within ERB, Inc as he claimed, 'ERB, Inc was displeased with National's stories and artwork on Burroughs' characters and disappointed that the company had not lived up to an apparently unwritten agreement to promote the lesser-known Pellucidar and John Carter features. ERB, Inc subsequently chose not to renew NPP's contract when it expired earlier this year.' Other writers would later claim that overseas publishers objected to Joe Kubert because – as they had previously printed Russ Manning's work from both Western comics and the newspaper strips, as well as locally-produced imitations of Manning – his style was too much of a contrast for their audiences. The fact that Kubert was adapting some of the same ERB books only recently tackled by Manning didn't help matters.

ERB, Inc president Robert Hodes was now planning a comic book publishing company of the corporation's own. Judging by the contents of an article about ERB, Inc in the 15 February 1975 issue of business and finance magazine *Forbes*, there was big money to be made in this area. The article stated that 250 newspapers throughout the world carried the Tarzan strip and that three million copies of Tarzan comic books, in 16 languages, sold worldwide each month. Hodes was quoted as saying, 'Comics now account for the most significant part of our revenues.'

Hodes figured that the editorial costs of what came to be called the 'Tarzan Art Studio' would be funded by the fact that ERB, Inc were already producing comics material for sale to foreign publishers. Mark Evanier was appointed managing editor of the comic book division in April '76, by which point production on the new material had already begun. Pre-contract agreements were made with a printer and a distributor. It was a scenario almost designed to make comics-reading Burroughs fans drool at the mouth: comic adaptations administered by people who would not be allowed to deviate from the principles established in the original Burroughs canon.

However, it seems that the corporation jumped the gun. Foreign publishers who owned the comic-book rights to Burroughs characters proved uninterested in the Evanier material, a reluctance which posed a potential problem because the foreign publishers' contracts gave them the right to generate their own material should they wish. Nevertheless, Evanier was authorised to continue and to backlog material. Enter Marion Burroughs. One of the first things she did when she decided to take up the reins of her inheritance was to order the termination of in-house comics material production.

Stateside-wise, this left ERB, Inc having to cast around for a new comics publisher. To some extent they were in a seller's market. Such was the pulling power of Tarzan and Korak at least that Western/Gold Key would almost certainly have welcomed them back. National Periodical Publications' president Sol Harrison had even indicated he would be prepared to submit to DC publishing stories produced by ERB, Inc., something else which suggests poor sales was not behind the DC cancellations.

Charlton Comics would no doubt also have been interested, although there would have been psychological obstacles to ERB, Inc working with a publisher that had comparatively recently provoked them into legal action. Brancatelli didn't mention in his article any possibility that ERB, Inc might be considering offering their properties to Warren, publisher of the magazine in which he was writing. Warren produced A4-sized comic books with glossy covers and black-and-white content. They were aimed at a slightly older market than usual for the genre because periodicals with magazine formats were not bound by the Comics Code Authority and were able to be slightly more daring. An adult-oriented Tarzan title to stand alongside Warren publications like *Vampirella*, *Eerie* and *The Spirit* might well have been a very good publication.

In the end, the corporation plumped for the obvious choice. An eager Marvel Comics had produced sample Tarzan material in 1972 when it was known that Western were being forced to relinquish the licence. However, they had lost out to what they wryly termed their Distinguished Competition. In some senses it was logical and even desirable that Marvel should now be given their chance. At this point in history, Marvel were considered the hippest of the American comic-book companies: their storylines were on a higher intellectual plane than most DC fare even if their sales figures were generally lower. Moreover, they were more associated than DC with comics based on licensed properties. In that field, they were just entering their pomp: their adaptation of new movie *Star Wars* was about to become one of the biggest-selling American comics of all time.

Marvel's adaptation of *Star Wars* was written by Roy Thomas, although that was less a reason for his being picked to script the new Tarzan title than his celebrated work on another of Marvel's licensed properties, *Conan the Barbarian*. The latter adaptation of the pulp sword and sorcery works of Robert E Howard (a Burroughs devotee, of course) had since its 1970 introduction taken the comics world by storm, and it seems it was the fact that Tarzan was another loinclothed non-superhero that prompted

Marvel supremo Stan Lee to give Thomas the gig. Thomas admits he was not overjoyed. 'I got a call from Stan personally,' he says. 'He said they were going to do that and the John Carter comic. I wanted to do John Carter and Marv [Wolfman] had already put in dibs on that.' However he does concede, 'I always kind of wanted to do Tarzan even though I wanted to do John Carter more.' As with apparently just about anybody who has written Tarzan comics, Thomas was steeped in the character and the works of his author: 'Stan had read Burroughs when he was young. Marv and I were both Burroughs fans ... I was fairly familiar with Burroughs ... It's not so much that you remain a fan exactly of the writing but you have to admire that imagination if you're into heroic science fiction or even just superheroes.' So impressive was Thomas' knowledge that Marion Burroughs was, he says, 'very enamoured of me for a short time.' He explains, 'Stan had me write a thing about how to exploit the other Edgar Rice Burroughs characters if it did well.' He wrote a 'long memo' about 'all the various series we could make out of it.'

Thomas had followed the DC book. 'Joe didn't keep enough of the dialogue and certain things like that for my particular taste,' he says, 'but Joe Kubert's my favourite comic book artist and I think he did a wonderful job on it in terms of the art. Probably the writing was pretty good too. It just was a little more spare than I was interested [in].'

John Buscema was chosen to be Marvel's Tarzan artist partly, admits Thomas, because he had been his long-term collaborator on *Conan the Barbarian*, although Thomas adds, 'And because John was one of the best artists around. John wasn't that eager to do Tarzan. He liked the character. He loved Joe Kubert's version. He felt like he had nothing to add to the character, but I think he did a pretty good job anyway. After the first couple of issues, though, he only did layouts. He wasn't very involved emotionally. He just adapted the books with a few notes from me and then I would do the dialogue.' In contrast to Kubert's 'snatched' style, Buscema was renowned for clean, bold lines and chiselled features. Asked if he gave Buscema any suggestions about how Tarzan should look, Thomas says, 'Not too much. I just left it to him, and he drew it to look rather like the character had looked in some of the earliest pictures by J Allen St John and by Foster in the comic strips. I may have suggested a leopardskin rather than the lion's hide [loincloth] that [you] saw in some of these comic books drawn by Jesse Marsh and others.'

Thomas set his Tarzan world in the era of biplanes, not monoplanes. He reasons, 'When you modernise Tarzan too much … you're messing up that character every bit as much as Johnny Weissmuller and the guttural, non-verbal approach that they had.'

The 'Fury-filled first issue' of Marvel's *Tarzan* was cover-dated June 1977 and, unlike the DC title, began its sequencing at #1. It featured a Buscema cover with a by-now very familiar image of Tarzan: astride a rearing lion, knife unsheathed. Thomas readily admits the homage to the Clinton Pettee *All-Story* picture: 'I especially wanted that. I just had him add a woman on the cover. I felt like that would be a good addition.'

The Filmation *Tarzan Lord of the Jungle* series was now playing on television, but although Marvel's book was subtitled 'Lord of the Jungle' throughout its run, Thomas says of the TV show, 'I'm not even aware of being aware of it and, if I was, I wouldn't have paid any attention unless they'd absolutely told me I had to. I wanted nothing to do with anything except the original work of Burroughs. And I really wasn't interested in making up new Tarzan stories right away, although I would have done some. I wanted to just adapt the novels, to pick up where basically DC had left off.' He adds, 'There were elements in the first couple of issues that are original simply because he's telling a story to somebody, but except for those minor incidents and a couple of things here and there in the first couple of stories, I didn't do anything original.' In the second issue, Thomas became the umpteenth comics writer to tell Tarzan's 'origin' story. He took a lateral approach by having Jane recount Tarzan's backstory in a sequence which employed just one speech balloon.

Impressive as dealing with that origin story in seven pages might be, that Autumn Thomas displayed even greater condensation powers in Marvel's youth magazine *Pizzazz*. Thomas explains, 'I wanted to do something different, so I thought, let's do the Young Tarzan and we'll make up little stories.' This series of brief peeks into Tarzan's formative years logically kicked off with an origin story. This time, Thomas managed to reduce the *Tarzan of the Apes* novel to one page of six panels. 'That was fun,' says Thomas.

The fact that American comics were cover-dated months past their actual newsstand appearance means that Marvel's *Tarzan* would have first gone on sale well before the stated June, but it's still an interesting coincidence that it was in that month that Britain got a new Tarzan publication in the shape of *Tarzan Weekly*. It's even more interesting that this publication from independent Byblos was one of the few products of the Tarzan Art Studio. Stewart Wales and co-editor Russ Manning put together a fine title, dripping with specialist knowledge, both in its strips and its text articles. An anthology, in the British tradition, *Tarzan Weekly* even featured a strip devoted to Akut, the Mangani from *The Beasts of Tarzan* and *The Son of Tarzan*. It deserved to last longer than the 20 issues it managed before becoming a monthly (a reduction in status, as this was a much less common publishing schedule for comics in Britain), which in turn dribbled away into irregular specials that staggered on into the early '80s. *Tarzan Weekly* suggested that, had it not been strangled at birth, the Tarzan Art Studio could well have created the greatest Tarzan comics of them all. To this day, however, although printed and translated throughout Europe, almost none of its work has been reprinted in the US.

In his stint on the Marvel Tarzan title, Thomas tackled *Tarzan and the Jewels of Opar*, *Tarzan Lord of the Jungle* and *Jungle Tales of Tarzan*. The comic lurched back and forth haphazardly between those Burroughs tales on occasion, but Thomas raises a different demerit when he notes, 'I think I kept too much of Burroughs' description in the captions, probably because I had been able to do that more with Robert E Howard because he had used a purple prose that lent itself to comic book adaptations. But Burroughs' prose really just told what was going on, so therefore you needed less of it. I wish I had done those adaptations a little differently, but it was still a nice book, especially the first two issues.'

Despite his adaptation orientation, there was one original Tarzan story Thomas would have definitely countenanced writing. Given that he was more interested in John Carter than John Clayton, it would have been logical for him to engineer a team-up between the two characters: Marvel's *John Carter, Warlord of Mars* had made its debut at the same time as the *Tarzan* title. Thomas: 'I wanted to do it. I remember reading the early science fiction fanzines in the early '60s about this book *Tarzan on Mars*, which I was very eager to see. When I finally did see it and read a little of it, it wasn't anything to write home about. It was a great idea. I've hated the fact that since then Dark Horse did it and I wasn't in on it.'

Neither that encounter between Burroughs' two greatest heroes nor any other Tarzan story was feasible from Thomas' point of view after he took a call from Marion Burroughs in, he estimates, late 1977. Thomas: 'Up to that time we'd had an excellent relationship. I knew her reputation for being difficult, but somehow or other I had managed to avoid any problems with her. They kind of left me alone, because I wouldn't have taken any guff from her ... Basically, she got unhappy because I adapted two or three of the stories from *Jungle Tales of Tarzan*, which I was told by our lawyers and so forth that had looked at the contracts that we could do. I don't know if they were wrong, but Marion called me up one day to complain about this. She said, "You can't do that." I said, "Well, they told me I can. Your beef is with the people back in New York, not with me. I obviously won't do it if they tell me I can't do it." Then she kind of accused me and even Buscema of plagiarising – didn't use that word, but that's what it amounted to – the work of Burne

Hogarth, because he had earlier adapted one of the same *Jungle Tales of Tarzan* in one of his hardcover books ... She was afraid of trouble with him, but she didn't say he had complained ... She said, "Even some of the wording is similar." I said, "Well of course it is. We were both adapting an Edgar Rice Burroughs story." She was a stupid, foolishly flawed woman. I knew Buscema didn't have the book and didn't even like Burne Hogarth. He was very much a Hal Foster/Allen St John fan. I really got upset at the veiled accusations, and I just hung up on her. I called Marvel and I quit the book effective immediately. The book lasted some months longer. I didn't mind quitting that much, but I wasn't going to deal with that idiot woman anymore ... Around the same time, I quit doing *Star Wars*. I wasn't interested in having somebody tell me what to do in the comics. Maybe if Stan told me I could take it, but I wasn't going to take it from Marion Burroughs and even from George Lucas ... Danton Burroughs apologised to me once or twice years later for her behaviour. I don't think she was good for that company, but she was there and at that stage there was nothing Danton or anybody else could do. She was the widow of the son of Edgar Rice Burroughs and that took precedence over him as the grandson. I don't think she was ever the fan that Danton was.'

David Kraft and Bill Mantlo succeeded Thomas in the writing duties on Marvel's *Tarzan* title. (Kraft also handled the *Pizzazz* strip following Thomas' sole Young Tarzan.) 'I guess they did fine,' shrugs Thomas. 'I never read any of the issues all the way through. I know Dave was assigned to rewrite one of my *Jungle Tales* near the end, made it look like he wrote it rather than me because they were trying to appease Marion Burroughs by changing the wording.'

Thomas blames neither those writers nor the introduction after his departure of non-adapted storylines for the fact that Marvel's *Tarzan* title was cancelled after 29 issues. (There were also three annuals. The *John Carter* title lasted 28 issues and three annuals.) Thomas: 'Neither the DC nor later the Marvel book sold particularly well, though I don't recall any sales figures.

They weren't disastrously bad but they weren't good enough. I was told this was true with Marvel – and perhaps it was with DC as well – that Edgar Rice Burroughs, Inc insisted on a high enough payment for it that made it more difficult for it to make a profit if it didn't sell exceptionally well ... We got *Star Wars* free. Conan was almost free – two or three hundred dollars an issue.' Gerry Conway agrees, the DC writer saying, 'The cost of the licence and the weak sales made it a poor prospect for either company economically. The only reason to do the book – at that time – was fan nostalgia on the part of the publishers and professionals who got a chance to participate.' Marvel did put out another Tarzan title in 1983, but whether or not the world needed yet another version of his origin story, as presented in *Marvel Super Special* and reprinted in two standard-length issues titled *Tarzan of the Apes* the following year, is a debatable point.

Thomas says, 'I remember Stan telling me he sat down with Marion Burroughs, and I don't know who else was there at the meeting, in New York and they thought they had everything all [sorted] out, and then they got a contract from Tarzana which almost [made it seem] like the whole conversation didn't happen, all the agreements weren't there. I always said that Marion Burroughs was the person who woke up in the night in a deep sweat fearful that somewhere in the world somebody besides her and the estate was making money out of Tarzan.'

Pretty soon, few would be making money out of Tarzan. Although Tarzan movies had been scarce in this decade, what with the Filmation series and the comics titles either side of the Atlantic, the years 1976 to 1978 had been fairly good ones for the ape-man. Yet the fact that he was now visible mainly in an animated series and in comics confirmed Tarzan's complete transmogrification from a character for adults into purely a children's icon. Moreover, from this point, after an almost unbroken half-century, there would be no regular American Tarzan comic books for two decades.

Meanwhile, although Ballantine continued to publish Tarzan paperbacks in the States, ape-man novels were becoming hard to find in the UK. Four Square – who had issued Tarzan paperbacks in the UK with beautiful painted covers – were in 1962 bought out by New English Library, who began reissuing ape-man tomes in the Seventies. It's unknown whether their apparent poor sales were caused by sloppy production methods – NEL paperbacks were notorious for falling apart because the glue used for the spines was sub-standard – but in any event the UK Tarzan book reins passed to Flamingo in the same decade. That the latter chose to use the great Burne Hogarth as cover artist may, oddly, have worked against them. In comics, Hogarth transcended the medium. On a book cover, his four-colour, cone-haired images of the ape-man against a pure white background merely suggested the books' contents were children's fare. Presumably, low sales accounts for the fact that Flamingo's ape-man publishing programme extended no further than the first four Burroughs Tarzan books.

It was all symptomatic of Tarzan's eclipse as a major cultural figure.

Aside from the Gene Roddenberry film, the other Holy Grail/running joke Tarzan movie project drooled over by Burroughs fans was a film written and directed by Robert Towne – celebrated screenwriter of the likes of *Chinatown* and *Shampoo* – that was intended to faithfully adapt the *Tarzan of the Apes* novel for the first time in the modern era.

Talk of that project first began appearing in print in the mid-'70s. In 1976, Danton Burroughs excitedly announced, 'Towne says he's going to give my grandfather's Tarzan to the people. I've liked some of the screen Tarzans, but none of them has been like the man my grandfather created. If you've read the books, you know that Tarzan was actually an English lord who was well educated and didn't use "me" in the nominative case.' It was indeed exciting news, if made less exciting by Danton's simultaneous declaration that he would be interested in taking the lead role. (He said he worked out a lot.)

The movie was subject to such delays and switchbacks in

fortune that for several years it seemed destined for the same fate as the Roddenberry film. While that didn't ultimately happen, it was unfortunately beaten to the screens by *Tarzan the Ape Man* starring Bo Derek. The latter 107-minute, August 1981 picture not only went in completely the opposite direction as regards fealty to the source, but may even be the reason the late-'70s saw Tarzan's last gasp as a major cultural figure.

Many a Tarzan/Burroughs fan would have been ecstatic at the news of a big-screen comeback for a character who had – Ron Ely pseudo-movies and Steve Hawkes ersatz movies excepted – sat out the '70s in that medium. Their ecstasy was to turn to horror. Although the 1959 Denny Miller film had been dubbed by Gabe Essoe 'Tarzan the Worst', this second re-make of the exalted 1932 Weissmuller flick, remarkably, stole that dubious crown.

The 1981 *Tarzan the Ape Man* is referred to in some sources as *Tarzan, the Ape Man* based on the fact that a comma appears in the closing frame of the film, although it's not visible on either the movie poster or in the opening credits. 'No comma on my script title page,' says Gary Goddard, writer of the film's screenplay with Tom Rowe. That, however, does not begin to address the contentious issues surrounding the project.

The movie was produced by Bo Derek and directed by the actress' husband John. An allusion to the perceived power balance within that professional relationship is made by the title card drawn by Frank Frazetta for their production company Svengali, which precedes the picture: it shows a smiling, naked Bo dangling her husband on puppet strings. Goddard says, however, 'It was really John's vision. Bo sometimes would sit in the meetings and would contribute some things. She was very much into creating her role, but in terms of the writing and directing she really let John do his thing.' Although that title card may be misleading, an unusual pecking order of a different sort is revealed in the credits: Bo Derek (Jane) is given star billing, Richard Harris (Jane's father) second billing and Miles O'Keeffe – who happened to play the title character – receives an 'Introducing' at credits' end. Additionally, the movie poster depicted Bo Derek swinging alone on a vine.

The movie could certainly be said to more than make up for the 22-year absence of Jane from the cinema franchise. It may be difficult to remember now, but at the time Bo Derek had a status in popular culture that justified the part of said poster's strapline which read, 'The most beautiful woman of our time ...' The film *10* (1979) had shot to prominence her chiselled beauty, incongruous cornrows and perfectly formed breasts. With her riding high on the fame thereby created, it didn't seem too outlandish an idea to build a new Tarzan movie around her.

Despite Jane's elevated position, the film was actually a dilution of the Dereks' original intentions. Explains Goddard, 'After Bo had done *10* and was a huge sensation, John had a concept for a movie that he called *Me, Jane*. It was the Tarzan story from a Jane perspective, which – when you look back on it – was ahead of its time, because it was before *Wicked*, it was before all of these other [projects] where you take existing fairytales and you turn them around, tell them from a different vantage point. The idea of *Me, Jane* was a great idea. However, they went to MGM to do this, and MGM found they only had very narrow rights. They had the rights to do a re-make of *Tarzan the Ape Man*. So the trick was to create a story that fulfilled John's desire to tell it from her perspective without veering from the essential structure from *Tarzan the Ape Man*.'

An opening voiceover conversation taking place in (we infer) a stuffy English gentlemen's club promises a 'bizarre adventure.' That, at least, can't be disputed. A clue as to the overall lack of judgment for which we are in has already been buffoonishly provided by the famous MGM lion producing not a growl but a Tarzan yodel. The story is set in 1910, i.e. one year after the concluding (African) events of the *Tarzan of the Apes* book. We don't get too much of an impression of the Edwardian era, the '80s-redolent hairstyle and moustache of supporting character Mr Holt (John Phillip Law) seeming particularly anachronistic. Although Bo Derek plays a character called, as in the first film version, Jane Parker, she is here journeying to Africa to find the father she has never known. Jane is an independently wealthy adventurer and assertive enough to shoot an intruder dead during the opening credits, but this feminism is later undercut by her unutterable lip-bitten coyness in erotic scenes with Tarzan.

James Parker – played by Richard Harris as an Irishman – left Jane's now deceased mother in the year after his daughter was born for reasons never adequately explained. In their soap-opera reunion, Jane suggests to her dad that he is 'a first-class bastard.' The viewer is left thinking, 'She came all the way to Africa to tell him that?' Despite her contempt for him, Jane insists on accompanying her old man on his quest to find the fabled elephant's graveyard. This is implicitly because she fancies Holt, although that sub-plot is not pursued. While on this trip, she hears a strange yodel and thereby learns of Tarzan, a legendary name – if one of varying pronunciation by the cast – that strikes fear into the native bearers.

When the party loses one of its men due to a frayed rope, Harris is seen screaming at the sky, 'Why did you *do* that?' According to Bo, this was the Dereks' moralistic replacement of the chillingly racist 'What was in that pack?' line in the equivalent scene in the original, but the celestial, impassive shaft of light shining down beside Harris, coupled with the actor's unemotional delivery, is guffaw-provoking.

The party comes upon an inland sea, where Jane elects to take a bath. Cue some nude aquatic frolicking befitting the sex symbol of the age. Although Derek is beautiful, there is no getting round the fact that when Miles O'Keeffe appears, chasing his pet lion along the sand, he is even more appetising. O'Keeffe was actually far from first choice. A late replacement, he had been the stand-in double for ex-boxer Lee Canalito until Bo reputedly decided the latter wasn't trim enough. Goddard even remembers another actor being in the running in the person of Klinton Spilsbury, who played the title role in the 1981 release *The Legend of the Lone Ranger*, but a previously enthused John Derek came back from a meeting with him with a changed mind. Bo thought a lot more of O'Keeffe's physique than she allegedly did of Canalito's, describing it in her autobiography as the most beautiful body she had ever seen.

O'Keeffe was a six foot three, 26-year-old former American football player and psychology student. His physical perfection – rippling, toned, muscular but not thickset – is topped off by a buttock-revealing loincloth and underlined by the fact that he carries himself like he's strutting down a Parisian catwalk. After calling off his oversized moggy, Tarzan wades into the surf and grabs Jane none too gently, but he is scared off by the report of a rifle as Jane's father and Mr Holt appear. Yet Jane goes from terror of Tarzan to fierce loyalty toward him in the blink of an eye: in the very next scene, she objects to her father stating the view that he is an animal.

The absurd is piled upon the ridiculous when the party sets off again and – as though this is a 1930s B-movie – James Parker vaguely remarks, 'Something's not right' as unseen hostile natives in menacing paint masks gaze at them. The attacks these natives mount on the party are assumed to be the work of Tarzan. Although Tarzan is innocent on that score, he shortly materialises again with apparently dubious motives, erupting from a river at which Jane is filling her flask and swimming off with her. On dry land again, Jane produces a gun and its report sends Tarzan packing – at which point Jane unaccountably pleads, 'Don't go!' The bad acting and incomprehensible motivation is joined by maladroit direction in a scene in which a python coils itself around Jane. Tarzan swings in on a vine and rescues her in an atrocious, confusing, repetitive, unexciting, overlong scene shot in the slow-motion that incomprehensibly keeps recurring. Tarzan falls ill from a snake bite, at which point his animal friends miraculously appear to help him, one of which is inexplicably an orangutan. It's as though the Dereks consider the audiences no more worldly than those of the 1920s. An elephant scoops the unconscious Tarzan up in its tusks and carries him off. This scene makes sense in the original, but here all the pachyderm is doing is taking Tarzan to a river different to the one in which he has just wrestled the python. This problem of scenes transplanted arbitrarily and illogically from the predecessor film afflicts the entire re-make.

Jane then becomes the predator. She strokes Tarzan's prone, unconscious body, the virgin revelling in never-before experienced sensations. When Tarzan awakes and moves away from her, Jane pursues him and sits beneath a tree in which he takes refuge. The next day, they achieve some sort of rapport, although a primitive one: Tarzan is mute throughout the movie (which at least gives a quasi-excuse for his backstory being unexplained). Notes Goddard, 'That is a decision that John made. I would have liked him to speak. He liked the idea of the silent, brooding embodiment of the male machismo … He wanted him to be this presence … In John's mind, he was making *Me, Jane*.' The pair engage in some idyllic frolicking and splashing, with Jane keeping up a commentary of babbling nonsense. In another snort-inducing passage, Jane bites her lip in delight as Tarzan's fingers inspect the contents of her blouse. It is the crassly adolescent polar opposite of the mature, beautiful sensuality of the nude swimming scene in *Tarzan and his Mate*.

Tarzan delivers Jane back to her father's party but is frightened away by their hostility. Cue the re-entry of the hostile natives, who slaughter some of the party and take the remainder, including the Parkers, back to their village. The fearsome, gargantuan and curiously punk rocker-like chief of the tribe almost idly impales James Parker on an elephant tusk before advancing menacingly on Jane, who has just featured in an extended scene in which her naked body is ritualistically washed, with her on all fours. Alerted by a chimp friend to Jane's situation, Tarzan swings in on a vine to confront the tribal leader. In another ineptly filmed and totally unengaging slo-mo action scene, Tarzan triumphs by snapping his enemy's neck. The tribe conveniently don't interfere as the pair fight, and then evaporate when the tussle is over. Tarzan throws his head back and yodels – as elsewhere, clearly an overdub of Weissmuller vintage. Despite the elephant tusk through his guts, Harris delivers an interminable death speech to his daughter. Even had that speech contained any trace of pathos, it would have been washed away by the section immediately following, in which another opportunity is taken to put Derek's chest on display as Tarzan washes Jane of the ceremonial paint in which she has been forcibly daubed. A quite pretty *From Here to Eternity*-esque Tarzan-and-Jane beach scene is then undermined by a lengthy closing credits sequence wherein a topless Jane is seen engaging in horseplay with orangutan and ape-man.

'I had the vision of, "I'm going to write the greatest Tarzan script ever, because I know Tarzan, I love the material,"' says Goddard. So where did it all go wrong?

The original script was by Tom Rowe. Goddard: 'He had done at least two drafts before me. I thought it was decent. The essential difference is I believe he was an older guy. He wrote from a different life experience.' He adds, 'We're credited together but we never met each other. The Writers Guild determined that we had a shared credit.' The 24-year-old Goddard was just starting his screenwriting career. He had got to know the Dereks via a Marvel Comics-related project called *Dazzler*. Goddard recalls, 'One day John says, "We're working on this project at MGM, *Tarzan the Ape Man*. We really like your writing and we're not that happy with the script that we just got and we'd like you to do a dialogue polish." So I started doing a dialogue polish of the entire script and I got about 70 percent through it, and by then MGM were anxious to get the movie into production. They said, "We really like your writing but we don't like what it's based on. We want you to do a whole new script from page one; start over, but you got to do it fast, and we want you to go with us to the Seychelles islands." I lived in the Seychelles islands with Bo and John in a villa for almost a month, and in the course of that month did almost three full rewrites of the script … The MGM head of production told me, "When you're done writing it and John approves it, our legal department has to vet it." It's tough enough to write a screenplay, but you have to write a screenplay with all these rules.'

Nonetheless, Goddard was ecstatic at the position in which he found himself. Not only was he working for the biggest female star in the world, but he was 'a huge fan' of Richard Harris: 'I wrote that character with his voice in mind and with his bombastic personality.' Additionally, 'If I didn't read all the Tarzan books growing up, I read most of them.' Goddard watched neither Weissmuller's nor Denny Miller's *Tarzan the Ape Man* in preparation: 'I did read the original script that we were basing it on, 'cause I had to know that script, but I was really trying to create this world that John wanted.' Of the latter he says, 'John had very specific ideas.' He adds, 'I think in my enthusiasm and excitement to make what I felt would be a great Tarzan film, I brought a lot of unique things to it.' However, Goddard had a shock in store. He says, 'I got the lesson you always hear from writers. I learned the writer is the most important person on the job until the day shooting starts, at which point he is now almost a non-entity.'

As a quasi-non-entity, Goddard did not attend the eight-week shoot in Sri Lanka and the Seychelles, where ex-Tarzan Jock Mahoney (credited as Jack O'Mahoney) was stunt coordinator. The shoot was chaotic. Not because the chimps bit, the elephants played up and the lion broke its leash and attacked Bo. Such animal-related misfortune goes with the territory with Tarzan films. Also not too eyebrow-raising was the funny-tummy trouble and the matter of an actor hired to perform in an ape suit resigning because Bo's nudity offended his religious sensibilities. Rather, the bedlam related to an overstretched, nepotistic crew that was the consequence of Bo firing people left, right and centre. In the first 15 days, Mrs Derek sacked 15 of the original Hollywood squad of 23. Canalito – let go on day three – was one of the few the Dereks decided needed to be replaced. Bo's mother added wardrobe and make-up to her existing role of hairdresser, while Bo's sister became assistant director. When the production manager subsequently left, she was replaced by Bo's Girl Friday.

As for Goddard's script, he got to find out what had been

done to it only when he attended a preview. 'I was all excited,' Goddard recalls. 'It starts unfolding and I'm like, "Did I write that? I don't think I wrote that."' At the end of the screening, he was 'stunned.' He recalls, 'I'm realising all my friends and peers are going to watch this and go "God, Gary wrote that, could you believe it?"' Yet he faced a dilemma: 'If you take your name off, you also don't get your residuals. Everything's tied to your screen credit. I just had to bite the bullet.'

He elaborates on the changes that had been made: 'John did have a penchant to improvise a little bit on a theme. While the basic structure remains pretty much as written, in some of the scenes a lot of the dialogue was improvised based upon what I wrote.' Other elements were wholly new. Of the risible celestial shaft of light and boobs-groping scenes, Goddard says, 'Neither of those are in the script! John considers himself an artist. He's a photographer by nature, so everything in his films is visual first.' Like many, Goddard was puzzled by John Derek's insistence on slow motion. He feels he came to understand it when he subsequently worked with the director on a picture called *Pirate Annie* that didn't get produced. He offers, 'John was afraid of action sequences, 'cause he didn't know how to shoot them, and the artistic part of him that believed a director must shoot every frame prevented him from [being] willing to hire a second unit director [to shoot them].'

Of course, for all anyone knows, Goddard's script as originally envisioned would have made an equally terrible movie. However, perhaps a yardstick for the way that he feels his vision was traduced is the section in which Jane is painted. In the finished product, the white paint is puzzling where it doesn't seem an excuse to show off Bo's bod. Goddard's original idea had a sophisticated hinterland, being based on the elaborate religious paintings rendered on elephants in India. Goddard also says, 'You wouldn't even realise [initially] she was naked: it would look like she's in this very elegant, embroidered, form-fitting gown, then when the camera moved in on it, only then you would realise that she's been decorated. It's a very beautiful thing. I was a little surprised when I saw the film that it was just all that white paint going on her. John said, "Oh my God, I was on such a tight schedule."'

Forgotten by history is the fact that the Dereks' *Tarzan the Ape Man* was a commercial success. Even despite an American 'R' rating unprecedented for a Tarzan flick, it pulled in $30m more than its budget. However, while one prominent critic – NBC's *Today Show*'s Gene Shalit – lauded it as an enjoyable, fun movie, the reviews were generally savage. Goddard doesn't blame Bo Derek's widely-derided acting: 'If you look at Bo in *10*, she's very charismatic. I think she had a lot of innate ability. Everyone in Hollywood wanted to work with her.' However, Goddard admits he was not surprised by the reviews. He says of Mr Derek's intentions, 'Maybe that movie done by John in his own artistic way would have been very cool, but trying to bend that plot of *Tarzan the Ape Man* into that really couldn't work, so he wound up with this hybrid that certainly didn't make the Tarzan fans happy, and I'm not sure that it made the Bo Derek fans happy.'

John Derek admitted that, before the film opened, he had had to edit out two minutes and four seconds of material that a federal judge had decided violated Burroughs' original contract with MGM. Although that contract had allowed – even insisted – on a certain distance from the books, it had also stated that the original story could not be drastically changed. There was further legal action. The fact that Tarzan didn't appear until over half-way into the picture, as well as the 'R' rating, led ERB, Inc to sue MGM over derogatory treatment of their character. Danton Burroughs: 'MGM had the rights to re-make *Tarzan the Ape Man* in perpetuity given to them from a contract that my granddad wrote. It was just a bad wording, so we took them to court to stop the movie. We stopped them. They can never do another re-make of *Tarzan the Ape Man*, but that one got out.' With a mixture of horror and admiration, Danton said, 'It was so unique. It's a cult classic.'

Although Danton lamented Tarzan's muteness, he also said,

'Miles O'Keeffe was just excellent.' Indeed. The film is a failure on almost every level imaginable, yet there is one shining exception to the overall ghastliness. No one – not Kamuela Searle, not Johnny Weissmuller, not Gordon Scott, not Mike Henry – had ever looked as good as O'Keeffe in a loincloth. Everybody questioned about him for this book enthuses over O'Keeffe. Denny Miller, star of the previous *Tarzan the Ape Man* as well as an expert on physical fitness, says of him, 'He looked better than any of us. He was really ripped.'

How ironic that the finest-ever visual representation of the ape-man should feature in the worst Tarzan movie of all time.

At the turn of the 1980s, former Top Sellers Tarzan comics editor Dez Skinn was running a design company called Studio System. One day a movie art director came into their offices in London's West End seeking illustrators. Skinn recalls, 'He said, "We're storyboarding a new movie called *Greystoke*." I said, "Oh, Tarzan." He said, "You know about it? How do you know about it?" I said, "Well, I don't know about it, but Tarzan was Lord Greystoke, wasn't he?" "Ah, thank God for that. Nobody's supposed to know about it." He didn't realise that "Greystoke" was a bit of a giveaway to a fan.'

The incident was an indication of the fact that the Holy-Grail Robert Towne-helmed Tarzan movie was nearing the end of its long, tortuous journey to the screen. By now, however, Towne was out of the equation. Recalls Skinn of the art director, 'He looked through the different artists that we had on our books and picked the guy who was drawing *Garth* at the time, Martin Asbury. So Martin storyboarded *Greystoke* for us for Hugh Hudson.'

Explained Danton Burroughs, 'What happened was, Bob Towne got into a fight with Warner Brothers so he stopped doing the rest of the screenplay, so that Warner Brothers only used half of it. Then Hugh Hudson had to finish the rest.' Hudson himself recalls things slightly differently: 'Robert Towne sold his rights back to Warner Brothers because he was making a film called

Personal Best and he needed another million dollars, I think. Warner Brothers agreed to give it to him if he gave up his rights in doing *Greystoke*.'

Offering the director's job to Hudson – whose work on 1981's *Chariots of Fire* helped win that production an Oscar for Best Picture – demonstrated a serious commitment to the property on the part of the studio. At one point, *Chariots of Fire* producer David Puttnam was even set to come aboard the project. Hudson: 'He pulled away from it. We tried to find a producer. In the end they said, "Well *you* do it." I produced it and directed it, but out of London where I had the Warner operation supporting me, so really it was produced by Warner Brothers.' Stanley S Canter was credited as co-producer, but Hudson says, 'I never met him. He got a credit because he was involved from the past.'

'All my life I've read them,' says Hudson of Burroughs' books. 'They were great. Certainly the first one or two. So many films had been made and television things and they always changed things ... I liked the concept of it, of going back and doing it for real. As real as you could do it ... It was a very interesting story about all sorts of things. I tried to deepen it as much as I could, make it about nature and nurture and all those things. He's an interesting invention, Tarzan. Although it's an invented character, it's like a mythic character.'

Hudson says of the script he inherited from Towne, 'It had the germ of a very interesting [film]. Half the film was silent: people speaking animal talk. There was no dialogue until they meet the white people, very little. I liked that concept. It's quite faithful to the original story ... He'd written half of the script ... He hadn't taken it back to England. He'd sketched out various ideas for going back to England and we followed some of them, and they were much in the style of what we finally did.'

Hudson brought in Michael Austin to finish Towne's semi-screenplay. Austin had previously written the Alan Bates movie *The Shout* (1978) and the Sean Connery vehicle *Five Days One Summer* (1982). Austin was not steeped in Burroughs like Hudson, but the director says he was a 'very witty man. Very witty dialogue ... We did it together, we structured and decided how to do it and we produced a screenplay which Warner Brothers liked.' Hudson says that, simply in order to remain faithful to the book, there was no thought given to setting the film in the present day. When it's pointed out that the ending of the film doesn't retain faithfulness, Hudson shrugs, 'We had to make it into a film.'

Hudson 'saw many' actors hoping to be the new screen Tarzan. (He was not aware of Danton Burroughs' interest in screen-testing.) He says, 'We finally tested four ... An American dancing as a lead with the Dutch Royal Ballet ... I think the name was Fahy ... Julian Sands, Christopher Lambert and Viggo Mortensen. We did proper tests. We built an area and we tested them all, and we picked Christopher Lambert.'

Christophe Lambert (first name later Anglicised for commercial reasons, surname pronounced 'Lam-bare') was born in 1957 and raised in Geneva. As a teenager, he moved to Paris. 'I'd been through four months of private acting school,' he explains. 'Then I did Le Conservatoire in Paris, which is like RADA in London ... I'd done at the time a movie, 1980, a French cop movie. Couple of small parts after that. I tested for *Greystoke* end of '81 ... The agent I had at the time sent me for three casting sessions, which was basically three hundred people in a room jumping up and down in front of the director and the casting director and some producers, just to see their physical ability.'

Lambert reveals, 'I had big glasses on. I was skinny as could be.' However, these things did not daunt him. 'It was life or death,' he reasons. 'I wanted to be an actor since I was twelve years old'. However, he wasn't impressed by the process he found himself within. 'After two minutes of jumping up and down, I got bored and I just sat down, saying, "Well, it's been three minutes, you can see that I'm fit." The casting director Patsy Pollack – British casting director – saw me because I was sitting down in the middle of people moving around. She told me the story afterwards: she said to Hugh Hudson, "You should screen-test that guy." And Hugh Hudson looked at me, looked at her like she was completely nuts. She said, "Test this guy. What you see in real life is not what you gonna see on the screen." So he said, "Okay." She was at the time the best casting director in the world.

'Half of the screen test was Tarzan in the jungle and half of the screen test was Tarzan in civilisation. There was always an animalistic side about the character, but he was wearing clothes when he was living in civilisation and he was muddy and dishevelled when he was in the jungle. I thought part of the attraction for this character is that the only thing he is is an animal: instinctive, feeling people and not trying to act the part. Not trying because suddenly you have a suit, you are somebody different. He was still genuine about where he was coming from and mostly about his instinct ability, feeling the people, sensing them instead of analysing them. That's what I believed at the time in life and that's what I still believe today: you don't have to talk to people to sense what they are.'

'He had a wonderful way of looking,' Hudson recalls of his impressions of Lambert. 'He had a gaze beyond the camera into the distance. It's only because he's myopic, actually. It was a very interesting look. And he was a complete loner.'

Lambert's Tarzan knowledge was not vast. 'When I was a kid, we didn't have TV,' he recalls. 'When I discovered TV I was in Switzerland with three or four channels. Whatever movie was on the TV was an excitement. I probably watched two or three of the Johnny Weissmuller movies. I liked them, but I can't say that I was crazy about them.' Once he had secured the role of the ape-man, he didn't feel inclined to broaden his knowledge by investigating the Edgar Rice Burroughs books. 'Everything was in the script,' he reasons. 'I understood what it meant, being torn in between jungle and civilisation.' This may be fair enough, but Lambert's lack of steeping in the character is revealed in his belief that Tarzan was raised by chimpanzees.

Whatever qualities Hudson may have seen in him, Lambert was a daring choice. In possessing no discernible biceps, he was unlike any previous screen Tarzan except the lamentable

Mahoney. Because of his apparent physical unsuitability for the role, some might suspect that Lambert's French accent played a small part in him being cast as a man who learns his English from D'Arnot, but Hudson says, 'No. It just was by chance.' With regard to Lambert's physique, Hudson says, 'He's not a bodybuilder – I absolutely specifically didn't want that. Johnny Weissmuller was a most magnificent-looking man and he wasn't overbuilt: he didn't have enormous pectoral muscles or six-pack stomach muscles.'

Lambert, though, didn't have the toned look that comes from spending hours in the swimming pool, so had to submit to a rigorous training schedule. 'In March of '82 I was in London and started to train heavily for *Greystoke*: chimping and physical training,' he says. 'My first introduction to chimpanzees [was] with a professor called Roger Fouts. We trained in Ellensburg [Washington], tiny little town with a big, big university [that] was training the chimps, teaching them sign language. After these 2½ months, I went back to London and I started six months of training at 4½ hours a day of pure gymnastic and 4½ hours in the afternoon of pure chimping, plus vines, leaning how to jump from 35 feet high. So it was a combination of circus, chimping, of gymnastic. It was a heavy training ... I wasn't using weights. He wanted lean muscles. He didn't want me being bulk. So I was training on Pilates, I was training on bars, rings. Lots of push-ups, pull-ups, press-ups ... After six months of that, I put about thirty kilos of muscle mass on my body. It's very difficult to look at yourself, so you don't notice that you're getting bigger, but you notice that you're getting stronger.'

In *Greystoke*, for the first time on film, Tarzan's tribe were depicted as the undiscovered Mangani species of the books, albeit not named as such. Moreover, improved production techniques frequently enabled their realisation to be convincing. 'Rick Baker was the chimp costume designer,' says Lambert. 'It took something like two years just to design the suits. You had a suit that was the body muscles, and then you had the skin that was very thin lace and every hair was put in the lace by hand. So you can imagine how long it took to do that ... When the chimps had the suits on and their heads on, 'specially in Cameroon, they could never shoot more than three minutes at [a] time. The heat was very oppressive, and physically it was incredibly demanding."

Hudson notes that using 'small people, dancers, mainly female ... we managed to create a species of ape which was about five-foot-four maximum, and we trained them for three months in a studio. They created a primate tribe with a hierarchy, an alpha male, children.' The sole exception was that the crew 'used chimpanzee babies.'

Lambert recalls, 'Peter Elliott was the lead chimp and he also taught us how to chimp – he's probably the specialist in ape body language ... I was always there because I'm part of the troupe.' The baby chimpanzees were chosen to be aged around a year-and-a-half when shooting started. 'We're just training in sweat pants and t-shirts,' says Lambert. 'One day after six months of training, we put all the gymnasts in chimp suits with the head on, and all the baby chimps – without being able to see the faces of the people – went directly to the people they had been training with. I was in shock when I was watching them.'

An indication of how realistic the ape suits were was provided by the shooting of a scene outside London's Natural History Museum when an ape runs amok. Lambert says, 'Peter Elliott with his costume was running into the crowd. They weren't extras, they were just people watching a movie being made. They were running away screaming.'

Hudson says of his apes, 'We did a very good job considering the period. They're not quite right, but even today they're pretty good. They're a little bit more primate than Stanley Kubrick's apes in *2001*, 'cause he had them slightly further advanced.' Hudson is not jealous that the film was made pre-CGI: 'I think what we did is totally acceptable now.' He adjudges the organic *Greystoke* apes to be 'actually better' than the computer-generated simians in 2011's *Rise of the Planet of the Apes*, of which he opines, 'There's something too perfect about it, something slightly mechanical.'

The fidelity to the source in this aspect goes only so far, though: the heart rather sinks when the mode of arboreal transit of the *Greystoke* apes – and therefore Clayton's – is shown to be swinging on a succession of conveniently placed vines as though this is just another Johnny Weissmuller flick. In response to the suggestion that he could have shown the ape-man swinging from bough to bough instead, Hudson says: 'I didn't want to do it. We could have done it. He managed to do it once, and it wasn't necessary to do it all the time.'

During his six months of training, Lambert saw Hudson just twice. The actor was amazed to find that the director was even more distant when shooting began in Cameroon: 'Looks at me in the morning and he's saying, "Good morning, Chris." In the evening coming back from the set, he goes, "Good evening, Chris. You be ready on set tomorrow for eight o'clock." That's it. And we're in the same hotel. Never a word ... For 3½ weeks, Hugh Hudson was putting me in a chair on top of the movie set. I was waiting ten hours a day, twelve hours a day on that chair, not shooting. After three weeks of that, I broke down to Ian Holm, saying, "Listen, I don't know what this guy's doing to me. If he doesn't like me, why did he cast me?" I was in tears. The day after that, I was shooting ... Because probably he said, "I might be pushing him too far."'

Nonetheless, the non-communication by Hudson continued. The director maintained it when the cast and crew relocated to Elstree Studios, England. The non-communication only stopped as production prepared to shift to a British stately-home setting. Lambert: 'One day, when we finished jungle in the Cameroon and the jungle in the studio – roughly five months of shooting – he took me by the shoulder and said, "Christopher, now you're going to civilisation, you and I can speak." That was his way. He said, "You don't talk to animals."' Lambert pronounces these mind games 'dangerous,' at least for him. 'On an emotional level, I'm always on the edge,' he says. 'I was raised as a kid with absent parents ... Commentation [sic] for me is very, very, very important.'

The jungle scenes required more make-up than might be assumed. Explains Lambert, 'It was impossible to get tanned. You need an absolute steady and matching colour. Therefore I had body make-up from head to toe. Then I had the mud. Then the hairstylist had to do my hair, put some mud in it, a special mud. Then I had about twenty scars all over the body. So it was taking three hours every day.'

Lambert was at least spared having to appear naked, unlike the actors who played Tarzan at younger ages in the film. 'The little kid at seven years old wasn't a problem,' he says. 'At twelve years old, they started to ask him to hide a little. And at 23, 24, they were saying, "No, this guy can't walk around naked." It was never a question. It was a definite "no" from the studio. Between you and me, I was happy. I'm very shy, so just to be in loincloth was extremely difficult for me. Naked, mighta died."

Hudson says that the actor's lack of either physique or screen experience did not cause him to regret casting him: 'His body was pretty good by the time we'd trained him and built it up. It was fine ... I think he was very good." He points out that Lambert was helped by being in the screen presence of the 'magnificent' Ian Holm and the 'superb' Ralph Richardson.

In fact, far more problems were caused the director by the woman cast as Jane. Lambert recalls at one point being introduced to Elizabeth McGovern, but in the end the role of Tarzan's love went to Andie MacDowell. Lambert was pleased with the choice: 'She was an extremely nice person. She was a big, big model at the time, so she could have been precious, she could have been whatever ... [There's] famous movie couples that couldn't stand each other. That doesn't mean that on the screen you didn't believe they were in love, but I think it's always easier for both of them if they at least like each other.' Hudson, though, came to regret MacDowell's casting. 'She was a model and she didn't know how to use her voice to portray the emotions,' the director says. 'We were in the middle of the shooting and we started to try things out. It didn't work, so I just let it go and did what I could ... So we overdubbed her with a very good actress ... It was a terrible blow for her no doubt when she realised that was happening ... However, she went immediately to acting and vocal school and she became a pretty good actress.' Lambert feels that the dubbing (which he is under the impression was due to her Southern accent) was an unnecessary humiliation for MacDowell: 'She was good acting the part. It did a lot of harm to her at the beginning of her career. I'd no idea about that 'til she was dubbed.'

Hudson was to encounter more problems after the wrap. Negative audience reaction at previews motivated Warner Brothers to order the chopping out of large chunks of the film. The studio's nervousness was understandable: they had spent a then-massive $46m on production, nearly a sixth of which had gone on Rick Baker's ape make-up and costumes. Hudson denies rumours about the length of that first cut: 'It was never three hours. [It was] two hours 40 minutes ... The demand from the studio was it should be made, maximum, two hours ten minutes, and [they said that] it was too violent.'

The makers of the first Tarzan picture had boasted in publicity about their star killing a lion on set, but Hudson – who shot only simulated wildlife death – encountered a problem that perhaps indicates the pendulum had since swung too far in the other direction: 'It was tested and people said, "It's too violent, it's awful, the animals killing each other." And then they watch it quite happily [in] David Attenborough shows ... You can't kill animals [in movies]. They don't mind *people* killing each other.' Hudson admits that, as he set about re-editing with a new bloodless remit, he wondered if the cuts were removing the entire point of the picture. In the end, though, he was happy with the compromises reached. He provides an example: 'You finally believe he is the king of the animals' kingdom. He gives a panther to them, he's proven to be a provider of meat.'

The film was finally released in March 1984. In being named *Greystoke*, it cleaved to the current fashion in cinema for single-word, myth-draped titles. However, a subtitle was appended:

The Legend of Tarzan, Lord of the Apes. 'That really annoyed Hugh Hudson,' says Dez Skinn. 'He just wanted to call it *Greystoke*, because he knew that "Tarzan" was as off-putting as it was commercial, because people'll go, "Ah, yeah, yeah, yeah – seen it, seen it, seen it, Tarzan, Tarzan, Tarzan."' Lambert, though, says, 'It's important and it makes sense to me that they put "Tarzan" in the title. "Tarzan" is a known franchise. "Greystoke/John Clayton" is not. But I think it was done in a very subtle way.' Not so subtle is the fact that, just to fully cover themselves, the studio authorised a movie poster containing a précis of almost a hundred words.

That this is a very different Tarzan movie is apparent right at the beginning, which consists of a still shot of a tree captioned 'OVERTURE', which lasts for one-and-a-half minutes to the accompaniment of classical music. Cinemagoers not already apprised of it by the reviews would have to watch the entire film to apprehend another arresting departure from all previous versions except for the silent-era movies and the Denny Miller film: nowhere is the word 'Tarzan' uttered. Says Lambert, 'Who's going to call him "Tarzan" with a troupe of chimpanzees? Where is the name coming from?' Hudson offers, 'We were trying to make a realistic story.'

Another caption tells us that the opening scene proper – the death of the baby of the character we know from the books as Kala – occurs in Equatorial West Africa in 1885. Many Burroughs fans would doubtless welcome the film being set in the era of the *Tarzan of the Apes* novel, but it's something of a mystery why filmmakers without exception have stubbornly resisted the 1888 date set by Burroughs for the sailing of the *Fuwalda*. The way the Mangani are depicted is a mixture of excellent (very good faces, especially the yellowed fangs of the elders) and laughable (sometimes they are as obviously men in hairy suits as the trapeze artists in the 1918 *Tarzan of the Apes*; Kala's dead baby looks like the doll it is).

We are then taken back in time and across to Scotland where Lord Jack (sic) Clayton is preparing to leave the Greystoke family seat for a trip to Africa. That no less celebrated an actor than Sir Ralph Richardson plays the kindly old duffer grandfather of the unborn hero is not incongruous. The cast is positively studded with renowned British thesps, James Fox, Ian Holm, David Suchet and Richard Griffiths among them. The Americans, meanwhile, are superstars in waiting: not only is Jane played by Andie MacDowell, but she is voiced by Glenn Close.

When we are witness to the aftermath of a shipwreck whose cause is not explained, it feels like one of those places where a large chunk of the film has been excised. However, Hudson reveals that the natural assumption that the book's mutiny was shot and then dumped is incorrect: 'We didn't bother to do that. We were going too high in the budget.'

The Claytons build a cabin in their new jungle home while sole fellow survivor Captain Billings sets off to seek help. He is never heard from again. From the 14-minute mark, when a newly widowed Clayton cries out when being killed by a bull ape, to gone the 31-minute mark, when other people arrive, there is no human dialogue whatsoever in a succession of generally touching scenes in which we see baby John Clayton being raised by Kala. That times have changed since that first filmed Tarzan origin story is evident in full-frontal nudity, portrayals of lactation and a scene in which a teenage Clayton urinates on the chief of his tribe. The teenage Clayton is played by Eric Langlois, who, for some reason presumably related to confused notions of decency, has his buttocks literally glued together. (Daniel Potts – the five-year-old version of the character – is afforded no such dignity in his manifold bending and crouching motions.) It is established in this section (if not quite convincingly) that the young jungle boy has an uncanny ability for mimicry of wildlife, from birds to big cats. The Cameroon panoramas are sumptuous sights (Mount Cameroon was handily in the process of photogenically becoming an active volcano) made all the richer by the Royal Philharmonic Orchestra-played John Scott score. However, the scenes beneath the jungle canopy look like studio shoots and have the sort of acoustics associated with swimming baths.

The boy Clayton is left grief-stricken when natives kill Kala. Wholesale editing presumably accounts for the natives' apparent lack of motive, but it's difficult to know where to lay the blame for the fact that the scene is so limp. When the accomplices of Kala's killer turn and run after seeing Clayton dispense with him with a single back-breaking manoeuvre, this is not the stuff of the naturalism that this movie claims as its currency but instead the corny coinage of old black-and-white Tarzans.

Up to this point, the narrative has been fairly close to that of the *Tarzan of the Apes* novel. Although Ian Holm is very good in his tetchy but noble interpretation of D'Arnot, it is with this character's arrival that the Burroughs influence begins to drain from the picture, starting with the fact that he is Belgian rather than French and his first name is Philippe rather than Paul. D'Arnot is heading a steamboat expedition whose task is to catalogue fauna for the British Museum. Shortly after discovering the late Lord Greystoke's decaying log cabin, the party is, in a powerful and distressing sequence, slaughtered by cannibals. D'Arnot flees and hides. One of the picture's most memorable scenes occurs here as he faints in disbelief when Clayton looms over his feverish form with a curious Mangani in turn peering over Clayton's shoulder.

This is the first time we have seen Lambert. The adult Clayton wears a headband, his mother's locket and a loincloth. Said clothing – aside from the headband – was of course explained by Burroughs, as was the fact that the protagonist was clean-shaven at this age. Neither are clarified here. Few cared much before, but this film's naturalism draws attention to such issues. Things get worse in this regard: when D'Arnot later teaches Clayton to shave, ludicrously we are supposed not to notice that he looks no different following the application of the razor. In later Tarzan films, with cinema ever more naturalistic and self-conscious about illogical traditions, that one or both of these issues remained unaddressed was increasingly jarring.

Lambert jars even without these illogicalities. He's not bad as such – and occasionally conveys well the man/ape duality of his character with his simian grunts, hops and bounds – but one can see absolutely no reason why Hudson was so smitten. Not only is he not quite handsome, there is a semi-moronic slackness to his lower lip. Physique-wise, he is completely unimpressive. That a genuine ape/jungle upbringing would not necessarily result in bulging biceps has been touched on here before, but so has the fact that cinema requires a visual shorthand for power, strength and bravery.

There again, it is never quite established in this film that Clayton is possessed of those attributes. We see him holding a dead panther around his shoulders, but not him slaying it. Not long afterwards, there is a battle between him and the film's equivalent of Kerchak in which the action is un-ferocious and clunky, and in which Clayton achieves his victory while out of sight. The latter in particular feels a cop-out: he is now king of his tribe and we are still being asked to take his fighting prowess on trust. His bull-ape victory cry, incidentally, is limp.

Clayton nurses D'Arnot back to health, starting by – in a nicely realistic touch – forcing on him live grubs. During their six months together in the jungle, D'Arnot starts teaching Clayton the English language. That Clayton's capacity for mimicry enables him to learn quickly and accurately we can accept, but hardly his rapidly attained smooth sentence construction. Tarzan initially resists D'Arnot's insistence that Kala was not his mother ("ow many uzzer white apes 'ave you seen!'), but ultimately elects to follow him on his trek back to where his own kind can be found. In another jarring jump-cut clearly brought about by imposed editing, Clayton and D'Arnot arrive at a decadent white settlement with Tarzan now somehow fully clothed. Here, Clayton's rescue of D'Arnot from a menacing gang involves another action scene whose toothlessness is down not to cutting but poor scriptwriting: instead of laying into the attackers Mangani-style with fingers and teeth, Clayton hurls a paraffin lamp and sets the place ablaze like some 1930s matinée idol.

Another huge leap in narrative takes us to the Greystokes' Scottish castle, where his Lordship is being informed that his grandson – whom he seems to confuse with his son, although that's never quite made clear – is on his way to the family seat. 'It's an extraordinary example of man's superiority over beast,' a servant tells him. 'Not only did he survive, he made himself their master. Their lord, as it were.' When his carriage pulls into the Greystoke driveway, in a sweet touch Clayton leans and peers out of the door at his new surroundings just like a wary animal might. Lord Greystoke is delighted at the 'return' to the vast family estate of the man he calls 'Johnny' and tickled pink by his childlike unfamiliarity with civilised ways, which renders him without pretension, malice or understanding of the fact that porridge doesn't go with kippers. Clayton takes to his Lordship too, but is even more intrigued by Jane Porter, who in this narrative is his step-sister. Jane deepens his knowledge of civilisation, language and, eventually, sex. She then rejects the marriage proposal of pompous Lord Esker (Fox). The latter takes out his frustration on a retarded member of the clan whose part has clearly been drastically whittled down in the editing suite. When Clayton rescues this man from Esker's whipping, we are by now not surprised that a warning growl is the puny extent of the action.

So intoxicated with joy is the grandfather by the continuation of his line, he decides to replicate a childhood pleasure of cruising on a serving tray down his castle stairs, with fatal consequences. Clayton – whose ambivalence about being in civilisation has by now been established – is distraught that he has come all this way to suffer a bereavement that mirrors his traumatic loss of Kala. Nonetheless, he becomes engaged to Jane.

The new Lord Greystoke – now short-haired – opens a section of the British Museum. Queasy at being surrounded by animal bodies and parts, he ducks into a corridor, where he hears a familiar animal cry. To his astonishment, he finds his distressed ape step-father – Tublat in the books – cooped up in a small cage. In a powerful scene, the two jabber at each other before Clayton releases the Mangani. The pair flee the building and make their way to the nearest jungle-like environment, a local park. They climb a tree together, Clayton – now fully reverted to his ape personality – snarling at encroaching parties. Suddenly, the Mangani topples from the tree, shot by officialdom.

It is the final straw. Lambert reasons of his character's emotional and physical journey, '[D'Arnot] was saying, "This is not your world, your world is out there." So that means you are breaking his life more than you think by saying, "What you live is not what you are." Wrong. What he lived is what he was. But he's taking the chance, saying, "Listen, if there is something out there, I want to know about it. I want to see it. Then I will make my decision." So he takes that risk, which is huge. And it's a disappointment. He needs to go back to his roots, the jungle.'

Clayton's declaration to friends and family of his desire to return to what he considers home is convincing enough, but ends with a ridiculous vista in which lights go out across his castle in quick succession – a massive edifice put on the same footing as the house of the Waltons. Clayton, D'Arnot and Jane travel to Africa, where Clayton spots a Mangani who, although wary of him at first, shortly welcomes him. Without a word to his human companions, Clayton strips off and runs into the jungle fastness. It's the end of a film that would be confused and compromised even without the imposed editing that reduced it to a still overlong 131 minutes.

Says Bill Hillman, 'Most dedicated fans agree that the first half of that movie was excellent. As soon as they took him to England it seemed to collapse. He wasn't the heroic savage and he was little more of a weak joke.'

Greystoke may be the first modern Tarzan film to attempt to be faithful to the source material, but the moral of its story is diametrically opposed to Burroughs' premise. 'He has a noble image and he returns to the head of his tribe in the jungle,' says Hudson. 'He's noble to the end but he doesn't want to deal with the rubbish that's tried to push down his throat by the society that they say he is among the elite of.' Lambert says something in the same vein: 'If you look at the dinner scene, if I want to eat my soup by gulping it from the plate, that doesn't mean it's bad. It's the way this guy is. He is not used to a spoon. And the grandfather, who is a real gentleman, is saying, "You know what? He is right. Why are we wasting time with good or bad manners? Who cares?"' Yet Burroughs' original story was predicated on the opposite belief: nature over nurture. In other words, his fine breeding means that Clayton's real tribe is in civilisation.

Elsewhere, *Greystoke* ends up rather suggesting something that many Burroughs fans dare not admit to themselves: that maybe Tarzan as a concept doesn't lend itself to a naturalistic adaptation. The paradoxically unconvincing nature of a realistically skinny Tarzan is just the start. Hudson lazily opting to show vine-swinging is another problem: the character swinging from bough to bough would probably have been too labour-intensive to achieve. Then there is the thorny issue of sex to which the naturalism makes one's mind stray: an adolescent boy who knew no better would surely have mated with a Mangani. The difficulty of explaining the non-simian sounding name 'Tarzan' is revealed by its very absence.

Hudson feels that the re-editing that saw the film's scheduled late-1983 release postponed cost the studio something more than the lucrative Yuletide market: 'If it had come out at Christmas I think it would have been more accoladed, but the whole nine months, ten months waiting and people had to remember it...' Nevertheless, it was the first Tarzan picture ever to acquire Academy Award nominations: Best Supporting Actor (Richardson), Best Adapted Screenplay and Best Make-up. The middle one is the most remarkable, considering the script-related compromises and cuts. It also made Danton Burroughs smile, because Towne had exercised his right to remove his name from the credits: 'The first half of *Greystoke* was excellent because Bob Towne did the screenplay, but he was so pissed at Warner Brothers he [had his work credited to] his dog, P H Vazak. So [the dog] was nominated for an Academy Award.' Had

Richardson won, his Oscar would have been posthumous: he died before the release of the film, which was dedicated to his memory. Hudson says, 'It should have won for visual effects. Rick Baker, who's a masterful man, he should have won.'

'I talked [of] sequels later on but I never got very far with it,' Hudson says. 'I was onto something else. I don't think the film made enough money to warrant a sequel, actually.' The film did reasonable box office, taking $42m in the United States in its first nine weeks on release and ending up the fifteenth highest-grossing movie in America that year. However, those figures are less impressive set against its unusually high production costs.

Lambert says he 'absolutely' would have agreed to a sequel if the right script had come along. 'There was talk,' he recalls. 'We had some scripts ... When I say some scripts, it's like pages of notes. Ideas. Tarzan fighting Germans during the Second World War, stuff like that ... But after two years, three years, four years, synopses, ideas, your life goes on and you do different movies and Hugh is not available, I'm not available, so it's natural you went away.' Now he considers this to be for the best. 'It was difficult to make a sequel out of a complete movie. And when I'm saying "complete," the story was a circle: he leaves the jungle, goes to civilisation, goes back to the jungle. So what do you do as a sequel? You see him again living in the jungle? You've seen it for half the movie. Some movies you just have to accept you shouldn't touch the movie and make a sequel.'

Asked if *Greystoke* fulfilled all his artistic hopes for it, Hudson responds, 'Yeah. I think it did. Absolutely.' As a man who hates to watch himself on the screen, Lambert feels less able to judge. 'I saw *Greystoke* once at a screening in Pinewood when the movie was finished,' he says. 'I don't know what this guy is doing on the screen. It's not me. He's a different person.' However, the feedback he has received has left Lambert sure of one thing: '*Greystoke* is important because, thirty years later, it's still a movie that people are talking about. When you talk to Tarzan fans, they're definitely saying that *Greystoke* is the best Tarzan movie so far.'

Those Tarzan fans less convinced of the movie's aesthetic merits might be interested in seeing a director's cut that presumably would not be blighted by so many of the structural weaknesses of the theatrical release. Hudson said in the lead-up to the 2012 Tarzan centenary, 'It is being proposed.' Surprisingly, however, he revealed that there was no extant copy of the original cut, saying, 'The material of the cut will be in the vaults somewhere ... It's all there to be got out and redone. It would be quite a job 20 or 30 years later, but it's possible. People are still around who would remember what to do.' This was all rendered moot when a director's cut of the film failed to appear at that hundredth-anniversary juncture, probably the only time it would have been commercially viable.

Flawed though it is, its ambition, production values and tilt at some form of faithfulness make *Greystoke* one of the four most important Tarzan films alongside the first Elmo Lincoln picture, the second Weissmuller film and a movie yet to come, Disney's 1999 animated feature *Tarzan*.

PART EIGHT: THE KELLER ERA

Following the big splash of *Greystoke*, things were quiet on the Tarzan motion picture front for 14 years. However, said film would seem to have worked to revitalise the commercial worth of the ape-man. That nigh decade-and-a-half saw plentiful activity surrounding the character in books, comics and live-action television.

There was also Tarzan activity in another, newer medium that would have been beyond even the imagination of the mad Martian scientists encountered by John Carter. The ape-man's image and double-outlined logo had long been seen on pinball machines. Come the late '70s, pinball machines were on their way to being superseded in arcades by video games. The latter generated unofficial items involving generic white jungle men in loincloths, at least one of which – *Jungle Boy* aka *Jungle King* – attracted a successful legal action by ERB, Inc. Before long, though, the serious video-game business was not coin-operated but home-based. In 1984 came the first officially sanctioned ape-man home computer game. Called simply *Tarzan*, it was released for the Commodore 64, BBC Micro and Colecovision platforms. Its sideways-scrolling gameplay – the ape-man collecting points by punching human and arachnid antagonists against jungle and lost city-ish backdrops to the accompaniment of bubbling synth music – was cutting-edge. However, this new entertainment medium boasted possibly the most ferociously rapid development pace in human history and, less than a decade later, graphics so fuzzy that a sprite recognisable as Tarzan only via his bare legs and chest would seem comically primitive. This quick-fire development of the medium can be followed through *Tarzan Goes Ape* (1991, platforms: Commodore 64, Sinclair ZX81/Spectrum), *Jungle no Ouja: Tarzan* (1994, Super Nintendo, Japan only) and *Tarzan: Lord of the Jungle* (1994, Gameboy). By the time Disney issued a product on PlayStation, Game Boy Color and Nintendo 64 to tie in with their 1999 *Tarzan* movie, home computer games were unrecognisable from the mid-'80s:

players could take a Tarzan sprite visually indistinguishable from how he appeared in the movie through 14 levels on the journey from child to adult, collecting points by bulldozing through fruit and tokens and throwing objects at monkeys that promptly exploded into butterfly swarms. The lustrous backdrops across which the sprite moved were also identical to those seen in the film, something that could be verified by comparing them with the movie scenes that were interspersed throughout the gameplay.

In the '80s, there was still space in this soon-to-be digital world for games on the printed page. 1985 saw the publication of *Tarzan and the Well of Slaves* by Douglas Niles, an instalment of the Endless Quest gamebooks published by TSR, famous for Dungeons & Dragons. As well as the usual interactivity that allowed the reader/player to choose the story's ending, this new series had an educational element. *Tarzan and the Tower of Diamonds* by Richard Reinsmith followed in the same series in 1986.

It's not widely recognised, but the period during which husband-and-wife production team Max and Micheline Keller held the ape-man screen rights is as distinct and significant a Tarzan era as those of Sol Lesser or Sy Weintraub. It was an era, though, that began unpromisingly.

Recalls Micheline Keller, 'My husband woke up with the idea about bringing Tarzan to New York.' The resultant *Tarzan in Manhattan* (on which Gina Scheerer was co-producer) went in completely the opposite direction to the period-and mainly jungle-settings of the last two live-action Tarzan projects, recasting the franchise as both contemporary and urban. Keller: 'We actually lived in Encino, so we only lived about ten minutes away from the Burroughs offices in Tarzana. He spoke with the president. Her name was Sandra Galfas. She said they were very particular who they licensed the rights to. They weren't sure they wanted to do it with an independent. Marion [Burroughs] was still alive and she said, "Well let me see some of their work," and

Gordon Scott (right) had an impressive physique. His most impressive ape-man picture was his fourth outing, Tarzan's Greatest Adventure (1959, below).

A lobby card for 1959's Tarzan the Ape Man (above), Denny Miller's sole Tarzan film. In Tarzan's Three Challenges (1963, below), it was painfully obvious that Jock Mahoney was the oldest Tarzan ever.

Unauthorised Tarzan in films (above), books (top right) and comics (right).

The first proper Tarzan comic appeared in 1947 (above). Western's DuBois & Manning '60s Tarzan comics adaptations (below) are classics.

Mike Henry – Tarzan from 1966 to 1968 – was like no cinema ape-man before.

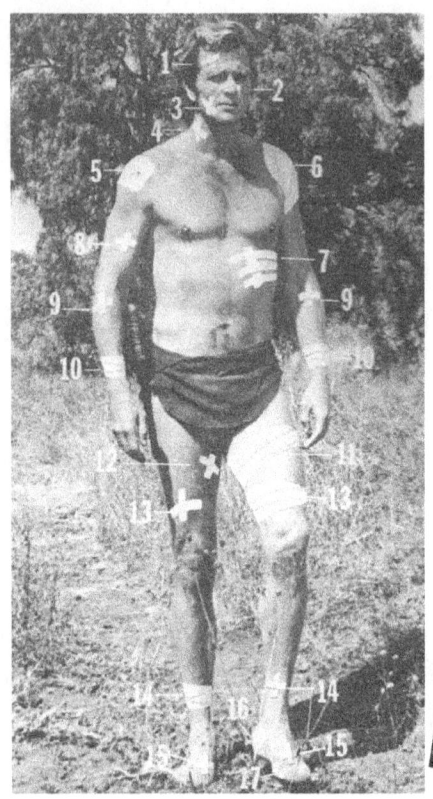 

Ron Ely played the ape-man in NBC's 1966-68 Tarzan TV series, which bequeathed both a memorable opening sequence (bottom) and a curious publicity photo (left). Tarzan En La Gruta Del Oro (1970, below) was one of two Steve Hawkes films of questioned legality.

DC Comics Tarzan artist Joe Kubert specialised in spectacular double-page spreads (above). Burne Hogarth's 1972 graphic-novel adaptation of Tarzan of the Apes featured utterly beautiful artwork (below).

Animated Seventies TV Tarzan from Filmation.

'After Pettee': the first depiction of the ape-man created a mini-industry of pastiche.

The film poster (above right) was the first indication that something was wrong with 1981's Tarzan the Ape Man. Miles O'Keeffe (right, with Bo Derek) was a great Tarzan in a terrible film.

The apes in 1984's Greystoke (above) were more impressive than either the physique of star Christopher Lambert (below left) or its prolix poster (below right).

TV Tarzan from Keller Entertainment. Scenes from Tarzan starring Wolf Larson (above) and Tarzan: The Epic Adventures starring Joe Lara (below). (Courtesy of Keller Entertainment Group, Inc.)

Left: a new era was denoted in 1984 by the first Tarzan computer game. Below: Tarzan and the Lost City (1998), starring Casper Van Dien, was theoretically the sequel to Greystoke.

Sony Wonder's Enchanted Tales Tarzan video (1999, above right) seemed to want only to be mistaken for Disney's Tarzan cinema film (other pictures), released the same year.

TV Guide insisted on Travis Fimmel's masculinity (left), but the WB's publicity release for its Tarzan show (above) seemed designed to make people wonder which one was Jane.

Disney's publicity release for the 2006 Broadway Tarzan musical adeptly incorporated both the lead actors and the show's splendid logo. Jenn Gambatese as Jane and Josh Strickland as Tarzan

Constantin's motion capture Tarzan movie (2013) was unexpectedly impressive.

The Legend of Tarzan (2016), starring Alexander Skarsgård (above and right), was the first film to name the Mangani, one of which was depicted in its poster (below).

The second decade of the 21st century brought the most energetic programme of Tarzan writing since the death of the ape-man's creator.

41 Entertainment/Netflix TV series Tarzan and Jane (2017). At top are (l-r) the Earl of Greystoke, Muviro, Jane and Tarzan. (Images courtesy of 41 Entertainment LLC.)

we sent over one or two of our TV movies. She liked the quality of our work, so she agreed to grant us a licence for a television series ... It was on the expensive side of what the licensing rights were for television products, but it was within the realm of what we could do.'

Says Keller of the long relationship her company ultimately had with the Burroughs estate, 'They had the right to read every script, [but] after the first few scripts they felt comfortable so they didn't bother. I think we still sent them over every script, but we never got any notes from them. They really let us do our thing.' However, there were limits to the corporation's *lassiez faire* attitude: 'Edgar Rice Burroughs, Inc had a series of rules that they gave us about what things Tarzan could do or could not do, and they were kind of interesting: no bad language, no sexual relations with Jane, no smoking, no alcohol...'

The Kellers commissioned a script by Canadian husband-and-wife team William Gough and Anna Sandor. Although this decision was based on their satisfaction with work the couple had previously done for them, Keller adds, 'William Gough I believe was a Tarzan fan.' Their work is a mixture of prose and film Tarzan: Kala features, if briefly, but so does Cheeta. No explanation is provided for Tarzan's fluency in English, his upbringing or his name.

Keller explains of the casting process: 'Agents were sending us actors and we just didn't find anyone we liked, so we had an open audition call in Hollywood and Joe Lara was at that open audition call. Interestingly enough, as was Wolf Larson, who we later used. Joe Lara, we just felt he had that animal magnetism.' Lara, a 26-year-old former model, has flowing locks, a chiselled face and a toned body. He looks the part in a way that Lambert didn't, but without conveying the impression of a body that could only have been honed in one of civilisation's gyms.

Tarzan is traumatised when hunters kill Kala and abduct Cheeta. His only clue to the perpetrators' identities is a matchbook from a New York nightclub. 'How do I get to New York?' he demands of an African friend in a scene that would have greater emotional impact were he not drawling in an accent that suggests he's never been beyond American borders. By a financial means not explained, Tarzan pursues the killers to civilisation, where he is initially dressed in jeans and T-shirt before switching to a loincloth. Setting off the loincloth is a pair of knee boots, which might sound unspeakable but actually don't look too bad, nor seem unreasonable considering the fact that the streets of Manhattan are quite possibly strewn with as many hazards as the average jungle floor. All Keller productions would depict the ape-man in such footwear.

As is traditional, Tarzan runs into Jane Porter. As is not traditional, she is a ballsy cab-driver. Jane is played by Kim Crosby, but more interesting is who didn't get the role. 'Our first Jane was almost Sharon Stone,' reveals Keller. The Kellers had worked with the then-unknown Stone on a TV movie, but their desire to employ her again was nixed by CBS when she declined to audition for a network she felt already knew her abilities. The network also rejected auditionee Teri Hatcher, soon to be famous as Superman's girlfriend Lois Lane. Jane's father is played by screen legend Tony Curtis. He is not anything as lofty as a professor here, but instead an ex-cop-turned-private-eye. Nonetheless, he insists on being called by full name 'Archimedes' not 'Archie'. Curtis hams up his boorish/endearing part – his character calls Cheeta 'Chiquita' and treats Jane like a 12-year-old – with a twinkle in his eye.

Tarzan in Manhattan was first broadcast by CBS on 15 April 1989 and ran to 94-minute (sans commercials). Its potentially interesting and amusing savage-in-civilisation premise is undone by the execution. The action – directed by Michael Schultz – is as anodyne as that of the average chase movie, and the fisticuffs marked by a markedly un-feral blandness. (Tarzan emits a bull-ape victory cry, but it's unimpressive.) Scenes such as Cheeta driving a car indicate that grit was not uppermost in the producers' minds. 'We were really looking for a family audience,' Keller says. 'Something that the kids could watch with their parents and an elder adult might enjoy because they knew the Tarzan legacy.'

The show is broadly similar to Weissmuller's *Tarzan's New York Adventure*, aside from the inclusion of a mild science fiction element in the shape of the discovery that the pseudo-philanthropic Brightmore Foundation that gets Cheeta in its clutches is conducting illegal experiments designed to transfer thoughts between animals. There is nothing in the script, though, as poetic or moving as Weissmuller's *Tarzan's New York Adventure* witness-box testimony. Moreover, the innocent-abroad premise was done much better before by the likes of *Catweazle* and *Man from Atlantis*.

That the ending sees Tarzan electing to stay in the Big Apple to work for Archimedes' security firm for minimum wage and all the bananas Cheeta can eat is not exactly logical, but of course was intended to set up a regular series. 'What we did discover out of that was that people really would prefer to see Tarzan in the jungle, so after we did the two-hour movie CBS did not pick it up as a series,' says Keller. 'That was a big, big, big disappointment.'

The Kellers went back to the drawing board to decide what to do with the rights they held. 'We had worked really hard, spent a lot of money in producing this pilot, much more than the network paid us, so it was quite heartbreaking, 'cause we were a small company,' says Keller. 'My husband just decided he was going to get it on the air by hook or by crook.'

As part of the Kellers' by-any-means-possible strategy, they gave Tarzan ideals that were the preserve of people considered peculiar when Burroughs brought the ape-man into a world where people with lion heads mounted on their walls and zebra pelts spread on their floors were more admired than despised. Keller: 'We decided to go with [a] Tarzan that would be helping to save the environment, and along the way we felt the show could also have a lot of nice comments about ecology and protecting animals and protecting rainforests and conservation and not polluting our rivers.'

Perhaps more important to their success than the concept,

though, was the couple's marketing. Keller explains of her husband, 'He actually ended up doing a series as an international co-production. I had a cousin that was French and we asked him to form a French production company, which he did, and then my husband sold [the series] to TF1 to come in as a partner. TF1 is the largest French station, government-owned. Tarzan is very popular in France. They even have a Tarzan museum. We did it as a French-Canadian co-production, and then it became a three-way co-production ... because neither of those countries had the kind of terrain that you needed ... We shot it in Mexico, so we had a Mexican producer come on board ... Officially, we were the developers of that series and not producers because Max set it up as a three-country co-production for the financing, which did not allow for American producers.'

The resultant series was called simply *Tarzan*. The French finance presumably accounts for why some sources render an accent over the second 'a', but it is not apparent in the show's title-sequence logo. It also accounts for the non-American main casting. 'We had to switch our Tarzan because, as an international co-production, neither of [the leads] could be American,' says Keller. 'Joe Lara was very American, so even though we would have loved to have kept him, we had to look for a Canadian actor or a French actor for Tarzan, and Wolf Larson was Canadian.' The apparently splendid poetry of the name of this 32-year-old graduate of *Dynasty*, who paid the bills when 'resting' by taking a multitude of calendar modelling gigs, is somewhat less impressive when it's revealed that Wolf is an apparently artful diminutive for Wolfgang, while his real surname is von Wyszeck. Larson's appearance was similarly less impressive than it at first sight appeared. Keller laughingly admits, 'He was not as rugged and wild as Joe Lara.' Although he was statuesque, buff and handsome, Larson's mane was clearly the product of one of civilisation's styling salons, something which compounded his blondness. Moreover, for UK viewers he bore a distracting resemblance to well-known DJ Pat Sharp. Jane Porter might have a very Anglo surname but is presented as a Gallic zoologist played by Frenchwoman Lydie Denier. The show's location dictated a geographical change, or at least fudging. 'We were shooting in Mexico so we made a decision that it would be generic jungle,' Keller says.

Rather unusually for an action-oriented drama series, each episode was only half-an-hour in length, making for screen time minus commercials of just 22 minutes. Once again, this is attributable to the exigencies of juggling the specific demands of investors. Keller: 'That's what TF1 wanted, and they were the first ones to come on board.' Complicating matters was the fact that Italian television – which had also purchased the programme before shooting started – insisted on an hour-long show. The Kellers addressed this by a device that made splicing easier: 'Every episode [had] a little tag at the end that ran it into another episode, talking about, "Now, we're going to go on to look for the poisonous egg," [or] whatever the next show was about.'

Many a Burroughs fan no doubt groaned when they saw that, like his predecessor, Larson sported knee-high boots. The actor revealed to *People* magazine that he changed his mind about going barefoot when he became cognisant of the poisonous snakes abounding in Cuernavaca, the area of Mexico where the first series was shot. Keller: 'The jungles are full of animals and very dangerous insects and we had people that were bitten by tarantulas. We just felt we would be putting him too much at risk to have him run around barefoot.'

The series swings back toward the Weissmuller Tarzan, featuring as it does a pidgin-speaking ape-man, Cheeta and the Weissmuller yodel. (Keller says of the latter, 'It was public domain. I think it might have even been mixed with a tiny bit of Joe Lara. Joe Lara did an amazing job too. Oh my gosh, we spent a lot of time on that yell.') However, Keller points out that there was at least one nod to the Burroughs hinterland: 'We did one episode where he got [out] a locket of his parents and he talked about having crashed and all of that. We did it as a plane crash as opposed to the shipwreck that was in *Greystoke*.'

Despite all the changes from *Tarzan in Manhattan*, the new production had something in common with its predecessor in the form of wholesome storylines geared toward the family. Eyebrows might be raised by the fact that Tarzan lives with a young man. However, his relationship with Roger Taft (Sean Roberge) seems as chaste as the one he has with Jane. The gauche Roger shares comic relief status with Cheeta, who usually closes episodes with some endearing action. Tarzan, who is teaching Roger his jungle lore, hangs around with a man from whom he learnt much of his, Simon (Malick Bowens). The latter character provides a framing device via voiceover readings from his journal. He is also the only black person in sight. Ron Ely guest-starred in a first-season episode.

The series began syndicated daytime Sunday transmissions in the US on 6 October 1991. (Its credits carried the pointed line, 'Based on the copyrighted Tarzan stories written by Edgar Rice Burroughs.') However, the American broadcast dates are pretty much irrelevant for this show, whose commercial achievements, although substantial, were in non-English speaking territories. Keller describes the programme as 'Tremendously successful' around the world: 'In France they put it on Christmas week around six o'clock and it just broke all records for TF1. Sixty percent of the televisions were tuned on to Tarzan every night, 'cause they ran it every night for the first ten nights. In Canada, it got more and more popular every year. Unfortunately, in America we had gone with a Spelling [distribution] company called Worldvision the first year and it just didn't work out financially. They wanted to lower the price so much for the second year. It was a shame, because I think it would have done the same as it did in Canada.' In the UK, the show failed to find a buyer until Disney launched their cable/satellite channel there in 1995.

Larson didn't want to return to Cuernavaca for the second season (Keller: 'It was very remote') so shooting was relocated to the more accessible, if less beautiful, Puerto Escondido. Keller: 'The third one we shot in Acapulco because we were going to be shooting a series called *Acapulco Heat* and so we felt that we could be preparing the other series while we were shooting *Tarzan*.' As with the first season, the second and third seasons of *Tarzan* each consisted (for most territories) of 25 episodes of 30 minutes' duration (including commercials). Simon disappeared from the series, replaced in season two by Jack Benton (Errol Slue) and in the third by Dan Miller (William S Taylor). Although both seasons again located receptive audiences across the globe, there was a five-year gap before the Kellers found anyone interested in following up the first season in the United States. By the time season two began its American airings on 28 September 1997 (season three was broadcast from 15 March 1998), the show was dead. 'I think the cost had just gone up and we might have lost one of the countries,' says Keller. 'It was really a financial decision. We just couldn't go into deficit on it.' However, the Kellers were not finished with the ape-man.

March 1992 marked the return of Tarzan comics to the American newsstands (not counting some '80s Blackthorne publications that reprinted newspaper strips in comic-book format).
'You've never seen Tarzan like *this* before!' declared the front cover of the first issue of independent publisher Malibu's five-part *Tarzan the Warrior*. It wasn't a lie. Writer Mark Wheatley and penciller Neil Vokes proffered a story involving such depressingly incongruous components as Bigfoot, a siren-punctuated car chase and shape-shifting aliens. The company's next mini-series in August – the three-part *Tarzan: Love, Lies and the Lost City* – did at least feature an adaptation of the *Jungle Tales* story 'Tarzan's First Love' amongst the furiously self-conscious re-imagining. Malibu's final ape-man offering was *Tarzan: The Beckoning*, a six-parter that straddled 1992 and '93.
Dark Horse was a publishing company established in 1986 with the twin objectives of treating comic books as being as valid as all other forms of entertainment and recognising the concept of the rights of creative staff, the latter a policy that in theory led to enhanced creativity. It seemed good news therefore that in

1995 the American Tarzan comic-book rights passed over to these hip new kids on the block.

Dark Horse's first Tarzan project was an anomaly. They were awarded the accolade of publishing the first unseen Burroughs Tarzan prose since 1964's *Tarzan and the Madman*. The story was issued across four monthly paperbacks, first issue cover-dated January 1995. This was of course in the tradition of the serialisations that, with a few exceptions, had preceded the book publication of all other Burroughs Tarzan tales. Illustrations by Arthur Suydam and Tom Yeates were deliberately designed to echo the style of the pulps. Subsequently, the work appeared as a deluxe Dark Horse hardback and a Ballantine paperback. All three editions appeared with the title *Tarzan: The Lost Adventure*. This of course was not the name given the story by its author, but the very fact that it had lain in a safe since 1946 demanded a mythos be attached to this previously untitled work.

As Burroughs' manuscript was a mere 83 pages, even had it possessed an ending it would have amounted only to a novella. In 1994, Danton Burroughs took over the running of ERB, Inc following Marion Burroughs' death. Spurning the option of just issuing the manuscript unfinished *a la* F Scott Fitzgerald's *The Last Tycoon*, he that year called Burroughs scholar and chronicler Robert R Barrett to discuss who would be an appropriate choice of writer to expand it to 200 pages and resolve its plot. Barrett's answer was Philip José Farmer. 'I began to heavily lobby Dan to get Dark Horse to hire Phil,' says Barrett. Barrett was not the only person to suggest that Dark Horse engage the services of Farmer. Another was author and comic-book writer Joe R Lansdale. Recalls the latter, 'I was on the phone with Jerry Prosser, who was working at Dark Horse. We were just talking about the project that we were doing at that time, which was a comic project. He said, "Do you know, we have the rights to the Tarzan book. We're looking for someone to do it." I said, "Oh my God, you got to get Philip José Farmer."' Dark Horse disagreed. Barrett: 'Finally Dan told me that Dark Horse on their own initiative had hired Joe Lansdale to rewrite Ed's portion of the novel and then to complete it. Both Dan and I were very disappointed that Phil wasn't chosen and, to my knowledge, Dark Horse never gave Dan an explanation as to why they had not chosen Phil.'

It's possible that the hatred of Farmer among some sections of the Burroughs fanbase may have turned off Dark Horse. However, the choice of Lansdale was a somewhat baffling one. Although Lansdale estimates he had by that point published – including under pen-names – 12 to 15 novels, they had been in the fields of mystery, horror and Western. However, there was some sort of logic to the decision. 'I'm a Tarzan and Edgar Rice Burroughs fan from day one,' says Lansdale. 'I was born in '51 and I started probably when I was about 11 or 12 ... I wouldn't be a writer had it not been for Edgar Rice Burroughs.' Accordingly, Lansdale was hardly going to turn the job down, even though he thought Farmer was a better choice and even though big bucks were not on offer: 'It was work-for-hire, which because it was Tarzan I was willing to do. It was way under my pay scale.' He was also not afforded much in terms of time. 'I had to turn it around almost immediately,' he recalls. 'It might have been six weeks, two months at the most ... I didn't have any time at all to prep outside of re-reading some of the Tarzan books.'

When Lansdale was sent a copy of the unfinished Burroughs manuscript, he concluded, 'I don't think it was something Burroughs planned to publish.' Although he allows, 'There were stretches in there when it just had the old Burroughs magic,' he says that overall, 'It was not outstanding. He whacked a lion on just about every page, or some kind of cat. I was very disappointed when I got it, to some extent.' His remit was not just to tie up Burroughs' dangling story threads but rewrite what was already written. 'They didn't think it stood up very well. It had a tired feeling. That's why it was in the safe. This comes from a fanatic Burroughs fan, but you find that it's very repetitious. A lot of the stuff, though, I just moved it around. There were also parts of it that were extraordinarily racist.'

He says the writing process was harder than it at first

appeared: "You were obligated to continue as was and stay in that tone. It would have been easier to write something from scratch, but it would not have been as wonderful as to have been someone who actually collaborated with Edgar Rice Burroughs.'

Of his development and plot resolution, Lansdale says, 'I didn't work it out at all. I don't outline any of my books particularly, because I get bored: by the time I outline it, I no longer want to write it. I followed what I thought was his lead, but as far as the stuff that was not in his manuscript, I just let it happen as I went.'

Lansdale was prevented from moving the ape-man into the modern world: 'I wished I could have updated [it] more. That was the one thing I was asked: to keep it in that tone ... I wasn't trying to copy Burroughs absolutely, because then if you did that people would say, "Well you tried to imitate him and you can't do that," which I agree with. I tried to capture the spirit of the Tarzan books as much as possible and yet somewhat bring my own brand to it without letting it override what the original was.' In what year did he consider the tale to be set? 'I thought it was just a mythical year, because Africa had changed a lot, but in my mind it happened sometime in the past.'

The joint Burroughs-Lansdale story sees Tarzan getting involved in the adventures of multiple safaris comprised of villains and explorers. Jane is absent but Nkima and Jad-bal-ja appear. Rewriting of even an inchoate and bitty manuscript inevitably aroused controversy (especially when ERB's original pages were subsequently privately published). Lansdale was accused of making Tarzan more vicious. This is something he disputes, saying, 'There's some pretty nasty stuff in the Tarzan novels.' However, some of the objections to elements introduced by Lansdale seem justified. Tarzan's fings-ain't-what-they-used-to-be musings on the modern world and how things might be better if he emigrated to Pellucidar are simply not within the ape-man's established frame of reference. That Tarzan is shown as being familiar with a fighting style learnt from a former Shaolin priest suggests Lansdale is trying to artificially fold one of his interests – kung fu – into another. The repartee between Tarzan and heroine Jean in which the ape-man's flirty banter drips with self-regard suggests the author is attempting to cram some James Bond in too. And would Burroughs have ever done anything so ludicrous as include a giant praying mantis versed in martial arts? Or refer to the jungle animal the 'croc'? As for Lansdale opting to exile Tarzan to Pellucidar at the end, it's almost as if a self-aggrandising author is seeking to block off the possibility of other writers having the chance to continue the ape-man's prose adventures.

Muses Lansdale, 'I felt that it's hard for people to believe in that Africa anymore, which was always an alternate universe really. There was a time when those books were written, and even into the '60s when I was a kid, that we still didn't know that much about Africa and still thought there was no telling what you might find. You might find a dinosaur somewhere there in the Congo. Then by the time that book was written we all knew that wasn't true and we all knew that that Africa didn't exist. So what I wanted to do was give the option of sending Tarzan to a place that was eternally that way, which was Pellucidar, an option for the readers to have the opportunity to believe that there was a world he could exist in that Tarzan would prefer ... I didn't think of it as exile. I thought [of] it as [offering] the possibility of a sequel where he could have more adventures, and if there was no sequel, at least we could all think, "Here is a world that would be full of adventures forever."' As for the Bond-ish flirty banter, he says, 'I was trying to update it a little bit.' The praying mantis he justifies by citing the ant-men, the Ho-don/Waz-don and other science fiction elements of Burroughs' Tarzan books. Certainly ERB, Inc had no problem with what he wrote. 'I never heard from the Burroughs estate,' he says. 'They had final approval and they approved it.'

As for his own evaluation of *Tarzan: The Lost Adventure*, Lansdale says, 'I didn't think it was [Burroughs'] best work, therefore I was limited for it to be my best work. I tried to do the best I could at the time. I wasn't trying to do it for old glory. I'm certainly not ashamed of it. It's certainly got its fans.' Some, of course, consider it blasphemy for Lansdale or anyone to presume to rewrite Burroughs. He responds, 'I didn't feel it was a sacrilege in the fact that it was unfinished, and Burroughs' work was often used to be filmed or to be made into comics, there were children's books of it, so he always designed his books as a product.'

Was he in a no-win situation? 'Yeah, I think I was.' However, Lansdale adds, 'I won better than I thought.'

After they had delivered Burroughs' enthusiasts their fantasy of unpublished Tarzan prose, Dark Horse followed it with a series of conventional comic books. If, that is, there was now any such thing.

In the period Tarzan had been away from the medium, comics had changed profoundly. In the 1980s, comic sales had begun to take a pummelling from arcade and computer games, which provided a similar fantasy tableau but with the exhilarating addition of interactivity. Meanwhile, comics were becoming both more adult and more specialist. Works like Alan Moore's *V for Vendetta* and *Miracleman* (both 1982), Frank Miller's *The Dark Knight Returns* and Alan Moore's *Watchmen* (both 1986) introduced edginess, moral ambiguity and post-modernism into the medium. Hand-in-hand with this raising of the age of the demographic went a rise in expense. Comics ceased to be casual purchases made by pre-pubescents in preference to a chocolate bar while mooching in what the British call sweet shops and the Americans mom-and-pop stores. Instead, they became the studiously collected and carefully preserved investments of people of student-age plus. They came printed not on the flimsy paper that was once considered all that they merited, but on thick, often glossy matter. Along with the higher grade of paper went deluxe formats, multiple cover variants and holofoil covers. They also sometimes came not in periodical format or frequency but bound as 'graphic novels'. Not only were they increasingly more expensive than traditional comics, but they were less visible. To buy them, one had to trek to a specialist outlet. In the States – where they are termed direct-market stores – such outlets were by 1992 responsible for 70% of all comic book sales, as opposed to 6% in 1978.

In the 1990s, the comics industry changed again as it began to be taken over by a new generation of writers and artists. This generational change completed the medium's journey from being populated by people – especially at senior level – who did not themselves read comics in their free time to being staffed exclusively by people who were also consumers. The fact of such people not being indifferent to the product they were purveying was ostensibly creatively ideal. However, it transpired that the latest generation possessed, hand in hand with love and respect for the medium, an unfortunate propensity to disappear up their own backsides. The new Tarzan comics perfectly proved this point.

Although the first Dark Horse product in June 1995 was straightforward enough, that would seem to be because *Tarzan: A Tale of Mugambi* – a one-off written by Darko Macan and illustrated by Igor Korde – was originally intended for publication by Malibu. The following month brought the Dark Horse style of – and the current general comics penchant for – what-ifs and parallel realities. *Tarzan vs. Predator at the Earth's Core* was a four-parter with scripts by Walter Simonson and art by Lee Weeks. That this mini-series saw Tarzan travelling to the Inner World was reasonable enough in light of the fact that Burroughs had once engineered such a crossover in his own work. However, as if the perils of the Mahars and Horibs were not enough, Dark Horse decided to throw in a monster from another creator's franchise, namely the man-eating alien that had first become famous in a 1987 Arnold Schwarzenegger movie, to which they held the comic-book rights. There's no denying that such team-ups are fleetingly intriguing, in the same way as can be fantasising about a football team line-up whose inclusions are not inhibited by era or nationality. However, whereas such fantasy-league team selections are impossible by definition, comic creatives have the means to put their dreams into action. The results are almost always proof that such dreams are best left to barroom debate. *Tarzan vs. Predator at the Earth's Core* was followed in January 1996 by another crossover four-parter, *Tarzan/John Carter: Warlords of Mars*, this one written by Bruce Jones and illustrated by Bret Blevins.

July of that year saw Dark Horse begin a monthly Tarzan title, the first American Tarzan comic with a regular schedule since Marvel's late-'70s book. This publication (which must have seemed boringly conventional to those who liked the Dark Horse crossover special events) lasted 20 issues.

Although they did issue a conventional adaptation of *The Return of Tarzan* as a 1997 three-parter, and although they handily reprinted European Russ Manning strips and long out-of-print Dell/Gold Key stories, Dark Horse generally seemed either unable or unwilling to refrain from indulging their tell-you-what-would-be-really-cool? fanboy whims. Tarzan met Carson Napier of Venus in a 1998 four-parter, re-visited Pellucidar in the anthology title *Dark Horse Presents* the same year, and in 1999 was in Pellucidar yet again in Mike Grell's four-part *The Savage Heart*. By the time of the four-part *Batman/Tarzan: Claws of the Cat-Woman* at the end of '99, there was a suspicion that inebriation and/or dare-you games lay behind story and team-up decisions. Overlapping with that book was Igor Kordey's *The Rivers of Blood*, a four-parter that appeared to display discipline in not shipping in characters from another universe – until the moment the reader discovered it had guest-starring roles for Carl Jung and Sigmund Freud. A two-part adaptation of Disney's concurrent animated Tarzan film the same year was unusual in being conventional and brief. It was back to chicken-dare in 2001 for the three-part *Superman/Tarzan, Sons of the Jungle*. Writer Chuck Dixon posited an alternate reality (i.e. an alternate fiction) wherein young Kal-El crash-lands not in Smallville but Africa, disrupting the mutiny that in Burroughs' book stranded John Clayton in the jungle and handing that fate of being raised by apes to the last son of Krypton. In a climax in

Opar, a Clayton who has grown up decadent encounters an apeman even more superhumanly powerful than Burroughs envisaged. As with so much of Dark Horse's Tarzan output, great talent, high production values and undeniable love for the source were invested in an enterprise that ultimately begged the question, 'What for?'

Of course, ERB, Inc may have cared less about such issues than exploiting their property. That the premium prices now commanded by comics had offset their increasing specialism meant that there was still big money to be made in the medium. Unfortunately, this bonanza was one in which Tarzan was unable to participate owing to the fact that his name no longer had the cachet it once did. *Sons of the Jungle* was to be the last official Tarzan US or UK comic until 2012.

In 1996, Max and Micheline Keller returned to the ape-man character with whom they had thus far had mixed TV success.

Following the savage-in-the-city angle of *Tarzan in Manhattan* and the eco-warrior approach of the Wolf Larson series, they now put a third spin on the character with *Tarzan: The Epic Adventures*. Micheline Keller: 'Our partner came to us with the idea of doing a [series of] one-hour [episodes]. The idea was to go back to the Edgar Rice Burroughs vision of a much more sci-fi Tarzan.' Keller denies assumptions that this series, preceded a month before by a two-hour telemovie, took its cue from recent sword, sandals and supernaturalism series like *Xena: Warrior Princess* and *Hercules: The Legendary Journeys* (the latter even similar in title construction). However, it certainly leaned toward a mysticism that was a half-way house between the Burroughs Tarzan novels of oddity-inhabited lost cities and the sword-and-sorcery domain of Conan. She also reveals that the Kellers' production partners – the Siegel brothers – were in the creative driving seat: 'Since we had done Tarzan so much, and I was doing *Acapulco Heat*, I thought, "Well, let them be in charge of this one."' Keller was not happy with the Siegels' decision to dispense with African wildlife ('Everybody loves the animals').

As a fan of family-orientated fare, she also didn't agree with the tenor of the series, saying, 'It's a more grown-up show. It's got a bit more violence in it.'

In casting, the Kellers returned to their first Tarzan actor: 'We took Joe Lara back because it was not an international co-production, so we could have an American.' Not that the *Tarzan in Manhattan* star didn't have to beat out competition like anyone else. Keller: 'There was a wonderful Australian that I considered very much. His name was Ingo [Rademacher]. He did a brilliant audition.' Mercifully, an ape-man with an Aussie accent was an absurdity that was not brought into being (even if it was only deferred). Lara, now 33, donned the loincloth and boots for a show that couldn't have been more different to his failed pilot of 1989. His flowing locks were immediately an improvement on Larson's in being both dark and alien to a hairdryer. Also making a return appearance from a previous Keller Tarzan project was Lydie Denier, the Wolf Larson series' Jane, who became in the *Epic Adventures* pilot Collette de Coude.

The pilot – titled *Tarzan's Return* and directed by Brian Yuzna – was broadcast on 28 August 1996. The script by Burton Armus featured the ape-man and his friend Mugambi following to Pellucidar Russian villains Rokoff and Paulvitch in pursuit of a crystal amulet stolen from the Countess de Coude. In the world at the earth's core (entered not via mechanised burrowing or a polar hole but a portal opened by the amulet), the ape-man encounters the Mahars (here an all-women race) and their enemy Jana, a beautiful savage.

The pilot set up the series quite well. However, its relatively high production values held out false hope: once into the weekly grind, a certain formulaicness and patchiness set in. There was, though, more fidelity to Burroughs in *Tarzan: The Epic Adventures* than in most modern live-action productions, as can be gleaned from the opening voiceover for each episode: 'Tarzan. Orphaned at birth in darkest Africa, raised by the great apes, he grew up in the primitive world of the jungle until fate brought him face to face with his past. Taking his rightful place as Earl of Greystoke,

Tarzan soon became disenchanted with civilisation. He returned home to Africa. Tarzan, Lord of the Jungle!' The silver Tarzan-with-lion series logo was based on the work of J Allen St John.

Yet the programme is Burroughs' Tarzan seen through a distorting lens. That the pilot featured elements or characters from the novels *The Return of Tarzan*, *The Beasts of Tarzan* and *Tarzan at the Earth's Core* indicated that the series' nearly 20 writers did not lack familiarity with Burroughs books. However, they seem to have been afflicted by production exigencies. D'Arnot, La and Amtorans also appear, but, as with the previously mentioned characters, not in the exact configurations and circumstances originally penned by Burroughs. Lara drawls in the traditional Tarzan actor's Americanese. Black marks to the producers, too, for in the episode 'Tarzan and the Demon Within' giving the ape-man a fear of enclosed spaces, something emphatically not in the prose ape-man's stoical psychological make-up. The same can be said of the way Tarzan is habitually depicted as wrestling with his man/ape dual nature. To be fair, such inner dilemmas do at least underline the adult orientation of the show: other producers wouldn't have bothered with such stuff in their pursuit of an excuse for fight scenes. (Another example of the older demographic tilted at is the thong sported by bad girl Mora in the pilot.) Also admirable is the decision to make this a period piece, even if the dialogue rarely conveys the early 20th century timeframe.

Leaps from even Burroughs' more fantastical Tarzan stories include spell-casting, power-thrumming crystals and a villainess shooting lasers from her eyes. Although these are a little too much, the overarching premise is on the whole more interesting than that of the Ron Ely series (debuted only 11 days amiss of exactly 30 years earlier), which looks earthbound and hidebound in comparison. The location shooting creates an additional layer of lushness. Keller: 'We initially shot the first two-hour at the Disney studios in Orlando, Florida, but that ended up being too expensive. We had to rethink it, so we moved it to Johannesburg and the series was shot in Sun City.'

With his creepy monsters and sweeping exotic sets, special effects supervisor John Buechler rises well to the challenge of the greatest volume of visual tricks yet required by a Tarzan project on a consistent basis, especially considering the low budgets with which he clearly had to work. Complementing his endeavours are some nicely exotic music and sound effects.

After the death of Edgar Rice Burroughs, the author's estate had waited 16 years before giving the go-ahead to a writer to continue Tarzan's print adventures. After a gap of another 30 years, it is almost beyond belief that, with the second official adult non-Burroughs Tarzan novel, ERB, Inc once again authorised nothing more than a novelisation.

Says Robert R Barrett, 'Ballantine/Del Rey received permission from ERB, Inc to have R A Salvatore write a novel based on the new Tarzan TV series, hoping to generate interest in the show.' Salvatore had been a published author for less than a decade but was already responsible for 20 books. His was a writing genre unmistakably in the same science-fantasy area that Burroughs had pioneered, but one that adhered to rules now codified to an almost absurd and anal degree, exemplified by an obsession with chronicling mystical quests in almost *de rigueur* trilogy or quartet format, with attention drawn to the number of each individual part as though it denoted a sociological milestone. Accomplished in his field then, Salvatore has gone on to achieve a plateau of success and influence within it for which there is possibly no suitable superlative.

Salvatore was a Burroughs fan, although he points out, 'I was always most interested in Pellucidar.' He explains of the way he got the gig to write a novelisation of the pilot of *Tarzan: The Epic Adventures*, 'I was working with Del Rey at the time, both for my DemonWars novels and some *Star Wars* opportunities. One of the editors, Steve Saffel, thought I'd be good for the job. I had never done a novelisation to that point, so I thought it might be fun.' Although an established writer of original novels, he says he did not consider a novelisation a demotion. 'It's hard to consider doing anything with the work of someone like Burroughs a step down. Don't get me wrong, I'm not big on novelisations and don't plan on doing any more unless the perfect project fell my way. But when it's a giant like Burroughs, or Lucas, well, it might be worth looking at the offer more closely.'

Salvatore had read neither the Fritz Leiber nor the Joe Lansdale Tarzan books, and he did not try to resolve the *Epic Adventures*' inconsistencies with the Burroughs oeuvre: 'I knew that this was being done with the blessing of the Burroughs' estate (his grandchildren, I was told). In that context, it's not really my place to come into a project half-way through and presume such things ... There were a couple of things that bothered me about the script and the director's cut, and I brought them up, but I was told that much of it would be fixed in production and, really, that was above my pay grade.' Salvatore states that he wasn't aiming his book at Burroughs fans: 'Since I expected that most of the people who watched the show would have no idea of Burroughs' original work, or even who he was (sad, but true), I was just trying to take that script and make it as fun a read as I could manage.'

Like Leiber before him, Salvatore did the best he could with the material he was given. His 280-page *Tarzan: The Epic Adventures*, published by Ballantine imprint Del Rey in 1996, follows the trajectory of Burton Armus' teleplay, but whereas Armus – a writing veteran of the likes of *Kojak*, *The Fall Guy* and *Knight Rider* – had to conform to anodyne American TV conventions, Salvatore was free to demolish them. His transposition of the narrative saw him inject into it something for which he is celebrated: mass, bloody and quasi-balletic fight scenes. 'Writing action sequences is my forte and my love,' he says. 'I want readers to experience a battle as if they're in it. I do this all the time. Other than that expansion, though, I really wasn't given much latitude.'

Salvatore reports that the book did not sell very well. 'I don't recall the numbers off-hand, but they were far lower than for anything else I've ever done.' However, this was not the main disappointment the project brought him. 'The biggest draw for me to take the job was the proposition of meeting [Burroughs'] grandchildren and discussing his work with them,' he says. 'It never happened.'

A range of action figures from Trendmasters, Inc was another tie-in attending *Tarzan: The Epic Adventures*. 'We really did try to do a big push,' says Keller. However, ratings for the series were disappointing. 'Worldwide, the show did not perform as well as the half-hours,' says Keller. 'I think it was because of lack of animals and that warmth there was in the half-hours.' Says Robert R Barrett of its performance in the home US market, 'It was not a show that was developed by any network. It was developed to be syndicated and purchased by any TV station that wished to run it – whether it was first-run or re-run ... There weren't many stations that purchased it.'

This was not the same as the Kellers losing money. The ape-man was still profitable enough for the pair to be eager to continue exploiting the TV rights they held to the character. Accordingly, when *The Epic Adventures* had run its course they started developing their fourth iteration of Tarzan. For their new live-action Tarzan project, the Kellers lined up Xavier DeClie to play the ape-man and planned the re-introduction of Jane, not seen in *The Epic Adventures* and referred to within it only as the ape-man's ex. Jane's role, it was announced, was to be given to a competition winner. Keller says, 'It was going to be a whole reboot again ... He was going to be back in the jungle, maybe a little bit more wild, more naturally animalistic.' However, the plans dissipated. 'We just didn't have the financing for it at the time.'

The Kellers thought of other ways of exploiting the character. 'We had almost reached an agreement with Sandra Galfas to do a Tarzan half-hour animated series,' says Keller. 'Then all of a sudden she said, "No, I'm sorry, we're going to go with Disney and they want to hold back on any other Tarzan projects." Can't blame them. [We were] very disappointed, because we actually had a company that wanted to do 65 half-hours.'

Thus came to an end the Kellers' association with the ape-man. Keller admits that their penchant for family fare sometimes worked against the Tarzan character. 'We did not portray him that savagely. We had a big discussion about whether or not he should eat [raw] meat and we felt that he should not. In the Burroughs books, he was chomping down all the time on animals. We never did the really rough, tough Tarzan.'

Nonetheless, the Kellers performed the crucial role of purveying Tarzan to a new generation. Nor did they do it by halves: the two TV movies and two TV series they produced over the course of a decade make them responsible for more Tarzan screen hours than anybody in history except Sy Weintraub.

Stanley S Canter may have been only the nominal co-producer of *Greystoke*, but he was certainly the driving force behind its (also nominal) follow-up *Tarzan and the Lost City*.

He had reputedly envisioned the project back in the mid-'80s but didn't formally acquire the rights until 1991, when he set about co-producing with Dieter Geissler and Michael Lakewith. By this time, of course, the original crew had scattered to the four winds and Christopher Lambert was too old to reprise the title role. Nonetheless, the film's visual effects supervisor Julian Parry later recalled that Canter habitually referred to it as *Greystoke 2*. However, while *Greystoke* was a much seen, multiple-Oscar-nominated movie, *Tarzan and the Lost City* is an uncelebrated project largely unknown to the general public.

On the surface, it is a promisingly Burroughsonian production. The film is again a period piece, taking place in 1913. Tarzan's alter-ego John Clayton is represented. Opar forms a crucial part of the story. However, the bad news starts with that generic title, which is admittedly Burroughsonian, but in a bad way: it could have served for any of half a dozen substandard Burroughs Tarzan books. Then there is the way scriptwriters Bayard Johnson and J Anderson Black engineer the ape-man's return to Africa on the eve of his wedding to Jane: a vision of things amiss back 'home' is projected across the ocean to the Greystoke family castle by Oparian shaman friend Mugambi via a lion's sight-line. This ridiculous fantasy device instantly undermines the film's grand ambitions and intended faithfulness to Burroughs. Additionally, there is a disconnect between this movie and the one to which it subtly affects to be a sequel. Tarzan had renounced both civilisation and Jane at the end of *Greystoke*. Additionally, he had not previously been portrayed as having any dealings with Oparians.

Perhaps the main fealty to *Greystoke* is a reluctance to use the Tarzan name. Although the opening crawl provides a new and not displeasing explanation for the origin of the ape-man's moniker ('The natives called him Tarzan'), elsewhere he is referred to as anything but: Greystoke, Clayton, John or (derogatorily) ape-man.

Nor does *Tarzan and the Lost City* possess *Greystoke*'s lushness. A theatrical release that can't attract Hollywood investors is almost always destined to look tatty. The South African location shots provide some attractive scenery, but this German-Australian enterprise otherwise reveals its poverty in such things as Germans playing characters supposed to be British, risible ape costumes and an Opar scaled down from a city to not much more than a pyramid.

The main casting is bad. Christopher Lambert may have lacked a lot, but we are instantly reminded by Casper Van Dien (Johnny Rico in the previous year's *Starship Troopers*) of at least what he mercifully wasn't: square-jawed, brown-haired and clean-cut. The actor is at least buff and boots-free. Also miscast are Steven Waddington (too gentle-featured to properly bring to life villain Nigel Ravens) and Jane March, the irregular angles of whose face have never been associated with Jane Porter's more apple-cheeked beauty.

Tarzan arrives in the Dark Continent in the middle of Ravens' plans to plunder Opar. The latter is here not a bestial dump but the cradle of civilisation. The ape-man is friendly with its inhabitants and resolves to stop Ravens. Matters, though, are complicated by his intended following him and needing to be rescued from peril herself. Not that Englishwoman Miss Porter is a helpless damsel: she sports a gun, slugs whiskey and puffs cigars, a feisty, modernistic view of womanhood that is at odds with the period setting but is a juxtaposition that will recur in Tarzan fare. Also anachronistic is an eco-warrior strain. The funny-endearing stunts engaged in by Tarzan's Cheeta-like chimp friend are redolent of the Weissmuller-era. The truncated, bloodless yodel Van Dien produces emphatically is not.

Where the film isn't mimicking *Raiders of the Lost Ark*, it descends into *Xena/Tarzan: The Epic Adventures* territory: Mugambi weaves magic spells. With one, he makes skeletons grow flesh and become fighting warriors. With another, he places Tarzan in a loincloth as if he is his Ken doll. (Up to approaching the hour mark, the most primeval Tarzan's appearance gets is a pair of cut-off trousers.) Mugambi's powers beg the question of why he needs the purely earthly help Tarzan is able to offer.

The throbbing native tableaux and the explosive bickering amongst the villains underscore the unfortunate fact that the weakest parts of the film are the ones involving Tarzan, which feature would-be cute anthropomorphism, uninteresting domestic notes and motivational nonsensicalities.

While some of Swiss director Carl Schenkel's transitions are rather clever, a scene in which the camera endlessly circles a bickering Tarzan and Jane is just clever-clever – and dizzying. The inaugural screen credit for scriptwriter J Anderson Black did not lead to better things – which would hardly have been a difficult achievement.

Initial reports suggested that *Tarzan and the Lost City* would be 102 minutes long, but upon its April 1998 release it mustered only 83. Some critics suggested that, sub-standard though it was, it sufficed as family fare. Canter seemed to indicate that this was his intention ('I structured the story on the action serials of the past, as I wanted to make a high adventure film with a really interesting love story'). However, that objective was undermined by a PG rating.

For Burroughs diehards, the film had one saving grace: Casper Van Dien was the first actor in the 80-year history of the franchise to attempt an English accent, even if the attempt was none too successful.

PART NINE: ENTER DISNEY

The '90s had been a good decade for the ape-man profile-wise, but 1999 was truly a Tarzan bumper year. The digital games *Disney's Tarzan* and *Tarzan Action Game* (platform: IBM-compatible PC) were just a fraction of it. A new Tarzan animated feature was released on video, a blockbuster Tarzan film hit the cinemas and, best of all for Burroughs fans, a brand-new Tarzan novel for adults made it to the bookshelves.

The least impressive of the bunch was *Tarzan of the Apes*, released on home video in March as part of the Sony Wonder *Enchanted Tales* series. (When DVD superseded the video medium, it was reissued as a double-set with, of all things, Moses story *A Tale of Egypt*.) Produced by Diane Eskenazi, its 1997 derivation and 48-minute length (i.e. about one hour if it had been interspersed with commercials) leads to the suspicion that it was a made-for-TV film that no television channel wanted and was put out three months before the release of the Disney Tarzan movie when the makers realised that they could ride the back of the latter's publicity and maybe even confuse some people into thinking that theirs *was* the Disney movie.

Although it's no Disney production, one can't quite see why it found no broadcasting takers. The animation is cheap but perfectly adequate, as is the soundtrack, which mixes public-domain classical anthems like 'Ride of the Valkyries' with three specially-commissioned songs (including a theme tune for the ape-man) in the mould of the set-piece numbers in Disney's *The Lion King*. Although it's aimed at pre-pubescents, there is even something in it for the grey-haired Burroughs fan in its faithfulness to source. Everything in Mark Young's script is much as it is in the novel *Tarzan of the Apes*, with what changes there are almost all due to the exigencies of aiming at a young target audience (Tarzan's father dies of natural causes, bloodshed is minimal), plot compression (the cabin is not built by Tarzan's father but discovered by him, Mangani become more conventional apes), political correctness (black maid Esmeralda becomes a cockney sparrer) and the need for a tidy resolution (Tarzan doesn't have to wait 'til the next instalment to get his title and the girl). The Samsonite Tarzan herein looks fine, although the ape-man is again given an illogical American accent (voice actor uncredited).

A Disney Tarzan movie – and the first animated ape-man story to be released in cinemas – was a somewhat different proposition. ERB fans might have blanched at the idea of a Tarzan cartoon on the grounds that it would continue the, for them, unwelcome shunting of the character into a juvenile market that his creator had never intended for him. However, way back in 1936 Burroughs had been all for an animated feature with plenty of humorous content, with his only caveat – expressed in a letter to one of his sons – that the 'cartoon must be good. It must approximate Disney excellence.' Then, as in 1999, Disney was a by-word for the best in animation.

The Jungle Book – that work with which *Tarzan of the Apes* has so much in common and from which it partly took its cue – had of course been the subject of a charming Disney adaptation (1967), so a version of the Tarzan story by the same studio seems so logical a step that it's surprising that it didn't happen sooner. No doubt if Disney did make a previous approach regarding licensing, the fact is lost in the mists of time and Cyril Ralph Rothmund's impenetrable filing system.

The screenplay for Disney's 85-minute film – titled simply *Tarzan* and released in June '99 – was written by Tab Murphy and Bob Tzudiker & Noni White. (In film-writing credits, an ampersand means a direct collaboration, an "and" delineates a separate writing process.) The opening is very clipped, involving an unnamed couple fleeing with their baby a ship aflame for unspecified reasons. They build a treehouse that would be implausibly elaborate even without their apparent lack of luggage and tools. Kala, meanwhile, loses her baby to a leopard (here given the generic Burroughs lioness name Sabor). Kala's tribe are neither Mangani nor chimpanzee nor an indeterminate species: for the first time ever, a Tarzan adaptation depicts the apes who raise him as gorillas. In the best scene in the movie, Kala tentatively opens the door of the eerily quiet cabin and finds another scene of devastation left by Sabor: bloody paw prints indicate that the shipwrecked couple have met the same fate as her infant. However, their baby is still alive and the instantly smitten Kala takes it back to her tribe. Her mate here is not Tublat but Kerchak. Although he is not the raging brute of Burroughs' original, Kerchak is gruffly uninterested in raising the human who he feels can never take the place of the child he and Kala have lost. When Kala decides to call the babe 'Tarzan', it is merely a conjunction of syllables carrying no meaning. 'Tarzan? Okay – he's your baby,' exclaims Terk, a sassy female youngster of the tribe.

We see Tarzan growing up in an Africa with no visible black people. With no explanation, he graduates from the nappy in which he was found to a loincloth. 'Why don't you just come up with your own sound?' Kala says to her skilled mimic step-son, and he does so in the form of a Weissmuller-like yodel that doubles as his victory cry later on in life. Terk is one of Tarzan's two lifelong friends, the other being an elephant named Tantor, who like, the rest of the depicted pachyderms, is red in colour. Despite his superficial assimilation, Tarzan is aware of being different to the apes, not least because of the non-acceptance of the stern Kerchak.

In another first for depictions of the ape-man, although Tarzan can stand upright, he is often shown walking on all-fours. It both makes sense and works visually. A more dubious innovation is his cruising down trees as though riding a wave. Although optically pleasing, this tree surfing brings another cinema-created nonsense to his arboreal travel mode to go with the vine-swinging (also depicted). This is particularly absurd considering that gorillas are amongst the few apes not comfortable in trees, with the only extended periods they spend in branches being when sleeping in nests.

As is now becoming the Tarzan norm, bloodshed is largely absent. For example, although as an adolescent Tarzan kills a menacing leopard with a spearhead he has fashioned to bring down fruit, he and his antagonist are discretely out of sight when the weapon is plunged.

When Tarzan is an adult, a small group of humans enter the jungle on a mission to study gorillas. Professor Porter and his daughter Jane – both English – are two of the trio. The third is a man named Clayton. This latter character has nothing to do with the Greystoke clan, for there is no Greystoke clan in this film and Tarzan's background remains unexplained. Clayton is ostensibly here for the same zoological purposes as his companions, although he is troublingly trigger-happy. When Jane gets detached from her party, Tarzan rescues her from a pack of baboons of the lesser-known Hades variety. He is entranced by the first hairless ape he can remember meeting and subsequently angry at Kala for not informing him that he is of a different species. In an unintended but perfect encapsulation of the inherent difficulties with the Tarzan name, there is an awkward moment when he tells Jane his handle: its humanistic enunciation is at complete odds with the simian jabbering in which he had just been engaging with the hell-baboons.

A montage follows in which the ape-man is taught by Jane of the world beyond the jungle via, amongst other things, a slideshow. (This is a Victorian-set tale, although the period is not laid on thick.) Jane also instructs him in the English language and good manners. Naturally, Tarzan picks them up with the traditional speed convenient to film plot. With the prospect of Jane's departure looming, a smitten Tarzan persuades her to stay by giving in to her entreaties to take her to see his tribe. This is something Kerchak has expressly forbidden. His consequent fight with Kerchak leaves Tarzan brooding on his identity. Kala enlightens him on this somewhat by taking him for the first time to his parents' cabin. Tarzan puts on his dead father's clothes and prepares to set sail with Jane for the world which he has decided contains his true kind.

On board ship, he walks into a mutiny engineered by Clayton, who is keen to acquire the bounty achievable through captured gorillas. When Tantor and Terk come to the rescue, Tarzan goes back to land ('I came *home*') and saves his tribe from the trappers, assisted by the demon baboons, who recognise a common enemy. In this battle, Clayton fatally wounds Kerchak, then, during a clash with Tarzan in the treetops, falls to his death. Before his life ebbs away, Kerchak awards Tarzan the accolade of calling him 'my son.'

Jane makes to leave, but in the rowboat heading for the anchored ship her father points out, 'But you love him.' When she swims back to shore, her father decides to join her. Cut to Tarzan, Jane and a loinclothed Professor Porter joyously swinging and tree-surfing, watched by Kala, Terk and Tantor. The movie ends with Tarzan and Jane on a high branch and the ape-man beating his chest as he yodels across the jungle.

The animation – directed by Chris Buck and Kevin Lima – benefits from computer techniques not in existence in the days of *The Jungle Book*. A process called Deep Canvas deploys CGI backdrops that have the lushness of an oil painting. However, the moody art on one of the film's posters was rather misleading. The characters superimposed on that rich, often gothic backdrop are possessed of the primary colours, doe eyes, toothpaste smiles, unthreatening anthropomorphism and tendency to comic pratfalls that we have long come to expect from Disney. We are also presented with the studio's customary playful incongruities, such as elephants bickering over whether or not piranhas are indigenous to South America and the usually unclothed Terk remarking that the dress she has borrowed from Jane is too revealing.

The only deviation from the Disney pattern is a bowing to current animation trends for the jaggedly exaggerated, and even ugly, something that gives Tarzan a projecting nose and pointy chin. (Curious considering the apparent template. Micheline Keller says, 'I think the look copies our Joe Lara. As did Joe Lara, because everyone was telling Joe Lara that it looked like him.')

Disney's *Jungle Book* is studded with memorable and iconic tunes like 'The Bare Necessities', 'I Wan'na Be Like You' and

'That's What Friends Are For'. It would have been reasonable for Disney to assume they would be delivered a soundtrack just as whistlable when they commissioned rock star Phil Collins to complement Mark Mancina's score: the ex-Genesis man and solo superstar had not shifted umpteen million albums for no reason, even if songs like 'In the Air Tonight' and 'Another Day in Paradise' are cut from darker cloth than the aforementioned jolly Terry Gilkyson and Sherman Brothers numbers. What Collins came up with was a set of the most perplexing anonymity: five bland songs – only two of which were sung by characters, the others being commentary on the action – that nobody could remember once they had left the cinema. Astoundingly, one of them – 'You'll Be In My Heart' – garnered Collins an Academy Award for Best Song. The film's most *Jungle Book*-like musical moment doesn't come from Collins but is an interlude at the landing party's camp in which the apes and Tantor bash out tunes on the likes of saucepans and typewriters.

Although the cast is, of course, unseen, it is still star-studded, including amongst its number Minnie Driver (Jane), Rosie O'Donnell (Terk), Nigel Hawthorne (Professor Porter), Brian Blessed (Clayton) and Glenn Close (the woman who was once the voice of Andie MacDowell's Jane here playing Kala). Yet having gone to the trouble of gathering together a bunch of largely English thesps, the producers lazily sag into the old, illogical he's-got-to-sound-American thought process by picking the very Californian Tony Goldwyn to voice Tarzan. On top of that, the ape tribe have a cacophony of working-class American accents.

A Disney cinema project is by definition a major release. Accordingly, this film put Tarzan centre-stage again. Although *Tarzan* had a large $150m budget, it achieved impressive returns as parents weaned on the likes of the Ron Ely series (but probably not the Burroughs books) dragged their kids to see it. There was a wave of Tarzan merchandise specifically related to the film, including a soundtrack, action figures, interactive computer software and McDonald's Happy Meal giveaway toys. There were also books for juveniles, aimed at a demographic even younger than that of the Tarzan Twins brace (e.g. the *Tarzan Jungle Jam* instalment in the Mouse Works Chunky Roly-Poly Board Book series). However, the real measure of the film's commercial accomplishments is its mildly astonishing number of spin-offs. Two further video games (*Disney's Tarzan Untamed*, 2001, for PlayStation 2 and GameCube and *Disney's Tarzan: Return to the Jungle*, 2002, for Game Boy Advance) was just the start of it. The film bequeathed a sequel (albeit for the home video market), a TV series and even a Broadway musical.

To the Burroughs fan fraternity, Disney's *Tarzan* was admirable more in theory than in reality. It was gratifying that new generations were being introduced to their hero via a blockbuster movie, but it was kid-stuff. Their ideal was a new Tarzan novel for adults that was something more than a fleshed-out screenplay. Almost unbelievably, in June 1999 they got their wish. Ratcheting up the dream-come-true factor for some was the fact that, in finally authorising an all-new, non-adapted adult Tarzan book, ERB, Inc also acknowledged the Tantor in the room, otherwise known as Philip José Farmer.

Although he had racked up over 50 published novels and was an acclaimed, if always controversial, novelist, Farmer must have thought his chance in this area had long gone: lifelong ambitions tend not to come true anyway, but are even less likely to be fulfilled when one is over 80. However, whatever his earthy leanings, and even arguably his desecrations of the ape-man in his previous books, the corporation decided that this time they could no longer ignore Farmer's credentials. Via his agent, Farmer had been lobbying Ballantine Books since the mid-1990s about the possibility of writing a new Tarzan novel. When he was rebuffed by Ballantine editor Steve Saffel in favour of the Salvatore novelisation, Farmer wrote to the fan magazine *Burroughs Bulletin* that his hopes of penning an original Tarzan novel had been 'blown away.' He elaborated, 'It's evident that the Ballantine editors are looking for stories to tie in with the TV

Tarzan series, which will be science-fictional and futuristic.' Judging by the tone of the rest of the letter, this was a matter of no little dismay to Farmer, who – lest we forget – had already seen the *Lost Adventure* gig go to Joe R Lansdale: 'My novel would take place in 1918, would be traditional, and would, I had hoped, sum up the Tarzan mythos and the Tarzan character. Also, since I've been reading the Tarzan books since 1928 and believe, in a sense, that Tarzan really exists, I'd hoped to add some insight into the persona of the Lord of the Jungle. But it's not to be.'

That wistful comment, however, was not the last word. In 1997, Robert R Barrett, friend of both Farmer and Danton Burroughs, was telephoned by the latter and informed that Saffel had contacted ERB, Inc with a proposal for a new Tarzan novel. Barrett was asked by Burroughs' grandson who would be a worthwhile author of such a book. 'I immediately told him that I thought that nobody but Phil Farmer should be chosen,' recalls Barrett. 'Dan agreed with me and [said that he] would pass on that recommendation to Ballantine Books.' Of course, this was an action replay of the situation with *The Lost Adventure*. This time, though, Ballantine did not ignore the endorsement the way that Dark Horse had. On 17 March 1997, Farmer wrote a thank-you letter to Barrett in which he said, 'I'm convinced that you played a large part in Ballantine deciding to let me write a new Tarzan novel.'

Asked why the corporation had never authorised an all-new Tarzan novel before, Barrett says, 'Basically those in charge at ERB, Inc didn't think that anyone could match Ed's original Tarzan novels. Which, in my opinion, is correct.' Farmer may or may not have agreed with that idea, but, as someone who had long been poring over Tarzan novels as obsessively as a teenager re-reads pop magazines, he was energised by the task at hand. Like plenty of Burroughs readers, he had been puzzled by the passage in *Tarzan the Untamed* wherein the ape-man discovers an ancient skeleton and, beneath one of its hands, a cylinder containing a map and a manuscript written in Spanish. Having set up a plot development, Burroughs promptly abandoned it. For a man like Farmer who had displayed a fixation with trying to reconcile the Tarzan novels' internal contradictions, it was a loose strand begging to be tied up. Having said that, the incident and its ramifications formed only a small portion of Farmer's eventual book rather than its crux, a change of plan that was the type of thing, Farmer explained to Barrett in a letter in November 1997, that was 'part of the fiction-writing process.'

When finally published, Farmer's book bore the title *The Dark Heart of Time*. As Tarzan is preoccupied with his search for the abducted Jane – Farmer's story took place between *Tarzan the Untamed* and *Tarzan the Terrible* – he naturally doesn't take time out himself to try to solve the mysteries of the cylinder stashed at the bottom of his quiver. However, when he is captured by a safari he inexplicably finds on his trail, he is informed of its contents by one of his Spanish-speaking abductors. Even at this point, the manuscript is an irrelevance compared with the fact that Tarzan has been taken prisoner and, more importantly, has been distracted from his hunt for his beloved. It gradually emerges that the man who has ordered his abduction is American tycoon James D Stonecraft, who is dismayed that his status as the richest man in the world cannot revive his fading health. He is pursuing Tarzan because he is convinced the ape-man possesses the secret to immortality. One of Stonecraft's employees is a being named Ben-go-utor, a halfway house between man and bear whose species is on the brink of extinction. Although Ben-go-utor initially uses his Tarzan-level spoor-following powers to help ensnare the ape-man, he does so under duress: his own beloved is being held prisoner. He eventually teams up with Tarzan. One aspect of the book that is authentically Burroughs-like is that the ape-man learns Ben-go-utor's language preposterously quickly. Another is ridiculous coincidence: at this point, Tarzan comes quite by chance across the lost city detailed in the Spanish manuscript. In another coincidence, he discovers there an ancient priestess called Rafmana who, as it happens, possesses immortality. She is the guardian of the Glittering Tree, which contains the mystical Dark Heart of Time.

The omission of the word 'Tarzan' from the arty-farty title was a mistake Burroughs would never have made. Farmer had drawn up a list of 11 possible titles, all containing 'Tarzan', but it was he – not Ballantine – who ultimately decided to truncate *Tarzan and the Dark Heart of Time*. A minor misstep, perhaps, but the writing presents more serious ones. Finally getting the chance to fulfil what he describes in the dedication as 'a 70-year-old ambition,' Farmer turns in a work less impressive than his pseudo-Tarzan material like *Lord of the Trees* and *Lord Tyger*. Although his plot is action-packed and often excitingly piles staggering quantities of peril on the ape-man, his narrative abilities prove unequal to those of Burroughs. Far from being marked by the smooth-flowing and evocative style of the latter at his peak, they are characterised – at least by this late point – by a fussiness that works against the action. Although never quite as momentum-crushingly pedantic as J T Edson in his Bunduki books, Farmer can't resist remarking on irrelevant matters during combat sequences. His prose is bitty, repetitious and sometimes confusing. The book could have happily lost a chunk of its nearly 300 pages.

Leaving aside the style, the content is speckled with things that give the reader pause. Explains Barrett, 'A whole series of letters between Phil, Dan and myself were sent, beginning in early 1998. Dan had asked me to read Phil's Tarzan novel and to point out any discrepancies between Phil's characterisation of Tarzan and Edgar Rice Burroughs'. I had told Dan that I would be happy to do this, but only if Phil was able to write the novel as he saw fit and not try to write it as Burroughs would. I pointed out a few instances in which I felt that he had Tarzan doing things that did not match up with Burroughs' characterisation. Phil changed most of these, only arguing on a couple in which he did not agree with me, and [neither] I, nor Dan, argued with him about them, letting them stand ... I'd rather not discuss what I suggested that he change in the manuscript or which of my suggestions he chose to ignore. There really weren't that many and they changed nothing in the story.'

Some of Farmer's tweaks to the Tarzan template are reasonable. Burroughs was an old-fashionedly 'proper' man even for his times and would never have shown Tarzan eating a rat or a rotting elephant. When Farmer does, we understand that this is exactly what someone with Tarzan's bestial upbringing would have done, even if we accept the notion of inherited nobility. Ditto for Tarzan's incredible cold-bloodedness and sadistic mischief: he wreaks havoc with his pursuers and former captives via such methods as killing one of their porters and tossing his decapitated head into their midst. There is a difference between logical projection, however, and making a character behave in ways that are not in his established nature. Farmer has the ape-man weeping when he sees Kala via the aegis of the Dark Heart of Time. Surely the world's self-declared foremost expert on Tarzan knows that he never cries? The other major liberty taken with the Tarzan template is dragging the ape-man into the realm of hardcore science fiction. It's interesting that Farmer had read Roddenberry's Tarzan screenplay, because he commits the same mistake the *Star Trek* creator did in introducing a stranded alien species. One of the two lost cities in the book is the City Beneath the Waters, established long ago by extra-terrestrials. Their Dark Heart of Time enables people who touch it to see beyond the confines of mortals. (Tarzan chooses to look at where Jane is being held, as well as at his ape step-mother.) Rafmana answers to the Ghost Frog, a hideous alien monster. People sacrificed to it end up in a living death in its belly. All of this out-of-place fantastical stuff simply feels impertinent. Moreover, although the strictures of writing an authorised Tarzan book meant that he had to 'behave', and so his customary sexual frankness, scatology and extreme violence are absent, Farmer throws in a sadistic ending that Burroughs would never have: Tarzan causes Stonecraft to drop dead of a heart attack by ringing him up and virtually saying 'Boo!'

Most importantly, the story doesn't make sense: there is no

reason for Stonecraft to believe that the ape-man possesses the secret of immortality either through his appearance (he is stated as being a mere 30, so wouldn't have looked suspiciously young) or – had Farmer chosen to go post-modern – the published chronicles of his adventures: this all takes place a decade-and-a-half before the appearance of *Tarzan's Quest*, the first place Stonecraft might have read that the ape-man does not age like the rest of us. Some have suggested that Farmer was leaving some dangling plot threads for a sequel. That the inconsistencies were more likely the product of ineptitude was revealed by a September 1997 interview, after *The Dark Heart of Time*'s completion but almost two years before its publication, where the author stated his lack of interest in a second book: 'I just wanted to write one, so I could fulfil a childhood ambition.'

The appearance of the Disney movie and Farmer's book in the same month was not the original plan. Farmer explained in a letter to *Burroughs Bulletin* that *The Dark Heart of Time* was originally due to hit the shelves not too long after *Tarzan and the Lost City*: 'It was rescheduled because the new Tarzan movie bombed so badly. Ballantine didn't want the book to come out on the movie's heels. Bad association. So the novel was reset to appear with the new Disney Tarzan animated film and the flood of children's items, games, T-shirts, toys, etc. The reasoning was that the book would be the only Tarzan item for adults to turn to.'

ERBivores (as they were now decreasingly called) had waited a long, long time for an all-new adult Tarzan novel – 35 years to be precise. Compounding their general disappointment when it did emerge was the fact that it was a dead-end. Some follow-ups to the Farmer book by other authors were envisaged by Del Rey but none appeared. 'Danton told me that the book did not sell that well, and because of that Ballantine/Del Rey chose not to commission further Tarzan novels,' says Barrett. The flat, unrevealing title of *The Dark Heart of Time* and the underwhelming cover art (a shaded human face and a couple of big leaves) can't have helped the novel's chances. (That the phrase 'A Tarzan novel' appears in a banner at the bottom is, one might uncharitably conclude, less to provide clarification than to pointedly slap a registered trademark symbol next to the character's name.) With this book, prose Tarzan once again sputtered to a halt.

Whatever the faults of Sony Wonder's, Disney's or Farmer's interpretation of the ape-man, 1999 had been a good year for the character. Although he could never recapture the extended period – amounting to four or five decades – when swinging on a pretend vine was a nigh-universal childhood rite of passage, in terms of profile Tarzan departed the 20th Century on a cultural high.

Tarzan: The Biography

PART TEN: POST-MILLENNIAL TARZAN

The first of the several spin-offs from the Disney Tarzan movie was a TV series from the same company. *The Legend of Tarzan* began airing on the United Paramount Network on 3 September 2001 and ran every day of the week except Saturdays. After a first season of 36 half-hour episodes, its second season was more of a coda, consisting of three episodes broadcast in the first week of February 2003, episodes that had previously been released on a home video called *Tarzan and Jane* in July 2002.

As with just about all successful movies that become television shows, *The Legend of Tarzan* was more of the same but diluted. Even the limited ferociousness of the parent movie was not going to be appropriate for a show aired on a children's channel, while its lush animation was not possible in the context of TV production budgets and timeframes. None of the film's stellar cast reprise their roles (Michael T Weiss takes over as Tarzan). Nonetheless, the kids of the Noughties were treated to a much higher grade of animated television Tarzan than their parents had seen as children when sat in front of Filmation's *Tarzan Lord of the Jungle*, even if the new series was shot through with more comedy and cutesiness. This upgrade was partly the consequence of CGI having made high-quality animation cheaper and quicker to produce and partly because of a raising of audience expectations that had long rendered risible the flavourless, formulaic nature of '70s American television.

The series is set after the events of the Disney *Tarzan* movie, taking place in the African home to which the ape-man returned with his new love at the end of that production. Terk, Tantor, Kala, Professor Porter and Jane form the supporting cast. The series opener was rather unpromising, consisting of an episode in which Tarzan is bitten by a venomous spider. Although it gives writer Gary Sperling a chance to depict Jane as a woman of action as she goes off in search of the antidote, the passive scenario for the ape-man rather works against the heroic Tarzan template. Subsequent episodes introduce Opar and La, the Waziri, the Leopard Men, Pellucidar, Nikolas Rokoff, 'One Punch' Mullargan and Stanley Obroski, although little like the way Burroughs first presented them. Keeping with the film's period setting, a pre-presidency Theodore Roosevelt also puts in an appearance, but a more surprising guest slot is that of Burroughs himself in the episode 'Tarzan and the Mysterious Visitor'. In real-life, Burroughs was never a visitor to the Dark Continent, but this story sees an author referred to as 'Ed' (later, his full name is displayed on the manuscript of his first Tarzan book) searching Africa for a reputed missing link. We are introduced herein to the man 'who had no business to tell it to me, or to any other' from whom Burroughs originally wrote that he 'had this story.' He is – at least according to episode writer Madellaine Paxson – a down-on-his-luck Samuel T Philander, friend of Archimedes Porter in the *Tarzan of the Apes* novel. The episode naturally takes liberties with inconveniently undramatic facts, but is also well-researched, identifying *A Princess of Mars* and *The Outlaw of Torn* as Burroughs works that pre-dated *Tarzan of the Apes*. Another episode – 'Tarzan and the Silver Screen' – recalls the post-modernist plot of the book *Tarzan and the Lion Man*, with Tarzan finding himself cast in a movie about himself. The thespian displaced by the ape-man seeks revenge.

Twenty-six different writers contributed episodes (sometimes in combination). The show's mix of seriousness and levity is demonstrated by the episode 'Tarzan and the Rift', which juxtaposes a story about the ape-man tackling sinister trappers with one about a wedge driven between Tantor and Terk by Tantor's new girlfriend.

In the middle of the roll on which Tarzan had been set through the aegis of Disney came another new live-action television depiction of the ape-man.

The series of one-hour episodes that debuted on 5 October 2003 on the new-ish American WB Television Network may have been unimaginatively titled *Tarzan*, but it was a show that was in some senses a real departure from previous depictions of the ape-man. WB's pre-publicity claimed that it was in the tradition of *Smallville*, their edgy, knowing Superman updating. Perhaps significantly, the WB pilot was originally titled *Tarzan and Jane*, for there was also a tinge of another TV re-imagining, namely the 1990s ABC series *Lois & Clark*, which put a contemporary and slightly feminist slant on the Superman franchise.

Producer David Gerber had an idea for a fish-out-of-water story involving Tarzan in New York. He met with young writer/producer Eric Kripke. The latter told Joe Nazzaro of *Starlog*, 'My epiphany was, "Let's view the story through Jane's eyes, because she's from civilization, so we can relate to her."' For the first time ever in any adaptation in any medium, Tarzan doesn't sport either a loincloth or singlet. Kripke explained to Nazzaro, 'Here are my rules: no loincloth and no jungle yell. He isn't Spider-Man, so it's important to keep his actions grounded.'

In this rejig, John Clayton is the nephew of billionaire Richard Clayton (Mitch Pileggi), CEO of Greystoke Industries. John was proclaimed dead when his parents' plane crashed in the Republic of Congo. Unbeknownst to the outside world, he was kept safe and raised by jungle animals, chiefly apes. Twenty years later, he was discovered alive and unwell (traumatised by his experiences, he initially barely speaks). Richard Clayton keeps John – who goes by 'Tarzan,' although the word is rarely uttered – locked up, ostensibly for safety reasons related to his savagery but in fact more to maintain control of the corporation to which John is the rightful heir. John's aunt Katherine, played by *Xena: Warrior Princess* star Lucy Lawless, takes Tarzan's side against her brother in the latter's quest to 'rehabilitate' John by civilising him.

Jane Porter (Sarah Wayne Callies) is an NYPD detective who lives with her younger sister Nicki (Leighton Meester) and works alongside black maverick Sam Sullivan (Miguel A Núñez Jr). She stumbles upon Tarzan after he has escaped his uncle's clutches and is living on the streets. Following an incident in which Tarzan saves Jane from falling off a building, the two are smitten with each other (not altogether convincingly). Tarzan proceeds to follow Jane around this urban jungle and help her solve cases. She often finds herself having to rein him in as he spurns society's laws and tries to mete out the sort of justice that prevails in the terrain with which he is more familiar. All this is underscored by a soft-rock soundtrack that is an integral part of a show whose intended demographic is largely teenage girls.

The show's star Travis Fimmel was a first on a couple of counts. Never before had an actor playing Tarzan had an Australian accent (albeit ineptly disguised). More to the point, never before had one looked like a girl. A Calvin Klein model turned thespian, Fimmel is not handsome but pretty, with sensual lips and cat-like eyes framed by cascading blonde tresses. The androgyny is part of an overall approach that seeks to undermine expected conventions.

Not that conventions can be completely subverted. The trouble with transplanting Tarzan to the big city is that the only way to meet a television drama series' necessity for conflict is to pit him against bad guys, and the easiest way to do that is to purvey what is effectively a cop show. Tarzan may have massive upper-body strength, refined tracking skills and a guileless perspective on morality and politesse, but he ultimately has to catch the villain in less than an hour against a concrete backdrop whose soundscape is punctuated by wailing sirens.

Micheline Keller reveals, 'We tried to give them advice. One of them called us and we said, "You know what? We found that the world really wants to see Tarzan in the jungle, not in the city." But they had their own concept that they were going with.' However, the producers sought to do more than the Kellers had in this context. That Tarzan is officially dead after an incendiary climax to the first WB episode, and subsequently wrongly accused of murder, adds a tinge of *The Fugitive* or *The Incredible Hulk* to the show.

Also different is the overall gloomy ambience and slow-burning character development, even if the intended sophistication is slightly undermined by such logic lapses as

Tarzan sometimes being unaccountably familiar with technology and social custom.

In 2008, Kripke – by now celebrated for a subsequent WB (later renamed CW) series, *Supernatural* – described his Tarzan show as a 'a piece of crap...' He did emphasise to Jason Davis of *CS Weekly*, however, 'I'll stand behind the pilot.' However, the structural strength of the pilot – the fact that it had a start, middle and conclusion – was also the show's undoing. Kripke: 'I was hungry to have anything in production, so I wrote a 50-page story that ended. Then it got made and ... it was all my dreams come true. They said to me, "Let's do 12 more." I said, "Uh, wait! What's the story?" So, Tarzan was a hell ride in every way, and we only did eight before they wisely put us out of our misery.'

Whether a piece of crap or a noble failure, the WB's *Tarzan* was gone in the blink of an eye. Although the pilot accrued a respectable audience figure of 5.5 million, by the fifth airing ratings had tumbled to 2.84 million, at which point WB pulled the plug, although it did broadcast the three other episodes on which production had wrapped. In contrast, *Smallville* outlasted *Tarzan* by eight years and triumphantly departed the stage at a time of the creators' own choosing.

Disney's animated sequel *Tarzan II* would perhaps have been more appropriately titled *Tarzan ½*. Its events occur part of the way into the studio's first Tarzan film at a point where the title character is still a young boy.

Only Glenn Close and Lance Henriksen (Kerchak) reprise their vocal roles from the first outing, with Alex D Linz replaced as young Tarzan by Harrison Chad. Brian Smith directed this 60-minute affair, which required the efforts of two writing teams, Jim Kammerud & Brian Smith and Bob Tzudiker & Noni White.

The film finds young Tarzan brooding over the fact that he is a substandard 'ape'. Subsequently, his lack of climbing prowess puts Kala in danger, in the aftermath of which incident Tarzan is temporarily beyond contact and therefore presumed dead. When he is about to return to his tribe, he hears some of the other mothers ruefully observe that Kala is probably better off without him. Distraught, he flees into the jungle. There he meets a gorilla family consisting of hulking but dim-witted brothers Uto and Kago and their controlling mother Mama Gunda. They are stranded in a barren valley by their fear of Zugor, a legendary monster reputed to guard its only entrance. Zugor is really a gnarled and lonely old ape practising a deception. He and Tarzan strike up a rapport when they realise they were both deemed burdens by their respective former tribes, although that doesn't stop Tarzan falling out with him long enough to utter a playful line that nods to decades of ape-man heritage: 'Me Tarzan, you grouch.' Tantor and Terk realise Tarzan is still alive and come to collect him, as does Kala when she belatedly hears the news. A battle royale ensures between all the parties before a spanner is thrown in the works by the fact of Mama Gunda and Zugor falling in love. The story ends with some of the tree-surfing that was a feature of the parent film, followed by a variation of the predecessor's finale: Tarzan on a high branch emitting a yodel.

There's a feeling of grand pointlessness to the enterprise: we know how Tarzan's life turned out from having seen the original film. However, the young intended audience was probably not agonising over that, nor the fact that this follow-up is no *Godfather Part II*, and more likely delighted by the above-average animation, good-heartedness, endearing characters and abundance of amusing scenes. Their mums and dads were probably more distracted by the two new songs Phil Collins contributed in the well-crafted-but-characterless style of the first film.

Ambitions seem to have been low for this project, as epitomised by the fact that its June 2005 release was not to cinemas. Notwithstanding the large market for such products, especially bearing the Disney brand name, issuing a film 'direct to video' (in fact, by then, DVD) is the embodiment of lack of confidence in its quality and/or commercial viability. Even so, Disney still saw further mileage in the character. Having portrayed Tarzan on film, television and home video/DVD, they were preparing to return him to the stage.

Once upon a time, Disney stage shows were limited to such delights as *Walt Disney's World on Ice*, wherein anonymous individuals dressed as the likes of Goofy and Donald Duck skated across rinks while performing vignettes from the studio's films. This all changed with *Beauty and the Beast*, the high-value 1994 production that, in reworking a Disney movie for Broadway, showed that a property could both have its life significantly extended and its cachet raised. Having found a new way to embed themselves into the American culture that they to many already epitomised, Disney proceeded to mine that new seam with a vengeance, their 1997 show *The Lion King* being particularly mind-blowing in its success. The Noughties saw their stage musicals achieve an even higher plateau, both domestically and abroad. In 2006/07, the number of Disney musicals on Broadway doubled to four. One of them was a production based on their 1999 animated *Tarzan* movie.

Tarzan: The Broadway Musical was reported to be one of the few Great White Way musicals to turn a profit before it opened. This was quite a feat considering it was also reported to be one of the most expensive Broadway productions of all time, with a budget between 15 and 20 million dollars racked up over the four-and-a-half years required to bring it to the stage. Nor was the demand for tickets a phenomenon that tapered off after the 10 May 2006 official opening: its theatre's 1,368 seats continued to be filled for every performance. By September, Disney's Dusty Bennett was informing Danton Burroughs, 'We broke the Richard Rodgers Theatre box office record in July and then went on to break our own record two more times throughout the course of the summer.'

Such receipts were the result of the customary care the company lavished on the show. Disney did not lazily stage the existing *Tarzan* film script. Instead, they started from scratch, hiring heavyweight dramatist David Henry Hwang (*M. Butterfly*,

Aida) to provide an original 'book'. Hwang admitted to *Disney Insider* that he wasn't too familiar with the Tarzan legend and said that he felt the previous versions in different media had served to obscure the original story. 'So I read the original novel by Edgar Rice Burroughs and looked again at the Disney movie, which I'd always loved,' he said. 'This was a story that excited me ... As a Chinese American, I particularly related to a man caught between two worlds (in Tarzan's case, between human and ape families), taking elements from each to become his best self.' The producers also packed the show with songs, commissioning nine more numbers from Phil Collins. The greatest amount of work that went into the show, however, related to the arboreal elements.

Edgar Rice Burroughs had once expressly agreed with the proposition that the people who staged the first Tarzan stage play had taken upon themselves an 'impossible' task. However, since 1920, times – and what was and was not impossible – had changed, with the talents of director/scenic designer/costume designer Bob Crowley and choreographer Meryl Tankard meriting credit alongside the technological progress. Bungee cords, nigh-invisible wires, hidden harnesses and a crevice-pocked bouncy castle-like set enabled the actors to give the impression of tree-swinging and tree-surfing. The new methods even facilitated them flying out over the audience. All of this was done without real leaves: deep green lighting and hanging artificial fronds created the jungle ambience. (Natasha Katz was nominated for a Tony Award for Best Lighting Design of a Musical.) A measure of the success of these effects is provided by the overwhelmed reaction of the presumably show-hardened reviewer of the *Daily Telegraph*, who gushed, 'The opening minutes of *Tarzan* are among the most exciting and inventive I have ever witnessed in the theatre. Bob Crowley has conjured up an astonishing succession of *coups de theatre*. They whisk us from a thrilling shipwreck to an amazing underwater rescue sequence, from a bird's-eye view of a tropical beach to a jungle full of gorillas swinging around like kids in an adventure playground.'

Some things, though, clearly remained impracticable: the character of Tantor was jettisoned.

Daniel Manche and Alex Rutherford were the younger versions of Tarzan (loinclothed for the sake of decency, if not logic), with Josh Strickland taking over as the adult ape-man. The latter's mane of dreadlocked hair was unexpected but somehow worked, and if the lack of bulge to his muscles seemed incongruous, it was soon forgotten about as he engaged in impressive flips, swinging and knuckle-dragging. Jane was played by Jennifer Gambatese, agreeably so according to critics, although she had to struggle against her frumpy if period-correct costume. The gorillas were represented more by suggestion than costume, with performers like Merle Dandridge (Kala) made simian only by the fur on their head-pieces, tops and skirts.

The Broadway production closed on 8 July 2007 after 35 previews and 486 performances. However, the show fanned out across the globe to appreciative audiences, with productions mounted in the next few years in Holland, Sweden and Germany. There have also been many regional US productions. Amongst the souvenirs and merchandise the show bequeathed was a soundtrack album and the behind-the-scenes book *Tarzan: The Broadway Adventure*.

As with the animated movie, that *Tarzan: The Broadway Musical* was not a faithful Burroughs adaptation was offset by the fact that it kept the Tarzan franchise alive. Nor did it merely introduce the ape-man to new generations: being the subject of a Broadway show meant Tarzan was taken to a higher grade of people than those to be found in the multiplexes.

On the downside is something exemplified by the fact that on the promotional poster for *Tarzan: The Broadway Musical* the distinctive Disney logo appeared above the title but Burroughs' name was nowhere in evidence. Tarzan had recently become more a Disney property than an ERB character.

In the run-up to the year that marked the centenary of Tarzan's first appearance came the announcement that there was to be a new series of Tarzan novels. However, a look beyond the surface facts threw up two unexpected details. The first was that the resumption of the franchise was not the idea of ERB, Inc but of an author who was initially unaware of the 100-year milestone. The other was that the new Tarzan novels – the first authorised by the estate since *The Dark Heart of Time* in 1999 – were to be geared toward children.

Liverpool-born Andy Briggs – the first British writer to chronicle the adventures of Lord Greystoke – started off in screenwriting, making contributions to projects like *Judge Dredd*, *Freddie vs. Jason*, *Aquaman* and the *Highlander* TV series (not all of which made it to the screen). He had also written children's novels and graphic novels.

As with most people under 50 (particularly in the UK), Briggs had only ever known a drought situation with Tarzan books. 'I got into Tarzan through the TV and the movies,' he says. His transition from idly thinking it 'would be cool to do something' with the ape-man to actively considering taking on the character came by chance. Briggs: 'I originally saw it on a list of titles that I got from a TV company who were looking for out-of-copyright properties that they can reinvent and do something with. I thought "Wow! Cool. It didn't occur to me that this is out of copyright." Then I looked into it and I discovered the hideous copyright mess where it's only out of copyright in America but in copyright the rest of the word. And then the word Tarzan is a trademark, so you can't do anything with that. That's what got me interested, and then I just started thinking about how it can be rejuvenated, how it can be brought to a new audience. This was well before I was even aware of the centenary. This was just a bit of a passion project.

'Originally I was noodling around with how to do it. I write movies, I go to the studios all the time, so do I go in at that level?' With a putative Tarzan movie from Warner Brothers having been in turnaround for several years, Briggs twirled his thoughts in a different direction: 'I thought, "If I owned Tarzan, what would I do?" You need to get in at the grassroots. You need to rebuild the brand up almost from scratch, with that wonderful legacy, so I thought a book would be the best way to do it. You could go straight in and do an adult book. Fine, it might find a market, but the smart way to do it is what they've done with the Young Bond series, the Charlie Higson books. If you want a property to survive, you start with the youngest audience you can feasibly work with.' Briggs decided that the field of Young Adult 'makes sense, because then there's a refurbished brand that you can build everything else on top of.' A recently codified genre, YA features protagonists of a similar age-group to its readership of people of roughly 14 to 21.

Briggs initially met resistance: 'I talked to all the major publishers and everyone thought it was really cool. Everybody knows Tarzan, everyone's looking for a brand. They just didn't think the estate would go for it. It was very demoralising. Eventually, I just thought, "Screw this, I'm just going to contact the estate directly." Contacted them, got my agent in LA to send samples over of my work, my résumé and things, and a half-a-page pitch of what I had in mind, and almost immediately got a reply back saying, "This sounds great. Come over to Tarzana." So I went over, I met with people from the office there, and it wasn't even a battle. I left very stunned, because I'd had such an uphill struggle with the publishers originally.' With ERB, Inc's imprimatur obtained, publisher Faber offered a deal for three books.

Perhaps surprisingly, Briggs found that the paucity of Tarzan in the media in recent times had not caused the character to drop off the cultural radar. 'When I've been doing all the visits around the country with my superhero books, I've been talking to younger readers ... Everybody knows who Tarzan is. Everyone knows his backstory, everyone knows the famous yodel, but very few of them have ever seen a film and virtually none of them have ever read the book. I find that fascinating, because I suddenly realised how imprinted Tarzan is on popular culture. I just think it's an image that you see subliminally. And some kids ... you play them the Tarzan yodel and [they] go, "Yeah, that is

George of the Jungle," and that yodel's not in the *George of the Jungle* film. It's a very strange thing. It's a kind of collective consciousness that's built around this character.'

The Tarzan Twins books excepted, Burroughs only ever wrote commercially for adults, but Briggs denies that aiming his Tarzan books at adolescents demeans the character: 'Let's put it this way. *Tarzan of the Apes*, it's a classic. Adults will read it. [But] the majority of people who'll read that book will be kids in school studying English Literature or American Literature. Same way, they are the majority of people who are reading Charles Dickens. They might have been written for an adult audience a hundred or whatever years ago, but that's not who reads them now.' He says of his Tarzan series, 'To say it's a kids' book – and this is the constant battle I've had with the publisher – is absolutely incorrect. We're just aiming it at the people who are actually just reading *Tarzan of the Apes* ... Some people have mentioned it should be for diehard fans, which is completely selfish because Burroughs himself was the master [of] flogging it off, licensing it off, as much as possible. It's incorrect to say he's a character for adults anymore. He's just become a character for everybody. Whether the book's marketed in the children's section, whether it's marketed in the adults' section, is irrelevant. In an ideal world, it will pick up in the YA section and then it'll just do what they did with *Twilight*, what they did with Harry Potter: they just stick a different jacket on it and it goes straight into the adults' section.'

Briggs describes his series as a 'reboot', terminology for a fresh start deriving from the computer age that was seven decades into the future when Tarzan first saw air. Some components of said reboot were bound to create controversy. His changes start with the fact that Tarzan is no longer a man born circa 1888. 'It [would be] a pointless exercise,' he says. 'You might as well just say, "Look, read the [original] book." Why do that? Why not just say, "If we're going to refresh this then it's going to have to be appealing to a contemporary audience." In that case we're going to have to bring it up to date and set it now and make sure we've preserved the original flavour of Tarzan.' However, Briggs seems to be hedging his bets somewhat when he insists that the period is left a little ambiguous: 'It's irrelevant when this is set. You really don't know, 'cause you're in a jungle.' Up to a point, anyway. Of Jane, he notes, 'She is a modern girl, therefore she has an iPhone.'

Briggs has dispensed with the concept of the Mangani almost completely. 'Because of the influence of the movies, we're just not going to get away with that,' he reasons. 'A new generation of people who've never read the original book [would] struggle to get into that, because [in] every movie, or most of them, they are gorillas.' Briggs has done his research a little better on wildlife: 'You're talking about a book that was published in 1912, when Burroughs had never been to Africa, there was no research done out in the wild on how great apes actually behaved, so there was a lot of liberties taken in the book that people just are not going to buy now.' With the example of Cheeta in mind, Briggs did investigate the possibility of portraying Tarzan as raised by chimpanzees, but he reveals, 'Every zookeeper and animal expert I spoke to referred to the chimpanzees basically being vicious bastards. They just seemed too extreme for their natural behaviour to take in this infant.' A small element does remain of Burroughs' vision of an ape species one step closer to man. Explains Briggs, 'The estate didn't want [me] to say they are just gorillas, so there are hints in the first book of them being a lot more intelligent.'

Angling the book toward the Young Adult market has necessitated another example of hedge-betting, this one concerning the ages of the central characters. 'Again, this was a huge conversation. The ages have been not addressed – skirted around, if you want to be very critical – but it's been done in such a way that it doesn't lock the character [of Tarzan] down.' When it comes to Tarzan's country of origin, though, Briggs has been specific where Burroughs was vague. 'It's set in the Congo because it's the one wide space which borders Rwanda and everywhere else. It's the last, biggest rainforest in Africa.'

Environmentalism is a big part of the series. 'Tarzan was for all intents and purposes the world's first eco-warrior,' Briggs asserts. 'He was the protector of the wild. He kills for food, he kills for safety, for protection. He doesn't go out and kill the animals just for the sake of it ... If you go in and start cutting down all the trees in Tarzan's territory, he's not going to stand there. He's going to destroy you.' However, Briggs does concede, 'It would be horrible if he vocalised this. If he went out saying, "Stop! Preserve the environment!"'

The first of the books, *The Greystoke Legacy*, appeared in June 2011, Briggs having agitated to resist the obvious publication date of 2012: 'I was banging my drum saying, "Look, surely what you want to do is build up a new fanbase, so when you go into the centenary, you've got all the diehard fans and then you've got this whole wave of new people."'

Briggs admits, 'As a fan, instantly, you're going to spot everything that's changed.' A *Star Wars* fanatic, he can to some extent sympathise. 'For a lot of things, I am a purist and I love the original, I hate people tampering with it.' However, at the end of the day, he makes no apology for his fine-tuning of Tarzan. 'There's [not] enough purists who are going to keep this alive. When all those purists die, Burroughs' original book is dead.'

The Tarzan story as recounted in *The Greystoke Legacy* features an aeroplane carrying Lord and Lady Greystoke – an English couple known for championing environmental causes – crashing in the country then known as Zaire, now the Democratic Republic of Congo. Her ladyship is five months pregnant and, although she lives long enough to give birth to a son (their name for him is not revealed), both she and her husband perish. The baby is brought up by a band of gorillas (referred to by the boy as Mangani) who make the plane-wreck their home. The boy next interacts with a human when a United Nations peacekeeper named D'Arnot enters his territory. The boy saves D'Arnot from a lioness. D'Arnot teaches the boy English. Making his way back alone to civilisation, D'Arnot tries to alert the

Greystoke family to the existence of an heir. When he is disbelieved, he returns to the jungle in search of the boy but dies there.

These events are not presented sequentially or directly, but rather pieced together across the course of the story by Jane Porter, teenaged daughter of an illegal logger. Jane encounters the ape-man when she gets lost in the jungle. Another teenager at the logging camp, Robbie, has a troubled past. The loggers' uneasy pact with local guerrillas comes to an end when each side starts suspecting the other of acts of sabotage and mischief: in fact, the culprit is Tarzan, taking out his anger at their despoilment of his locality. The book climaxes with a scene in which Tarzan calls upon lions, elephants and gorillas to demolish the guerrillas' camp and rescue their prisoner loggers, about whom he has taken a more lenient view due to his fondness for Jane. The latter feels the same way for him, shaken out of her insular adolescent mentality by the beauty and danger of the jungle, demonstrated to her by her brave but lonely new friend. The narrative ends with Tarzan disappearing back into the jungle but with Jane feeling she has not seen the last of him.

As ever, it's intriguing observing the decanting of the Tarzan legend into the modern world, but also as ever some of the tampering is irritating. Additionally, in changing elements, Briggs gets into trouble. He has Tarzan eating meat because Burroughs' ape-man was raised by the omnivorous Mangani – but how would a man raised by gorillas, a species whose consumption of living things extends only so far as insects, have developed a taste for animal flesh? Although Briggs' depictions of Tarzan's arboreal abilities (a matter of downwards jumping as much as swinging) are impressive, they are again not consistent with ground-based gorilla behaviour. Tarzan's name, meanwhile, is not explained.

Tarzan is clad in a ragged pair of cargo shorts, origin unstated. He is, in other words, a wild variant on a cool teenager. Gruesome though this particular piece of updating is, it surprisingly set a trend in Tarzan projects.

Briggs writes competently, if never particularly sparklingly. However, his writing has a layering that Burroughs' did not. While the author never set foot in Africa, Briggs did travel to what he doesn't call the Dark Continent. This means he is able to offer dense, accurate detail about wildlife (if sometimes dropped in heavy-handedly) and to evocatively convey what a sticky, sweaty place Africa is. Meanwhile, he has clearly done his research on logging outfits, capturing their diesel stink, fly-by-night nature and mercenary ambience. His gorillas are lovely and admirable without being sentimentally anthropomorphic, and his portrayal of the Greystokes' moss-covered, wrecked plane as an improvised gorilla home is charming. In contrast to this believability, Briggs' depiction of a lion zigzagging to dodge a gunman's bullets is the kind of nonsense that Burroughs, even with his limited knowledge, would never have proffered.

There are two severe faults with *The Greystoke Legacy*. First, Briggs doesn't actually seem to know what to do with Tarzan. The character is virtually a guest in his own book. Admittedly, the inclusion of lengthy material about jungle interlopers that not only keeps Tarzan off the stage but is in itself rather boring is something of which Burroughs himself was frequently guilty. However, the ape-man at no point drives the narrative: he is unseen until past the 60-page mark, and when he does appear is presented through the eyes of others. Not until gone 200 pages are we made privy to Tarzan's point of view.

The other glaring problem is the restrictions imposed on the author by that orientation toward the young. There is no real hint of sexual attraction between Tarzan and Jane. The ape-man fights lionesses but miraculously manages to triumph over them without recourse to fatal wounds, while a battle for supremacy with gorilla character Terkoz is settled – Filmation cartoon-style – by Tarzan using a lasso to cause his opponent to punch himself in the face. The nadir of the pussyfooting comes after a passage wherein Tarzan slashes a lioness across a flank with a rare use of his knife: Briggs feels compelled almost to apologise for it, insisting it is 'fair retaliation' for the big cat having raked its claws across the ape-man's back. The morality is moreover a strange one, for human deaths of a grisly nature are quite happily presented for the young readers' edification.

All of this might seem to demonstrate the fallacy of Briggs' theory of keeping the character alive via YA, and illustrate that raising the young on Tarzan is of no use whatever if targeting them necessitates undermining the character's whole savage, bloody premise. Yet the book did well enough to generate two sequels. *Tarzan: The Jungle Warrior* (July 2012) sees Tarzan traveling across jungle and savannah to rescue a baby gorilla snatched by a hunter. Jane is meanwhile investigating Tarzan's past and weighing up whether it would be the right thing to do to reunite him with the Greystoke family. *Tarzan: The Savage Lands* (2013), like its immediate predecessor, came adjacent to a series title: 'The New Adventures of Tarzan'. It finds the current Lord Greystoke seeking out his wild cousin to eliminate him from the hereditary line, while Jane and Robbie – wishing to warn Tarzan – stumble on the city of Opar.

'It proved there was a huge demand to see Tarzan in a contemporary environment,' says Briggs. 'Most bad reviews came from a small yet vocal minority of older generation of Tarzan fans who usually claimed "It's not Burroughs" … It was never intended to be. Those negative views definitely put some of the new younger readers off.' Nonetheless, more YA Tarzan books are in the offing. 'I am not quite ready to take my hand off the tiller just yet,' says Briggs.

In January 2012, the ape-man returned to Dark Horse comics. First came the three-part *Dark Horse Presents* story 'The Once and Future Tarzan', written by Alan Gordon and illustrated by Thomas Yeates, a project which saw the ape-man travel in time to the half-flooded ruins of a future London. This was followed by a far more conventional Tarzan comics project. Graphic novel *Jungle Tales of Tarzan* (2015) was an adaptation written by Martin Powell and illustrated by various artists. It was then back to crossovers with the mini-series *Tarzan on the Planet of the Apes*.

Writers Tim Seeley and David Walker and artist Fernando Dagnino posited a universe in which Tarzan and Planet of the Apes-franchise character Caesar are raised as brothers but separated by slave traders, reuniting when war is raging between man and simian.

Dark Horse, though, were just one of three simultaneous official publishers of Tarzan comics, a situation that was a marked contrast to the days when ERB, Inc moved exclusive official titles from publisher to publisher.

One of the alternative publishers was Dynamite Entertainment, whose relationship with ERB, Inc started off on the worst terms imaginable. In December 2011, Dynamite launched an unauthorised Tarzan series, seeking to claim public-domain usage rights. However, with the Tarzan name being the trademark of ERB, Inc, they were careful to title the series *Lord of the Jungle*, with the name Tarzan mentioned nowhere on the covers. In 2012, they were served by ERB, Inc with a writ. The case was settled in 2014, by which point Dynamite had also issued the six-part Tarzan/John Carter crossover series *Lords of Mars*. Details of the settlement were kept secret, but its unexpected upshot was that Dynamite now had ERB, Inc's imprimatur for both Tarzan and John Carter comics, something that seems related to ERB, Inc's frustration with Marvel, now owned by Disney. Marvel owned rights to the John Carter character but had seemed to lose interest in them after the failure of the 2012 *John Carter* film. 'It was important to us that we reacquire the comic book and comic strip rights from Marvel Entertainment so we could reintroduce them in the market place,' said Jim Sullos, ERB, Inc president.

Dynamite subsequently published the ongoing series *John Carter: Warlord of Mars*, *Swords of Sorrow*, a female-character 2015 mini-series in one issue of which Jane Porter (as it called her) teamed-up with ancient Egyptian demon hunter Pantha, and six-part mini-series *Lords of the Jungle* (2016), in which writer Corinna Bechko and artist Roberto Castro paired Tarzan with Sheena. However, the word Tarzan could still only be found in sub-titles of Dynamite ape-man covers, presumably due to Dark Horse's prior claim to the character.

As is now the norm, Dark Horse and Dynamite made their titles available not just as printed comic books and book anthologies, but as downloads. Comics which consist of nothing more than digital files are less cost-intensive than traditional paper comics: artists and writers still have to be paid, but distribution, warehousing and third-party retailers are not part of the equation. Accordingly, in 2014 ERB, Inc decided they had little to lose in setting up the Edgar Rice Burroughs Digital Comic Strip Service. The beauty of the low-cost digital model was evinced by the fact that not only did the service proffer weekly doses of iconic ERB properties like Tarzan, Mars, Venus, Caspak and Pellucidar, and some middlingly well-known works like *The Lad and the Lion*, *The War Chief* and *The Mucker*, but even adaptations of real obscurities like *The Girl from Hollywood* and *The Outlaw of Torn*.

Many Burroughs fans had literally died waiting for a John Carter movie: it took fully 100 years for one to make it to the screen. That is if you don't count – and most Burroughs fans don't – a low-budget production called *Princess of Mars*, released direct to DVD in 2009 and predicated on a cop-out premise of a Mars in a different solar system.

John Carter, released in March 2012, was a very different proposition: a big-bucks motion picture made by the golden-touch Pixar studio. Directed by Andrew Stanton, the film was quite good, although with the richest irony felt second-hand in places simply because of all the other media properties that had taken their cue from Burroughs' character down the years. It also served an important additional role in generating newsprint and web stories in which asides like 'based on a book by the man who created Tarzan' were inevitably prominent.

Al Bohl's *Tarzan: Lord of the Louisiana Jungle* had its premiere the month after *John Carter*. The documentary revolved around the filming of the first Tarzan movie, which took place in Bohl's home state. Bohl explains, 'I was having breakfast with some men in South Louisiana and one of them told me he was from Morgan City and that they'd made the Tarzan movie there in 1917. Then he said, "Do you know, they brought in monkeys and apes for that movie just for background? When they got ready to leave, the [animals] wouldn't get back in the cages so they just left them." So that just really excited me to realise that there might still be monkeys down in the South Louisiana jungle.'

In September 2012 came *Jane: The Woman Who Loved Tarzan* by Robin Maxwell, both the first Tarzan novel told from Jane's point of view and the first Tarzan novel written by a woman.

Maxwell was once a screenwriter. Although her success in that field seems to have been limited (CBS Movie of the Week *Passions* is the only example she lists on her website at the time of writing), she has subsequently enjoyed considerable success in the field of historical fiction with such works as *The Secret Diary of Anne Boleyn* and *The Queen's Bastard*. In 2010, she published *O, Juliet* in which she told in novel form the story of Romeo and Juliet. As with the Andy Briggs series, her Tarzan tome was the idea of the author, not the non-proactive ERB, Inc. Says Maxwell, 'My agents and editors were saying, "Well, what's your next book?" My husband said, "What's another literary love story?" and about three seconds later I just blurted out, "Tarzan and Jane." He kind of laughed it off. I thought, "This is a real great idea." Nobody's better at doing a woman's point of view of either history or literature than I am.' However, Maxwell was cognisant of the difference between reworking the unequivocally public domain Shakespeare and taking on Tarzan: 'I knew that you messed with Edgar Rice Burroughs' estate at your own peril.' She instructed her lawyer to write to ERB, Inc president Jim Sullos. Maxwell: 'Before I knew it, Jim and my lawyer were on the phone and Jim was asking me, "Well okay, what's your great idea?" 'Cause all I had said in the letter was that I had a new twist on the Tarzan story. I just said, "The Tarzan story from Jane's point of view," and he went through the roof. He just said, "Oh, that's fantastic." He liked the romantic angle of it. He read some of my work, so I went in and pitched to him in Tarzana for five hours.'

Of course, to some extent, Maxwell's idea was merely the literary equivalent of Bo and John Derek's movie. That picture being such a sore point with the corporation, some might be surprised that ERB, Inc were so receptive to her proposal, but she reasons, 'I have a track record. I'm considered one of the queens of historical fiction, and I have a body of work behind me. Having heard my take on the story, he knew I wasn't going to make it into a mash or something they were going to be ashamed of.' By this point, Maxwell had read *Tarzan of the Apes*, but she admits that when the idea first came to her she had not consumed any Burroughs, although she had enjoyed Tarzan comic books as a girl and seen many Tarzan movies from the Weissmuller era onwards. For those who doubt the suitability for adventure works of someone with her back catalogue, Maxwell asserts that her grounding as a screenwriter taught her how to write action-oriented narrative.

Maxwell was pleasantly surprised at the serendipity of her timing: 'The day that [Jim Sullos] asked me on the phone "What's this about?" that's when he told me the hundredth anniversary was happening.' Less of a pleasant surprise were the terms to which she was required to agree. As with previous continuation Tarzan novelists, she had to cede to ERB, Inc copyright and a percentage of royalties and to agree to conform to the estate's Tarzan Universe dictates. 'There's about 20 rules which you may not break,' she says. "Tarzan cannot drink, he cannot smoke, he cannot be a racist. Tarzan cannot do anything to harm another human being unless they're bad. Things like that.' This caused a temporary hiccup: 'The last one was Tarzan may not have illicit sex. This was going to be an adult novel and it was going to be a romance between a sexy man and a virgin, but a full-blooded woman. Here they are alone in the jungle going through incredible adventures and they were going to make love, there was no two ways about it. I said to Jim, "If they cannot make love in this book, then I'm not writing a book." So he had a talk with the Burroughs estate and came back with a compromise: Tarzan may make love, but it must be done tastefully.'

However, these were merely the first hurdles to publication. Maxwell found that despite her track record and having 'top agents' in her employ, obtaining a publisher was difficult. 'The rejection letters were, "We don't think there's a market for Tarzan books" or, "We don't know how to sell this,"' she recalls. Although the book found a buyer following a reworked pitch and a second round of applications, science fiction and fantasy specialists Tor are not the level of publishing outlet to which she is used. Surprisingly, though, *Jane* was perceived far more attractively as a talking book: 'Audio books are huge and getting huger, and there was actually an auction for *Jane* and I ended up getting a huge audio book deal.'

Maxwell admits she took 'tremendous liberties' with her telling of the Tarzan story, but points out, 'it was all authorised by the estate.' She reasons, 'Being a historian and a bit of a science buff, I wanted to keep it as close to reality as possible. I felt that it was really implausible that if Tarzan was taken by the Mangani at age one, he would have been able to relearn the English language. So I decided Tarzan was four years old when his parents got murdered in front of him. Jane ... helps him remember who he is. When he meets her, he doesn't have anything but Mangani language.' Another alteration revolved around the implausible coincidence with which adapters have had problems as far back as the 1918 *Tarzan of the Apes* movie: that a party that happens to include a Greystoke is marooned on the very shore on which Tarzan's parents were stranded. Instead, a party devoid of Greystokes but containing Archibald Porter and his half-English, half-American daughter Jane – herself an heir to a title – come upon Tarzan's home. Maxwell makes that home, incidentally, in Gabon.

Although Maxwell's book is set in the same period as *Tarzan of the Apes*, her Jane is somewhat different to Burroughs' heroine, starting with the fact of her education. Says Maxwell, 'During those years women could not graduate. They could only "audit" classes at the University. During the week she lives on campus with the women attending Newnham College. She is allowed to audit Professor Archimedes Porter's gross anatomy laboratory – human anatomy – for medical students because Archie is her father. He moved mountains to make that happen, and it's causing quite a stir among the male students. When she goes home to their Cambridge greathouse on weekends, she is his assistant in the home laboratory where he works as an enthusiastic amateur in palaeoanthropology ... Jane is a very precocious woman of her time ... She's dissecting a human cadaver when we first meet her ... She was a one-off as an Edwardian woman. Didn't care for the life of the peerage. They had a name for it: a New Woman.' However, this is no anachronistic ladette: 'She's of the peerage herself. She's a dignified woman.'

Some of Maxwell's changes seem to stem partly from an inchoate and incomplete knowledge of the Burroughs Tarzan. For instance, in her retelling, Tarzan has an adoptive half-sister and playmate to whom Maxwell gives the name Jai. 'That was a character in something else,' she says vaguely. Further changes clearly derive from modern PC culture. 'There are no cannibals in this,' says Maxwell. 'The Waziri are the only native tribe in it. They are peaceable because there's no other tribe around and Tarzan has a friendly relationship with them. I did not want to show him killing native people.' Is that realistic? 'Well, the way I have it written it is.' Maxwell's text pointedly refers not to the 'jungle' but to the 'forest'. As for Tarzan killing animals, Maxwell explains, 'He does, but not in the same way that he does in the ERB books. He's a kinder, gentler Tarzan.'

The demographic research Maxwell conducted reveals interesting facts about Tarzan's diminishing position in popular culture. "I discovered that only people over 60 had even possibly read the ERB books. Virtually all of them had seen the Weissmuller-Maureen O'Sullivan movies. They had a very distinct and sometimes passionate admiration for Tarzan. If they read the books, they thought highly of ERB too. Then the next down is the 35-60 age group. They were young and watching movies at the time of *Greystoke* and that abomination starring Bo Derek. They did not mostly read the ERB novels. Then the youngest age group, 18-35, they certainly didn't read the books, but what they saw movie-wise was the Disney animated features. They saw *George of the Jungle*, but a lot of them can't even make the distinction between Tarzan and George of the Jungle … Luckily the 60-plus men and women happen to be a big group of readers.' However Maxwell and Tor did not aim exclusively at the oldies. Like the Dereks, Maxwell had the idea of using *Me, Jane* as a title or component thereof. The idea was discarded because it was felt it would not have resonance for the young.

In Maxwell's take, Archimedes Porter has conducted numerous searches for Darwin's missing link. In Summer 1905, Porter changes to Gabon the location of his yearly African expedition after a man named Ral Conrath convinces him that this is the most likely location of his Holy Grail. In fact, Conrath is a scoundrel who is really seeking a legendary ancient city awash with gold and needs a plausible cover story to effect entry to the region. Conrath also has designs on Porter's daughter, and convinces him that Jane's own anthropological expertise makes her presence on the trip necessary.

Once in Africa, the Porters' party encounter Paul D'Arnot, who is here a rather wretched, drink-sodden character, lured against his better judgment into helping Conrath. Maxwell throws into the brew the murderous colonist machinations of King Leopold.

A strange loinclothed man saves Jane from being eaten by a leopard, a fate to which she has been left by Conrath after confronting him about his dirty dealings. That the animal from which the ape-man saves Jane is not the traditional lion/lioness illustrates that this narrative strives to be scientifically and geographically accurate. As the man who identifies himself as 'Tarzan' nurses Jane back to health, Jane in turn helps him recover his memory and ability to speak English.

Tarzan and Jane end up having sex, although the ape-man is sensitive and patient about the process. A plausible reason for the incongruous chivalry of a jungle-raised man is suggested by the fact that, in this text, Tarzan has seen tribe chief Kerchak force himself on both his human mother and female members of the Mangani tribe. However, Maxwell fails to explicitly draw this link.

When Tarzan brings her to meet the folks, Jane realises – whatever Conrath's deception – that his Mangani tribe is indeed a missing link, although she concludes it may well be the last tribe of its kind. Positing the Mangani as equidistant between man and animal gives a plausibility to their human-esque words like 'tar-zan', but Maxwell rather undermines the authenticity by suggesting that Kala's unusual intelligence makes her as an individual her species' next step in evolution. In one respect, though, Maxwell went with the flow of scientific discovery: 'Right when I was about to start writing the section where Jane meets the Mangani, a *National Geographicals* [sic] magazine came out and it was about a missing link fossil that they found in Ethiopia. This one was called *ardipithecus ramidus*. It was an erectus. From the neck down it looked human except the fingers were simian and the big toe was perpendicular to the rest of the toes. The face looked like a chimpanzee. So I used that as the basis of the Mangani.'

Tarzan ends up saving Jane from the rapacious Kerchak, after which he triumphantly eats Kerchak's heart, although there is no bull-ape victory cry. Tarzan and a now proudly bare-breasted Jane catch up with Conrath in the fabled gold-bedecked city, which is named Opar and is here a Pyramid-dotted outpost of Ancient Egypt. The pair commence battle with the aid of the tribe Tarzan thinks of as Waziri after the name of their chief. However, the city's volcano takes care of most of the villains, choosing at that point to erupt and destroy Opar.

When Conrath gets swallowed up by boiling hot lava, he follows D'Arnot – whom he has murdered – into eternity. Also not surviving the book are the Mangani, possibly wiped out by disease, conceivably one brought from civilisation by Jane.

The book's ending finds Tarzan working as Jane's episcope operator: on the couple's excursions from their Kenyan base, she is a traveling lecturer on the missing link. Crowds refuse to believe her even when confronted by Kerchak's skeleton. Edgar Rice Burroughs, catching one such lecture and engaging her in conversation afterwards, is given an idea for a follow-up to his recent pulp debut *Under the Moons of Mars*. 'Change, enlarge, and embellish upon what I've told you as you see fit,' Jane tells the burgeoning literary talent.

Although it has a period-correct strait-lacedness, *Jane* also takes us earthy places into which neither Burroughs nor many other writers in the early 20th century would have dared stray. Miss Porter's thoughts include: 'I felt clean and dry below, and detected no unsavory odors from my nether regions;' '…the man's arse, I thought, was one of the Seven Wonders of the Natural World;' 'I wrapped my arm around Tarzan's waist, breathing in his rich, musky scent;' 'And I wanted him rough. Craved him inside me. Moving hard.' It's even stated that Jane finds herself turned on by Tarzan's devouring of Kerchak's heart.

Feminism is retro-projected onto the story. Jane bristles at the conventions that restrict both her ambitions and waist. Although Tarzan is Jane's protector in the 'forest', she is often the dominant force in the relationship. For instance, Tarzan is childlike and supplicant as she reads to him from books and his parents' journal. Jane provides Tarzan archery skills following the apeman's failure to learn how to use a stolen bow and arrow. Alice Clayton is a plucky castaway, rather than the shrinking violet of *Tarzan of the Apes* who dropped dead from the shock of seeing a Mangani. Even Kala is a libber in the way she stands up to Kerchak's bullying. Tarzan adopts a loincloth (one which, by the way, leaves his buttocks exposed) not because of the example taught him by the books in the cabin, but because Kerchak's brutal mating methods have made him ashamed of his own sexuality. The feminist theme, though, is repetitive, and undermined by the fact that it's difficult to perceive the materially privileged Jane as too much of a victim.

It's that privileged terrain which makes the first hundred pages, mostly set in civilisation, hard-going. Nonetheless, the book's mainly first-person narrative is competent, if sometimes melodramatic. It cleverly sprinkles in well-researched historical detail, even if the dialogue often groans with exposition. It flits back and forth in time, but doesn't feel particularly disjointed. The dairy entry in which John Clayton, Sr realises that he and his wife are doomed – 'What is that! A sound on the roof? A falling frond? Dear God, dear God, they are footfalls' – is genuinely spooky.

Ironically, though, the best part of the book is a vivid, remarkably bloody and decidedly Burroughsian passage in which Tarzan fights with Kerchak for possession of his father's hunting knife. A flashback, it has nothing to do with Jane.

In December 2013 came the first motion-capture Tarzan movie. It was billed in some places as *Tarzan 3D*. In conventional cinemas and on television and DVD it, naturally, became merely *Tarzan*, so will have been confused by many with the 1999 Disney movie.

Motion capture, a most peculiar phenomenon of modern cinema, is essentially a halfway house between live action and animation. It involves actors playing scenes while covered in pick-ups so as to provide a computer programme the outlines of their bodies. Digitally projected onto those body outlines are chosen features and textures, and, behind them, preferred landscapes. The archetypes of cartoons – exaggerated and distorted facial features, lush-verging-on-impossible vistas – can thus be combined with the attributes of live action: fine detailing and naturalistic body movements and expressions.

The main creative wellspring of this *Tarzan* movie seems to be Reinhard Klooss, who directed, co-produced with Robert Kulze and co-wrote the screenplay with Jessica Postigo and Yoni Brenner. Although the movie was made by German production company Constantin Film, there is nothing Teutonic about it. Nor, unfortunately, is there anything English about it: the movie gets off to a depressing start when it's revealed that the hero is a New Yorker called John Greystoke, Jr, aka 'JJ' (Craig Garner). Also groan-making is a jarring and pointless science-fiction strand: JJ's father is an adventurer seeking a meteor that once crash-landed in Africa and which is reputed to have magical properties.

It is while pursuing his interest in the meteorite that Greystoke, Sr meets his death in a helicopter crash in which his wife is also killed. JJ is the only survivor. By a remarkable coincidence, the ambitions to be both ape and 'king of the jungle' that JJ harboured in civilisation come true when he is adopted by Kala, a gorilla who has just lost both mate and baby. (The fact of the name of Kala and other apes, as well as lots of exposition, is provided by an omniscient narrator.) JJ now starts thinking of himself as 'Tarzan,' a name he had previously devised – he fancies it means 'ape with no fur' – when playing with his toy gorilla.

Young Tarzan (Anton Zetterholm) roams the jungle in shorts that are the only tangible remnants of his civilised self. When he is a 19-year-old, his apparel switches to a loincloth which – like his clean-shaven face – goes unexplained.

Peter Elliott, who played a *Greystoke* Mangani, provides choreography that makes the movements of the gorillas very convincing, and those of Tarzan satisfyingly equidistant between gorilla and man. The ripple, gloss and fine detail of the gorillas' fur is something that would be impossibly labour-intensive through conventional animation. It is in depicting Tarzan's arboreal activities, though, that the benefits of motion capture really become apparent, and where the movie springs to life. This technology enables the best-ever representation of Tarzan in the treetops. Motion capture's blend of artificiality and realism is usually a strange contradiction, but it turns out to be perfect for showing Tarzan swinging and somersaulting through the branches with a combination of athleticism and elegance.

Although he also uses vines, this Tarzan is even sometimes shown swinging from bough to bough. Not only is the canopy rendered beautifully, it is panned across spectacularly. Live-action footage, with all its practical limitations, has never provided anything as impressive in any Tarzan vehicle.

Jane Porter (Spencer Locke) first appears as a young teenager when her explorer father James – a former colleague of Greystoke – brings her on a trip to Africa. Tarzan rescues Jane from peril. They meet up again when Tarzan is nineteen after Jane – now a conservation campaigner – is taken on a trip to Africa by current Greystoke Enterprises head William Clayton. The latter wishes to take advantage of the energy potential of the meteor, whose location he has latterly discovered. It's hoped that inviting along a civilian with a plausible interest in the region will shield the company's activities from competitors.

Despite an impressive body, the late-teen Tarzan (Kellan Lutz) has a slightly gormless face, a common, and quite befuddling, feature not just of motion capture but – as seen in the Disney *Tarzan* – modern animation *per se*. His yodel is yet another Weissmuller-lite affair.

Considering the demographic, it's understandable that there is little bloodshed. Although Tarzan does despatch one crocodile, he is shown scaring off a second with a mere yell. In his showpiece showdown with mortal enemy Tublat, he ostentatiously refuses to stab him with his father's hunting knife. There is, though, a little sauciness. Investigating her tent, Tarzan discovers one of Jane's bras and concludes that it's a slingshot. He also tries to watch Jane undress.

Its breathless pace renders the film slightly simplistic, but the kids-oriented vibe makes this not matter too much. There is even in some respects a greater realism, hence maturity, than in most Tarzan pictures: because this is the first film adaptation in which Tarzan is older than a baby when stranded in the jungle, his later transition from feral back to civilised is far more plausible.

The realism makes the science-fiction elements all the more regrettable. The meteor transpires to be not just magical but sentient. Moreover, a creature resembling the acid-spitting dinosaur from *Jurassic Park* puts in an appearance, while a scene very similar to the 'pit' section of the 2005 *King Kong* finds Tarzan in a valley battling plants and animals mutated to freak size and fearsomeness. The latter vista of fantasy flora and fauna, though, does for once enable the producers to give Tarzan licence to slaughter.

There are some knowing nods to Tarzan film history. Tarzan and Jane engage in a swimming reverie, albeit clothed and to a rock-song backdrop. For the first time ever in a Tarzan film project, the line 'Me Tarzan, you Jane' is spoken, and, furthermore, repeatedly.

A surprisingly enjoyable hour-and-a-half ends in rather feeble and pat fashion when Tarzan uses his yodel to summon gorillas, snakes and birds to overcome Clayton's avaricious employees, a dominion over beasts which may be a tradition in the film franchise but has not been established in this particular narrative. Moreover, Clayton's retreating 'copter is brought down by a rock hurl that is impossible even for the mighty Tarzan.

It's interesting what a difference the prestige and might of an organisation like Disney seems to make to a movie's fortunes. In content, timbre and quality, Constantin's *Tarzan* is rather similar to the 1999 *Tarzan* from the House of the Mouse. Yet whereas the latter film did well in both reviewers' columns and box offices, Constantin's notices were unenthusiastic to rotten, while receipts in cinemas were so disappointing that the film failed to secure a wide US theatrical release before transferring to availability via streaming, download and DVD.

It's doubtful that Burroughs fans lost sleep about the fate of the Constantin project. What they wanted, and had wanted for nearly two decades, was a new, live-action Tarzan movie.

This was not least because of the new potential created by advancing technology. By this point, it was astonishing to realise that *Greystoke* – the yardstick for modern live-action Tarzan cinema – was more than a quarter of a century old. The science of movie production had moved on massively since 1984. Superheroes had come into their own because the advent and increasing sophistication of computer technology meant that literally anything seen in comic books could now be exhilaratingly replicated on screen. Those same modern capabilities could, theoretically, for the first time do justice to the animalistic essence of Tarzan novels. Proof of this seemed to be provided by the way the title character in *X-Men Origins: Wolverine* (2009) bounds across a battlefield employing all four limbs in a motion startlingly animal-like. Further proof was offered by the way the CGI chimpanzees in *Dawn of the Planet of the Apes* (2014) adeptly propel themselves through branches.

Producer Jerry Weintraub spent the early years of the 21st century trying to get a live-action Tarzan film off the ground. By July 2016, when the project finally reached the screens (standard, 3D and IMAX 3D), Weintraub had been dead for a year. He at least passed away secure in the knowledge that *The Legend of Tarzan*, as it was titled, was directed by a prestigious name indeed: David Yates, who had helmed four of the colossally successful Harry Potter films.

'I used to watch the black-and-white Johnny Weissmuller movies on the telly at Christmas time,' recalls the English-born Yates. 'The BBC used to run them a couple at a time. They were always very charming and enjoyable, but I wouldn't say I was a fan. Just something that was entertaining to watch on a Saturday morning.' Yates also feels he viewed an episode or two of the Ron Ely TV series, again more with casual interest than passion. When Yates read the *Legend of Tarzan* script by Adam Cozad and Craig Brewer, he was drawn to the project by the fact that, 'All my preconceptions about Tarzan as a character and as a story were blown away. It felt very entertaining and thoughtful and fun. It starts when he's a lord and you realise he's quite sophisticated and he's settled and created a life for himself in London. So it was a lovely antidote for all the preconceptions that people have about "Me Tarzan, you Jane" and the wild ape-man in the jungle.'

Yates wasn't worried about the ape-man's decreasing visibility over recent decades. 'I saw it as an opportunity, really, because I think he's an enduring character and I felt he was ready for a reintroduction,' he reasons. 'He's such an extraordinary character. His world is amazing. And so it was really an attempt to reboot that story and that character and that world for a generation that hadn't experienced it. And for a generation who may have done before, we wanted to make a movie that was more exciting than what they'd seen previously.'

Although Yates insists that the development hell through which the movie had suffered is not that uncommon in Hollywood and that there were good reasons for the delays ('It's a difficult thing to make interesting again when there are all those old preconceptions about it'), he does implicitly acknowledge that him being one of the world's most successful directors gave the project new impetus: 'I had a very good relationship with Warner Brothers and they trust me and support me. It was pretty much a sure thing once I said yes, as long as we could figure it out for a budget that made sense to the studio. That process in itself took about a year. It's challenging. It's a big complicated movie, it's quite epic, involved loads of visual effects. In fact, it had more visual-effect shots than some of the Potter movies I've made.'

Those who imagine that said year involved sitting around crunching numbers would be wrong. Explains Yates, 'We'd recce Africa. We'd cost the designs. We'd go to visual effects [specialists] around the world. We'd pitch visual effect shots and sequences. We'd get them to cost them. We'd meet actors. It's quite a dynamic process. You're basing the figures on real-world variables. You're looking at a ton of stuff. You're effectively in pre-production. You're hiring people. You've got a crew with you already. So all that process of budgeting involves a lot of people and a lot of research and a lot of stuff that eventually ends up in the movie. It's almost like making a film in itself.'

Yates says he didn't consider many actors for the lead role before plumping for Swede Alexander Skarsgård, famous as vampire Eric Northman in TV drama *True Blood*. 'It was a very short list. Initially, I would get a list of actors who could all possibly be a Tarzan. From a very early stage I felt Alex was the guy. I did meet a couple of other guys, but that was really politics for the studio, in terms of the studio said, "Would you mind meeting such and such an actor? We think they're great, just see what you think."'

Of Skarsgård, Yates says, 'He just had a sense of otherness. He's an incredibly fine actor. He'd done some very interesting independent work, as well as dabbled in a couple of studio pictures. I liked the fact that he was Scandinavian, so he's got this weird, rootless quality about him.'

Although actors' ages are an important issue in an era in which pictures are so often made with a view to a series, Yates says he was not put off by the fact that Skarsgård was approaching forty. 'When I first met him, he came to my apartment in London and tapped on the door and my first thought was, "God, he's a *boy*. He's so young. We'll have to beef him up. This guy's gonna need a lot of training." He just has this evergreen quality. You just have to go with your gut.'

Boy he may have originally looked, but by the time shooting commenced Skarsgård was unmistakably a man. 'He worked for months and months and months every single day with a Scandinavian trainer,' recalls Yates of the process that gave Skarsgård one of the most drooled-over physiques of 2016.

Attention was also paid to Lord Greystoke's intonation. 'We did a little bit on the accent,' says Yates, but adds, 'I wasn't too fussed about him sounding clipped and English. I liked the idea that his accent was sort of somewhere between here and there. So a sense of being a Brit, but he's had a weird upbringing, he's a child of Africa. He didn't grow up and go to Eton and all of that.'

Despite ultimately going with what was essentially his first choice as the ape-man, Yates insists that he interviewed thespian studio suggestions with 'a very open mind.' As proof of this, he cites his acquiescence to the casting of Margot Robbie as the ape-man's spouse. 'Again, they didn't say, "We really want you to cast her," they just said, "We think she'd make a great Jane, see what you think."'

The colonialist inhumanity of King Leopold – condemned even by Burroughs in *Tarzan of the Apes* – is becoming a motif in modern ape-man interpretations. Like Maxwell's *Jane* novel, *The Legend of Tarzan* uses the Belgian monarch's murderous behaviour as a story crux. Christoph Waltz – the current go-to guy for playing movie villains, fresh from the part of Blofeld in *Spectre* – takes the role of Belgian captain Léon Rom. Despatched by Leopold to find diamonds to alleviate his severe financial difficulties, Rom is a cross between effete and ingeniously vicious (he strangles people with a rosary). His search for the gems takes him to Opar, in this version a village populated by a black tribe who resemble Burroughs' Leopard Men and are headed by a chief named Mbonga (Djimon Hounsou). The latter happens to bear a grudge against Tarzan: the ape-man killed his son for slaying Kala. Mbonga promises Rom all the diamonds he desires if he can bring him Tarzan.

Back in England, where he has been settled for eight years, Tarzan is invited by Leopold to tour the Congo. The monarch apparently wishes to acquire validation by exploiting the celebrity Tarzan possesses, one that extends to the ape-man having appeared on the cover of *Punch* magazine. The script doesn't make it clear whether this is a pretext related to the Mbonga situation.

It also doesn't enlighten us as to why United States diplomatic envoy George Washington Williams (Samuel L Jackson) says, 'You are Tarzan. Lord of the apes, king of the jungle. Me Tarzan, you Jane.' Notwithstanding Tarzan's celebrity status, where would he have heard this iconic phrase? Still, it can now be said that it has appeared in two Tarzan films in the space of 2½ years after only having featured before in the franchise's almost century-long history in popular misconception.

For purposes of furthering its own trade interests, the British government is keen for him to take up Leopold's offer, but the ape-man is reluctant. His hair may remain shoulder-length and he may instruct his butler to serve him his eggs raw, but he has quite taken to civilisation. 'My name isn't Tarzan,' he airily declares. 'It's John Clayton the third. Son of John and Lady Alice Clayton. Fifth Earl of Greystoke. Member of the House of Lords.' His mind is changed by Williams when the latter explains that his government suspects that one method by which Leopold is strengthening his interests is slavery.

There follows one of several moodily-shot origin flashbacks. When Kala adopts the helpless baby Tarzan, she is not motivated by having lost a child of her own. Akut is here Tarzan's stepbrother. Even had these deviations from source mattered much, they would have been compensated for in the eyes of Burroughs purists by the fact that, for the first time ever in filmed Tarzan, the species that fosters the ape-man is verbally described as Mangani.

Tarzan's knuckles are deformed, him explaining to some children, 'I grew up running on all fours. It changed the bone structure.' As ever, the new Tarzan's yodel is a pale imitation of Weissmuller's – yet the screenwriters have the cheek to portray Rom remarking of it, 'It sounded different than I thought. Better.' As in *Greystoke*, Tarzan can imitate wildlife to a parrot-like degree.

Something that completely fails to materialise is a further step in Burroughs faithfulness enabled by technology. The shipwreck that stranded the Clayton family – so easy to conjure via the marvels of CGI – is not even shown (not even, as in *Greystoke*, in aftermath). The CGI-generated Mangani might be big, fierce and sharp of tooth but are never quite as impressive as the best prosthetics-created *Greystoke* apes. As for that dream of a liveaction Tarzan swinging from bough to bough, it comes as an unspeakable disappointment that Yates not only portrays him travelling on vines but swinging in an unusually sideways, looping fashion that seems deliberately redolent of Spider-Man, a recent cinema sensation.

Tarzan at age five and eighteen are played by Christian

Stevens and Rory J Saper respectively, both nude, but shot discretely rather than in Hugh Hudson's full-on approach. Skarsgård is a good adult Tarzan. He looks nothing like his age. He is reasonably handsome and has a body that is, in one respect – the abdominal muscles – even more impressive than Miles O'Keeffe's. He also proffers a more than passable English accent. (Joking reference seems to be made to the fact that he is conscientious enough to pronounce zebra in the English way – 'zeb-rah' – not in the American manner much of the crew would have been using: 'zee-brah'.)

Although American-accented, this movie's Jane spent part of her youth in Africa: she and Tarzan first met when her father was teaching English in a village. She accompanies Tarzan on his return to the continent.

When Tarzan reaches Africa, Cozad and/or Brewer mash up fauna from different terrains as cavalierly as did Burroughs, with – considering modern knowledge – far less excuse. Moreover, whatever the animal – carnivore or herbivore – Tarzan is shown to be mates with them all.

Principal photography was done in Hertfordshire in the UK, but the Congo exterior background footage was shot in Gabon. Yates' African photography – landscapes and animals – is sumptuous and exciting. Particularly impressive are scenes involving unsettlingly man-sized ostriches and ferocious-looking hippos. However, his action sequences – wherever shot – are disjointed, confusing and full of pointless slow-motion. It's also quite arresting that there is nothing in the animal scenes as impressive as a 2011 Kerala Tourism television advertisement with the strapline 'Your Moment is Waiting', which contained an image of a woman beatifically leaning her head against the trunk of an elephant that is resting on its belly, ears contentedly flapping, a vista strikingly like a transplantation of several scenes written by Burroughs involving Tarzan indolently lying on Tantor's back scratching his ears. It's peculiar and frustrating that no Tarzan movie has ever contained anything so beautiful and so suggestive of oneness with nature as this mere commercial.

When Tarzan sets off in search of a kidnapped Jane, he seems no more adept on vines than the natives in his party. In fact, we only really get the impression that Tarzan is anything extraordinary in a scene in which he, single-handedly and unarmed, lays to waste a train carriage full of Belgian soldiers. Elsewhere, the fashions and exigencies of the modern era simply prevent him being too impressive. When he is reunited with his Mangani tribe and compelled to battle Akut, for instance, he does not use the knife that in such showdowns was once *de rigueur* but is now deemed inhumane. Unsurprisingly, he loses – which begs the question of how a weapon-spurning Tarzan was ever able to become 'Lord of the apes, king of the jungle.' Moreover, when Tarzan is confronted by Mbonga, he is not shown overcoming him but supplicating to him and conceding he was wrong. In a 21st century in which the world is making recompense for past maltreatment of native Africans, the fact that Mbonga's son slew the only mother Tarzan had known has to be made less important than the fact that Mbonga's son was supposedly too young to know any better.

In preparation for his fight with Akut, Tarzan strips to his breeches, which end, Victorian-style, just below the knee. He remains dressed like that for the duration, making this the first loincloth-free ape-man theatrical release since Frank Merrill's *Tarzan the Tiger* in 1929, aside from what Yates terms, 'A little homage to the loincloth at the end, when he's swinging through the jungle with all the apes.' Yates reasons that the breeches were, 'Again, in the spirit of moving it on and making it feel more resonant and contemporary. And this story did not require him to wear a loincloth. It was not really about that stage of his life.' However, he betrays the fact that part of his rationale is rooted in his lack of knowledge about the source material when he appends of Tarzan's childhood, 'It's absurd to have a loincloth in the jungle because the primates that take care of him, they don't know how to make loincloths.'

Considering all this updating, it is ironic that it is the

antediluvianism of the climax which undermines an above-average Tarzan actor, high production values and an interesting new take on the ape-man. Tarzan somehow summons hordes of lions and wildebeest to help him defeat the villain. That the creatures, instead of battling each other, obligingly destroy the town where Rom is assembling a mercenary army is as corny and nonsensical as all those Weissmuller climaxes where the day was saved by the arrival of elephants equipped with anthropomorphic sentience.

The ape-man provides an explosive Bondian climax by interfering with the pressure gauge on Rom's steamer. With missions accomplished – Rom ends up inside a crocodile and Jackson has enough evidence to indict Leopold – Tarzan for some reason remains in Africa, where one year later (and with the ape-man still dressed in nothing but breeches) Jane has a healthy baby. (Earlier on, it is implied that Jane once had a miscarriage.) Hozier's 'Better Love', played over the closing credits, provides the ape-man another anthem, even if its relationship to his bio seems nebulous.

Strangely, this film boasts several similarities to 1998's *Tarzan and the Lost City*, the last live-action ape-man cinema outing, among them a frock-coated Victorian England opening, Tarzan sporting a pony tail in civilisation, Tarzan in breeches and the whiff of 1930s serials.

However, there has been a big societal – or at last media – change since '98. Political correctness so suffuses its every frame that *The Legend of Tarzan* ends up almost an apologia for the Tarzan character and its history. This serves to diminish both logic and excitement. Not only is Tarzan barely allowed to be the savage primeval that has always been his essence, but the script is heaving with anachronisms. When she finds Tarzan intimately sniffing her when they first meet in Africa, Jane – as though fresh from a sexual-harassment seminar – says, 'I'm not sure my father would find this very appropriate.' Jane is ludicrously 21st century, snarling defiance, spitting in faces, head-butting, and punching with a closed fist. George Washington Williams is played absurdly by Jackson: although he (like Rom) was a real person, it's impossible to believe Williams would have been as bellicose and jive-talkin' as a Tarantino character. Not only is the Leopold-related anti-slavery storyline achingly right-on, it requires juggling the chronology (the action is set in 1889, shortly after the ape-man was born in Burroughs' first Tarzan novel) and changing Tarzan's nationality (i.e. he now seems to be Congolese instead of the previously theorised Angolan, Gabonese or Kenyan). There is even a soliloquy about the immorality of the treatment of the American Indians.

The film's endless self-consciousness about conforming to what are considered acceptable attitudes by modern society – or at least an influential component of its commentariat – is summed up in the speech by Jane that gives the film its title. It is used twice, in slightly different iterations. It first appears as, 'They're singing the legend of Tarzan. For many years he was thought to be an evil spirit. A ghost in the trees. They speak of his power over the animals of the jungle. Because his spirit came from them, he understood them. And learned to conquer them.' The reprise closes the 110-minute picture. Here, the final line is pointedly changed to, 'And learned to be as one with them.'

All this trendy recalibration cut no ice with the critics. Reviewers more than ever before had problems with the premise of a white man being the king of the jungle. They further suggested that the very fact that the screenwriters had felt obliged to jettison some of the Tarzan hallmarks showed that it would be better not to make ape-man pictures at all rather than attempt to update the concept. That is, when they weren't adjudging the film nonsensical and corny.

Yet *The Legend of Tarzan* defied the poor box-office expectations engendered by the largely unfavourable reviews. 'We did quite well,' adjudges Yates. 'I think the movie made 356 million dollars at the box office. It's not a huge blockbuster, but it's pretty respectable. So there was an audience for it. I'm very proud of the film and we had some wonderful feedback from fans of Tarzan. And people who didn't know anything very much about Tarzan seemed to respond to it really well.'

The film, though, did not achieve Yates' apparent objective of riding the superhero wave. As Yates says, 'There's a number we had to cross to be able to justify making a further film and we didn't quite hit that number.' He is referring to the fact that prospects for a sequel fell foul of the same contemporary movie-studio metrics that did for *John Carter*: the rigid financial formula which dictates that a motion picture has to earn back twice its budget to be granted a follow-up. 'It's a business fundamentally,' Yates shrugs. Some might suggest that Yates' own business sense is awry: it seems staggering, considering the lack of principal shooting in Africa, that the director managed to rack up production costs of $180m.

The Tarzan live-action rights will remain with Warner Brothers for several years. Considering that *The Legend of Tarzan* did find an audience, it's possible that, even if there is not a direct sequel, there will be another Tarzan picture relatively soon. However, if the Tarzan property comes to be perceived as tainted by failure, it may once more lie fallow for decades until rediscovery by a new generation of filmmakers. Should that far-future project fail once again to be a Burroughs-correct depiction of the ape-man, it will be commensurately more disappointing to the aficionados.

'It has always proven hard to make an ERB [adaptation] that's true to the book,' mused Michael Moorcock, albeit before the release of *The Legend of Tarzan*. Speaking of his experience of devising a script for the 1975 film version of *The Land that Time Forgot*, he notes, 'The director was able to change the ending and get rid of some of the story's idea through editing.' He summarises, 'I suspect such disappointments will be forever with us.'

The Tarzan centenary briefly saw a renewed interest on the part of mainstream publishers in reissuing ape-man novels. In November 2012, Gollancz put out the deluxe hardback *Tarzan of the Apes & Other Tales: A Centenary Edition*, embossed with gilt versions of the Tarzan logo and iconic ape-man-with-lion J Allen St John image. While nobody was expecting a '60s-style Burroughs boom, it's startling how quickly things went from covetably deluxe to quasi-ephemeral: subsequent Tarzan reissues were done via the Gateway imprint of Gollancz's parent company Orion, whose mission statement is, 'to ensure that the great works of SF & Fantasy's heritage are not lost to the harsh economic realities of modern commercial print publishing.' Which means, of course, eBooks, as cheap to manufacture and market as digital comics.

In 2013 Baen published a multiple-author collection of short stories titled *The Worlds of Edgar Rice Burroughs*, edited by Mike Resnick and Robert T Garcia. It followed 2012's *Under the Moons of Mars: New Adventures on Barsoom*. They were available in print – or hard copies to use the modern parlance – but the fact that the 2013 book had just three Tarzan tales suggested, like the Andy Briggs novels, a lack of confidence in the existence of the once-considerable audience for adult Tarzan prose. However, in May 2015 came *Tarzan: Return to Pal-ul-don* (Altus Press), not only an adult ape-man novel, but the start of the most energetic programme of Tarzan writing since the death of ERB. It was the first of a new series called "The Wild Adventures of Edgar Rice Burroughs" intended to also take in the other worlds devised by the ape-man's creator.

Will Murray is a pulp historian and novelist who has written several Doc Savage continuation books. In *Return to Pal-ul-don* he has the ape-man, as in *Tarzan the Terrible*, accidentally visiting the 'Land of Men' during a time of global conflagration in the outer world. This, though, is a different World War, the second, placing the story adjacent to *Tarzan and the 'Foreign Legion'*. Lord Greystoke is despatched by the RAF to retrieve a crashed military aeroplane which happens to have come down in the vicinity of Pal-ul-don. 'Tarzan and the Secret of Katanga', a short-form sequel by Gary A Buckingham, appeared in a deluxe hardback version of the book. Murray's second Tarzan book appeared in November 2016. *King Kong vs. Tarzan* (also Altus was the sort of fantasy-league crossover that the public is more used to seeing in comic books.

Murray had an existing relationship with Altus, but other continuation works would be published by ERB, Inc themselves, who had an ambitious programme with which they felt no mainstream publisher was likely to be able to keep pace.

Tarzan on the Precipice by Michael A Sanford appeared in May 2016. Set between *Tarzan of the Apes* and *The Return of Tarzan*, and between the ape-man's renouncing of his birthright and return to Africa, it sees him take a detour to Canada with vague plans of looking up Paul D'Arnot's brother. There, he stumbles upon a lost civilisation – surrounded by a thorny thicket like that encircling Minuni – consisting of the descendants of a Viking settlement. Also resident in the crater are the region's variant of Mangani – outsiders call them sasquatch.

In December 2016, came *Tarzan Trilogy* by Thomas Zachek. It contained three new ape-man novellas set in the mid-20th century. *Tarzan: The Greystoke Legacy Under Siege* by Ralph N Laughlin and Ann E Johnson appeared in May 2017. Set in the 1970s and 1980s, the story features a Tarzan who is now a great-grandfather but still virile and active. His son Jack runs the Greystokes' African estate, grandson Jackie administers the Greystoke Trust in London and Jon, Tarzan's great-grandson, has just graduated from college. At the start of the tale, Jon has not yet embraced his African heritage because his mother (Jackie's Swiss wife) wants nothing to do with that continent, raising her son instead in London and Switzerland. Famous real-life gorilla researcher Dian Fossey makes an appearance in a narrative that sees Tarzan traveling to London, Paris and Moscow to work out why the Greystoke family is under attack on several fronts. Sullos opines that it is 'unlike any other Tarzan novel and will become a seminal story to carry Tarzan and the Greystoke Trust into the late 20th Century.'

The proliferation of new ape-man books could one day mean that continuation Tarzan novels dwarf in number the original Burroughs canon, a situation that already exists with James

Bond, another franchise that took a long time to implement a full-fledged continuation publishing programme after a hesitant start. The difference is that the Fleming legatees have hit upon a lucrative way of perpetuating prose James Bond: hiring literary novelists of the stature of Sebastian Faulks and William Boyd to write a single 007 novel, thus ensuring each time out both wide publicity and sales to people beyond the Fleming fanbase. For the Burroughs estate, it is too late, and Tarzan of too old a vintage. The 1966 Fritz Leiber *Tarzan and the Valley of Gold* novelisation could have inaugurated such a programme, but many of the name authors who were brought up on Burroughs, and who would be obvious candidates to participate, are now dead. One feels, however, that the corporation can do better than pulp-revivalist writers like Murray, previously self-published authors like Zachek, or in the case of Sanford, a retired dentist.

Whatever the failings – commercial and/or aesthetic – of the latest two cinematic Tarzan ventures, the ape-man continues to be considered a commercial screen property.

As proof, in January 2017 came 41 Entertainment's television series *Tarzan and Jane*, commissioned by Netflix. It was yet another ape-man milestone: the first Tarzan screen vehicle whose initial transmission consisted of a streaming over the internet, a concept which when *All-Story* printed *Tarzan of the Apes* in 1912 would have been no more comprehensible to civilised man than to the Mangani.

The series was the idea of Avi Arad – ex-head of Toybiz and Marvel Studios – and developed and co-executive produced by he and Allen Bohbot. Kaaren Lee Brown was head writer and story editor. *Tarzan and Jane* uses the type of computer animation pioneered in *Toy Story* (1995) and popular since, in which characters look more three-dimensional than those in traditional painted cel animation, but at the same time as curiously unreal as moving dolls. The first series was eight episodes (all available to watch on the same day, as per Netflix's policy) of half an hour each (including commercials).

The series' origin story spans the first three episodes. It starts with the crashing in an African jungle of an aeroplane containing baby John and his relief-worker parents. The orphaned John is rescued by gorilla Kala. When Kala (for no discernible reason) takes the baby to a Waziri shaman, the latter injects him with a combination of ancient medicine and the experiments of British scientist Archimedes Porter. The injection involves various types of animal DNA: 'mighty lion, great gorilla and racing cheetah.' These not only save the boy's life but unexpectedly grant him those animals' powers. When he calls on those powers, he physically changes: cheetah's claws sprout, enabling him to climb trees and even cut open car roofs, his eyes grow large and grant him a lion's night vision, his muscles visibly balloon when using the strength of the gorilla...

The shaman is worried about the unforeseen consequences of anyone else having access to the transformative effects of the medicine ('The world is not yet ready for him') and accordingly ensures Porter is told that John has died. He gives the baby to Kala to raise, although John maintains contact with local civilisation. 'Tarzan' is the name given the boy by the Africans, which means in their parlance 'child of the jungle'. The boy spends his early years in apparently the same loincloth in which he is wrapped at the human-simian handover. Andy Briggs might find it interesting that the teen ape-man is depicted running around the jungle in cargo shorts. By now, Tarzan is speaking English with an African accent. His African peer 'Muviro Waziri' educates him. The young Tarzan has little dignity, blowing raspberries to indicate displeasure. He at least grows out of that, but there is no improvement in his feeble yodel. With Weissmuller's powerful yell so iconic and freely available to anyone working with ERB, Inc, one wonders why producers so seldom avail themselves of it.

While in Africa, Tarzan meets Dr Porter's daughter Jane. The latter's assumption that Tarzan is inarticulate enables a play on the classic dialogue between the two characters: Jane introduces herself by saying 'Me, Jane;' Tarzan responds, 'Me, Tarzan.' Jane is subsequently shocked to find he is perfectly fluent in English, although not half as shocked as the viewer will be when in civilisation his African accent changes instantly to an English one.

That transition from real to urban jungle is brought about by the uploading to the internet of tourist drone footage of a mysterious feral boy. It is seen by Tarzan's billionaire grandfather, Earl Greystoke, who instantly notes the resemblance to his missing son. The 15-year-old Tarzan (voiced by Giles Panton) is at first not happy to be retrieved from his African home, but softens when he begins to feel a familial connection. He ends up at private school Burroughs Academy, in whose uniform he is only visibly wild via his quasi-dreadlocked hair and disinclination to wear shoes.

One of his schoolmates is Jane (Rebecca Shoichet). As in Constantin's film, Jane's dad is, like so many contemporary fathers, estranged from the mother of his child. Whereas Jane's dad is an upright white Englishman, her flighty actress-turned-reporter mother is a black American. The political correctness doesn't end there. As the series title suggests, Jane is depicted as on the same footing as Tarzan despite the fact that this incarnation of the ape-man effectively makes him a superhero. Just as she in Africa was instantly swinging on a vine as adroitly as the boy raised in the wild, in civilisation Jane keeps pace with Tarzan's climbing powers. She does so via a suit whose underarm flaps preposterously enable her to fly.

One episode commits the error of having Tarzan reminisce about orangutans, but the depictions of London at least are reasonably authentic in terms of settings, traditions and accent, and only a pedant might point out that car-bound British police officers don't wear helmets or that UK billionaire's buildings do not feature giant vanity signage. When Tarzan and his schoolmates have a kickabout (another sign of the authenticity is them playing soccer, not American football), the ape-man is – even after a century – gifted a new attribute: he's revealed to be a great goalie.

Muviro (Doron Bell) is also in London, having gained a scholarship. He, Tarzan and Jane soon end up in battle with villains in Tarzan's nature-oriented wheelhouse. Along with their tussles with animal poachers, the trio are having to deal with the background machinations of Tarzan's evil cousin, who is trying to bring about the Earl of Greystoke's ruination.

As in the Filmation animated series, there is no sex or violence. Tarzan triumphs via methods like commanding a rhino to demolish the cages of poachers and unleashing hornets on baddies. Meanwhile, the closest the two leads come to romance is an exchange accompanied by a meaningful look at the end of episode eight: 'We do make a great team, Jane'/'No doubt about it, Tarzan.'

The animation is merely good rather than great: actions such as climbing, swinging and pouncing are lazily concertinaed. Meanwhile, Kala is mysteriously brown-furred. Faces are, though, at least natural looking instead of grotesque or comical.

Many things don't make sense. How is Tarzan so conversant with society's customs, technology and argot? Why would Tarzan be so adept in the trees if raised by ground-based gorillas? How is he able to befriend predatory animals like panthers? Some of these nonsensicalities are of course in the long tradition of Tarzan on film, but part of the explanation seems to be the fact that the intended demographic is unprecedentedly young. Certainly, the older palette will find much of this stilted and dull. Nonetheless, it can be reasonably entertaining, even sweet, for older viewers, not least because there are occasional winks to them, such as the crack Jane makes about the smell of Tarzan's feet.

Tarzan and Jane essentially demonstrates that there are always new ways to move around the furniture of the Tarzan legend. Such rearranging will almost always upset the purist, but is probably the only way to achieve the wish that unites every ERB fan: to keep Tarzan alive.

PART ELEVEN: SWINGING INTO AN UNCERTAIN FUTURE

While Tarzan continues to exist as both cultural icon and commercial property, there is no getting around the fact that the trajectory traced by this book is of a figure of incrementally decreasing profitability and relevance, one whose continued existence is only made possible by being traduced.

Tarzan never seemed a figure of the Edwardian era, which very slightly preceded his first appearance, nor of any other specific timeframe. Whereas Sherlock Holmes is rooted in Victoriana, Tarzan has lent himself to endless updating. At any given point in time, there was somehow always something contemporary about him, even if his muscular values far predated and were often in opposition to those of soft modern society.

That situation no longer prevails. The low cinematic profile in recent decades of a character who once dominated the flicks is quite startling. In the 52 years between 1918 and 1970, there were 42 official Tarzan cinematic ventures, including the two Ron Ely pseudo-movies and the two marginally differentiated Herman Brix films, but not including the two questionable Steve Hawkes films nor serial versions of ventures also released as features. Since 1970, there have been six, two of them not live-action. From once being perceived by movie studios and producers as a commercial certainty, Tarzan is now viewed with financial scepticism. Roy Thomas, Marvel Tarzan comics writer, says, 'Several decades ago I remember reading that the three most famous characters on the face of the planet earth were Tarzan, Superman and Sherlock Holmes. Even if Superman might still be in there – I don't know about Sherlock Holmes – I doubt if Tarzan is. And if he is, it's just a faint memory of him, 'cause he's an idea whose time has gone.'

The idea of a man who is a friend to all those creatures of the jungle with whom he is not tussling to the death is anthropomorphic illogicality of the kind that many people now accept only in cartoons. Furthermore, the careless approach to zoology of the old Tarzan books and movies – the nonsensical throwing together of plains and jungle animals (and sometimes African and Asian wildlife) – no longer washes. And yet, what kind of Tarzan would it be without lions and elephants in the frame?

Additionally, many people feel that the whole Tarzan story is rooted in the assumptions of imperialism. Even leaving aside the frequent racism to be found in Burroughs' prose, the very notion of a white man being king of the jungle is one that seems, in some way that is perhaps not fully explainable, to be critical of black races.

An inherited title like Lord Greystoke does not imply the exalted position in the human race it did even until relatively recently. In 1999, the number of hereditary peers permitted to sit in Parliament's second chamber was reduced to a mere 92. Stripped of the implication of legend-shrouded, passed-on power, the peerage was massively diluted in allure, with 'lord' left as little more than a fancy-pants title.

Moreover, Tarzan's stamping ground of Africa does not have the mysterious associations it once did. 'I've been in Africa, I spent a couple of weeks in Kenya driving around,' says Thomas. 'You'd be hard-pressed to find much jungle there. The animals have to get used to you driving within 50 or a hundred feet of them or else they wouldn't survive, 'cause there wouldn't be any tourism there if you couldn't drive around and suddenly around a corner see a pride of lions or an elephant. You just can't [set] it in Africa anymore. If you do, you're ignoring the facts that any halfway intelligent schoolchild would know. You might be able to find a way to do a story or two now and then and assume that there's some jungle somewhere that's been kept away, but it wouldn't be that vast.'

Additionally, Tarzan is limited today in what he can do in that jungle. As far back as the mid-'80s, Hugh Hudson was apprised of the fact that the public did not find acceptable depictions of the death of animals at Tarzan's hands, regardless of the imperatives of realism. In the early 20th century, carnivorous African wild animals had associations of menace. In the latter part of that century, as the dwindling of their numbers caused by hunting and habitat-destruction became public knowledge, that perception underwent such a change that they actually became objects of pity. In an age where wildlife is seen through a prism of the assumptions of conservation, the idea of an animal being killed by a man wielding a knife is not exciting but grisly. Yet a Tarzan who cannot plunge his father's blade into the hide of Bolgani, Numa, Sheeta or Mangani even in self-defence is truly a pointless Tarzan. The loinclothed backwoods policeman role to which this would reduce him has been tried before – principally in the Ron Ely TV series – and been found wanting. That all the post-Mike Henry Tarzan cinema projects have proffered Tarzan only in bland form may well explain the very paucity of post-Mike Henry Tarzan cinema projects.

As might cultural time and tide. Movie Tarzan Denny Miller was a professional habitué of nostalgia events. He noted, 'We go mainly to Western film festivals. They're coming to see people they watched with grandmother and grandfather and their mother and father on black-and-white television. Some of them bring their kids, and their kids aren't interested in cowboys. Their heroes are astronauts and spaceship guys. Those are the cowboys and the Tarzans of yesteryear. The youth of today, in this country anyway, are no longer [into] cowboys or Tarzans because they've grown up without them.' Gary Goddard, co-screenwriter of Bo and John Derek's *Tarzan the Ape Man*, puts it in the more clinical terms of an industry insider. 'A fundamental paradigm shift happened after *Star Wars*,' he says. 'Most people tell you Westerns died because of *Star Wars*, because *Star Wars* is to some degree a Western but it's disguised as something else. The kids didn't want six-shooters anymore after that, they wanted lightsabers. *Star Wars* spoke to a generation. The nature of the Tarzan-type hero is perhaps a product of its time.' 'I think other noble savages have taken his place to a degree,' says

Michael Moorcock. 'Conan and various other fantasy creations. The appeal is a powerful one and in American literature goes back at least as far as Fenimore Cooper. *Star Wars* has taken over to a degree, but the role of romantic hero as some kind of outcast seems to have been taken over by various vampires and wolfmen for the moment ... I'm not sure his time has passed, but he would probably operate better in the denser parts of the Amazonian forest. Somewhere we could find a lost city or two without losing our sense of wonder ... I'd love to see an intelligent movie or HBO series, say, which dealt with the shrinking Congo and the plight of the great apes in the ongoing civil wars in that region. Tarzan is still a good poster boy for ecological preservation, respect for wild animals and our duty to be good stewards for the planet. He doesn't have to be pious about it. He, of all people, can get angry and fight against armies conscripting boy soldiers and so on – maybe having been asked to come by the Waziri. Maybe the only way it could be done would be by a black author. Readers seek their escapism in different ways these days in fantasy and SF, but if Tarzan became more up-to-date he might turn into something less escapist, better able to face the Matter of Africa.'

Regardless of what happens with Tarzan in the cinema, the prose Tarzan will never be as big again, and not merely because its originating author is dead. The decline of prose Tarzan began with the waning of the pulps, an extended freefall that actually started not long after Burroughs placed his first novel with *All-Story*. The paper shortages of the Second World War further damaged the market. Over the coming years, the decline was exacerbated by the expanding entertainment options available to increasingly affluent Western societies. Pulps did not survive to the '60s in a recognisable cultural form or newsstand format. Possibly the primary type of mass entertainment in 1912, they are now all long gone.

The '60s may have seen a Burroughs boom but it was also the end of the line for mass-market Tarzan books. In the 1970s, men's action-adventure novels briefly became a flourishing industry.

One might have thought this was the perfect backdrop for another ERB boom, or at least a Tarzan boom in which a chosen author could continue the ape-man's adventures in the manner of L Sprague de Camp's extrapolation of Robert E Howard's Conan stories. However, the paperbacks shifting huge quantities at this point in history were gratuitously violent, profane and exploitative of human foible – in other words, full of all the things Burroughs' square-jawed, moralistic prose was not. In any case, the men's action-adventure novel wave drained away rapidly: in the next decade the market was decimated by home video. Even without that invention, the prose Tarzan would have suffered along with all other literary characters: books have now been completely eclipsed by film, comics, television and digital games in a culture where reading prose is not cool.

In 2008, Danton Burroughs was anxious to emphasise to this author, 'We're still protected in England until the year 2020,' a reference to the fact that in Britain copyright is creator's-life-plus-70 years whereas in the States copyrights on works published before 1923 have unequivocally expired. American copyright law has changed since the upheavals of the 1960s, with authors' works protected until 70 years after their deaths if published in 1978 or thereafter. This does little good for Burroughs' heirs, though. Although works published after 1923 but before 1978 are protected for 95 years, it all becomes rather meaningless in light of differing copyright laws in different countries and the ability created by the World Wide Web to circumnavigate the notion of sales territories.

In the last years of Danton's life came the confluence of increasing numbers of Burroughs works falling into the public domain, the expansion of the internet and the rise of inexpensive print-on-demand technology. This confluence served to give occasion to both Burroughs fans and the merely opportunistic to offer their own versions of ERB books. Said Danton, 'We don't like it, but this is the way copyright law is.' The only substantial protection ERB, Inc have derives from their canny decision to trademark the word 'Tarzan', something the inheritors of the estates of the creators of Sherlock Holmes and James Bond failed to do with their properties. ('John Carter' and some place names from Burroughs' books are similarly protected.) As Bill Hillman points out, 'If you're endangering contracts with Disney, MGM or major comic book companies, you have to defend it.' While this should ensure a legal deterrent to too much unauthorised exploitation, one is tempted to think that ERB, Inc might even be nostalgic for the days when the number of people who actually wanted to exploit the Tarzan character vastly outnumbered that today.

Perhaps, though, this is a rather over-dramatic analysis of the health of the Tarzan franchise. Danton certainly didn't feel any particular financial pinch on the part of ERB, Inc in 2008, with the John Carter movie in preparation, the live-action Warner Brothers Tarzan being planned and even a Carson of Venus movie on the theoretical horizon. 'It's never-ending,' he said. 'It still keeps us busy. There's still interest out there.'

Since then there have been two Tarzan cinematic releases and a tide of new Tarzan books and comics. Productions of the Disney Tarzan stage show continue to be mounted across the world. The character lives on in countless other, often unexpected, ways. A 2017 Google Alert for mentions of 'Tarzan' on the internet yielded new results every day. Everywhere, the ape-man's recognisability is confirmed by the fact of people and things continuing to be named after him by either headline writers or civilians: a naked rock climber, a flamboyant Ghanaian politician, a monkey seen exploring a backwater of Fort Lauderdale, a canine contestant in the Puppy Bowl, a type of suede wedge sandal, a freestyle swimming technique, an eleven-year-old child found living wild in India, a robot designed by a US university to swing between cables to monitor crops, a documentary on the relationship between humans and monkeys with a Soviet Union allegory titled *Tarzan's Testicles*... Moreover, it is obvious from the remarkable number of erotic Kindle books featuring Tarzan in name, image or circumstance that the ape-man is a significant sexual fantasy figure, straight and gay.

This is all astonishing because when Tarzan first appeared more than a century ago, it was in a world with vastly different technologies, assumptions and traditions. The world of 1912 had no radio or television, nor motion pictures that today we would not find risible. Universal suffrage existed in neither the USA nor Britain. Courtesy of pre-industrialisation, Africa was a largely unknown continent. With the exception of just two countries, that continent was the property of far-off white European nations and would remain in that colonised state for four decades. The concept of racism as a pejorative was in its infancy, as were the notions of ecological preservation and animal rights. Life for most of the people in the industrialised West was poverty-stricken and drab. That they sought out adventures set in a far-flung and more colourful land was as much to do with obtaining solace as aesthetic pleasure. In light of all of that, it can be posited as a triumph that Tarzan has not gravitated to the status of a creation about which a consensus has emerged that he is merely historical, like the Three Musketeers, or simply offensive, like Fu ('Yellow Peril') Manchu, Bulldog (enemy of 'wogs' and 'dagos') Drummond and the Scarlet (friend of the decadently cruel) Pimpernel.

'I don't think it's dated,' says Christopher Lambert. 'Don't try to make the character of Tarzan Indiana Jones, because that's dated. If you make a new movie about feelings, about emotions, about sadness, about tears, about pain, about joy, about being a chimp – that is not dated.'

Notwithstanding his comments above, Goddard says, 'I think all the themes still work, stories work. What would bring it back is a re-telling that would speak to today's audiences. Look what they did with [Guy Ritchie's 2009 film] *Sherlock Holmes*. They basically kept Sherlock Holmes but they added almost a steampunk quality. That was a huge hit. Sherlock Holmes is a pretty stuffy character as written. All of a sudden he's embraced by a new generation. A filmmaker has to come along who has a voice, an interesting point of view, who retains the Tarzan basic mythology, the basic elements of the character, and then layers in something that speaks to today's generation. Certainly, there's enough stories of Tarzan you could actually do that.'

He summarises, 'Tarzan is perennial and the basic idea is very strong. I believe Tarzan is timeless.'

APPENDIX: TARZAN IN THE MEDIA

BOOKS

By Edgar Rice Burroughs
1914: *Tarzan of the Apes* (McClurg)
1915: *The Return of Tarzan* (McClurg)
1916: *The Beasts of Tarzan* (McClurg)
1917: *The Son of Tarzan* (McClurg)
1918: *Tarzan and the Jewels of Opar* (McClurg)
1919: *Jungle Tales of Tarzan* (McClurg)
1920: *Tarzan the Untamed* (McClurg)
1921: *Tarzan the Terrible* (McClurg)
1923: *Tarzan and the Golden Lion* (McClurg)
1924: *Tarzan and the Ant Men* (McClurg)
1925: *The Eternal Lover* (McClurg)
  Note: Tarzan makes cameo appearance only.
1927: *The Tarzan Twins* (Volland)
  Note: book for children.
1928: *Tarzan, Lord of the Jungle* (McClurg),
1929: *Tarzan and the Lost Empire* (Metropolitan)
1930: *Tarzan at the Earth's Core* (Metropolitan)
1931: *Tarzan the Invincible* (Burroughs)
1931: *Tarzan Triumphant* (Burroughs)
1933: *Tarzan and the City of Gold* (Burroughs)
1934: *Tarzan and the Lion Man* (Burroughs)
1935: *Tarzan and the Leopard Men* (Burroughs)
1936: *Tarzan and the Tarzan Twins, with Jad-bal-ja, the Golden Lion* (Whitman)
  Note: book for children.
1936: *Tarzan's Quest* (Burroughs)
1938: *Tarzan and the Forbidden City* (Burroughs)
1939: *Tarzan the Magnificent* (Burroughs)
1947: *Tarzan and the 'Foreign Legion'* (Burroughs)
1964: *Tarzan and the Madman* (Canaveral)
1965: *Tarzan and the Castaways* (Canaveral)

(Features 'Tarzan and the Castaways', 'Tarzan and the Champion' and 'Tarzan and the Jungle Murders')

Note: with the exception of *The Tarzan Twins, Tarzan and the Tarzan Twins, with Jad-bal-ja, the Golden Lion, Tarzan and the 'Foreign Legion'* and *Tarzan and the Madman*, all the above initially appeared in magazines first, often in significantly different form and sometimes under a different title.

By Fritz Leiber
1966: *Tarzan and the Valley of Gold* (Ballantine)
    Note: novelisation of motion picture of same title.

By Douglas Niles
1985: *Tarzan and the Well of Slaves* (TSR, Inc.)
    Note: role-playing book.

By Richard Reinsmith
1986: *Tarzan and the Tower of Diamonds* (TSR, Inc.)
    Note: role-playing book.

By Edgar Rice Burroughs and Joe R Lansdale
1995: *Tarzan: The Lost Adventure* (Dark Horse)
    Note: Burroughs uncompleted manuscript finished, amended and expanded by Lansdale; initially appeared in magazines.

By R A Salvatore
1996: *Tarzan: The Epic Adventures* (Del Rey)
    Note: novelisation of television pilot of same title.

By Philip José Farmer
1999: *The Dark Heart of Time* (Del Rey)

By Maude Robinson Toombs
2006: *Adventures of Tarzan* (ERBville Press)

Note: collation of newspaper serialisation of novelisation of 1921 serial of same title.

By Arthur B Reeve
2008: *Tarzan the Mighty* (ERBville Press)
Note: collation of newspaper serialisation of novelisation of 1928 serial of same title.

By Andy Briggs
2011: *Tarzan: The Greystoke Legacy* (Faber and Faber)
2012: *Tarzan: The Jungle Warrior* (Faber and Faber)
Note: books for children.

By Robin Maxwell
2012: *Jane: The Woman Who Loved Tarzan* (Tor)

By Andy Briggs
2013: *Tarzan: The Savage Lands* (Faber and Faber)
Note: book for children.

By Will Murray
2015: *Tarzan: Return to Pal-ul-don* (Altus Press)

By Michael A Sanford
2016: *Tarzan on the Precipice* (Edgar Rice Burroughs, Inc)

By Will Murray
2016: *King Kong Vs. Tarzan* (Altus Press)

By Thomas Zachek
2016: *Tarzan Trilogy* (Edgar Rice Burroughs, Inc)

By Ralph N Laughlin and Ann E Johnson
2017: *Tarzan: The Greystoke Legacy Under Siege* (Edgar Rice Burroughs, Inc)

MOTION PICTURES

Tarzan played by Gordon Griffith (as a boy) and Elmo Lincoln
1918: *Tarzan of the Apes* (National Film Corp.)
1918: *The Romance of Tarzan* (National Film Corp.)

Tarzan played by Gene Pollar
1920: *The Revenge of Tarzan* (Numa Pictures)

Tarzan played Gordon Griffith (as a boy) and P Dempsey Tabler
1920: *The Son of Tarzan* (National Film Corp.)
    Note: serial; also released in feature format.

Tarzan played by Elmo Lincoln
1921: *Adventures of Tarzan* (Great Western)
    Note: serial; also released in feature format.

Tarzan played by James Pierce
1927: *Tarzan and the Golden Lion* (R-C Pictures)

Tarzan played by Frank Merrill
1928: *Tarzan the Mighty* (Universal)
    Note: serial.
1929: *Tarzan the Tiger* (Universal)
    Note: serial.

Tarzan played by Johnny Weissmuller
1932: *Tarzan the Ape Man* (MGM)

Tarzan played by Buster Crabbe
1933: *Tarzan the Fearless* (Principal)
    Note: serial; also released in feature format.

Tarzan played by Johnny Weissmuller
1934: *Tarzan and His Mate* (MGM)

Tarzan played by Herman Brix
1935: *New Adventures of Tarzan* (Burroughs-Tarzan Enterprises)
Note: serial; also released in feature format.

Tarzan played by Johnny Weissmuller
1936: *Tarzan Escapes* (MGM)

Tarzan played by Glenn Morris
1938: *Tarzan's Revenge* (Principal)

Tarzan played by Herman Brix
1938: *Tarzan and the Green Goddess* (Burroughs-Tarzan Enterprises)
Note: largely footage previously seen in *The New Adventures of Tarzan*.

Tarzan played by Johnny Weissmuller
1939: *Tarzan Finds a Son!* (MGM)
1941: *Tarzan's Secret Treasure* (MGM)
1942: *Tarzan's New York Adventure* (MGM)
1943: *Tarzan Triumphs* (RKO)
1943: *Tarzan's Desert Mystery* (RKO)
1945: *Tarzan and the Amazons* (RKO)
1946: *Tarzan and the Leopard Woman* (RKO)
1947: *Tarzan and the Huntress* (RKO)
1948: *Tarzan and the Mermaids* (RKO)

Tarzan played by Lex Barker
1949: *Tarzan's Magic Fountain* (RKO)
1950: *Tarzan and the Slave Girl* (RKO)
1951: *Tarzan's Peril* (RKO)
1952: *Tarzan's Savage Fury* (RKO)
1953: *Tarzan and the She-Devil* (RKO)

Tarzan played by Gordon Scott
1955: *Tarzan's Hidden Jungle* (RKO)
1957: *Tarzan and the Lost Safari* (MGM)
1958: *Tarzan's Fight for Life* (MGM)
1959: *Tarzan's Greatest Adventure* (MGM)

Tarzan played by Denny Miller
1959: *Tarzan the Ape Man* (MGM)

Tarzan played by Gordon Scott
1960: *Tarzan the Magnificent* (Paramount)

Tarzan played by Jock Mahoney
1962: *Tarzan Goes to India* (MGM)
1963: *Tarzan's Three Challenges* (MGM)

Tarzan played by Mike Henry
1966: *Tarzan and the Valley of Gold* (Banner Productions-Allfin, A.G.)
1967: *Tarzan and the Great River* (Banner Productions)
1968: *Tarzan and the Jungle Boy* (Banner Productions)

Tarzan played by Ron Ely
1970: *Tarzan's Deadly Silence*
1970: *Tarzan's Jungle Rebellion*
    Note: above two releases spliced episodes from television series.

Tarzan played by Steve Hawkes
1970:   *Tarzan En La Gruta Del Oro* (*Tarzan in the Golden Grotto*)
1972:   *Tarzan Y El Arco Iris* (*Tarzan and the Rainbow*); also known as *Tarzan and the Brown Prince*
    Note: above two releases of questioned legality.

Tarzan played by Miles O'Keeffe
1981: *Tarzan the Ape Man* (MGM)

Tarzan played by Daniel Potts (as a boy), Eric Langlois (as a teenager) and Christopher Lambert
1984: *Greystoke: The Legend of Tarzan, Lord of the Apes* (Warner Bros.)

Tarzan played by Casper Van Dien
1998: *Tarzan and the Lost City* (Warner Bros.)

Tarzan played by Tony Goldwyn
1999: *Tarzan* (Disney)
   Note: animated motion picture.

Tarzan played by Craig Garner (as a boy), Anton Zetterholm (as a teenager) and Kellan Lutz
2013: *Tarzan* (also known as *Tarzan 3D*) (Constantin Film)
   Note: motion capture motion picture.

Tarzan played by Christian Stevens (as a boy), Rory J Saper (as a teenager) and Alexander Skarsgård
2016: *The Legend of Tarzan* (Warner Bros.)

TELEVISION PRODUCTIONS

Tarzan played by Gordon Scott
1966: *Tarzan and the Trappers* (NBC)
   Note: TV movie; also released in cinemas.

Tarzan played by Ron Ely
1966: *Tarzan* (NBC)
   Duration: two seasons (57 episodes).

Tarzan played by Robert Ridgely
1976: *Tarzan Lord of the Jungle* (title changed to *Batman/Tarzan Adventure Hour*, then *Tarzan and the Super 7*) (CBS)
Duration: four seasons (36 episodes).
Note: animated series.

Tarzan played by Joe Lara
1989: *Tarzan in Manhattan* (CBS)
Note: TV movie.

Tarzan played by Wolf Larson
1991: *Tarzan* [First-run-syndication in US]
Duration: three seasons (75 episodes).

Tarzan played by Joe Lara
1996: *Tarzan's Return* [First-run-syndication in US]
Note: TV movie, pilot for *Tarzan: The Epic Adventures*.

Tarzan played by Joe Lara
1996: *Tarzan: The Epic Adventures* [First-run-syndication in US]
Duration: one season (20 episodes, excluding pilot).

Tarzan played by Michael T Weiss
2001: *The Legend of Tarzan* (United Paramount Network)
Duration: two seasons (39 episodes).
Note: animated series.

Tarzan played by Travis Fimmel
2003: *Tarzan* (WB Television Network)
Duration: one season (8 episodes).

Tarzan played by Giles Panton
2017: *Tarzan and Jane* (Netflix)
Duration: [unknown]
Note: animated series.
Note: series streamed over internet.

VIDEO/DVD RELEASES

Tarzan played by [unknown]
1999: *Tarzan of the Apes* (Sony Wonder)
   Note: animated feature.

Tarzan played by Michael T Weiss
2002: *Tarzan and Jane* (Disney)
   Note: animated feature.

Tarzan played by Harrison Chad
2005: *Tarzan II* (Disney)
   Note: animated feature.

RADIO PRODUCTIONS
(Note: English-language productions only.)

Tarzan played by James Pierce
1932: *Tarzan of the Apes*
   Duration: 77 episodes.

Tarzan played by Carlton KaDell
1934: *Tarzan and the Diamond of Asher*
   Duration: 39 episodes.
1936: *Tarzan and the Fires of Tohr*
   Duration: 39 episodes.

Tarzan played by Lamont Johnson
1951: *Tarzan, Lord of the Jungle*
   Duration: 75 episodes.

Tarzan played by Rod Taylor/Ray Barrett/Lloyd Berrell
1950s: *Tarzan, King of the Apes*
   Duration: 1,000+ episodes (estimated).
   Note: Australian production.

STAGE PRODUCTIONS
(Note: excludes regional productions.)

Tarzan played by Ronald Adair
1920: *Tarzan of the Apes* (London)
  Duration: [unknown]
1921: *Tarzan of the Apes* (New York)
  Duration: 14 performances.

Tarzan played by Josh Strickland
2006: *Tarzan: The Broadway Musical* (New York)
  Duration: 486 performances.

NEWSPAPER COMIC STRIP

Daily strip
1929: *Tarzan* (Metropolitan Syndicate/United Features Syndicate)
  Duration: has run continuously since 7 January 1929 with the exception of 17 March-9 June 1929.

Sunday strip
1931: *Tarzan* (Metropolitan Syndicate/United Features Syndicate)
  Duration: has run continuously since 15 March 1931.

COMIC BOOKS (USA)
(Note: regularly published, American hard-copy Tarzan titles only.)

1947: Dell (131 issues.)
1962: Gold Key (75 issues.)
  (Note: numbering continued from Dell title.)
1972: DC (52 issues.)
  (Note: numbering continued from Gold Key title.)
1977: Marvel (29 issues.)
1996: Dark Horse (20 issues.)

SELECTED BIBLIOGRAPHY

BOOKS
Star Trek Creator: The Authorized Biography of Gene Roddenberry; David Alexander; Boxtree; 1994
Gene Roddenberry: The Myth and the Man Behind Star Trek; Joel Engel; Virgin; 1995
The Book of TV Lists; Gabe Essoe; Arlington House, 1981
Tarzan of the Movies; Gabe Essoe; Citadel; 1968
Mother was a Lovely Beast: A Feral Man Anthology; Philip José Farmer; Chilton; 1974
The Big Swingers; Robert W Fenton; Prentice-Hall; 1967
Kings of the Jungle; David Fury; McFarland & Co; 2001
Tarzan: The Centennial Celebration; Scott Tracy Griffin; Titan Books; 2012
Tarzan on Film; Scott Tracy Griffin; Titan Books; 2016
Master of Adventure: The Worlds of Edgar Rice Burroughs; Richard A Lupoff; University of Nebraska Press; 2005
The Battle of Hollywood; James H Pierce; House of Greystoke; 1978
Edgar Rice Burroughs: The Man Who Created Tarzan; Irwin Porges; Ballantine Books; 1976
Tarzan Forever: The Life of Edgar Rice Burroughs; John Taliaferro; Scribner; 1999
Tarzan – Giant Book; Various; Williams; 1971
On Tarzan; Alex Vernon; University of Georgia Press; 2008
The Tarzan Novels of Edgar Rice Burroughs; David A Ullery; McFarland & Co.; 2001

PRINT ARTICLES
'Bo Derek Takes to the Jungle to Bring "Tarzan" Back Alive'; David Lewin; *The New York Times*; 19 July 1981
'Edgar Rice Burroughs In The Funnies!'; Alberto Becattini; *Alter Ego* #129; November 2014
'James Bond of the Jungle!'; Anthony Petkovich; *Filmfax* #127; 2011

'The Legend Of Tarzan: behind the scenes with director David Yates'; Owen Williams; *Empire*; July 2016
'Planet Of The Ape-Man'; Owen Williams; *Empire*; September 2012
'The Tarzan Art Studio'; Henry G. Franke III; *Alter Ego* #129; November 2014
'Tarzan's New York Adventure'; Joe Nazzaro; *Starlog*; November 2003
'Tarzan's Travails'; Joe Brancatelli; *Eerie* #79; November 1976

WEBSITES/WEBPAGES
angelfire.com/blog/moviejungle
boxofficemojo.com
collider.com
disney.go.com/disneyinsider
edgarriceburroughs.blogspot.com/2011/08/filmations-tarzan.html
doctormacro.com
epguides.com
erbzine.com
herocomplex.latimes.com
famous-and-forgotten-fiction.com
ibdb.com
ibelongwithyou.com
leylander.org/intercom/Tarzan (from an article originally published in *Comic Book Marketplace* #42)
moviehole.net
newspaperarchive.com
philsp.com/magazines.html
pjfarmer.com
tarzanmovieguide.com
terrororstralis.com
tvtropes.org
weirdscifi.ratiosemper.com/tarzan/cartoon.html

www.ingramcontent.com/pod-product-compliance
Lightning Source LLC
Chambersburg PA
CBHW032028150426
43194CB00006B/197